EXPLORING
THE NC500

David M. Addison

Other Books by
David M. Addison

An Italian Journey
A Meander in Menorca
Sometime in Sorrento
Bananas about La Palma
Misadventures in Tuscany
An Innocent Abroad
Confessions of a Banffshire Loon
The Cuban Missus Crisis
Still Innocent Abroad

EXPLORING THE NC500

Travelling Scotland's Route 66

David M. Addison

Exploring the NC500: Travelling Scotland's Route 66 by David M. Addison

First edition published in Great Britain in 2017 by Extremis Publishing Ltd., Suite 218, Castle House, 1 Baker Street, Stirling, FK8 1AL, United Kingdom. *www.extremispublishing.com*

Extremis Publishing is a Private Limited Company registered in Scotland (SC509983) whose Registered Office is 49/51 Horsemarket, Kelso, Roxburghshire, TD5 7AA, United Kingdom.

A CIP catalogue record for this book is available from the British Library.

ISBN: 978-0-9934932-4-9

Typeset in Goudy Bookletter 1911, designed by The League of Moveable Type.
Printed and bound in Great Britain by IngramSpark, Chapter House, Pitfield, Kiln Farm, Milton Keynes, MK11 3LW, United Kingdom.

Cover artwork is Copyright © Lukas Hejtman at Shutterstock Inc.
Cover design and book design is Copyright © Thomas A. Christie.
Author image and internal photographic images are Copyright © David M. Addison and Fiona J. Addison.
Incidental vector artwork from Pixabay.

Map of Route NC500 and its surroundings

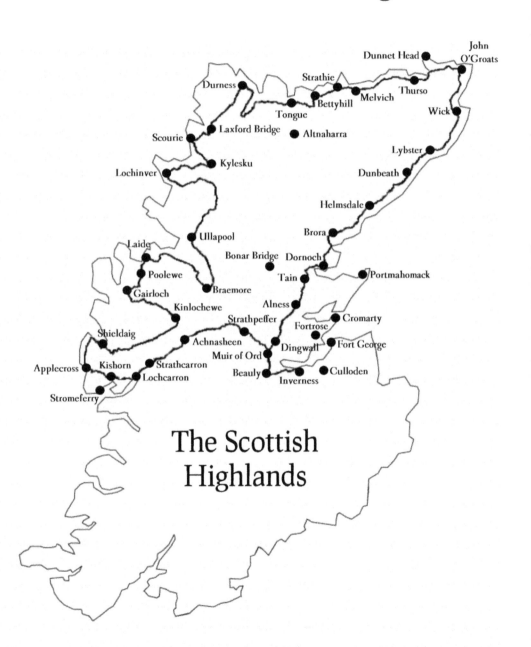

The Scottish Highlands

Contents

Acknowledgements

My thanks are due to many websites, too numerous to name and wherever possible, I traced back to the primary source.

Grateful thanks to the following for their assistance in providing me with information, or for pointing me in the right direction, or for their help in other, more practical ways. In alphabetical order they are:

Fiona Addison, Jacquie Aitken, Ruairidh and Kate Cameron, Barbara Cohen, Jill Ferguson, John and Marjorie Gunn, Jane Kitchener, Neil King, Jim and Moira Leslie, Maureen McCluskie, Rosemary McIntosh, Paul Monk, Les and Marjorie Pike, Elliot Rudie, Shirley Stephenson, Jason Uybch and Jackie West.

The image of the Daniel Stone (National Museum of Scotland Catalogue Reference number NMS.X1B127) on page 64 appears by kind permission of Groam House Museum. *www.groamhouse.org.uk.*

The image of Cromarty Courthouse on page 72 appears by kind permission of the Cromarty Courthouse Museum Trust. *www.cromarty-courthouse.org.uk.*

The image of the Strathpeffer Pump Room interior on page 98 appears by kind permission of The Real Sweets & Gift Company, The Pump Room, Strathpeffer. *www.strathpeffer.org/realsweets.*

The images of the St Kilda mailboat on page 242 and the dogskin buoy on page 244 appear by kind permission of Strathnaver Museum. *www.strathnavermuseum.org.uk.*

Site of the Battle of Culloden

Fort George

Duke of Cumberland's Bastion

Kerb Cairn

Inverness Castle

The Stone of the Brahan Seer

Spa Pavilion, Strathpeffer

Home of Hugh Miller

EXPLORING THE NC500

Travelling Scotland's Route 66

Chapter One

Inverness: Monsters, Myths and Writers

ANYONE who is unfamiliar with Inverness Castle, but who is familiar with Shakespeare's bloody play *Macbeth*, may be in for a very big disappointment when they see it for the first time. With its battlements and round towers, it looks just the sort of thing you might build for the children on the beach if you had time enough and skill. And it is decidedly pink. You just can't imagine Macbeth living in a *pink* castle for God's sake!

But possibly most disappointing of all as far as the aficionado of castles along the NC500 is concerned, is that it now serves as the sheriff court. Thus if you have a burning desire to see what it's like on the inside, you had better start studying for a law degree, although another possible, quicker solution occurs to me – but of course I couldn't possibly advocate such a method.

It dates only from 1836 and is built on the site of a former fort, and has absolutely nothing to do with the place where King Duncan was oh, so foully murdered by the wicked, treacherous and tyrannical Macbeth. Sportin' Life in *Porgy and Bess* famously and sagaciously remarked, "the things that you're liable to read in the Bible, it ain't necessarily so," and this observation was never more true than in Shakespeare's version of events which, he in his turn, got from Holinshed's *Chronicles*.

The historical Duncan may, or may not, have been slain by Macbeth personally but it was not murder: they were combatants on the battlefield. There are no contemporary accounts to support the Shakespearean Macbeth or "MacBheatha" to give him his Gaelic name, as a tyrannical despot, but there are a host of writers who came along hundreds of years after his death who fed the myth and of whom Shakespeare was merely the most successful.

Alas, poor Macbeth – and Shakespeare himself said it, through the mouth of Antony: "the evil that men do lives after them; the good is oft interrèd with their bones". And, making allowances for the mores of medieval

Scotland, the real Macbeth was actually quite a "good" king in Sellar and Yeatman terms, encouraging Christianity and going on a trip to Rome in 1050, good Catholic man that he was. You can only afford a luxury like that if you feel things are safe and secure at home. Which they were. He ruled for 17 years from 1040 to 1057 and was not, according to the word of W. Shakespeare Esq, killed in single combat by Malcolm but in battle against his army at Lumphanan.

Down below where the castle sits aloof on its grassy mound, the peat-coloured River Ness flows equally uncaringly and at a fair lick on its way north to be swallowed up by the Moray Firth. Surprisingly shallow at this point at least, it looks as if you could easily wade across it and, even if you are as lacking in inches as I am, you would not be not in any danger of getting your knees wet.

To the south lies the first (or the last) of the lochs that make up the Caledonian Canal, arguably the most famous loch in Scotland, if not the world, on account of its famous (and mythical resident). Loch Ness of course. Twenty-three miles long, it is incredibly deep, an average depth of 600 feet with a recently-discovered greatest depth of 786 feet, but even then it is still only the second deepest loch in Scotland. That honour belongs to Loch Morar, which at its deepest, is over an astonishing 1,000 feet and what's more, also claims to have a monster named "Morag" which seems to me to be something of an oxymoron.

Loch Ness is also the second largest loch (after Loch Lomond) in terms of surface area: 22 square miles, and – this is the thing that is really staggering – I am reliably informed by the Gazetteer for Scotland that all the fresh water from all the lakes (as the Sassenachs call them) in England and Wales could be poured into it with room to spare.

And talking of fresh water, I am much less reliably informed about the origins of the loch but which I repeat here for the benefit for those of you who like a folktale. Once upon a time there was a green and fertile glen (valley to those Sassenachs) which had a magic well and which provided a never-ending source of fresh water to the dwellers of this demi-paradise. But the deal was you had to remember to put the lid back on when you had drawn off as much water as you needed as otherwise it would continue to gush forth like the magic porridge pot.

One day a young woman, on hearing her baby crying in distress, did not hesitate. She rushed to find out what ailed the child and in her haste and in her panic, flung aside the lid to the well which landed she knew not where. By the time the child was comforted, it was too late. The lid could not be found and the well continued to pour out water. The residents of the glen were forced to take to the hills, higher and yet higher, from whence they uttered the cry, "Tha loch nis ann! (There is a loch there now!)" That is how the loch came about, and that is how it got its name.

And as well as there being a great quantity of it, the water is also as "murky" as the hell Shakespeare's Macbeth feared and which also helps feed the monster myth – as do the numerous hoaxes which have been perpetrated over the years, even by respected naturalists like Sir Peter Scott although he denied it strongly. But then, as Mandy Rice-Davies famously remarked in a totally unconnected scandalous event, "He would, wouldn't he?"

Sir Peter was a co-founder of the Loch Ness Phenomenon Bureau and in 1975 after a diamond-shaped flipper was photographed in the loch, on that scant evidence, he was able to reconstruct and paint (he was a very talented artist) the whole monster – a plesiosaur, which, with its long neck and small, snakelike head, fitted in well with previous sightings. In order that it could be registered as an endangered species, he gave "Nessie" the scientific name of *Nessiteras rhombopteryx*, ancient Greek for "the monster of Ness with the diamond-shaped fin". It seemed the most exciting of breakthroughs until you are made aware that this is an anagram of *Monster hoax by Sir Peter S.*

Hoaxer or believer? Reader, you must decide for yourself. But you would believe St Columba, wouldn't you? A holy man like him wouldn't tell a porky pie would he? He was the very first to record a sighting of the monster in 565 AD.

The story goes he ordered one of his men to swim across the river (not loch, note) to fetch a boat. During the course of his swim, the poor man was confronted by the monster which seemed to have every intention of devouring him whole without even bothering to taste him first. Columba was not slow to act: he made the sign of the cross and ordered the monster to "Leave that man alone!" He was used to being obeyed and the monster did as it was told. In fact Columba looked so scary it has scarcely dared raise its absurdly little head above the waters since.

If you do trust Sir Peter, then you should know that the plesiosaur, along with its cousins, the land lizards, became extinct about 65 million years ago when the asteroids that rained upon the nascent planet we call Earth, brought an end to the Mesozoic Era and ushered in the Cenozoic, or the Age of the Mammals. This is the one we are in today and we are the masters now, just as the dinosaurs were then. Who's to tell who will succeed us, but please let it not be the termites. I am all for voracious readers but a termite's idea of a good book is to devour it, literally.

"Nessie", if she does exist, must have a very long pedigree, must be a many-generation descendant of some miraculous survivors of that catastrophe –

even Methuselah didn't quite last a millennium, falling short by a mere thirty-four years. Since the catastrophic calamity that spelled the extinction of the lizard race (or almost did if you are a believer), and for a period of two-and-a-half million years or so, ice advanced (and retreated again) from the North Pole and buried what is now known as Scotland under a two-mile-thick sheet of ice.

About 10,000 years ago, in this seemingly unstoppable march of ice, glaciers gouged out "Nessie's" home, so I think it's safe to say we have a problem as far as the survival of anything is concerned, let alone a relic from a bygone age. I'm sorry if this incontrovertible truth disappoints the romantics but it should not deter you in the least from coming to Scotland – there is a great deal to be seen, never mind a monster that never is.

However, if you insist on being an incurable romantic and want to try your luck at a spot of monster hunting, it's only fifteen miles from Inverness to Drumnadrochit and Urquhart Castle where the loch is very wide and from where you get a good view up and down practically the entire loch. So should "Nessie", somehow having got wind of your visit, come up to have a peek at *you*, this is the best place to shoot her. But only with your long-distance lens please, not your high-power velocity rifle. You may be on a monster hunt but remember she is an endangered species.

In the likely event you are unsuccessful in your mission and should Inverness Castle not have lived up to your expectation of what a Scottish castle should look like either, then Urquhart Castle most certainly will satisfy your romantic requirements. It dates from the 13th century with several extensions being added over the following three hundred years. It has also seen more than its fair share of wars during that time, so it's not surprising it looks a little bit battle-scarred. But that all adds to its appeal, especially when you factor in the beautiful backdrop in which it is set.

But that is not on our itinerary on this occasion and, given that our grand scheme is to explore Route NC500 mainly from a historical perspective, the first thing that is on our agenda – here in Inverness – is to explore the old town. Dylan Thomas famously began *Under Milkwood* with "To begin at the beginning"; the King of Hearts advised Alice to do the same; Julie Andrews put it more musically to the children in the *Sound of Music*, though she added the tautological "very". It sounds like very good advice to me, therefore we direct our steps towards Abertaff House, the oldest house in Inverness.

It was built in 1592 and is situated in Church Street. This was the town house of Colonel Archibald Fraser of Beaufort and Abertaff. His father was Lord Lovat who was executed for his part in the '45 Jacobite rebellion. His is an interesting story and we will come back to it very soon but, staying with the house in the meantime, it is a two-storey affair, set back from the street and very easy to spot with its dazzlingly-white harling and crow-stepped gables. The restoration has been so successful it looks much younger than its 400 and more years.

What's particularly interesting about it, halfway down one side (the south) is the semi-circular tower that houses the "turnpike stair" (think of a corkscrew) on top of which, somewhat comically, is perched what looks like a doll's house, actually called a "cap house". A rectangular stone set into the nearest gable-end bears a heart with the letters AS and HS on either side. How romantic!

A plaque on the same wall tells us the house is now owned by the National Trust and although we are members, which means it would cost nothing to get in, we will not be paying a visit. That's because it used to be the Trust's offices, but since they moved to new premises it has been closed to the public. Which is a bit of a shame really: I would have loved to have visited the doll's house – even if, like Alice, I did have to crouch as I went though the door.

As for Lord Lovat, the 11th Lord, he has the unenviable distinction, at the age of eighty, of having his head chopped off on Tower Hill in 1746 – the last person to meet his maker by this particular form of execution in that particular place. His head wasn't all he lost that day: he lost the title as well. That's the price he paid for being on the losing side in the Jacobite Rebellion the previous year.

His father, the 10th Lord, was the first of the Lovats not to inherit the title by direct descent. He must have felt the title lie rather uneasy upon his shoulders, for in order to make it more secure, he abducted and forcibly married the widow of the 9th Lord, Amelia Murray.

They were no mean family, the Murrays of Atholl, and they took a pretty dim view of this. Lovat, or Simon Fraser, to give him his baptismal name – or "Simon the Fox" as he was also known – was forced to flee. He was tried, found guilty *in absentia*, attainted (which means not only he but his descendants forfeited the right to the title), and sentenced to death. On this occasion however, he escaped the ultimate punishment by offering his services to the Government side in the '15 for which he was duly pardoned. In a long legal battle, many years later, his right to the title was confirmed – only for him to throw it away again thirty years later, as you know.

But Abertaff House is not the only charming house on Castle Street. Just a few hundred yards away is the three-storey Dunbar Hospital with the same white harling. Above the arched gateway is the Dunbar coat of arms. Provost Alexander Dunbar was the philanthropist who donated the building to the

Burgh as an almshouse and hospital. It is said to have been built from stones recycled from Oliver Cromwell's Fort (1658). It's good to see the boot on the other foot for a change, Cromwell being notorious for having knocked about a good few buildings in his time, as Marie Lloyd's music hall song put it.

The Hospital dates from 1668 and in its lifetime served many purposes, some at the same time: grammar school, weigh house, library, school for young ladies and a female work society (whatever that is exactly), and once again a hospital in the 19th century when a cholera epidemic broke out in the town. In my view, the windows are what contribute most to its charm: tiny dormer ones in the roof, small square ones in the middle, and rectangular ones on the bottom.

All that is very fine and, taken as a whole, Church Street is a very fine street indeed, better by far than the present-day Main Street, which even the most devoted and died-in-the-wool Invernasian would have to admit is unremarkable. It does have one remarkable feature, however. On a building, on your left, if your back is to the river, carved into the stone, are no fewer than seven quotes from the Bible: two from James, one from Matthew, three from Revelation and last and not least, one from Habakkuk.

They are all to do with reasons why you should be good and I would say the tone is rather threatening, as if whoever was responsible for putting them up there reasoned that if a bit of scaremongering was what it took to save your immortal soul from perdition, so be it. I quote the verse from Habakkuk: "Woe unto him who that giveth his neighbour drink, that puttest thy bottle to him and makest him drunk also". If you want to check it out, it's Chapter II Verse 15, and you'll find it doesn't stop there.

What does all this say to the visitor to Inverness? What impression does it give of the place? And note this: this writing on the wall is not on a church as you might expect, but on a building you might see on any street in any city. And furthermore, if you assume these texts must have been chiselled out more than a century ago, they have not been allowed in the least to fade into the façade. The letters have been picked out in white and, what's more, are in block capitals, not so much speaking at you but shouting. It seems a God-fearing sort of place, a place where zealotry is alive and well and where the spirit of John Calvin looks down on his legacy and sees that it is not just good but very good.

Back on Church Street by a happy coincidence, is another very fine building and one that would make Habakkuk splutter into his mineral water. It's a bit of a youngster compared to those we have just been admiring earlier, dating only from 1840. Its present name is *The Kings [sic] Highway*. Church Street, referred to in charters of 1240, used to be the main thoroughfare in Inverness, hence the name of the building which was built as a hotel, as it still is today. Since 2011 it has also been another link in the Wetherspoons chain – for the uninitiated, purveyors of real ales and providers of food at budget prices. Some dishes even include a free pint. What is there not to like, and yet my Missus, for some reason, does not.

What I like about the Wetherspoons chain (apart from the prices and the beer of course) is each pub puts its location into its historical context for the benefit of any patrons who might be interested. This establishment does not disappoint, even if the price of a pint here is more than I am accustomed to in my local. Over in a secluded corner, framed and illuminated, are engravings depicting Inverness of old featuring a stone seven-arched bridge and the towering, wooden "Macbeth's Castle". Interesting though that may be, of more interest to me are the portraits of celebrated travellers who came here.

In the beginning there was Daniel Defoe (1660-1731), novelist (his *Robinson Crusoe* (1719) is regarded as being the first novel), journalist, political pamphleteer and – perhaps most intriguingly – secret agent, or spy.

"Defoe" was his pen name; his actual name was "Foe" and no friend to Scotland, or so many Scots believed, though he himself would claim the precise opposite. He was very active in promoting union with England (what later became the Treaty of Union of 1707), writing widely on the reasons in favour of it, even starting up his own newspaper, *The Review,* as a propaganda machine. He was sent to Scotland by the English government to do what he could to promote the cause. In Edinburgh he found violent demonstrations against the proposed Union but, somehow inveigling himself into the posts of advisor to the General Assembly of the Church of Scotland and certain committees of the Scottish Parliament (who were unaware he was reporting back to England), he managed to have some influence.

Amongst his prolific outpouring of prose, between 1724-1727 Defoe wrote *A tour thro' the whole Island of Great Britain, divided into circuits or journies.* He called Inverness "Inner-Ness" and heartily approved of it. He praised the fertility of the soil and the cultivation of it, considering it to surpass the rest of Scotland. But what impressed him possibly even more was the quality of spoken English, though he did not go quite so far as some did in saying it was the equal of London's. Though before the good citizens of Inverness get too puffed up, he attributes this to Englishmen: three regiments of Cromwell's soldiers who, after they were disbanded, settled in the area with their wives and children and passed on to the locals how to speak proper.

Defoe goes on to say the people have much of the English way about them in the manner of their dress and customs, eating and drinking. He mentions a "stately stone bridge with seven arches", at the northern side of which lay the "frightful country". This side civilisation; that side barbarians. That is the way he saw it, much like the way the Romans viewed Antonine's Wall.

If he were to come back today, given his pro-English and Union stance, since the upsurge of support for the Scottish National Party in recent times and the renaissance of nationalism, Mr Foe or Mr Defoe, would be well advised to come under a different alias altogether. As a contemporary Unionist put it, had his true purpose been discovered, he would have been "pulled apart by the Mob". Daniel in the Scottish rampant lions' den indeed.

Next in the frame is Thomas Pennant (1726-98). Naturalist, zoologist, antiquarian, travel writer and gentleman, he deserves to be better known today than he is. A real "lad o' pairts" as we say in Scotland, only they wouldn't have said that about him as he was Welsh. Travelling from his home in North Wales on horseback, he made two journeys to Scotland in 1769 and 1772 – quite an undertaking in those days. Inverness was the most northerly point of his first tour. He returned by Loch Ness and it must have been very disappointing for him, being the naturalist he was, that Nessie did not pop up to say hello and thus make his day.

He was accompanied by his faithful servant, Moses Griffiths, (1749-1819), who sketched the flora and fauna along the way and whose illustrations appear in the books. And get this – in colour! Pennant described the scenery and the people he met, just like I intend to do on the NC500 – though you couldn't say he influenced me in any way, as that was always on my agenda. He did, however, influence Samuel Johnson, so much so that it was partly his writings that encouraged him to leave civilised London for barbarous Scotland.

Pennant had his Griffiths and, more famously, Johnson (1709-84) had his Boswell (1740-95), whose name has since come into the language as being synonymous with being an indispensable companion and biographer. Johnson was the most celebrated man of letters of his day: novelist, poet, essayist, critic, biographer, political pamphleteer and most notably, lexicographer. His dictionary appeared in 1755. He had a very superior attitude towards Scotland and the Scots. His famous dictionary definition of oats confirms this: "A grain which in England is generally given to a horse but in Scotland supports the people." His view of Scots as some sort of lowlife is supported by Madame Piozzi (née Hester Thrale), who records that on being asked by a Scot what he thought of his country, Johnson replied that it was "very vile".

Madame Piozzi also gives us this gem from Johnson: "Knowledge was divided among the Scots like bread in a besieged town, to every man a mouthful, to no man a bellyful". Coming from someone who thought London was the centre of the universe – the greatest thing before sliced bread, on the face of it – it seems surprising he should embark on this trip at all, let alone with a Scotsman as his travelling companion.

In 1773, the unlikely pair set out to tour the Western Isles and both wrote books about their travels. Johnson published his *A Journey to the Western Isles of Scotland* in 1775; Boswell's better-known *Journal of a Tour to the Hebrides* appeared in 1785, the year after Johnson's death. Was that what he was waiting for, fearful of what the famous critic might say?

Perhaps mercifully, Johnson has little to say about Inverness in his *Journey* but, not altogether surprisingly, he agrees with Defoe about the "elegance" of the language.

They visited "Macbeth's Castle", which Boswell thought Shakespeare described perfectly when he wrote: "This castle hath a pleasant seat". He reports that just as they came out of the castle, a raven perched on one of the chimney pots and croaked. This immediately brought to his mind what was running through Macbeth's:

> *The raven himself is hoarse*
> *That croaks the fatal entrance of Duncan*
> *Under my battlements.*

It may have happened or it might just have been another excuse for Boswell to show off his Shakespeare.

In the morning they set off for Fort Augustus via Loch Ness, where not a sign of the monster was seen or even given a mention. Thus our paths diverge and probably just as well, as to follow in their august footsteps would not be something I'd undertake lightly.

Chapter Two

Culloden: The Death of a Dream

I T'S noon on April 16th 1746. Across Drummossie Moor two armies face each other. On the left, with their backs to Inverness, but facing the driving rain, the exhausted, cold and hungry Prince Charlie's men; on the right, the Duke of Cumberland's paid recruits, well-fed, well-trained, rested and raring for a fight.

Well, who would you put your money on if you were a betting man?

The previous evening the Hanoverian troops had celebrated the Duke's 25th birthday, the feast washed down with a tot of brandy to toast the Duke's health. As they celebrated, little did they know that it had been Prince Charlie's plan to spoil the party. Under cover of darkness, he had planned to launch a surprise attack at Nairn some twelve miles to the east of Culloden where the Duke was camped. In a pincer movement, Murray, the Prince's general, was to veer round to the left and attack the government troops from the rear while the Prince would launch a frontal attack.

In a series of mishaps that foreshadowed the disastrous events of the following day, the enterprise was doomed from the start. For one thing they set off too late and for another, Murray's men made heavy weather of the terrain in the darkness. Eventually he realised they were never going to reach the enemy in sufficient time to attack before dawn and decided to abort the mission, sending a message to the Prince to that effect. However the message never got through and the greater part of the army carried on before it dawned on *them* that they were on their own and turned back. It was hardly the best of preparations for a battle.

But worse was yet to come. For a thousand and more of these exhausted and ravenously hungry Jacobites, this was to be their last day on earth and if not this, the next, as the dying and the wounded were butchered on the field or hunted down and dispatched without mercy by the dragoons.

It had all been so promising not so long ago. Ever since he raised his standard in Glenfinnan in August 1745, Charles had been at the head of a victorious army that in fifteen short minutes had defeated the Hanoverians under General Cope at Prestonpans to the east of Edinburgh. Although they occupied the city, with their light artillery, they were unable to take the castle. The Prince, winning the argument over Murray who wanted to stay and hold what they had, decided to march on London, convinced he would gather support from English Jacobites on the way and not least, support from the French who would launch an invasion.

It all went very well. In two weeks they reached Derby, picking up 250 men at Manchester. At Derby however, only 125 miles from the capital, they stopped to take stock and in a heated council of war, Charles, against his wishes, was persuaded by Murray they should advance no further and return to Scotland. The hoped-for uprising of English Jacobites had failed to materialise in the hoped-for numbers, nor was there any word of the French having landed and all the time was the threat of government forces treading right behind them.

In the meantime, central Scotland was back under government control and even in the Prince's heartland of the Highlands, the government was recruiting clansmen to its side. Murray was right after all, though ironically, it could be argued that it was only a matter of timing: the Jacobites had advanced so rapidly the French hadn't had enough time to arrange for their army to be transported across the Channel. However, once they heard of Charles' retreat, that put paid to any plans they did have to invade.

It was another might-have been moment, but on the way back to Scotland, things still went well for the Jacobites, Murray defeating the government troops under General Hawley at Falkirk, though it could be said they failed to pursue their advantage and allowed Hawley and a good part of his army to escape to Edinburgh. Into the breach rode the king's youngest son and blue-eyed boy, William Augustus, Duke of Cumberland. His seemed an awfully young head to count on to ensure the crown remained on his father's. Young, certainly, but not inexperienced. Already, by the tender age of 22, he was a major general, and as Commander-in-Chief, led the so-called "Pragmatic Army", a confederation of British, Hanoverians, Dutch and Austrians, to defeat at the hands of the French at a little place called Fontenoy in Flanders during the War of the Austrian Succession.

So now, here they are, ready for the showdown, the two twenty-five year-olds and distant cousins, Cumberland and Bonnie Prince Charlie, facing each other on Drummossie Moor. The site of the battle, on the west of the River Nairn was chosen by the Prince on the advice of John O'Sullivan who said the ground would not suit the Hanoverians' cavalry or artillery. O'Sullivan, now the quartermaster-general for the Jacobite troops, had been an advisor of Charles ever since he landed in Scotland and a man in whom he had absolute trust.

Ironically, Charles also put more trust in his own judgement than in Murray's, the seasoned campaigner and man of war. He did not see eye to eye with him in the matter of tactics, especially. Actually it seems Charles was blind to the fact that it was Murray whom he had mainly to thank for the Jacobites' success, for the morale-boosting victory at Prestonpans, for choosing the route to Derby via Carlisle and not Newcastle, and leading them back to Scotland again – well, actually bringing up the rear-guard, the more difficult and dangerous job as they had intelligence that Cumberland was snapping at their heels. And indeed there was a skirmish at Clifton Moor which Murray won. Meanwhile, Charles and the main army proceeded to Carlisle and thence to Stirling, where against Murray's advice, Chares laid siege to the castle.

As to the choice of battlefield at Culloden, Murray argued precisely the opposite from O'Sullivan. He contended that the flat and treeless Drummossie would suit the Hanoverian cavalry and infantry right down to the ground (if you forgive the pun) and furthermore, was unsuitable for the Highlanders' famous and feared weapon of mass destruction – their charge. Instead he advised, if fight they must, then let it be the other side of the River Nairn, where the boggy ground would impede the charge of the Hanoverian cavalry and where the Jacobites could have taken up position on higher ground to await the enemy.

What neither of them knew was that in Aberdeen, Cumberland had been disciplining and training his troops, honing them into a well-oiled military machine. In particular, he had an answer to the Highland Charge. Instead of attacking the man in front of you, so he instructed, stick your bayonet into the man on the right as he lifts his sword arm to smite your neighbour down. However, in the event, hundreds of Jacobites never got within a bayonet's length of the British soldiers – they were cut to ribbons by musket fire and grapeshot as they charged.

Charles would not be moved, preferring to listen to O'Sullivan. The hot-headed Young Pretender was always spoiling for a fight and had had to be persuaded before by Murray and others that that was neither the time nor the place. But this time he got his way. His faith in O'Sulivan was severely misplaced: whose fault was it the Jacobites were starving and had to forage for food on their return from the aborted attack on Nairn, such rations as they had still in Inverness? And whose fault was it that their meagre artillery, compared to the Hanoverians', had been issued with the wrong size of shot? And whose fault was it that he didn't even think it was necessary to inspect the proposed battlefield?

It was yet another might-have-been moment – if only he had listened to Murray who advocated retreating to the Highlands to regroup, gather their strength and live to fight another day. As it happens, reinforcements were on their way, but luckily for them they never made it to the killing field in time. Yet perhaps if the Murray plan had been adopted it only would have prolonged the inevitable – the Jacobites would still have been defeated in the end. Instead what happened here was a quick death for the Jacobite cause. It was all over in less than an hour with twelve-hundred Jacobites, and quite possibly a few hundred more – no-one is sure of the exact numbers – who laid down their lives for Charlie on Culloden moor.

And so, now here we are, standing where the last battle on British soil took place, trying to imagine the scene, that day nearly three hundred years ago.

They make it so much easier for us these days, the National Trust for Scotland. I remember coming here years ago with my parents, when I was still in short trousers and clambering onto Cumberland's Stone from where he was said to have commanded the battle. I sincerely doubt it: he would have had a better view from his horse. Besides, he was carrying a war wound: he was shot in the leg at the battle of Dettingen during the War of Austrian Succession and it's hard to imagine him managing to climb up there. For the present day visitor, the best overview of the site by far is from the roof of the visitor centre – except not for us on this occasion. It is closed. The gods are at it again.

I also remember you could drive right up and park next to the memorial cairn that was erected by Duncan Forbes, the last laird of Culloden, in 1881. Now you get to it by walking along a meandering path where it stands midway between the front lines of both armies. Forbes also erected the stones that mark the places where the clans fell, the clan identified by the sprigs the dead wore on their bonnets. It's all part of the Trust's plan (and a very good plan it is too) to restore the battlefield as far as possible to what it was like in 1746. It's an on-going project: the heather and gorse and self-seeding trees will insist on growing on the grassland where before the battle, sheep safely grazed.

We do not head straight for the cairn as many may be tempted to do as it seems a more obvious objective, but make our way from the government lines which are nearest the visitor centre and across no-man's land to where, in the distance, a blue flag beckons us. It marks the Jacobites' lines. But we do not go alone. We are accompanied by an audio-visual guide which gives us details of the battle, all the better for us to understand the scene before our eyes. It is all part of the entry price, which to us as NTS members, is nothing at all – the best bargain in Scotland.

As well as making sense of the battle formations and proceedings, it also lets you hear eyewitness accounts, from both sides, of some of the participants. That's the sort of thing that really makes history come alive. In my school days, in history, all we were told about were kings and queens and prime ministers and emperors and their interminable bloody wars and hardly anything at all about the ordinary people. That's what should really interest us about the past – people like us. After all, most of us are ordinary: we were not born to rule or command, especially if you are a man, and married.

We come to what is known as the Culwhiniac enclosure, built of stone and part of which has been reconstructed. It could have been a good defensive position for the Jacobites but Murray realised he couldn't spare the men to hold it and had wanted it demolished. But of course his royal master and quarter-master general knew better. On the right flank of the Jacobites, it was an impediment to their advance, funnelling them through the gap between another stone wall on the left flank, but even worse, just as Murray feared, as the Hanoverians advanced, it turned out to make very handy cover from which they could mow down the retreating Jacobites without fear of reply. Shooting fish in a barrel springs to mind as does the retort, "I told you so", as Murray might have said to Charles about his decision to fight on Drummossie Moor. He might have been able to do so a year later when they both happened to be in Paris – only the petulant Prince, philanderer and drunkard, refused to meet him, never having forgiven him for not agreeing to march on London.

It's good to have someone to blame for your failure to have carried the day. It couldn't be *his* fault after all: he was appointed by God who reigned in heaven, his master in the firmaments. (And where was He at Culloden?) No, it's got to be Murray's fault as he had gone against his will so many times in the past. And just look at the circumstances to which he had now been reduced – *persona non grata* in France and living in Rome instead of London, where he would have been ruling the United Kingdom if only Murray had listened to him!

As you take the trail through the heather that grows so incredibly high (could it possibly be fed by the nutrients from that blood-drenched ground?), you can't help but be impressed by the way the Trust has presented the formation of the battle lines. The heather and grass has been cut back so you can walk along them, and all along the way there are slate tablets which bear the names of the clans or regiments and the number of men who served. And not a one that does not have a sprig of heather on it. Some are mixed with wild flowers that also grow in profusion here and are bound together with blades of grass. A sign perhaps that the visitor or visitors have become incredibly moved, moved to make a spontaneous gesture of respect. Other visitors have clearly come prepared: the sprigs of heather and wild flowers entwined have been bound by a strip of tartan ribbon. There is even a bunch of red roses wrapped in cellophane.

Alas there are no poppies here, as in Flanders, which would be fitting, but I remember this is September. There are, however, thistles which have flowered and are seeding, and that I think, is even more appropriate: the emblem of Scotland shedding its seed on the ground just as its sons shed their blood.

Having said that, we should bear in mind that although the Jacobites thought they were fighting for independence from England and the dissolution of the Treaty of Union and the restoration of the Scottish Parliament, their leader, the man for whom they were prepared to die, and did, had a greater prize in mind. His ultimate aim was to restore the Stuarts to their rightful place on the throne of the United Kingdom. Which goes some way to explaining his desire to take London rather than remaining in Scotland to consolidate.

On the left of the battlefield I notice the ground is very boggy indeed, the very thing Murray wanted, but this is on the Jacobite side of the fence so to speak and absolutely hopeless for the Highland Charge. The idea was that once you saw the whites of the enemy's eyes, you discharged your musket (if you had one) then rushed forward as fast as you could, trusting to luck that you would not be cut down in the first volley of enemy fire and you would make it through to the next hazard – being impaled on a bayonet of sharp steel.

Eventually we come to the cairn with its topknot of greenery and at the bottom, the plaque that in block capitals bears the date of the battle and the legend: "The Graves of the Gallant Highlanders who fought for SCOTLAND & PRINCE CHARLIE are marked by the names of their clans". And at the bottom of that, more posies of heather and wild flowers. They too have laid down their lives.

Predictably, at these grave markers, there are more flowers, even at the stone that says "Field of the English. They were buried here." It's good to see that some respect is shown to the other side but alas, the stone is guilty of perpetuating a myth, a belief held by many that this was a battle fought between the Scots and the English. Nothing could be further from the truth. For one thing there were, on the Jacobite side, the Irish Piquets and the Royal Ecossais, a unit of the French army, composed mainly of Irish and some Englishmen who claimed they had been press-ganged or were prisoners of war.

But the biggest surprise of all for some visitors must surely be that on the so-called "English" side there were no fewer than four Scots units and one Irish. On the front line, on the left, were the Monros [[sic]], 426 of them, my grandmother's ancestors. My grandfather's, the Gordons, weren't there at the fight, but had they been, they would have been on the Jacobite side. That's what happens in a civil war: family fights family, though it was to be two hundred years later before I came along to make the link between the families on opposite sides of the divide.

The illustration of how a family could be split could not be better illustrated than by the story of Anne Mackintosh and her husband. She was for Bonnie Prince Charlie; he was on the government side, a captain in the Black Watch and what's more, he was also the clan chief. It would seem to be an understatement to say she put her marriage on the line when she raised the clan in support of Charles. She recruited four or five hundred men, half of whom were in time to see action at the Battle of Falkirk. The other half she wisely kept at home. You can imagine her husband and his bosses wouldn't have been best pleased with her. The cockles of Charlie's heart, by contrast, must have been considerably warmed after his disappointment after Derby.

In her turn, he probably charmed the pants off her, so to speak, and maybe he actually did. Her husband was twenty years older than her and Charles, it was generally agreed, was said to be charming and charismatic, though in all the portraits I have seen of him as a young man he looks extremely effeminate. He called her "La Belle Rebelle" which has a nice ring to it, I must admit.

His name has been passed down to us Scots as "Bonnie Prince Charlie" and peddled as some sort of romantic hero and there is nothing in the Scottish psyche at least, that we like better than a failed romantic hero. But as his later life testified, there was nothing in the least romantic about Charlie. And here's another thing to be borne in mind. "Charlie" sounds affectionate, diminutive, as if the heir to the Stuart throne was a man of the people, the sort of bloke that since he had the cash, would be happy to splash it about, put his hand in his pocket and buy everyone in the pub a pint or a dram of *uisge beatha*, while being equally happy and at ease with slurping up the claret with the aristocracy.

The less-than-romantic truth is the Gaelic word for "Charles" is "Tearlach" and I would be the last to blame anybody, given the mysteries and complexities of Gaelic orthography, for not realising that that comes out as "Charlie" when spoken by a speaker of Gaelic. Thus it turns out his greatest supporters were not being so familiar after all.

On 16th February 1746, Charles was mixing with the aristocracy, as usual, staying with Lady Mackintosh at Moy Hall, just to the south of Inverness, when the commander of Inverness barracks got to hear of his presence and sent out a party to arrest him. Imagine what a feather in his cap it would have been if he had carried that off! And imagine how, if he had, while it may not have altered the course of history exactly, it's pretty safe to say there would have been no Culloden. The whole thing degenerated into farce when, having got wind of the planned arrest themselves, while Charles scarpered, Anne sent out her servants to make a right royal hullabaloo in the bushes. The commander's men thought they were outnumbered by the entire Jacobite army and returned, Princeless, to Inverness. This little-known episode and footnote in history became hyperbolically known as the "Rout of Moy".

A different and ironic twist took place a month later when Captain Mackintosh himself was captured. Instead of throwing him in the clink and throwing away the key for good measure, Charles turned him over to his wife for safekeeping with the words he "could not be in better security or more honourably treated". After everything that had happened you can imagine their exchanges might have been enough to blister the paintwork. But we don't have to imagine it. Somewhat disappointingly, if there is nothing you like as much as a good domestic, she is recorded as merely and meekly having said, "Your servant, Captain", while he replied, "Your servant, Colonel". It's an enjoyable story and it would be nice if it were true, but somehow I don't believe it unless they were keeping their powder dry until the servants were out of earshot.

Although she obviously wore the trousers in Moy Hall, unlike Joan of Arc, Anne was not allowed to ride into battle at the head of her troops. That honour fell to Alexander MacGillivray, chief of Clan MacGillivray of that ilk, and chief of the Chattan Confederation, an alliance of twelve clans, uniting for mutual protection.

"Colonel Anne" aside, however much he wished it to be so, Prince Charles Edward Stuart was not universally popular in Scotland. In fact he should have realised that – away back in the Prestonpans days when the citizens of the capital did not exactly welcome him with open arms and he had to force his way into the city. But of course he was in the Lowlands where many were doing very nicely out of the Union, thank you very much. It is estimated that between three-quarters and two-thirds of those who made up the Jacobite army were Highland Gaels and either Catholic or Episcopalian.

Now we are standing before the Well of the Dead where a stone marks the spot where the aforesaid chief of Clan MacGillivray fell. There *is* a well there, or a spring (though I for one wouldn't care to drink from it), so the stone is apposite enough. But actually, I wonder if the "Wall of the Dead" would not be more appropriate, for the fighting was particularly fierce here, the bodies piled high, the Jacobites having to climb over the bodies of their comrades to get at the enemy. This was where the Jacobites broke through on the extreme left of the government line, only for the second line to advance and surround them.

And so we come to the Old Leanach Farm, rectangular, with a short stubby projection at the front, to form an L. The walls are made of boulders and, like a Beatle haircut, the untidy thatched roof comes down to meet the top of the walls underneath which the little windows peer myopically out. The front (and only) door comes right up to the thatch and anyone over six foot would have to duck if they didn't want to crown themselves on entering.

On the gable ends, above the stone walls, the pitch of the roof is filled in with divots of turf. At the back, where there is a single small window, the western corner has been shored up with stone buttresses. Originally the house would have been a T-shaped structure but at sometime in the past, the western gable was demolished to form the L-shaped structure we see today. There is no sign of a chimney now and if there were not one in 1745, this would have made it a "blackhouse", typical throughout the Highlands and where the interior walls were whitewashed to help you from bumping into folk through the miasma of peat smoke which was expected to find its way out through the thatch. A 1797 coloured lithograph of the battle featuring the cottage does show a central chimney but we can't rely on the artist's accuracy here: his main subject was to show the battle raging all around and the cottage was merely incidental.

There does, however, appear to be a chimney in a photograph of the last resident, Bella MacDonald, taken outside the cottage sometime before her death in 1912. (Yes, unbelievably, it was still occupied up till then.) After her demise, the cottage was taken over by the Gaelic Society of Inverness and gifted to the NTS in 1944 by the landlord of Culloden, Hector Forbes, the descendant of Duncan who built the cairn and erected the grave markers and who possibly had the cottage restored at the same time. Good man, Duncan! When I was here as a boy in the early Sixties it served as the visitor centre. Some difference to the present one built in 2007!

It looks perfectly charming, the sort of image you might put on a chocolate box, but looks can be deceiving. The cottage bears a horrible history. During the battle, being situated in the Hanoverian lines, it seems likely that it was commandeered as a field hospital. After the battle, over thirty Jacobite officers and men were found in a barn. They were barricaded in and it was set on fire. And in another atrocity in the aftermath of the battle, twelve wounded men were discovered being sheltered by a local woman. They were promised if they surrendered without a fight, they would be given medical treatment. They weren't. They were shot in front of the woman's eyes.

Atrocities such as these began right after the battle and went on for months afterwards. On the day after the battle, the wounded and the dying on the field, or wherever they were able to crawl for concealment, were hunted down and shot or bayoneted. "Butcher" Cumberland, having earned that nickname as a result of these deplorable events, gave as an excuse that according to a copy of Murray's orders, which somehow happened to fall into their hands, that "no quarter" was to be shown to *them.* The only thing is that these orders did not bear Murray's signature and "no quarter" was an obvious insertion by a person or persons unknown.

Culloden was Cumberland's only victory, so no great military strategist he. You could say Charles more or less handed him Culloden on a plate. In 1757, during the Seven Years' War, Cumberland was head of an Army of Observation, a confederation of German states whose mission was to defend Hanover from attack by the French. He snatched defeat from the jaws of victory at Hastenbeck and with his father's permission, sued for peace at Stade and signed the Convention of Kloster-Zeven. His army was disbanded and much of Hanover was occupied by the French. When he came back to London, the former blue-eyed boy was greeted by George II with the words: "Here is my son who has ruined me and disgraced himself." The King renounced the Treaty, appointed a new commander and the following year, the French were driven out of Hanover. See what a difference a good general can make, Charles Edward Stewart!

The final irony is, only a year after Culloden, the government went to the Highlands in search of recruits to serve in India. You might cynically conclude this was another method of subjugation: if they were over there, they couldn't be here. Ten years after Culloden, Jacobites also fought for Britain in the Seven Years' War. (It should really have been called "The First World War", with theatres in Europe, North America, South America, the Caribbean, India, the West Indies and West Africa.) And ten years after that, former Jacobites fought with distinction in North America during the American War of Independence, where once again they found themselves on the losing side.

As everyone knows, Culloden spelled the death knell of Jacobitism in Scotland. And from his base in Fort Augustus at the south-west end of Loch Ness, Cumberland made sure it was so. Apart from the torching of crofts and chapels and looting, the government lost no time in rushing through laws designed to snuff out all traces of Highland culture. By the Disarming Act of

1746, as well as not being allowed to wear tartan, the clans were also not allowed to possess weapons, even if they had not fought against the government – or even if they had fought for it. Under the umbrella of "weapons" came the bagpipes. Which maybe goes to show Cumberland was not all bad after all.

The Heritable Jurisdictions Act of 1747 severely diminished the power of the chiefs. And just in case anybody got any ideas, barracks were built, most notably the redoubtable Fort George which was completed in 1769. There was also a massive expansion of the road network which General Wade, after the previous rising in 1715, had built all over the Highlands. Thus troops could rapidly be deployed to any trouble spots and snuff out any incipient rebellion. You can still see some of Wade's forty bridges today, most notably that over the Tay at Aberfeldy, and still drive along some of his (upgraded) 240 miles of roads. They were the wonder of their day. Not since the Romans had the roads been so good.

And so, having completed our tour of the battlefield, we make tracks to the visitor centre where we began and hand back our audio-visual guides. I may have given the impression that we made a beeline for the battlefield but however egocentric it may be, the first thing I wanted to see was our names on the ceiling of the café, our reward for making a donation toward the cost of building the visitor centre.

We soon realised it was a hopeless task to spot them amongst the rows and rows of names like a list of the victims on a First World War memorial such as Thiepval which, at least, are alphabetical. In fact it would be easier to find a name there as here, the names are not alphabetical, but in the order in which donations were received, presumably. The NTS had pledged £800,000 towards the £10 million cost of the centre. I am really glad to find so many names, even if it does mean ours are lost amongst them. Fortunately the nice lady at the desk has a file and can tell us, and others like us, where to look so we can crane our necks and bend our backs like a limbo dancer to see our names.

Ah, there we are, column seventeen. Fame at last. Well, the grandchildren at least might come one day when we are no longer around and look for granny and grumpa amongst the many up above even if our names never were recorded by St Peter in his book. Well, mine at least.

Mission accomplished, we entered the museum. Really you could be here all day and still not read and touch and see and listen to everything. I don't suppose you could say there is too much information like you want to do to people who want to go into the finer details of their operations or the condition of their bowels, but you could certainly spend hours in here before you get to the battlefield itself.

The visitor begins with an explanation of the background to the battle, placing it in its historical context. John Donne famously wrote that "no man is an island", and our island is no island in that context either and the visitor, if he curbs his impatience to get to the battle and battleground itself, might be surprised to learn that the Jacobite rebellion was just a piece of the jigsaw in the greater European picture, the northern frontier against Public Enemy Number One – France.

The French victory at Fontenoy in 1745 encouraged Charles to believe that the time was ripe to launch his campaign to regain the throne, convinced he could count on French backing. Meanwhile, across the Atlantic, France and Britain were locked in a struggle for territory in North America. Most significantly, the French loss of Louisbourg on Cape Breton Island in the strategic Gulf of St Lawrence gave them a dilemma. Support the Young Pretender by launching an invasion of England or try to retake Louisbourg? After Charles retreated from Derby, they decided to send the army across the Atlantic rather than the much shorter hop across the Channel and thus ended any hope for Charles of French support.

Meanwhile, on the other side of the world, the British lost Madras to the French and in 1748 as a sort of quid pro quo, the British gave them Louisbourg back in exchange for their precious Madras, the East India Company's headquarters in southern India.

The visitor will also learn of the aborted night march to Nairn and the decision at Derby before reaching the so-called "Immersion Theatre" by means of the '45 Corridor – on the red side, or corner so to speak, the government or Hanoverian side, on the blue, the Jacobites. I wouldn't be surprised if the theatre is the highlight of the visitor centre for most people: theatre in the round, you are in the thick of it as the Jacobites charge, are mowed down, repulsed and shot down by musketeers from behind the wall of the Culwhiniac enclosure.

When you come out you can hold a musket yourself, feel the weight of it and then thank your lucky stars you didn't have to march carrying it as well as all the rest of your kit. Other weapons are available to try but not for the taking away: they are firmly chained down.

So much to see, so much to read, so much to do (for many of the displays are interactive) it's difficult to decide where you should focus your attention, but most people will probably be drawn to the large tabletop with an animated display which shows how the armies were lined up and how they were deployed during the battle. It is a very fitting preparation for going out onto the battlefield itself. We should know: that's exactly what we did.

The centre may have cost the best part of £10 million but it's been money very well spent. And just think: our contribution might have paid for a label next to some exhibit or other! Hmm. Now I wonder which one it was...

Chapter Three

Clava Cairns: A Mystery in Stones

THE B9006 takes us forward to the past and past Cumberland's Stone, if you can find it – and if you don't, like us, what does it matter? It's only a stone, a glacial erratic with a myth attached, whereas this place, just a stone's throw from Culloden, gives you a wonderful feeling for that material. Masses and masses of stones: tall ones, short ones, skinny ones, huge fat ones, big ones, medium-sized ones and little ones – more than you could possibly count, and some small enough to put in your pocket.

And that's just what someone did. We are at Balnuaran of Clava, a 4,000 year-old early Bronze Age or late Neolithic Age cemetery. Time passed. No-one noticed the theft. Then one day the Inverness Tourist Board received a heavy parcel. When they opened it, they were astonished to find a stone inside. It was accompanied by an anonymous letter from a Belgian tourist who explained he had pocketed the stone as he thought it might be a stone-age tool and would look perfect on his mantlepiece. He went on to say he was returning it as he believed it carried a curse. Since it had been in his possession he had suffered a series of misfortunes: his wife had become seriously ill, his daughter had broken her leg, he had broken his arm, and he had lost his job. He requested the stone be taken back from whence it came.

Dear anonymous Belgian, you did the right thing in the end and I hope you and your family are having a curse-free life now. And I have news for you. Even if you had provided your name you probably would have had as much chance as breaking into the top five of most famous Belgians in the world as the proverbial snowball in hell. (Well how many can you think of?)

We have no such nefarious intentions as the anonymous Belgian but we have our own curse to bear – the midges. Apart from them, it is a very pleasant place indeed to sleep throughout eternity, a shady nook with the River Nairn tinkling nearby. Pity about those accursed midges, but I suppose if you are dead they wouldn't bother you any more but they are a perfect pest for the living.

The Belgian was by no means the first to desecrate the site. The Victorian owner of the land did far worse. He drove a road through it (the one that took us here) – you can see a standing stone on the other side of the fence and another on the other side of the road. Showing a complete disrespect for this ancient monument, he moved others out of the way and used some of the smaller ones (a good many actually), to build a wall. He also planted the trees we see today. See how tall they have grown!

So, as well as all those other outrages, he is also largely to blame for making this sanctuary a midge-infested area too. There wasn't a single one at Culloden just a mile or so up the road. Thank you very much indeed.

Before any professional examination of the site was made, there were some amateur excavations whose findings went unrecorded. Now the site is in the safe hands of Historic Scotland and like so many of its other sites that are in ruins, entry is completely free and open all hours. But if it eases your conscience any and makes you feel happier, a notice on the gate tells you where to text a donation of £2. Isn't modern technology a wonderful thing? And wouldn't the people who built this site be amazed?

There are three cairns, each enclosed by a circle of standing stones or "kerb stones". Even before you pass through the entrance gate, your eye is attracted to a massive hump of stones on your right, for all the world looking like a bleached white whale, as if Moby Dick had somehow been washed ashore here and not decayed.

Impressive certainly, but when you go round to the left, you discover a passageway and realise this huge pile of stones must have been higher still when first built. Like Maeshowe in Orkney, it once had a domed roof and you reached the central chamber by crawling along the passage on your hands and knees. That it is roofless now is good news for the modern visitor as (s)he can walk right in and thanks to the open skylight so to speak, see the interior very well.

You can see how the walls have been constructed with courses of larger stones and the gaps filled in with smaller ones. The passageway, not more than a foot wide, is clearly defined by two rows of massive boulders chosen for their natural smoothness. Its height I judge to be about three feet, so not for the claustrophobic, all those who crawled along here when the roof was in place, especially when you remember you are heading into the even deeper dark, black as death itself, with tons and tons of stones resting above your head.

Who these architects were we just don't know since they did not know writing and the bodies that once occupied these cairns, and who might have provided some clues, have long since turned to dust, along with any grave goods that might have been buried with them. Well, that's not quite accurate. In 1950 archaeologists found some minute traces of cremated bone – not even enough to make a handful of dust, the sum total of finds in the cairn.

However, because the Clava complex shares some similarities with other sites of the same era, the experts have concluded these burial chambers were not for mass burials, but contained only two or three bodies, presumably people of some importance, such as chiefs or priests. Whoever they were, they must have regarded them with a great deal of respect to have expended such an enormous amount of effort. Carrying all those stones up from the riverbed is one thing, but just think of the supreme effort it must have taken to manhandle those massive boulders from their original location, wherever that was, into such a precise position – and we haven't even started talking about the standing stones which encircle the mound. If you look closely, you will see they are graded in height with the tallest two, seven or eight feet high, facing south-west and flanking the entrance to the passage.

And there is something else too which is not immediately obvious. The line of three cairns are orientated NE-SW and here's the cunning thing – at the midwinter sunset, on the shortest day of the year, the rays of the setting sun would pierce the passageways and illuminate the back wall of the chamber just as it does at Maeshowe. And like Maeshowe, these cairns would have been visible for miles and miles around, there being no trees hereabouts in those days.

We may not know much about the people who built these cairns, but anyone can see they were far from primitive. Because of the orientation of the passageways, it's safe to say if they were not sun worshippers in the modern sense of the term, lying prostrate on continental package-holiday beaches, all the while anointing themselves with the holy suntan cream – the sun must have had a special signifance for them since they took such care to orientate the passageways with such precision.

We need to pause and look at it from their end-of-time's telescope for a moment. If we dread the long winter nights and long for the return of spring, imagine what those people in this northerly latitude must have thought about the encroaching winter. The people who know about such things tell us that when this site was in its prime, the climate was warmer but wetter. Still not nice without central heating. After the winter solstice, they knew things could only get better – it marked the slow return of that life-giving, life-affirming, warming sun. The bones of the dead, they were sure, would appreciate a little warming even if it did not penetrate to the marrow.

To help with our understanding of the site, there are very helpful noticeboards with artists' impressions of what the cairns looked like when they were first constructed. They also draw our attention to the mysterious circles or cup marks which you can find in several stones dotted about the site, if you forgive the expression, for that's exactly what they look like – polka dots, laboriously carved out of the stone and without any sort of recognisable pattern. There are no signs of any tool marks; the holes are completely smooth so a great deal of time must have been spent getting them like that.

What they really are, no-one knows, not even the experts. Their best guess is it's some sort of primitive art and who am I to say they are wrong? But if it *is* art, what it means, if anything, is a complete mystery – just like I feel when confronted with a piece of 20th or 21st century abstract art. They might be disappointed if they ever find out the answer, like you are when the secret of a conjuror's trick is revealed to you. You would have preferred the mystery.

I have a humble solution to proffer. I think it could be some sort of board game. They remind me of the holes I saw set into the pavement in the Forum in Rome. At first I thought they were some sort of urban graffiti but actually they were board games where bored citizens passed the time by having a game of marbles or whatever it was while their wives were shopping for a new *tunica* or handsome new slave. And for what it's worth, I am also reminded of the *Solitaire* I used to play as a boy where the many, many holes were filled with marbles and the object of the exercise was to get your marble, the last marble on the board, into the hole in the middle.

But that can't be what these holes are, because the game I described requires a cruciform shape and I can't see that, or any other shape for that matter, in any of these stones. Nevertheless, I humbly pass on the suggestion to the experts that that's what these holes are – some sort of game and they have absolutely no meaning, religious or otherwise. After all, wouldn't you just love, in those dark, prehistoric days, to have some sort of recreation? And what better than by inventing a game that would puzzle archaeologists for tens of centuries to come?

Although it remains to be seen what the experts make of my modest proposal, they do agree these stones probably were carved by a people before the cairn-builders. Since the "cup marks" stones seem to be randomly incorporated into structures all over the site, that seems eminently logical to me. I mean, if you were looking for stones to build your cairn and this was near to hand, despite it looking like a broken bit of *Aero*, wouldn't you rather use it than have to lug a heavy stone all the way up here from the river bed?

What the experts *have* discovered and what is a bit difficult for us to see today, given the ravages of time and erosion and the lichen invasion, is the place colour and texture played in the architects' plans. We are told for example that red stones were used for the back of the chamber where the sun would illuminate them, while, for the rising sun, they chose "white" stones with quartz. Good morning, bright star! We say hello. You shine above us and our stones twinkle below.

The red at the back of the chamber is more noticeable in the SW chamber than in the NE where, if I hadn't known to look out for them, I would not have noticed particularly the red stones among the "white" and would have put it down merely to random chance. Similarly, the experts tell us the standing stones that encircle the mound are graded in size with the largest being nearest the entrance. Yes, true enough, now you come to mention it.

What we can't see, no matter how hard we look, is around the cairns, it seems these people built a platform as far out as the ring of standing stones. That's an incredible amount of stones! As well as acting as a buttress (not that I thought they would have needed it), it also created a stage on which we are told they probably performed rituals or perhaps conducted funerals. They found seashells and cremated bones amongst the rubble.

Today all that remains to be seen of that is the odd stone scattered about and very much at risk of disappearing beneath the turf forever. Was this where the Victorian laird got the material for his walls and road? We are not told if these platforms were covered with turf but I presume not, and if we were awestruck when we first arrived at the amount of stone and stones in this place, imagine what it must have looked like in 1871 before he came along! Talk about stone the crows! More a case of there being more than enough to kill a murder of the blighters!

And there's more – much more! Between the two chambered cairns there is another sort of monument carefully positioned so as not to impede the rays of the setting sun from entering the passageways. Unlike them, this cairn did not have a roof or an entrance. You have to imagine two rings of boulders with a hole in the middle, like a doughnut. The archaeologists think there was a fire in the middle which is why they called it the "Ring of Fire". They found traces of burning in the centre as well as some human bones. The space between the two circles was filled in with stones and what's more, the colour scheme to which I've already alluded was recreated here to create segments, like slices of cake, with alternate pink and white stones. What can it all mean?

I have a theory. Yes, another! These "slices" of different-coloured stone resemble rays emanating from that central, empty core. Could that, especially when a cremation was in progress, possibly represent the sun and, when the poor deceased was reduced as near to ashes as he could possibly be, could it not symbolise his returning to the heart of that life-giving force at the centre of their universe? It's only a suggestion.

The experts think this monument underwent a later stage of development. The central hole was filled in and an outer circle of stones was added and some were linked by pathways to the inner circles, making it look more than ever like rays emanating from the centre – but why only some of them? My guess is these later people were turning to a new religion (they found a Pictish cremation nearby) and the filling in of the hole had something to do with the sun playing a less important part in their culture.

Before we go, there is one other monument I must tell you about – the Kerb Cairn. Stay with me, it won't take long.

It's not much to look at now, only a small ring of boulders. Amongst all these massive amount of stones it looks completely insignificant, but thanks to the artist's impression on the noticeboard nearby, we can see that once upon a time in the past, about a millennium after the two large cairns and the Ring of Fire, it was a structure of at least some minor significance. But how strange, as the song has it, the change from major to minor! What does this puny little grave have to tell us about these peoples' evolving society?

Like its predecessors, the stones were graded in height with the largest to the south-west, to welcome the setting sun. Yes, I can just about see that, though I wouldn't have noticed it if it hadn't been pointed out to me – especially as one of the biggest seems to have toppled over into what would once have been the grave.

They also used their ancestors' mixture of colours: red, pink and white, but they are even harder to make out, being very much overgrown with moss. A flat red stone is meant to represent a lintel – a lintel into a place so small and so shallow that a passageway was not only unnecessary but impossible. And another thing: it is not aligned to the south-west. It's a sign that although vestiges of the old traditions lingered on, the times, they were a'changin'. The Pictish cremation discovered near the Ring of Fire is testimony to that.

This "lintel" stone has one clearly defined ring on it, but look more closely and you will see the vestiges of more, which the enemy of us all, time, has worn away. Was it by accident or by design that this stone with the "design" on it was placed here? It all adds to the mystery.

If you were to continue a little further down the road, on the one that the laird made, in about half a mile or so, you would come to another cairn, only much smaller and in a pretty ruinous state. It's called Milton of Clava. There may have been more cairns once but there is not much to see now, only one tall standing stone and a few depressions in the ground where cairns may have been once upon a time. Potentially more interesting, but not by much, are the foundations of a rectangular building which the experts speculate might have been a chapel. It hasn't been excavated yet but, according to the noticeboard, it might be medieval. Thus this holy site continued to have religious connections a thousand years after the cairn builders.

You may be disappointed by what this site has to offer compared to its neighbour just up the road; in fact it doesn't even to begin to compete with it, but it does have something to offer which the other doesn't – a splendid view over the fields to the magnificent Nairn, or Culloden, viaduct. Graceful and elegant, it strides across the valley in twenty-eight elegant arches. At 1785 feet long and 312 feet high at its highest, it is the largest viaduct made of bricks and mortar in Scotland, built for the Highland railway in 1898.

It was not designed by Telford as many people suppose, but by Murdoch Paterson. It was begun in 1893 and not quite complete in 1898 when he died aged 72. I would say that's some monument to be remembered by, but there are many, many more. As railway fever took a hold of the Highlands, there is hardly a railway bridge or a station or station buildings (many of them on the 500), that does not bear Mr Paterson's fingerprints. That's some legacy to be proud of. Everybody has heard of Thomas Telford but who has of Mr Murdoch Paterson?

Step up and take a bow, sir! Your time has come!

And our time has come too. Time to move on – to visit William Skinner's finest achievement. It was the wonder of its age, and it still inspires awe today. William Skinner, I hear you ask? Perhaps if I give you his full title – Lieutenant-General William Skinner? No, still doesn't ring a bell? Well, we're going back to the much more recent past, back on the Culloden trail again. We're making for Fort George and Skinner was its designer and chief engineer. Designed to accommodate 1600 troops, defended by more than 80 cannons, it is the biggest and best artillery fortification in the entire UK and the equal of many in Europe besides. Not that there was any prospect of another insurrection anyway, but one look at it by claymore-wielding Jacobite diehards from the Highland heartlands would have been enough to have sent them homeward to think again.

Skinner's name deserves to be better known, don't you think?

Chapter Four

Fort George: The Subjugator of a Nation

IN Maths I was taught (and one of the few things I remember), that the shortest distance between two points is a straight line and I know it makes sense, but it has always struck me how tedious, to put it mildly, it must have been for foot-soldiers on the march to see that ribbon of road unwinding endlessly before them. Maybe it was a blessing if all you could actually see was the back of your comrade's neck and resign yourself to the mind-numbing beat of the tramp, tramp, tramp of your feet.

It's on one such long and unwinding road we are rolling effortlessly along now at a pace the soldiers who marched down this road would never have believed possible, and yet it still seems to take an age before we arrive at that narrow point we saw in the distance. It could be a Roman road, but isn't; it could be one of General Wade's, but isn't. What it actually is, is the B9006, and the Ordnance Survey map also tells us it's an Old Military Road. What it does *not* tell you is the name of the man who built it and thus his name also is condemned to obscurity like Murdoch Paterson's, although like him, you will find his handiwork all over the Highlands. The man in question was Major William Caulfeild ⟦sic⟧.

Caulfeild became Wade's assistant in 1732 and succeeded him on the latter's death in 1748. Caulfeild continued working until his death in 1767 aged 69, and with that came an end to the road-building project in the Highlands. He had completed his life's work. In his younger days he must have had a pretty good working relationship with Wade since he named his second son after him. And further evidence of admiration for his boss's work is that Caulfeild is attributed with having composed the immortal lines:

> *If you had seen this road before it was made,*
> *You would lift up your hands and bless General Wade.*

But, as things turned out, it was a case of the apprentice surpassing the achievements of the master, for Caulfeild actually ended up building three times more miles of road than Wade (900) and hundreds more bridges (600). So the chances are, should you find yourselves on an Old Military Road, you are not on a Wade road at all but a Caulfeild, just as we are now.

At the end of it, and taking twenty-one years to build, Fort George sits on a peninsula jutting out into the Moray Firth like a big, squat toad with a pointy bottom. The yards-thick battlements bristle with cannons but not a single one was ever fired in anger. Amongst a host of other defences, in a zig-zag arrangement, there is not a wall that any attacker would not come under fire. No wonder no-one bothered. And here's the great thing for the visitor today: not much imagination is required to imagine it as it was then, because it remains pretty much the same today as it was in its heyday.

With astonishing accuracy, the original estimate was for £9,673 19s 1d. (Wouldn't you just love to know what that penny was to be spent on?) In actual fact the final bill came in at £200,000, almost £20 million in today's money. Some things never change. The building of the Scottish Parliament Building, completed in 2004, was three years late and at an eye-watering £414 million, an incredible 400% over budget. Which makes the more recent Edinburgh trams fiasco seem minor by comparison. At £776 million, it was only twice the estimated cost. After a catalogue of delays, the tramline eventually opened in 2014.

Still, the money was well spent on Fort George if it subdued the natives. And it did, though the expression "taking a sledgehammer to crack a nut" springs to mind. Fort George never saw any action, not in the immediate aftermath of Culloden or later, though there was just a slight chance if things had gone differently, it might have been called into service in 1759 during the Seven Years' War when the French made serious plans to invade England. This time the boot was on the other foot: the French were looking for support from the Jacobites. How much support they would actually have got is doubtful and how effective it would have been even more so. In any case it was never put to the test. The twin prongs of the French fleet were defeated at the battles of Lagos off the Portuguese coast and Quiberon Bay off Brittany. Never again would the French raise an army or even so much lift a finger to help the Stuart dynasty. (It was about this time that Bonnie Prince Charlie found himself a guest who had overstayed his welcome in France and he moved back to Rome, the city of his birth, where he died in 1788.)

When Lieutenant-General William Skinner designed this fort he did not start from scratch but built it on past good practice, the so-called *trace Italienne*, or "star fort" shape, a defense against cannon and mortar fire and which he adapted to suit this site. A cannonball can make a nasty hole or inflict serious damage on even a six-foot-thick wall, so naturally you don't present the enemy with such an easy target. For this reason, the buildings are set well back from the entrance, not even seen, hidden from view behind a glacis (a sloping earthen rampart) and defended by triangular-shaped ravelins, ramparts (there's more than a mile of them), ditches, bastions, demi-bastions and casemates, to name but a few. (You really need a glossary to understand the defences here.) The excavations were used to construct the glacis, ravelins and ramparts. The bricks for the walls, and I wouldn't like to begin to count them, were made on site, a proper little brick factory. They must have baked them by the dozens.

From the car park, we pass through a covered passage and find ourselves in an open space where the ravelin guardhouse now serves as the visitor centre. And still we can't see the buildings in the interior of the fort! The eye is drawn to an incredibly white drawbridge at the end of which, set in a massive wall with a green fringe on top, is the main entrance with on the pediment, George II's coat of arms. Through the open door, at last, you can just about make out some buildings on the other side of the arch, your first glimpse of the inner fort.

It's when we set foot on the drawbridge that it really hits me just how hard a place like this would be to capture. Should the attackers somehow make it this far they would be confronted with a yawning chasm, ditch, dry moat, call it what you will, by any name you would care to call it – it would present a serious obstacle to any attacker. But let us suppose, in some mad moment, someone had forgotten to raise the drawbridge, five cannons on each side of the flanking bastions on the ditch would blast you and the bridge to kingdom come. And that's not all – incredibly, the ditch could be flooded at high tide through sluices, so what it really should be called, to add to your collection of military terms, is a *batardeau.*

Thankfully Historic Scotland makes it so much easier for us nowadays to gain entry to the fort. All you need is the price of a ticket and it's *Open Sesame.* We don't even need that, being members. Couldn't be easier. A piece of cake and another bargain not to be missed.

But before you enter the fort, stop a moment and look closely at the Royal Coat of Arms in the pediment above the arch. There's a mistake. Can you spot it? Starting in the top-left quadrant and moving clockwise are the royal arms of Scotland "impaling" England, then moving clockwise, France, Ireland and Hanover. Which one is wrong? Just in case you don't know what Scotland "impaling" England means in this context, let me enlighten you. It's a lot less painful than it sounds. "Impalement" in heraldry simply means the splitting of an escutcheon (shield) to show a union, with the position of honour being on the right, the *dexter,* and the other, of course, being the *sinister.*

It's not easy to spot and, if the language of 18th century fort defences takes a bit of getting your head around, the language of heraldry is more likely to bash in your brains – especially if you have let your medieval French lapse. Around the lion, *rampant, gules,* there should be a double border (*tressure*). So now you know. Furthermore – the *tressure* should be *flory counter-flory,* which is to say decorated with fleurs-de-lys facing alternately inwards and outwards. It symbolises the Auld Alliance between Scotland and France.

And now at last, when you step inside the fort proper, ahead of you lies a vast green sward – the parade ground, where they also hold the Highland Tattoo. This three-day event celebrating Highland culture has just finished evidently as men with tattooed muscles (is it a job requirement?) are dismantling scaffolding. And as you walk on, it's like entering a small town with serried houses, row upon row. They are Georgian of course, but look incredibly modern, not in the least like the two-and-a-half centuries old that they really are.

At the end of Main Street, so to speak, is an arch with a clock standing between two rows of buildings. On the left was the bakehouse; on the right the brewery. Through the arch is the chapel, the last building to be completed, and not in Skinner's original plans. He had other priorities of course. His plan was that the soldiers' spiritual needs would be attended to by the minister of nearby Kirkton. To attend that church would still involve a bit of a tramp, and I for one would rather have put my feet up on the day of rest. In 1777, the minister of Ardersier took over the chaplaincy. So you see, Fort George was a self-sufficient unit, and if it came to the bit could withstand a siege – probably the only option open to attackers since they couldn't get in.

And if the way we had come was considered the fort's weakest, most vulnerable side, and if you thought that was impossible or next to impossible – it was even harder to attack from the sea. This we can see for ourselves as we stand on the toad's head, the Point battery with on either side, like its eyes, Prince Frederick William's demi-bastion on the left and on the right, that of the Duke of Marlborough's. The front legs have two full bastions, Prince William Henry's on the left and Prince Henry Frederick's on the right. On the back left leg is the Prince of Wales' bastion and on the right, the Duke of Cumberland's. Its bottom I have already mentioned – the ravelin at the entrance. It is without question the most formidable toad in Scotland and something I wouldn't dare to meddle with, just like our prickly emblem, the thistle, whose motto *Nemo me impune lacessit* you don't need to be a Latin scholar in order to get the message.

We reached the Point up a grassy slope but nothing that an electric wheelchair can't handle, for one has been abandoned at the top. But how odd! Where is the driver? Can't be far away, unless – oh my God, unless he or she got out for a short walk and either was blown (it is pretty windy up here) or fell over the precipice in a fit of vertigo. It's a long way down; the chapel looks like something out of a miniature village. But it's all right. I spot another scooter zipping along and the driver is a young person, wearing a uniform – a member of staff. Right enough, it must save a lot of time getting around the 42-acre site and a damn sight more fun than riding a bicycle. And if, like me, you have no idea what an acre looks like, think of a football pitch and you'll not be far out.

There's a good view from the Point. To the west, the mountain ranges of Wester Ross ripple into the sky. That's where we will be not so long from now. Much closer, just across the narrow firth, is the Black Isle and almost opposite, Chanory Point where people go to see the dolphins putting on an aerial display, or as I once saw on TV, perhaps passing a porpoise about, tossing it through the air from one to the other as if playing a game of basketball. If the dolphin fans are really lucky, they may even see one pull a bird under the water to drown it, not because they have any intention of eating it, but just for fun and because they can. They are said to be supremely intelligent creatures, practically as intelligent as us – the masters of their element. I can believe that: it takes a certain kind of intelligence to invent a game called "Pass the Porpoise".

In 1881 the fort became home to the Seaforth Highlanders which was an amalgamation of the 72nd and 78th Highlanders. In 1961 they were amalgamated again with the Cameron Highlanders to become the Queen's Own Highlanders. Then in 2004 (do try to keep up) they amalgamated yet again with the Gordon Highlanders to become the Highlanders, the Royal Regiment of Scotland, and this is where the third battalion, known as the Black Watch, is based. That is history I suppose, as what differentiates the present from the past is just a matter of time. But the time we are most interested in is the 18th century, and well done Historic Scotland, for setting aside some rooms so we can see what life was like for the soldiers who manned this fort in the aftermath of Culloden.

Our way to see them takes us past the chapel designed by the famous Adam family: John, James and Robert, Scotland's premier architects of the time. Their father, William, was awarded the contract to build the fort. And very pleasing the chapel is too, on the inside especially. Very plain, very simple, very light, very airy, and very, very white. I like it a lot. There is an upper gallery supported by Doric pillars, on either side of the nave where the rank and file sat, in the body of the kirk. The officers sat in box pews on the right which unfortunately have been removed. And there is no mistaking this is a church for the military, for regimental colours are hanging from the gallery with more in the apse where the communion table is housed, and in the aisle to the left there is a pyramid of four regimental drums.

Most intriguing is the three-tiered pulpit. On the bottom the precentor stood to lead the singing of psalms. There is no organ or any instrumental accompaniment; that could be a distraction from the Word which is all there was in the beginning. As a matter of fact, the Church of Scotland only adopted hymns in 1861 and it took the Free Church another eleven years to be convinced the singing of hymns was not sinful. In the middle stood the reader and on the top tier of course, was the minister. Above him there used to be a sounding board; now it's just the lemon ceiling with its white mouldings and shaped like your palate. I bet the acoustics in here are very good indeed and made the sounding board redundant.

Leaving the chapel, we make our way to the historic barracks rooms, built of red sandstone, which displays three periods and two classes of accommodation. First is the Rank and File Room of 1780, just eleven years after the fort's completion. It certainly is Spartan but what else would you expect in those days for those at the bottom of the pecking order?

What *is* a surprise is to see a woman in a shawl slaving over a cold stove where a long-handled pot, probably containing soup or a stew of some kind, sits on a hot plate at the side. Behind her, a soldier, resplendent in his uniform and a pair of cross-gartered stockings that Malvolio would have given his eyeteeth for had they been the right colour, is sitting on a wooden bench on a bare wooden floor at a wooden table. In front of him, on top of a wooden plate, is a wooden bowl. (What would they have done without that material?) She looks incredibly dowdy, while he, in his bright-red tunic with white frogging, looks like a peacock, just as nature intended, in the bird world at least.

But what about her? What on earth is she doing in this world of men? Well, strange as it may seem, one percent was allowed to bring wives, and even the kids. They were permitted to do chores for the men, for which services the army generously granted them half rations. They slept with their husbands in the same room. That explains the blanket, draped like washing on a line, over the bed in the corner. It's not a lot of privacy that's for sure, especially as the blanket only covers the top third of the bed.

The soldiers slept eight to a room, in a double bed. I bet they didn't tell you that when you took the "king's shilling" – that you'd have to sleep in the same bed as a possibly flatulent comrade who snored and kept pinching the blanket. I suppose it was a bed, at least. Pity the kids who had no beds at all and slept where they could. The troops, it seems, did not suffer them gladly; in fact it seems they regarded them as a constant source of irritation.

We know this soldier's name – Private James Anderson, born in Dundee in 1758. He enlisted in 1780 and received what must have seemed to him unheard of riches – five guineas – out of which he had to buy his uniform and equipment. The army giveth and the army taketh away. I don't know what that left him with (probably not a lot) but one thing it did allow him to do was wear the kilt which had been circumscribed in 1746, as you may remember my telling you earlier.

He was only here for six months undergoing his training, then he was posted to India. Join the army and see the world. He had to march to Queensferry, a mere 150 miles (God bless Caulfeild) where he took he took ship to India. The voyage took over a year but dismiss any thoughts of a relaxing cruise, playing quoits on the deck, getting a tan, and all the while the pay was going on. One in five never made it to India alive. And of course, when you got there, there was another kind of death to face. Maybe James got lucky when he got a bullet in the thigh and was repatriated to the Chelsea hospital and eventually discharged, not just from the hospital, but the army. He made his way back to Dundee and what happened to him after that we are not told but I imagine it would have been difficult for him to get a job with his gammy leg, despite being only twenty-eight.

It's only a couple of our steps to step forward eighty-eight years, to the Rank and File Room 1868. The fireplace has gone and it's a lot less crowded with only five beds. That's because there are now married quarters and a mess room, not to mention improved culinary arrangements, so soldiers no longer had to do their own cooking. I would certainly say that was a reason for celebration. There were other advances too. To relieve the boredom, there was a library and sports facilities. There was even a savings scheme, though it is hard to see the rank and file soldier (or the officers for that matter) being able to contribute much to it: the pay had not gone up in the past hundred years.

Despite all this, it still looks pretty Spartan. The wooden beds have been replaced with iron ones that are hinged in the middle to create more space when not in use, but even better, they are single. What luxury, just think of it – a bed to yourself! There's even a shelf above the bed where you can stow your stuff. And the wooden plates have been replaced with crockery. Also, on the table, a galvanised iron bucket and basin and a couple of scrubbing brushes. They may have a mess room but that's no reason why this should be one too.

At the table a soldier is reading a letter. Impossible to tell from his expression if it's good news or bad. Actually it's a letter from his sister in which she says that "aunty" was sorry to hear he had enlisted but thought it was the "best that he could do, like many a good man." His name was George Moffat, born in Leith and who enlisted in the 79th Cameron Highlanders in December 1867. Just like James Anderson before him, he was posted to India, but this time the voyage only took forty days. He served four years there in a policing role as there were no battles to be fought, before returning to Britain. In 1879 he was posted to Egypt where he saw action in the battle of Tel-el-Kebir (1882) and the Nile (1884-85), where he was wounded and repatriated to a hospital in England. Two months later he was back in Fort George. He ended his career at Edinburgh Castle and died in 1910. Seems funny a career like that should take us into the twentieth century.

We, however, have taken a step back to the past. We are in the 19th century, in 1813 to be precise, and here is Major Andrew Coghlan seated at a table on which there is a portable writing desk. A china cup and saucer and milk jug stand on a green cloth. How civilised! Imagine having a whole room to yourself! The thing that really catches the eye in it is the four-poster bed in the corner. Well I suppose it is not a proper four-poster, the canopy only comes halfway down, but it is a double bed and what's more, he has it all to himself. Note too that the windowpanes are larger and are fitted with shutters and between them is a chest of drawers made of mahogany, not just utility. And get this: in a crystal decanter, port, and on a silver tray next to it, a whisky decanter and glasses. Yes, an officer's life for me!

In fact Major Coghlan was not just any officer: he wound up as head honcho here, or rather that is what he was as we see him now. No wonder he's got the best bed and room in the entire barracks. He ended up as a Lieutenant-Colonel and retired on full pay in 1827. He died in 1837 aged 70, regretting he wasn't dying on the battlefield. Spoken like an officer and a gentleman, sir!

His career began in 1791 in the 72nd Regiment of Highlanders when he enlisted as an ensign, or junior officer. In 1795 he became a lieutenant and was made a captain a year later. His first posting was to India where he was at the siege of Balangore and Savendroog and he fought in the battles of Seringapatan and Pondicherry where he was wounded and invalided home for six months' leave.

He bought a commission in 1807. Imagine being able to do that! (The practice persisted until 1871.) That made him a major. He ended up at the second battle of Buenos Aires that same year (part of the Anglo-Spanish War of 1796-1808) where the British, under the command of Lieutenant-General John Whitelock, were repulsed by, amongst others, 800 African slaves and the inhabitants, who poured pots of boiling cooking oil on top of the would-be invaders' heads. (I wonder if Whitelock bought his commission.) In 1808-09

Coghlan commanded the 45th in Spain during the Peninsular War. (The British were always fighting a war somewhere in those days.) He was wounded twice, once in the head. After that he was transferred to the 21st Foot and became the commander here. Actually, as he sits at his desk now, he was just about to pack his bags, promoted again, this time as Lieutenant–Colonel of the York Chasseurs.

And so we say goodbye to him and the historical barracks rooms and make our way across the street to the Grand Magazine which held over 2,500 barrels, each containing 100 pounds of gunpowder. They had certainly learned something since the Jacobites blew up Fort Augustus during the march north from Derby and on their way to their ill-fated date with destiny at Culloden. Probably it was a lucky hit, a mortar bomb happening to hit the gunpowder store which blew the whole thing up. No chance of that happening here, or even them blowing themselves up by accident. It was built into the bastions whilst the interior of the fort was protected by a blast wall. It was fitted with copper air vents and a blast door. Inside, the floor, the barrel racks – everything was made of wood to avoid creating a spark. The men who worked in here had to wear special shoes and even clothes without metal buttons.

We're all but finished now. We're on our way out. I would have liked to have visited the dog cemetery for some reason I don't even understand myself, except I am very fond of cemeteries. It's on a ravelin on the north side and closed to the public, for some reason I don't understand either. Instead we pass through the sallyport in the casemates on the southern side and come to the harbour which is all silted up and has not been used in an age. This was where supplies came to the fort, so much easier than taking them in by Caulfeild's road, no matter how good it was, for its day.

We missed them on the way in, so now we visit the guardhouses and the "black hole", otherwise the prison cell, now painted white and featureless. What had this little barrel-vaulted room witnessed in the past, before the prison cells, the former provision stores, were built in the nineteenth century? Drunkenness was the major cause of indiscipline. Sentries were supposed to be on the lookout for "whisky women" smuggling the national drink into the fort. In 1831, one soldier, David Abernethy, recorded his misdemeanour on the wall of his cell, chipping it out laboriously. His time was not wasted: we know his name today. He got sixty days for being drunk on guard duty. At least it passed the time. He did not tell us what he got for defacing army property.

In the officers' austere guardroom, a row of fold-up metal beds like we had seen in the 1870 barracks room, are lined up like a row of soldiers. They don't look very comfortable, and they aren't. I know because I feel one of the mattresses. Just as I thought. Straw, very thin, very, very scratchy and very, very lumpy with one thin blanket to cover you. Even at the height of a Scottish summer that seems inadequate; in the depths of a Scottish winter where the wind comes sweeping in from Siberia, it's no wonder they called it "Camp Misery".

I would call it a miserable existence: up at 5am to be ready for nearly two hours' drill at 6, breakfast, followed by more drill at 10 for two more hours, two hours off for dinner, then more drill at 2 for two more hours. And no doubt the drill sergeant bellowed at them to march at the double too.

After that you were done for the day, free, to do – nothing. What *was* there to do in this isolated, wind-swept place that must have seemed like a prison camp? They could hardly walk into Inverness for a quick pint. No wonder they were bored out of their skulls; no wonder they turned to stronger stuff whenever they could get their hands on it and people like David Abernethy ended up doing time.

Chapter Five

Avoch: The Great Explorer

TODAY we are going to be circumnavigating the Black Isle, which, sandwiched between the Moray and Cromarty Firths, is neither an island nor black. It's also, strictly speaking, not on the NC500, but then neither is Culloden or the Clava Cairns or Fort George for that matter. But the NC500 is not the be-all and end-all; it offers bewitching detours and this is another for us on the trail of the past.

We soar over the Moray Firth on the Kessock Bridge and cross the busy A9 towards Munlochy Bay. Shortly afterwards we arrive in the little village of Avoch (pronounced Och). We are on the trail of a very famous man, the first man to cross the North American continent, more than a decade before Lewis and Clark went to explore, for Jefferson, the pig-in-the-poke that he had bought from the French in 1803. Some pig! Some poke! At a stroke it doubled the size of the nascent nation, extending it from the Mississippi to the Rockies. Some number cruncher has calculated that it worked out at 3 cents an acre. It is known to history as the Louisiana Purchase; I would call it the bargain of the century.

Of course it took a Scot to show the way, though his way was rather more north than that of Lewis and Clark. His name was Alexander Mackenzie, not the second prime minister of Canada who also came from Scotland (unsurprisingly enough), but the fur trader, turned great explorer, who was born in Stornoway in 1764. In 1774, after his mother died and hard times having hit the Hebrides in general, he and his father, accompanied by two aunts, set sail for New York to join an uncle of Alexander's who had gone before, so to speak.

No sooner were they beginning to settle into their new life, or so it seemed, than the American War of Independence broke out and in 1776, both his father and his uncle did what they saw was their patriotic duty and enlisted in the King's Royal Regiment of New York. No Jacobites they. In fact, during the '45 Rising, young Mackenzie's father, when he was just a teenager, enlisted as an ensign in the British army to protect Stornoway from that other set of revolutionaries. For his own protection, young Alexander was shipped off to Montreal with his aunts, as being a loyalist was not a popular choice amongst the colonists of New York State.

A few years later he became apprenticed to a fur trading company which merged with the North West Trading Company and in 1789, under its auspices, Mackenzie left Fort Chipewyan on Lake Athabasca in Northern Alberta, along what the natives called the Deh Cho River. In the quest for ever-increasing trade and profits, and acting upon what turned out be unreliable information from his somewhat louche boss, Peter Pond, Alexander's mission was to find a navigable route to the Pacific. Thus he became an accidental explorer.

At first all seemed well but then, to his intense disappointment, the river swung north and ended up in the Beaufort Sea, not the Cook Inlet as he had hoped. It may have been a disappointment then, but think of the joy it must have brought when the river was renamed in his honour. At over 1,000 miles, it is the longest river in Canada. In fact, in the entire North American continent, only the mighty Mississippi is longer. That's some legacy. Better by far than being known as the famous fur trapper, Alexander Mackenzie.

In 1792-93 the indefatigable Mackenzie tried again, journeying down the Slave River to a fork in the Peace River where he and his companions overwintered at the tongue-twisting and appropriately-named Fort Fork before setting out again the following May. They took the Parsnip River, crossed the continental divide and reached the Fraser River, but were advised by some friendly natives to continue no further but to turn back and go overland as the natives downriver were hostile. In any case, they were told the river was unnavigable in places. So that was that.

Thus Mackenzie was forced to take what was known as the "Grease Trail". Whilst the Silk Road sounds exotic and enchanting; the Grease Trail sounds slippery and distinctly unappealing, but better by far than being porcupined with arrows and your crowning glory adorning some brave's belt. The reason for the name is because long before a white face ever darkened the continent, there was a system of trails whereby the natives of the west coast traded the eulachon (a fish like a sardine) for furs and other commodities with the natives in the interior. At first sight this seems a bit strange, for did the natives in the interior not have fish aplenty in their own rivers and lakes? Furthermore, by the time the fish reached the interior, they would have been a bit sniffy to say the least. So what was so special about the eulachon?

Well, it was a very oily fish and it was the oil that was sought after. To get the oil, according to an ancient recipe, you buried the fish for a week until they were nicely decomposed, then you poured boiling water on them and skimmed off the oil. Actually the early explorers called it the "candlefish" as, during spawning especially, it was very fatty indeed. What you did was you dried it then threaded a wick through its mouth and poked it out through its bottom. And there you have it, the first scented candle in Canada. What a useful fish it was to be sure.

Eventually Mackenzie and his merry men (who probably were far from happy at having to retrace their paddle strokes), arrived, with the help of friendly tribes, in the Bella Coola Valley. In borrowed canoes and accompanied by guides of that tribe, they paddled downriver and eventually, "like stout Cortez... star'd upon the Pacific." Thus Mackenzie gets the credit and the fame as being the first man to cross the continent twelve years before Lewis and Clark.

As a matter of fact, before they set off on their own expedition of discovery in 1804, Jefferson presented the duo with a copy of the great Scot's account of his travels which had been published in 1801. It rejoiced under the title of *Voyages from Montreal, on the river St. Laurence, through the continent of North America, to the Frozen and Pacific oceans; in the years, 1789 and 1793; with a preliminary account of the rise, progress, and present state of the fur trade of that country.* I suppose an epic journey deserves a title nearly as long but if I had been his editor, I would have been looking for something a bit more snappy. Still, you can't deny it does what says on the cover and you know exactly what you are getting when you buy it – unlike the Louisiana Purchase.

But long before the publication of that runaway bestseller, Mackenzie also did another piece of writing – he recorded his feat on a stone: "Alex Mackenzie from Canada by land 22nd July 1793". Although he was actually from the Isle of Lewis, he wrote "from Canada" because that was the name given to the former French territory in southern Quebec where Montreal is situated on the St Lawrence and from whence his transcontinental journey had really begun (as it says on the cover).

In 1802 he was knighted and was elected to the Legislative Assembly of Lower Canada (parts of present-day Quebec, Newfoundland and Labrador) as opposed to Upper Canada (mainly present-day Southern Ontario). He served for four years from 1804 to 1808 but his heart wasn't in it. Four years later he returned to Scotland but the story is not over yet. It was a new beginning.

It is a truth universally acknowledged that a young girl in possession of a great fortune must be in want of a husband and Geddes Mackenzie was a fourteen year-old heiress. She inherited her fortune via her grandfather who had inherited it from Admiral George Geddes Mackenzie who, by the simple expedient of marrying his cousin, contrived to become his brother-in-law. The fortune bypassed Geddes' father, a prosperous merchant in London, as he was unfortunate enough to predecease his father. With his legacy, Geddes' grandfather bought the Avoch estate which, on his decease, was passed on to Geddes and her twin sister, Mary.

Shortly after he returned from Canada, Alexander married Geddes as you will have guessed. You may find this somewhat shocking, as at forty-eight, he was nearly three times her age. Not that money had anything to do with it; he was not in want of a great fortune himself, which is how he was able to buy Mary out and thus Geddes became sole owner of the estate. Actually that is being economical with the truth; it meant *he* became lord of the manor, as according to the prevailing practice of the time, the wife's possessions were his also. It was not until 1893 that women gained full control of the property they brought to the marriage as well as what they inherited during it – eighty years too late for Geddes.

Actually, it seems to have been a happy enough marriage, in the short time it lasted, Alexander not having been in the greatest of health. Towards the end of his life, he was reduced to a diet of water and sops from which he thought he was deriving some benefit, and had even given up the booze. Not much of a life. Eight years after his marriage, he died in 1820 of chronic nephritis near Dunkeld. He was on the way back to Avoch after having consulted his doctor in Edinburgh. A fearsome journey by coach even for someone in good health. He was only 56.

But before that fatal day which condemned Lady Geddes to the appallingly-named status of being Alexander's "relict" for forty years, they had a daughter also named Geddes, and two sons, Alexander George and George Alexander, just to ring the changes a bit. What this tells you is that although Alexander may have explored the continent from sea to shining sea, when it came to the matter of names, he showed a distinct lack of imagination. We might say "they", if his wife had any say in the matter. One benefit for her was she didn't have to change her surname on marriage (which would make her a thoroughly modern woman today) and neither did her sister who also married a Mackenzie and, you'll never guess, had a daughter named Geddes. Twins tend to do similar things like wearing the same sort of clothes, even identical ones, but this is carrying imitation a bit far don't you think?

What Alexander and Geddes's three children had however, unlike their cousins, was an uncertain number of half-sisters and half-brothers roaming around the Northwest Territories, as it seems Alexander had at least two native "wives". We have some details about one daughter, Julie, who was born in 1806 and whose mother, Marie, was an Inuit. To his credit, it seems

Alexander continued to make provision for his families across the seas once he returned to Scotland.

And so, having crossed a continent and an ocean, home from the hills and the seas, here lies the explorer whose life's journey began in the Hebrides. Like Hamlet's father, he is now exploring "the undiscover'd country from whose bourn no traveller returns." We will all be explorers of that mysterious land ourselves one of these days, some of us sooner than later and some sooner than we expect, unfortunately.

It might come as something of a surprise to many, as it was to me the first time I came here, to stumble over the famous man sleeping the big sleep in this quiet, out-of-the-way spot so far removed from the river he "discovered". If you wish to pay your respects, you will find him quite easily in the cemetery. Just follow the path and you'll discover him off to the right in a stone enclosure erected by Geddes in loving memory. She is there herself now but it was a long, lonely sleep he had of it before she joined him sixty years later, in 1880.

Far from being a sad place, it is colourful and cheery and the casual traveller, happening to pass by, might wonder why this death should be celebrated with the hanging out of so many flags, the maple leaf of Canada and the fleur-de-lis of Quebec amongst them. Fortunately for them (not having read this book), there is a plaque which gives a potted history of Sir Alexander's explorations in English and in French, as is the custom in Canada where even the back of the cornflakes packets is written in French – though Francophones think it's the front.

Chapter Six

Fortrose: The Countess, The Wolf, and The Seer

I T'S a quaint little town, Fortrose, with, at its sleeping heart, the ruined red sandstone 13th century cathedral. But before building began on that there was a 7th century church founded in nearby Rosemarkie by St Curadàn, aka St Boniface, and there had been a bishop there since the 12th century at least.

For the present ruinous state of the cathedral, apart from Old Father Time, we have to thank the usual suspect, Oliver Cromwell. He gets the blame of having stripped it of stone and wood for the construction of his fort in Inverness in 1653. But the rot had really begun, literally, almost a century previously when during the Reformation, William, Lord Ruthven, stripped the lead from the roof for his own little dwelling.

Once upon a medieval time, Fortrose Cathedral was a place of some importance. At its peak, it was bristling with canons, twenty-one of them no less (and it wasn't even a fortified building), not to mention five vicars (who deputised for them), and not forgetting – of course – the boss, the Bishop of Ross, whose territory extended as far north as far as land could go and as far west as sea would allow.

And it still was a place of importance in the sixteenth century, for in 1564, Mary Queen of Scots slept here. But perhaps we should not be too surprised at that: she slept around a bit, just about everywhere in Scotland in fact. Not in flight this time, this was just part of the job: her royal progress after her return from France in 1561, introducing herself to her subjects – a queen to be seen.

What the bishop and the canons made of having to put up the royal guest, I do not know, but only the most loyal of subjects would have greeted the announcement that she was going to descend on them for a few days as a cause for celebration. Rather it must have been something to dread as the royal household with its numerous retainers descended like a flock of locusts and ate you out of house and home. And let us not forget the sanitary arrangements were not as they are now. They stank you out and moved on.

Sometimes it is a great advantage to be a poor humble peasant: you don't have to worry about her majesty dropping in for a cup of tea, never mind B and B. But there was something they *did* have to fear, as did their lords and masters: the Great Leveller, aka the Grim Reaper. Legend tells of the appearance of the pestilence in the shape of a miasmic ball which the canons somehow managed to capture in a blanket and, with due ceremony, buried in the cathedral green. The ceremony they used was "bell, book and candle", normally reserved for excommunication.

Not something that the good and those who kept their noses clean had to worry about, but in 1797, some nosy workmen doing some repair work on the south aisle opened one of the sarcophagi. They were in for a shock. Instead of a rickle of bones and a handful of dust, what they found, to their surprise, was a perfectly preserved corpse wearing a red mitre, a red silk tunic, underneath which was a white nightie. He was also wearing white silk stockings, white gloves and by his side, a painted wooden crosier. From these clues they were able to deduce they were looking at the body of bishop, looking as fresh as the day he died. Unfortunately there was no-one around to recognise him, so who he was exactly, we don't know for sure. There are a couple of contenders: he was either John Fraser (d.1507) or Robert Cairncross (d.1545). Whoever he was, it is a pity for him he was not identified as he should really have gone on to sainthood – an uncorrupted corpse being one of the tests.

As it happens, there are some workmen here now. It's hard to tell what work they are here to do as they are merely loitering with intent at the moment, but presumably it's to do a bit of preserving after their own fashion. One method that was implemented some time ago was to fence off what is left of the cathedral's interior to prevent visitors from tramping about the place and who therefore must peer at the remains through railings like an exhibit at the zoo. Not that it costs anything to do so. Like many of the ruinous sites under the care of Historic Scotland, entry, as far as it goes, is free.

But it's our lucky day. I get chatting to the foreman and when I tell him about my book, he produces a key from his cavernous pocket, unlocks the gate and allows us to step inside for a few minutes.

So it's thanks to him I now find myself standing next to the most famous dead resident still remaining in the cathedral: Euphemia, Countess of Ross (b. circa 1344, d. circa 1395). Who, do I hear you say? She may be a footnote in history now but she was famous in her day and this is her story.

She was a countess, not by marriage, but in her own right; another heiress, like Geddes Mackenzie, and once upon a time she mingled with the great and the good. She also mixed with the bad, especially the very bad. Now here she lies, life's fitful fever over long ago, the stone effigy capping her tomb which is much less well-preserved than the bishop's body reputedly was when he was dug up. I wonder if anyone ever thought of having a peek inside *her* sarcophagus. I expect they did and, if they had found anything unanticipated, I'm sure we would have heard about it.

She married Sir Walter Leslie to whom she had a son, Alexander, and a daughter, Mariota (anglicised into Mary or Margaret), who married Donald of Islay, Lord of the Isles, a grandson of Robert II (1316-90) – incidentally the first monarch of the Stewart (Stuart) dynasty that was to last more than three centuries, give a hiccup or two. On Walter's death, in 1382, Euphemia married again, this time unhappily to the fourth son of Robert II, aforesaid. The new husband was known variously as Alexander Stewart (1343-94), the Earl of Buchan, but most famously as the "Wolf of Badenoch". History does not tell us what Euphemia called him in private but it's not hard to imagine what it was when you hear what happened.

It must have seemed a good idea to her at the time, an upwardly good move, to marry into royalty. It certainly was a good match for *him*, as without having to bother with all that tedious robbing, raping and pillaging to acquire more territory, the Earldom of Ross passed into his hands (at least for his lifetime), while other lands she owned like Lewis, Skye and the town of Dingwall now became his in joint ownership, which of course meant they actually became his, he being her lord and master. Then two days after the marriage, the king conferred upon him the title of the Earl of Buchan. If Alexander's star was in its ascendancy, Alexander, the son's, was in the wane, his inheritance severely depleted by the marriage. Thanks, mum.

Euphemia lived to regret her decision herself. The marriage wasn't a failure due to the seven-year itch syndrome, as the Wolf had a mistress of long-standing and by whom he had seven children. He had none at all to Euphemia. Chance would be a fine thing. He didn't give a fig what other people thought; he brazenly continued living with the mistress. Seven years after the marriage and after an appeal by Euphemia to the Bishops of Moray and Ross, they ordered the Wolf to return to his rightful lair. He promised he would, but he didn't, the liar.

In November 1389, the Bishop of Moray excommunicated him for desertion. The following Spring, in retaliation, the Wolf descended upon Forres and sacked it, then marching east, destroyed Pluscarden Abbey on his way to

Elgin where he set fire to the city and the cathedral, the so-called "Lantern of the North". It certainly burned very brightly that night, June 17th 1390, as did much of Elgin.

Euphemia's response was much more measured. She began divorce proceedings at the papal court in Avignon, and in 1392 the marriage was annulled. For those of you who like a happy ending, she also got all her lands back.

As for Alexander, her son, it ended happily for him too. Or did it? He married Isabella, the daughter of Robert, the Earl of Fife (1340-1420), from whom Euphemia had had a great deal of support during her troubles with her husband. But the plot thickens. Fife was also the king's second son and her brother-in-law, and just as greedy for land and power as her ex-husband, though he went about it in a more subtle way. In actual fact, things worked out better for him than he could ever have foreseen.

Alexander was reinstated as the Earl of Ross but died in 1404 leaving a young granddaughter, Euphemia, as his heir. Fife generously and altruistically, ever the doting grandfather, stepped up to the plate and thus gained control of the earldom. Her aunt, Mariota, and Donald, Lord of the Isles, had something to say about that however. It all ended in tears and with a great deal of blood at the Battle of Harlaw, near Inverurie, in 1411. I'll just leave it at that and not complicate matters even further by going into further details as this particular family feud is not really part of our story.

But before all this, and as a consequence of Alexander the Wolf's rapacious methods in the north and his father's apparent condoning of them, the king's eldest son, John, the Earl of Carrick, the future Robert III, and with the agreement of the King's Council, not so much offered his father early retirement in 1384, but presented him with it and took on the role of the Guardian of Scotland.

Meanwhile, the Wolf's power continued to grow, taking lands from the Earl of Moray, amongst others. Unlike his brothers, who regarded him as the black sheep of the family, the king, far from regarding him as a sheep of any hue, let alone one in wolf's clothing, in 1387, aged seventy-one, appointed the blue-eyed boy the Justiciar North of the Forth. That had a nice ring to it, but what sounded especially good to the Wolf was it meant he was now legitimised, the judge and the jury – the top lawman in the north.

Following the death of Carrick's chief ally, James, Earl of Douglas, at the Battle of Otterburn in August 1388, and as the year drew to a close, Fife staged a coup in the King's Council and took over the Guardianship. He lost no time in setting about dealing with his upstart of a younger brother. Within days, he had removed the favoured one as Justiciar and installed his son, Murdoch, in his place. You can imagine how, when he heard the news, it was enough to make the Wolf choke on his cornflakes.

Then, in 1390, the king died. The king is dead. Long live the king! Well, no, not exactly. Although Carrick, as eldest son, assumed the title of "king" and for a reason you will see later, changed his name from John to Robert, the real Robert, aka Fife, remained as Guardian and the *de facto* ruler of Scotland until his death in 1420 at the age of eighty.

There is an interesting legend attached to the Wolf's demise in 1405. The story goes that one day a tall stranger dressed in black knocked at the door of Ruthven Castle, demanding a game of chess with the Wolf. The game went on for several hours until eventually the stranger won. He announced his victory in the most dramatic of manners. There was a sound of thunder and a flash of lightning, then the stranger disappeared. In the morning, the Wolf and all his men were found dead. The retainers were all burned black, whereas the Wolf's body was unmarked except for one curious thing – the nails in his boots had all been drawn out.

That's what you get when you play chess with the Devil, but God knows, the Wolf gave him a good run for his money before he lost to his professor of evil. His effigy, clothed from top to toe in a suit of armour, lies on top of his tomb in Dunkeld Cathedral, which seems a strange sort of place for such an unholy terror as he to while away eternity.

There used to be another famous person buried here, in Fortrose, an earlier Guardian of Scotland as it happens – Sir Andrew Murray (1298-1338). I only mention him in the passing as his bones were later reinterred in Dunfermline Abbey. His second wife was Christina, Robert the Bruce's sister. In 1332, he was made Regent for the boy king, David II, and following his release as a prisoner of war, resumed the Guardianship again in 1335 and which he retained until his death at Avoch Castle, also known as Ormonde Castle. Nothing of that remains now except a grassy mound, another of the places that claim the doubtful distinction of making a contribution to the masonry of Oliver Cromwell's fort in Inverness.

In another chapel is a triptych of white marble slabs cataloguing the deaths of some of the Mackenzies of Seaforth. Above the middle panel is a crown and between the spaces on either side is a stag's head. According to the story, in 1263, a certain young man, Kenneth, son of Colin of the Aird (not Colin Fitzgerald as is popularly believed), saved Alexander III from being gored by a rutting stag. He leapt between them, shouting *"Cuidich 'n Righ! Cuidich 'n Righ!* (Help the King!)", and with one blow of his trusty sword he severed the stag's head from its body. The king lived to die another day when, on a wild and stormy night, he fell off his horse at Kinghorn in Fife and broke his neck, thus plunging the country into a crisis of succession which, in due course, led to the appointment of John Baliol as king, and the Wars of Independence. And it was actually because of Baliol's unpopularity that John, Earl of Carrick, styled himself Robert III.

You can imagine this brave deed did no harm at all to the fortunes of young Kenneth. The grateful king bestowed upon him the lands of Kintail. He became the ancestor of the Mackenzies of Seaforth and the founder of the dynasty at Brahan Castle near Dingwall. And that is why *Cuidich 'n Righ* became the motto of the Mackenzies of Kintail and the *caberfae*, or stag's head, their family crest.

Now here lies that particular line of Mackenzies. The monument tells me he is beneath my feet so I tread softly so as not to tread on his dreams, though "nightmares" might be more the *mot juste*. Francis Humberstone Mackenzie, 21st chief of the Mackenzies, first Lord Seaforth and Baron Mackenzie of Kintail, who "departed this life" in 1815 aged sixty. The stone then goes on to list his sons who all preceded him: William as an infant in 1786; George in 1794 aged 6; Francis in 1813 aged 18 and the second William in 1814 aged 24. As the stone sums up: "In them terminated the male line of the Earls of Seaforth, Viscount Fortrose". It's a sad tale for sure: all heaven should weep at the death of even one child before its parents, but you might rightly suppose to have four precede you is a burden beyond bearing. Sir Walter Scott, no less, was moved to write a lament:

> *Of the line of MacKenneth remains not a male*
> *To bear the proud name of the Chief of Kintail.*

Not one of Sir Walter's finest couplets I would argue; to my ears it has much of that rhymester, McGonagal, about it.

If you have walked around as many cemeteries as I have and paused to read the gravestones, you will have found childhood deaths not an uncommon phenomenon, especially in bygone days. I have a particular reason for mentioning these deaths, however. The curious thing is they were predicted centuries beforehand by the Brahan Seer and well known in the Highlands long before they came to pass. Unfortunately none was written down at the time to authenticate the prediction.

The Seer predicted that when a "deaf and dumb" chief of Mackenzie was born, the male line would become extinct and the estate would pass into the hands of a "hooded woman from the east" who would kill her sister. "Deaf and dumb" is an unfortunate pairing of words which was common usage in the past, as if they were inseparable and indivisible and carrying connotations of stupidity, even idiocy. Sadly, you occasionally hear some people lump them together, even today.

He was not born unable to hear, but Francis had a severe attack of scarlet fever when he was twelve which left him deaf and his speech affected. In addition to this, at this time, the Seer foretold there were to be four other Highland chiefs who would suffer from deformities: one would be buck-toothed; one would be hare-lipped; one would be half-witted and one would be a stammerer. Contemporary accounts testify that Sir Hector Mackenzie of Gairloch was buck-toothed; Chisholm of Chisholm was hare-lipped; Grant of Grant was half-witted and Macleod of Raasay stammered. (It's not much of a choice, but which would you rather be?)

On the death of Francis in 1815, the chieftainship of the clan passed to Mackenzie of Allengrange although the estate was passed on to his oldest daughter (he had six), Mary Elizabeth Frederica, the recently widowed wife of the celebrated Vice-Admiral Sir Samuel Hood, who returned from the East Indies wearing her widow's weeds. She was therefore "hooded" as the Seer predicted, firstly by the bonnet she would have been wearing, as well as being "Hood" by name. As for killing her sister, there was nothing sinister about that. One day she was out driving when something spooked the ponies and they took off. Mary failed to control them, the carriage overturned, and they were both thrown out. Mary survived; her sister, Caroline, did not.

I am standing close to her now where she lies next to her father. Her tombstone tells us she was "summoned by sudden and awful accident: departed by faith and hope to her heavenly home 21st April 1823 in the 35th year of her age". I hope she did not get a disappointment when, and if, she discovered there is no such place as heaven. Poor Francis certainly did get a disappointment, to put it mildly, for this stone also records the death of another of his daughters, the second, Frances Catherine, who died in 1810. He must have thought he was cursed – and when you remember the prophecy, maybe he was.

Mary's memorial stone is on the other side of their father's. After her name and date of birth (1783), there follows a glowing tribute to her which goes on for sixteen lines (no small matter when you are chiselling the letters out of hard marble) before we are told she died at Brahan Castle in 1862 aged 79.

In a letter to his friend Mr Morritt, Sir Walter Scott, although an admirer of Lady Hood (as she was then before her remarriage), feared her estate management skills would not be up to the task and so it proved. Bit by bit, the lands were sold: what remained of Kintail (which her father had had to sell due to his mismangement of *his* estates in the West Indies), Ross, much of Glenshiel, the Church lands of Chanonry, the Barony of Pluscarden and the Isle of Lewis. That's a fair skelp of land. The castle itself was demolished in 1951 and used as the foundations for the new bridge at the village of Conon Bridge. *Sic transit gloria mundi.*

But what of the Brahan Seer (1630?-1677?)? Yes, I agree, that's a lot of question marks and that's precisely my point. We don't really know for sure, but to begin at the ending, he had a gruesome death, so we are told, and now we're off to visit the site where it took place – Chanonry Point.

The car park is very crowded because of the scores of people who have come in the hope of seeing the dolphins putting on an impromptu display of aquatic aerobatics. The firth is very narrow at this point and a good place to spot them. Fort George is just across the water but hardly anything of it is visible apart from the grassy ramparts. No wonder no-one bothered to attack it. Those who come to see the dolphins, you must suppose, think they have a much better chance of achieving their mission or otherwise why would they decide to come here in such numbers?

There is a memorial plaque crafted by the boys of Fortrose Academy attached to a boulder which reads: *This stone commemorates the legend of Coinneach Odhar better known as the BRAHAN SEER – Many of his prophesies were fulfilled and tradition holds that his untimely death by burning in tar followed his final prophecy of the doom of the House of Seaforth.*

He was born Kenneth Mackenzie in Uig on the Isle of Lewis and became an employee of his namesake, Kenneth Mackenzie, the third Earl of Seaforth (1635-78). According to legend, his wife, Isabella, who was reputedly very ugly and therefore a bit paranoid about the Earl being attracted to other ladies, asked if her husband (who was supposedly in Paris on business at the time), was well, and then went on to press the Seer for more information. He reluctantly admitted her husband was having a dalliance with another lady. You might have thought he, of all people, would have been able to foresee the consequences of such a confession and prevaricated a little. But maybe he was like George Washington and could not tell a lie. Or a Seer has to tell it like it is, part of the deal of being given the gift.

William Congreve (1670-1729) gave to the world, "Hell hath no fury like a woman scorned" and Isabella lashed out in anger at this defamation of her husband's character, though actually the confirmation of her worst fears was nearer the mark. She not so much shot the messenger, but much more inventively had him put head first into a spiked barrel of boiling tar. And what she did to her husband on his return, if that is what she did to the messenger, God only knows. However I am happy to tell you that this story, at least, is probably a work of fiction. There are no contemporary written accounts as you would expect there to have been had there been any foundation in fact.

But what of the legends themselves? Have they any substance? Apart from the prophecies aforesaid, there are a good many others such as the Battle of Culloden, the Highland Clearances, The Caledonian Canal and much, much more. I think we would do well to be cautious. For one thing, Coinneach Odhar (Kenneth the Sallow) made his prophecies in Gaelic and translations can be open to misinterpretation at the best of times, let alone when you are depending on what was heard, not read. Furthermore, who has not played "Chinese Whispers" and not been amazed (and amused) by the convoluted results, and that just in the space of two minutes, never mind two hundred years of being passed down from ear to ear?

The gift of the "Second Sight" may be something of a mixed blessing (though it is generally regarded as a curse), but hindsight, which most of us have, is a wonderful thing and therefore such things as the prediction of "black rain which would make Aberdeen rich" can be tied in to the discovery of North Sea Oil. Similarly, his prediction that when the fifth bridge over the Ness was built there would be worldwide chaos, was followed the following month by Hitler's invasion of Poland. In actual fact the contract had been awarded for the building of the fifth bridge but construction had to be suspended because of the outbreak of hostilities. Close, though.

We are indebted to the Seer's biographer, Alexander Mackenzie (1838-98) for writing down these predictions, albeit a couple of centuries after the prophet's death. Here is just one more, if you please. In his biographer's day, there were eight bridges over the Ness, but the Seer predicted there would a ninth and when that happened "the Highlands will be overrun by ministers without grace and women without shame". Well there *are* nine bridges now and I don't know anything about the ministers, but I'm sure if the Seer could see some of the women of Inverness today with their skimpy attire and tattoos that's exactly what he would think of them.

On the manner of the Seer's death, Parliamentary records dated 1577 show papers were issued for the arrest of a Coinneach Odhar on a charge of having supplied poison to a certain Catherine Ross, who wanted to dispose of her stepchildren so her own hellish brood would inherit her husband's fortune. Coinneach Odhar was very much a second choice, the lady having employed no less than twenty-six witches previously. Some of them were arrested and burnt at Chanonry Point despite their incompetence. There is no evidence of the same fate having happened to Coinneach Odhar, but you can see how this event and his name might be conflated with the Brahan Seer who died a century later. They might even have been related: grandfather and grandson perhaps.

To make his propecies, the Seer is thought to have used an adder stone, revered by the Druids, a stone with a natural hole in the middle, through which he was able to see his visions. When he found it, he looked through the hole (who wouldn't?) and was blinded but given the gift of second sight as a sort of compensation. In popular belief, the stones were created by a knot of serpents who became bonded by slime and saliva. The hole was created by their tongues, flickering in panic as they attempted to find a way out of their entanglement.

And should you, as you walk along the shore at Chanonry Point on the lookout for dolphins perhaps, cast your eyes to the ground, and should you happen to come across a stone with a hole in it, you have a choice. You can either pick it up and look through the hole or fling it as far into the firth as you can. It is said that before his dreadful death, that is what the Seer is supposed to have done – flung the accursed stone as far as he could into the water, where it has never been seen again.

But one of these days might it not be tossed up by a gurly sea onto the beach? It might even be there now, just waiting for someone like you to come along and pick it up.

Dolphin watchers beware. You may see more than you bargain for.

Chapter Seven

Rosemarkie: The Stone and The Picts

I T'S just a stone's throw, with or without a hole in it, to Rosemarkie on the other side of the V-shaped Point. The A832 takes us alongside the broad sweep of the bay with an enticing-looking sandy beach on our right, but we are not in the least seduced by it. For one thing it is not the kind of day for a paddle, let alone a swim, not even to feel the sand scrunch between your toes. We are on the trail of the Picts. First stop, the award-winning Groam Museum to see its collection of Pictish stones.

Who were the Picts? Well, that's a very good question. From my primary school days I knew the Romans called them "Picti" or "painted people" on account of their custom of painting their bodies before battle, if not before. And if today's tattooed women (never mind the men) would have shocked the Seer to his foundations, it's easy to imagine how they put the fear of death into the Roman soldiers, battle-hardened and well-disciplined though they were.

And a death sentence it must have seemed for them to leave behind those sunny climes where the fig, the grape and the pomegranate grew, to be uprooted and posted here, to the northern frontier of the empire with its drizzle, rain, sleet and snow. Then, in the summer, at the height of the battle season, the Picts called up the auxiliaries, their secret weapon, those blasted little blighters, the midges, who bit them to death.

The Pictish Chronicle, Scotland's answer to the *Anglo-Saxon Chronicles*, only not so exciting and written in Latin in the third quarter of the 10th century, has some interesting things to say about the origins of the ancient Scots. (We'll get to the Picts presently.) It tells us they came originally from Scythia (a vast area to the north of the Black Sea, stretching east through what is present-day Kazakhstan and beyond) and got their name from Scotta who was their queen and a daughter of one of the Pharaohs. A long, long time ago, they arrived in Ireland in "the fourth age of the world", that is to say in the times between the biblical David and Daniel.

The Scythians, the *Chronicle* goes on to tell us, are born with white hair because of the perpetual snow in their land. Because of that they were known as "Albani" and the Latin for "white", as I am sure you remember from your Latin at school, in its feminine form, is *alba,* which, as I am sure you also know, is the Scottish-Gaelic word for "Scotland". Another physical peculiarity about these people is they have brightly-coloured pupils which means like moles, they are able to see better by night than by day.

The demise of the Picts (to begin at the ending), the *Chronicle* informs us, was due to Kenneth MacAlpin (d. 858 AD) who destroyed them: "For God, to punish them for the fault of their malice...because they not only scorned the Lord's mass and injunctions; but also were unwilling to be reckoned equal to others in the law of impartiality".

In actual fact, the Picts were a confederation of peoples whose heartland was Fortrui, which, most historians agree, was situated in present-day Moray and Easter Ross. They emerged towards the end of the Iron Age, which in Scotland, was from 700 BC to 500 AD. We know most about them, not from themselves, but from what other people have said about them, like the Romans and ecclesiastic writers of whom Bede is the best known. But this is the question: just how much can you trust the reports? As the quote from King Kenneth testifies, who of us would choose our obituaries to be written by our enemies?

They are as dead as the dinosaurs now, the Picts, but like those primeval beasts, they did not truly die. Whilst the dinosaurs reinvented themselves as birds, the Picts merged with the Gaels of Dál Riata. Together they formed the Kingdom of Alba. Some historians, for one reason or another, not trusting the *Chronicle* to the letter, think the Picts conquered the Scots and not the other way about. And just to make matters even more complicated and confusing, it is possible that "Alba" was merely a translation of the Gaelic word for "Pictland" – so it and its people never disappeared at all!

Whatever the truth may be, Kenneth MacAlpin was styled the "King of the Picts" and became, as I also remember being taught in primary school, the first King of the Scots, circa 843, and thus he had it both ways.

In 906, his grandson Constantine II (d. 952), the King of Alba, met Bishop Cellach at Scone, near Perth at the "Hill of Belief" quite possibly the very same spot as Moot Hill, where according to tradition, Scottish monarchs were crowned on the Stone of Scone, aka the Stone of Destiny, until it was removed by Edward I, "The Hammer of the Scots", in 1296.

Anyway, at the meeting in 906, it was agreed between the king and the bishop that the "teaching of the faith, and the rights of the churches and the gospels, [[were]] to be protected equally with the Scots, *pariter cum Scottis*", as the *Chronicles* put it. The precise interpretation of the last three words is a matter of dispute, but what it tells me is Constantine may have been the King of Alba but it's the Scots who ended up being the ones who bequeathed their name to the land. The irony is the Scots were actually Gaels from Ireland, immigrants who settled in Scotland about 500 AD and who called their kingdom Dál Riata, as I said before.

The Picts may not have left us much about themselves in the written word but what they have left us are some fabulously carved boulders and stone slabs and the latter is what we are off to see at the Groam Museum. This curious name comes from the Gaelic and means "boggy ground", but you know you are firmly on the right road when you see the rather forbidding eyes of the Plough Inn gazing down at you from the end of the somewhat narrow High Street.

The museum is small, intimately small, but its two floors are packed with enough information to keep the serious student happily engaged for weeks, what with video films of the Picts and the Brahan Seer and old photographs packed away discretely in albums which you are at liberty to peruse to your heart's content. But what you can't help but see, the moment you step through the door, is the jewel in the crown of the museum, the Rosemarkie stone.

There it stands, nine foot high (and that's with a bit broken off at the top), a red sandstone monolith with beautiful, intricate carvings. It was unearthed in what is now the churchyard of the parish church before it was built. High on the upper part of what we are told is the front of the slab, amongst all the circles, whorls and loops and in stark contrast to that, the eye is drawn to a plain, equal-armed cross in bas-relief against a plain background. Those who know about such things tell us that the stone can be dated to sometime after 750 AD.

Obviously the Picts in these parts had been converted to Christianity by then, but when they made this great leap of faith is not exactly clear. Two or three years after he came to Iona in 563 AD, Columba, Loch Ness Monster-tamer and missionary, tried converting Bridei (d. 584) the king of the Picts, whose fortress was at Craig Padraig near Inverness. He found Bridei was made of sterner stuff and not so easily intimidated as Nessie. Bede, however, tells us St Ninian (d. 589) had converted the southern Picts, so it might be that by the time of the Rosemarkie stonemason, the community may have been converts for a century or more.

In 710, after the Synod of Whitby in 664, in which it was decided to follow the Roman brand of Christianity rather than the Celtic, the Pictish King

Nechtan decreed that his subjects should follow the Roman rule. It was all very complicated, concerning such apparent trivia as the correct style of tonsure, that is to say, to shave or not to shave the forehead – but centred around the date of Easter, when to fast and when to feast. It was a burning issue at the time and a matter of some great importance because, if you got it wrong, you might burn in hell forever. As King Oswiu of Northumberland put it: "I dare not longer contradict the decrees of him who keeps the doors of the Kingdom of Heaven ⟦St Peter⟧ lest he should refuse me admission".

In actual fact I wouldn't be surprised at all to learn his wife had quite a big part to play in all of this as she followed the Roman tradition whilst he followed the Celtic, which meant every so often, according to the vagaries of the lunar cycle, he was celebrating Easter while she was still fasting in Lent. That's no way to run a household, especially a royal one. The next time a conflict in dates would arise would be in 665 and I think it is an interesting coincidence that the great and the good from both sides of the divide met before that fateful year to resolve the thorny issue. And to this day, as you know, Easter is a still a moveable feast, Easter Sunday being the first Sunday following the first full moon after March 21st. It all sounds very pagan.

There is another cross on the reverse, lower down, in the bottom half of the slab. The square in which it is set has the appearance of being bolted to a mesh-like surface by four enormous studs. Like the other cross, the arms are of equal length, but it is much more ornate with four squares on each of its arms with projecting tabs like pieces from a jigsaw puzzle.

And "puzzle" is the appropriate word, for the top half is decorated with Pictish pagan symbols. There are three crescents with their horns pointing downwards, though only the tips of the topmost remain. We don't know what that looked like, but while the one in the middle is solid with criss-cross lines on it, the bottom is a delicate filigree of inter-connecting loops, like petrified lace.

Between the two crescents are the so-called "double discs" with their associated Z-rod, while crescents are invariably accompanied by V-rods. Scholars think they might represent a broken arrow and the crescent a shield, maybe to commemorate a victorious battle. The Z is reversed actually, but that's all right because between the horns of the crescent are what look like a couple of pizza cutters yet which we are told are actually mirrors, and it would look like a Z if you looked at it through them, wouldn't it?

There is also meant to be a comb, but all I can see is a diamond ring where the V-rods come to a point. And here is *my* point. Just as the critics have written more words than Shakespeare ever did about what *he* meant, digging ever deeper into the text and coming up with things I am sure the maestro never intended – if I can see a diamond ring in a Pictish carving when they never dreamt of such a thing (as far as we know), who's to say it is *not* there, if I can see it?

What the Picts meant by these carved stones no-one really knows. Some experts hazard a guess that they had something to do with celestial stargazing, of which the ancients did a great deal as they pondered the wonder and the mystery of the universe. For the curious, it might be irritating not to know the answer to so many riddles, yet I think that is to look at them through the wrong end of the telescope so to speak, and far from detracting from the stones, the mystery adds another layer of interest.

Some slabs unmistakably portray hunting scenes, but this certainly does not do that, making it one of the most enigmatic of all Pictish sculptures. Whatever it means, it certainly is beautiful, not an inch of it, even the sides, that has not been lovingly carved by the hand of a master stonemason. And that, ultimately, is how we should look at this stone – as a thing of beauty, and who would disagree with that?

Keats memorably wrote "A thing of beauty is a joy forever", and this wonderfully carved stone has been doing that for one-and-a-half millennia, apart from the time it spent underground before its resurrection, of course. Keats also said, in the last two lines of *A Grecian Urn*, and I think this hits the spot exactly:

> *Beauty is truth, truth beauty – that is all*
> *Ye know on earth, and need to know.*

And if this stone could speak, like the urn in the poem, it might have said to Dr Johnson, who thought Scotland a primitive, uncultured sort of place, especially the Highlands, "So, tell me, sir, are you still of the opinion I was made in a land peopled by savages?"

It's not the only example of a Pictish cross, here in the museum. There are fragments of others, including the one that has come best to symbolise Pictish art where the meeting point of the arms of the cross is encircled by a ring like a halo. Normally they are elaborately carved (and there is nothing wrong with that), but this is plain and enormously pleasing and the only one I have come across.

What draws the eye more, however, is another stone which I find rather amusing despite the seriousness of the subject. Actually it's a cast. The original came to light in Rosemarkie cemetery and currently resides in the exalted

surroundings of the National Museum of Scotland, exhibit NMS.XɪBɪ27, should you wish to seek it out. It depicts a man about to be devoured headfirst by an animal. The quality of the carving is very naïve. I suppose the man's name *could* be Daniel and the animal *could* be a lioness but, if it is, it's a very unconvincing one – more like a hound of an unidentifiable species. This impression is borne out by another animal of the canine sort beneath its lower jaw, its ears pricked back as if it had caught sight of a deer or some other sort of prey.

As for the human, he's even less convincing. He may have a man's head, but no man ever had a body which projected from his neck at an angle of ninety degrees like his unless his neck was broken. He has a very pointy beard and, despite what is about to happen to him, he doesn't look in the least alarmed, let alone terrified. He is gazing down his very large pointed nose with wide-eyed equanimity – which is when you notice that the tip of it is in contact with the animal's tongue and, although it has some very sharp-looking triangular teeth, its jaws are not open to gratefully receive the man-food. The man is more in danger of being licked to death than being devoured.

What this scene suggests to me is a hound happy to see his master as it means he will soon be released and a-hunting they will go. In fact, the more I look at it, the more I think that's what it is. The gums (yes, the artist has carved them) are pulled back in a grin rather than a snarl. And if the man's name *is* Daniel, and this is supposed to be a depiction of him in the lion's den, the reason for his fearlessness is because this is a snapshot of the scene just after the angel had appeared and told the lions to leave him alone and he knows he is not going to be turned into cat meat. But as anyone who has ever been licked by the household moggy knows, it's not a very pleasant experience and having the end of your nose rasped by a recently-tamed big cat would have made your eyes water, not to mention being poleaxed by its breath.

Joking apart, I like the way that Daniel's stylised eyes (let's call him that) are a mirror image of those of the big cat below (let's call *it* that), which replicate that of its mother (let's call *her* that). And then there is the parallel line created between the end of the cat's snout and Daniel's very flat forehead.

The artist had to have that of course, otherwise they would have been conjoined and that wouldn't have done at all from an artistic point of view. But look at the line created by the base of Daniel's nose, then trace it down to the top lip where the jutting Jimmy Hill chin begins – and what have you got?

To me it is a representation of north and east Scotland with its flat top, then the curve of Caithness angling down to the Moray Firth, then along to the bulge of Buchan before it sweeps down at forty-five degrees to Fife. And what is that, when it's at home, as the saying has it? Pictland. The home of the northern Picts, that's what it looks like to me.

Of course you may think I am reading things into it and maybe I am, but as I said earlier, while the artist may not have intended this, if I can see it, who's to say it's not there? This fragment may look naïve but may also have hidden layers.

You couldn't do better than come and see it for yourself – see what *you* think.

Chapter Eight

Cromarty: The Good Samaritan, The Eccentric, and The Good Laird

The road swings inland, taking us away from the coast. When next we see it again, it is a surreal landscape that greets our eyes. If, like Rip van Winkle, you had been asleep for the past twenty years, you might be forgiven for thinking the aliens had landed in the Cromarty Firth, their monstrous machines knee-deep in water and their skeletal ribs towering into the sky. Less fancifully but equally improbably, they could also be launch pads, the gantries ready to receive rockets bound on our own quest to find extra-terrestrial life. Or they could just be giant Meccano sets. What they really are of course, are oilrigs, a dozen of them having come back to nearby Nigg, just across the bay, for maintenance or refurbishment or simply to shelter for the winter from the North Sea which can be a perilous sort of place at the best of times.

It's a sign of the times actually. Time is money as far as these immensely expensive rigs are concerned and all the time they are here means they can't be out there in the North Sea earning their corn, returning the massive investment in them, drilling for black gold to make the wheels of industry go round. Times have certainly changed since the Seventies when you would be lucky to see even one rig after the newest-to-be-built disappeared over the horizon, bound for oilfields new. Now the fabrication yards have reinvented themselves as wind turbine manufacturers. It's an ill wind...

At the corner of Church Street in Cromarty a blue plaque has been placed on the wall of a house, now an antique shop. Erected by Ross County Council, it pays tribute to James Thomson M.D. 1823-1854 who was born here. He was "A GOOD SAMARITAN to wounded enemy Russians at the BATTLE OF ALMA in the Crimean War".

After the battle, "Alma" became a very popular girl's name as well as being adopted by a whole host of pubs, and of course there is the Pont de l'Alma in Paris which, since August 31st 1997, became famous for quite another reason. The "real" Alma, the inspiration for this rash of tributes, was actually the first fully-fledged battle of the Crimean War (1853-56) in which our former bitter enemies and rivals of not so long ago, and now our allies – the French – took on the Russians, our friends and allies-to-be in a not so far-off future global conflict. As for the Crimean War, of that it could be said that never, in the field of human conflict, was so much owed by so many clothes: the cardigan, raglan sleeves and the balaclava.

The Crimean War began over a religious dispute (so what's new?) in a distant land, the Holy Land in fact, over the rights of Christians. The French supported the Catholic Church while the Russians favoured those of the Eastern Orthodox persuasion. But that was really just an excuse. What it *really* was about was an attempt to prop up the declining Ottoman Empire and put a peep to the Russians who were getting a bit big for their boots. As far as the battle of the Alma was concerned, that was a result of the Allies' attempt to take the strategic port of Sevastapol. The Russians were outnumbered 2:1 and the carnage was dreadful: nearly 6,000 Russians were killed, with more than half as many on the Allies' side. Not all of them died as a result of combat however. An unspecified number were carried off by cholera. What they fought and died for – Sevastapol – only fell eventually after a siege lasting a year, in 1855.

Long before the Geneva Convention was ever even dreamed of, after the battle was lost and won, after the 44th Regiment had left the field, the lad from Cromarty, James Thomson M.D. volunteered to stay behind and do what he had been trained to do, to tend to the wounded – about 700 Russians. He saved the lives of about 400 and helped get them to Odessa, from whence they were sent homeward to fight again another day. That's "the pity of war" as Wilfred Owen said. But what's even more of a pity is that only fifteen days after his noble deeds, Thomson died at Balaclava aged only thirty-one, of cholera. He was buried by his trusty servant, McCarthy, by the shores of the Black Sea. There is something terribly poignant about that.

Back in Scotland, at Forres, a fifty-foot high memorial was built to honour the Good Samaritan. Forres is rather a long way from Cromarty, on the other side of the Moray Firth in fact, but the owner of the land and the prime-mover for funding the memorial, Sir James McGrigor (1771-1858), the former Director-General of the Army Medical Department, could not agree on a site and that is why it is there and not in the town of his birth. Which is another pity. A plaque on the monument tells us that Thomson died from "the effects of excessive hardship and privation", but since he had been working in the cholera wards at Balaclava for thirty-four hours before his death, I think I know which version I am inclined to believe. The same monument tells us that his life was "useful" and his death was "glorious". Once again, I think I know which of those statements I agree with and which I don't.

We know that the more famous man whose house we have come here to see used to live in this street, but before we get to his former residence, we are tempted by another attraction and like Oscar Wilde, who memorably said he "could resist anything except temptation", we give into it right away.

It's Cromarty Courthouse, dating from 1773, and you can't miss it with its whitewashed façade and imposing tower on which sits, like a thimble on a finger, a smaller octagonal tower of brick with a clock and domed roof. With its arched windows on the upper storey, square ones on the bottom and the half-moon window rising above the full-arched window on the tower, it's a very attractive building indeed, architecturally speaking. If the interior is only half as good, we are about to see something special.

It's another award-winning museum, just like Groam, a mere seven miles away. Once upon a time it really was a courthouse and just as the Rosemarkie Stone is the premier exhibit of the Groam museum, so the actual courtroom is the main attraction here.

But first of all you must meet Sir Thomas Urquhart whose life and times were extraordinary. He's sitting at a little table covered with a blue cloth at the bottom of the spiral stone stairs. This little tableau is a symphony in blue and white. Sir Thomas is wearing a shiny light-blue costume with a great deal of lace about it, at the neck, the cuffs, the sleeves and down his front. It looks as if the hair may be his own and not a wig, for the ringlets have become unruly and to complete the picture, he has a very scary, black drooping moustache straight out of the 1970s. He's holding a box that says "Donations" and you don't argue with a moustache like that even if he doesn't meet you in the eye.

He looks every inch a Cavalier, the complete antithesis of a Roundhead, and that's precisely what he was. Born in 1611, he went to King's College Aberdeen aged eleven – a precociousness that manifested itself in his later writings. A committed royalist, he was knighted by Charles I, declared a traitor by the Parliamentarians, and fought at Worcester in 1651, the loss of which battle meant it was all over for Charles II and the Royalists – or so it seemed. You might have thought it was all over for Sir Thomas too, but the charismatic figure was paroled by Cromwell and he returned to Cromarty.

This potted biography portrays a colourful-enough life but that's not why he is remembered today, or should I say, forgotten – by most people anyway. His chief claim to fame is as the translator of Rabelais (149[4?]-1553), only he out-Rabelaised Rabelais, so to speak. Both were fascinated by the origin of language, in words and their etymology. He thought spelling (yet to be codified in Rabelais' day) should reflect the Latin and Greek origins of the words rather than take a simplified form. Which is all very well for brainy folks with a classical training.

For an ex-monk, Rabelais was extremely bawdy (but there's no-one as zealous as the converted) full of sexual innuendoes, double entendres and the downright dirty. Urquhart's translation added something like 70,000 additional words to the original text in the same style and with added smut. But that's not all Urquhart did that deserves his being better known.

Although born with a silver spoon in his mouth, he was a real "lad o' pairts". In 1645, he wrote a tract on trigonometry (yawn!) called *Trissotetras* in which he invented a new terminology to describe what he was banging on about (the title gives you a flavour of his style), with the result that it was doubly incomprehensible but a very good soporific and essential bedtime reading for insomniacs.

He followed that up with *Pantochronachanon* (1652) and, if you have a smattering of ancient Greek, you might just be about able to see where he is coming from here. It's a genealogical work, in which he traces his ancestry back through 153 generations to Adam and Eve. Some felt touched by the hand of history and possibly altered its course – take for instance the several-times great-granny who found Moses amongst the bulrushes. Critics scoffed and mocked and said no-one could be *that* great and this, more than anything, made him a subject of ridicule. But in actual fact he might be the one having the last laugh, laughing at them for taking the book seriously, not seeing it for what it really was, an elaborate practical joke.

What he *was* serious about, long before Esperanto was ever dreamed about, was creating a universal language. Or was he? Whereas the idea behind Esperanto is its simplicity, Urquhart's *Logopandecteision* (1653) was extremely complicated. He explains: "It hath eleven genders, seven moods, four voices, ten cases, besides the nominative, and twelve parts of speech; every word signifieth as well backwards as forwards." Enough to keep the language teachers busy for years – if only he had got around to writing a grammar book – so he was quite possibly just having us all on again. In addition to that, he took a delight in coining new words and expressions. His slang words for "penis" are many and most imaginative, but this is not the place to tell you what they are.

From all this you might conclude Urquhart was either a genius or stark, staring bonkers. He would certainly have been placed on the Asperger's scale, and pretty high up too, if such a thing had been around in his day. He had first promulgated the idea of his universal language in his previous publication, *The*

Jewel (1652), at least a title you can read and remember. But wait a moment; it was also called *Ekskybalauron*, the most impenetrable title of them all. The subject of this work was a potpourri of anecdotes designed to be "a vindication of the honour of Scotland". Prankster perhaps, eccentric certainly, to which you can certainly add patriot, unless of course, you were on the Parliamentary side during the Civil War.

Urquhart's life was certainly colourful but not always happy. When his father died in 1642, his main legacy was a large number of debts as well as a clutch of creditors. It was at this time Sir Thomas somehow suddenly developed an unquenchable thirst for foreign travel and spent the next three years in Europe. But a greater misfortune was to befall him after the battle of Worcester when he lost all the manuscripts he had taken with him on the campaign thinking they would be safer with him than left behind in someone else's care, worse than forfeiting his property which he also lost after the battle. I'm not sure he might not have preferred to have lost his life. No worse calamity can befall an author than he lose his words and have to start all over again. Actually losing the precious papers wasn't half so bad as the ignominious use to which some of them were put. Deemed to be nothing but a lot of old rubbish (as you can imagine), some were used to light pipes while others came to an even more ignominious end. As Sir Thomas himself delicately put it: "for inferior employment and posterior uses".

But in the end it did end happily for Urquhart. He was able to resurrect his writings and lived to die another day nine years after the battle, in exile in Holland. He is said to have died laughing when he was told of the restoration of Charles II. It brings a new meaning to the expression "he died happy". That said, he doesn't look too amused at the moment, looking down his moustache at the coins we drop into his box without uttering a word of thanks or acknowledgement even. We leave him to his gloomy contemplation and pass on up the stairs, heading for the courtroom.

On the way there is much to read about the life and times of Cromarty, famous for fish, its harbour a gateway to Scandinavia, Holland and beyond. In fact at one time Cromarty rivalled Inverness as the foremost trading port along the Moray Firth. You would never think so now. All this and more you can learn about, such as how, in the First World War, Cromarty served as a naval base and on 30th December 1915, HMS Natal blew up with the loss of 421 lives, including some civilians who had been invited aboard for a party. Nothing to do with the German war machine. An internal combustion fault.

As soon as you enter the courtroom, straight ahead of you, on the bench, are seated three figures. In the middle is the sheriff, resplendent in red, looking

suitably stern and in command of the situation. On his right with a face as long as a wet Sunday afternoon, is one of the lawyers, for the prosecution I imagine, with a very fluffy white wig. On the sheriff's left, the other lawyer has no wig at all, which is a pity as he is having a very bad grizzled-hair day indeed. He is looking down despondently at the woodwork, not daring to lift his eyes to the defendant in the dock who has his back to us so we have no idea how he is responding to the proceedings. His hair, which is also very untidy, has been bunched back with a white ribbon, so you can see he has made at least some sort of an effort to create a good impression.

In the witness stand is a woman dressed in a plain brown gown with a white cloth covering her hair, giving her something of a nun-like appearance. She looks a poor sort of soul and is leaning on a stick. If you only saw her from the back you might have assumed she was quite young, but from where we are standing we are presented with her profile and are able to see that the shoulder-length hair escaping from and tied back beneath the headscarf is not even grizzled but pure white. Is she an abused wife whose husband has been maltreating her for years? But was that even an offence in those days, whenever those days were – judging by the clothes at least two centuries ago. What is it all about? What exactly *is* going on here?

Fortunately we don't have long to wait to find out the answers. Some cunning mechanism triggers some sort of device (Big Brother is watching you), and we have only a short time to take in the scene before the court springs to life. That's the advantage of coming off-season. We have the whole museum to ourselves, never mind the courthouse, so we don't have to worry about creeping in at the back like burglars to eavesdrop on the proceedings.

At the risk of spoiling the story for you, should you decide to pay a visit, I will tell you what's happening. I reckon that's better than your dying of curiosity if you aren't able to go to Cromarty anytime soon. I am also mindful of the cat, which, although it had nine lives, we all know what got it in the end.

The year is 1776 (a significant date in American history, note), and Cuthbert (!) MacKenzie is in the dock. Lord George Ross, that overall good bloke, the laird of Pitkerrie and Cromarty, is presiding. Just as there are good wives and bad wives (one of my great-grandfathers thanked God he had a good one), there are good lairds and bad lairds, and God knows we are going to come across a bad one before very much longer, but Lord George was a good one.

He bought the Cromarty estate in 1765 and built the Courthouse from money granted by the Commissioners of the Annexed Estates, in other words land forfeited by those on the losing side of the '45. (To the victor go the spoils.) He also built the sandstone pier; provided a lot of employment to the people by building a hemp factory, later turned into a ropemaking factory and now transformed into local authority housing. Not least, he built a brewery, now a residential centre for students of Robert Gordon's University of Aberdeen when on their field trips. Now you see why I say Lord George was a jolly good sort and why, if you are in need of a toast, especially if you come from, or live in, Cromarty, you should drink to his health. The truth is, however, he had an ulterior motive – he thought beer the lesser of two evils – it would wean the men away from whisky.

As for the case over which the well-intentioned laird is presiding, it's an old, old story. Late on a Saturday night and the early hours of Sunday morning, after a night's carousing, a fight broke out between a dozen or so "English speakers" and some Scots. Cuthbert took exception to being called a "hielan' bugger" although, given his name, it might have been the insult to his sexuality rather than his parentage that he took exception to. In any event he was arrested, found guilty and fined 2/6, no mean sum in those days, the said moneys going to charitable causes, whatever they were. Not a battered wives' refuge presumably.

After this drama is played out, we are free to move around the courtroom. Cuthbert, it turns out, is wearing a high collar and his left hand is bandaged and in a sling. It looks as if he had managed to make contact with the face of one of those who insulted him anyway. There must be some comfort in that despite his present predicament.

I'm not going to tell you the part the lady played in the story (I've got to leave something for you to find out for yourselves) but I must tell you more about Cuthbert's story because everyone likes an unhappy ending, don't they?

He joined the 71st Regiment of Foot, aka Fraser's Highlanders (got to pay off that fine somehow), but soon he was in trouble again. In 1777 he deserted from Fort George before being sent to the revolting thirteen colonies in America. He was arrested in Cromarty, thrown in the clink at Fort George, the very cell we had visited, and sentenced to between 500 and 1000 lashes, to be administered over several months – they weren't complete sadists, the British army. You may not be surprised to hear some died before their sentence was completed. As to whether Cuthbert survived his lashings, my lips are sealed.

A wooden board in the courtroom lists some key dates in Cromarty's history beginning in 1598 when a new Mercat Cross was erected. The next entry is 1611, when the "Great Eccentric", Sir Thomas Urquhart, was born. Then in 1643, an interesting little item about three people who died in the castle after accidentally consuming poison intended for the "mad young laird of Calder" who was married to Thomas's sister. Thomas is entirely above suspicion in this little unfortunate accident as he was not even in the country at the time. So whodunit and why? The contemporary historian, John Spalding, gives us a clue. Speaking about the intended victim, he tells us that following his marriage "thereafter he became mad, and of whom his lady had no pleasure". Just for the record, the lady's mother was also present – not that I'm implying anything...

Then in 1672, the board records the "bizarre suicide" of Sir John Urquhart who stabbed himself to death with the best silver at Cromarty Castle. All right, I made up the bit about the silver, but he did use knives and even forks from the cutlery drawer. So who's the mad one now? I never heard of anyone pricking themselves to death.

Now we are going downstairs to see the cells. A prisoner is reclining on a bed covered with straw. Nothing so grand as a mattress, just plain straw like you would provide for a pig in a sty. He's eating his rations. You might have expected them to be meagre but I think they were surprisingly generous. See what you think. Here are the rations laid down by prison regulations in the 1840s:

Breakfast consisted of porridge, 8 oz of oatmeal along with three quarters of a pint of milk; dinner was two pints of barley broth with twelve ounces of brown bread. That's almost half of one of today's small loaves, which according to the adage, is better than no bread at all, but I would say was quite a lot. Not only that, but there was a choice. If you preferred, you could have 3lbs of potatoes with 6 ounces of bread and three quarters of a pint of milk!

Supper consisted of 2lbs of potatoes or porridge made from 6 ounces of oatmeal with half a pint of milk. It was even specified what the broth should be made from: 3 ounces of barley and 1 ounce of peas; or 2 ounces of marrow bones; or one head of an ox; or 1 ounce of hough or neck or other meat; or half an ounce of dripping – along with vegetables of various sorts – onions, leeks, carrots, cabbage and turnips. Fine cuisine it is not, nutritionists would dismiss it as stodge while the consumers probably thought it was boring but I wouldn't have thought anyone complained about being hungry.

Hanging from the wall is what is known as the "jougs", an iron collar with an iron chain which would have been attached to the wall of the church or mercat cross and hence our slang term being "put in the jug". It was used for offences against the church as well as breaches of common law. The object of the exercise was to name and shame. Everybody knew why you were there – fornication was a common offence and where, but for the grace of God, it might be you there next week. Churchgoer, as you pass by on your way to make your devotions, you would be wise not to mock too much.

There are some exhibition rooms down here too where you are given a fascinating insight into the times. In 1843 for example, Margaret Cameron from the neighbouring parish of Resolis was arrested, taken to Cromarty and jugged-up for rioting when a new minister was appointed. The following day a crowd marched to the Courthouse to demand her release. It so happened a wedding was going on, and the wedding guests joined in the fun and broke the doors of her cell down.

A century earlier there was the case of Margaret Simson [sic] who, in 1736, was accused of slander against Donald Robson who was an elder. In those bad old days, the Kirk and the Presbytery exerted enormous power and poor Margaret was sentenced to excommunication which was truly the worst thing that could happen to you, worse even than death because eternity is a long, long time to burn in hell.

But it's the venom of the way the sentence is passed that is really astonishing. It runs: "In the name of the Lord Jesus Christ [the Presbytery] excommunicate the said Margaret Simpson and deliver her to Satan for the destruction of the flesh that it may be a means if possible to bring her to repentance for the salvation of her soul".

You can practically see the righteous and the saved wringing their hands in glee at her misfortune.

Chapter Nine

Cromarty: The Geologist and The Genius

THE charming whitewashed thatched cottage with the crow-stepped gables is where a famous man was born on October 10th 1802. It was built at the end of the 17th century by his great-grandfather with money he made as a sailor, or booty he made as a pirate. No-one, we imagine, would be proud to be descended from a robber on the High Street demanding money with menaces, yet the same person on the high seas brandishing a cutlass becomes a pirate, which has a certain romantic cachet amongst young boys especially, who would love to boast they had a real-life pirate in their family. And this is exactly what our man did in his book *My Schools and Schoolmasters* (1854) where he describes his ancestor, John Feddes, as the "last of the buccaneers" and tells us the house was built with "Spanish gold".

In the same book, Hugh Miller, for that is the mystery man's name (if you have not already guessed), tells us about a great-uncle who sailed around the world with George Anson (1697-1762), later First Lord of the Admiralty. He also had another great-uncle who drowned in a storm and a grandfather who also perished at sea. That is a couple of catastrophes to be sure, but which the hard-hearted Lady Bracknell would describe as "carelessness". I am reminded of Aesop's fable, *The Pilot and the Passenger,* where during a storm, the latter was amazed to see the former totally unafraid despite his father and grandfather both having been drowned or "drowndead", as Mr Peggotty put it better. The pilot responded by asking the passenger where *his* father had died. "In bed," he admitted, to which the pilot replied that by the same logic, he should be afraid to go to bed at night.

We do not know if Hugh's grandmother ever heard of the fable or spotted a flaw in the logic, but in an attempt to avoid history repeating itself, she sent her son into the country to work on a farm well out of the sight of the sea, but her efforts were in vain. Salt water evidently coursed through his veins and the lure of the sea proved too strong. He too had an adventurous life, seeing action against the Dutch and deserting from the Royal Navy. With his savings he bought a sloop, was shipwrecked and survived, though the boat did not.

That's his house next door, between the birthplace and the Courthouse, the imposing two-storey Georgian house built a century after the cottage. Talk about being upwardly mobile! But alas things are not as they seem. In order to partly finance his new vessel, he had to rent out the new house. There was some comfort I suppose, in that he had the cottage to fall back on.

There were rich profits to be made by entrepreneurs such as he, conducting import/export businesses around the British coast and beyond. That is why, as you stroll around Cromarty, you will see other grand Georgian houses and at the other end of the spectrum, humble fishermen's cottages, a combination which makes this one of the most interesting and best-preserved villages in the Highlands and well worth a detour from the NC500, a sort of climax to your Black Isle tour.

Like the pilot in the fable, Mr Miller senior, shipmaster and shipwreck survivor, was unfazed by this misadventure but was unlucky enough to be shipwrecked a second time in 1807 and this time unfortunately followed the family tradition of following his ancestors to a watery grave. It was only five years after the birth of his famous-to-be son, Hugh. No trace of him or his ship was ever found again, Davy Jones' locker remaining firmly shut. From riches to rags, the widow and her family of three were suddenly plunged into even deeper poverty, not to mention grief, just when they hoped their fortunes were on the turn. How the gods love to toy with us for their sport!

So, at the tender age of five, young Hugh was left fatherless and with an uncertain future. What's a poor widow to do, but remarry, and reader, she did, though as a single mum with three children (and before Internet dating), it must have been difficult. It was twelve years before the right man came along.

Hugh married too. His bride was Lydia Fraser who was nine years younger than him and looked even younger than her age. It was a long courtship. Her mother did not approve of him, a humble stonemason with no prospects. (Look for the notches in the beam of the cottage which mark each day when the love-struck loon did not see her.) Then Miller got a job sitting behind a desk, adding up figures in a bank which Lydia's mother deemed much more acceptable. Three years after getting the most boring job this side of hell, the couple finally tied the knot in 1837.

But I get ahead of myself. In Scotland, ever since the Reformation in the middle of the 17th century, the law required every parish to provide a school, unlike England and Wales where it was not until 1833 (Dr Johnson, please note) that the state stepped in to ensure schooling was provided for the children of the poor. This pioneering system meant that the peasant's son could rub shoulders with the laird's son and thence go on to carve out fame and fortune for himself in the world. And they did: Thomas Carlyle, David Livingstone, Robert Fergusson, Robert Burns and many, many more. But not Hugh Miller. You will see why later.

After attending a dame's school, where he learned to read, that open sesame to all learning and knowledge, not to mention the joy of reading for its own sake, Miller moved on to the grammar school where amongst other things, he was exposed to such delights as the Catechism (Protestant version), Book of Proverbs and the New Testament. Try feeding that diet to today's kids! No wonder he played truant so often.

From the school windows the pupils could see the "silver darlings", the herring, being landed and gutted on the beach. And just yards from the front door, if not in their sight exactly but certainly within hearing range, that was where they took the pigs to slaughter, sometimes as many as a hundred in a day. Unlike the lambs in the simile who presumably lay down their lives with scarcely a bleat of protest, the squealing of the poor porkers must have been terrible to hear and, with the best will in the world, must have been a great distraction from learning anything.

Another unsavoury practice was the annual cockfighting contest, run by the schoolmaster and who charged the boys twopence per entry. A nice little sideline to boost your (meagre) salary. To his credit, Miller was not an aficionado of this "sport". In fact he did not get on very well with the dominie at all. He was hardly a model pupil. The truanting was by no means the worst thing he did. He once stabbed a fellow pupil in the leg, albeit after being provoked, and after a physical fight with his teacher, stormed out and never came back. He was fifteen. It was not until 1972 that the statutory leaving age in Scotland was raised to sixteen, so he was well within his rights to leave.

His education did not stop when he left school of course, just as it does for all of us; it was merely the end of the formal part. From an early age, Miller was somehow drawn to rocks and armed with a chisel and a mallet that belonged to his illustrious buccaneering great-grandfather, he went around chipping bits off boulders of different sorts he found on the beach such as mica, porphyry, garnet and so on. This much amused those who had come from the village to collect seaweed and who thought this a most peculiar pursuit and mockingly asked him if he was looking for "siller". Each to their own. He collected rocks and showed them to anyone who would care to look. The geologist had been born. It was Wordsworth who told us "the Child is the Father of the Man". I am sure there is a great deal of truth in that.

If Miller was unfortunate to lose his father at such an early age, he was lucky to have uncles, one of whom, his Uncle Sandy, had fought with Nelson and must have had some very interesting tales to tell. You can just see the young lad sitting by the old man's knee listening, absorbed, to tales of derring-do. He was also very religious, as those who go to the sea in ships tend to be. He certainly was an inspiration to the lad, seems to have been a fount of all knowledge. In particular, he was a keen amateur naturalist who taught his nephew all he knew.

Apart from the words of wisdom received from Uncle Sandy and others, Miller turned to teaching himself from books borrowed from villagers. That is why, strictly speaking, we can't really call him a "lad o' pairts", though we would have to agree the system did give him the vital start of learning how to read. And if the reading fare at school seemed stultifying at best, imagine how the young Hugh must have lapped up *Sinbad* and *Aladdin* and other tales, as well as when he was older, the voyages of Drake and Raleigh and Anson, the latter in whom he had a personal interest, as you know. And all this we know from the autobiography aforesaid and in which he also regales us with this spooky tale.

On the night his father perished, though he and the family did not yet know that he had, the same storm that was responsible for his demise was also responsible for blowing the door of the house open. Hugh's mother told the lad to shut it but imagine his horror when, in the doorway, he saw a sodden severed arm pointing a finger at him just an inch from his chest. Naturally he turned and fled in terror and the maid was dispatched instead. She too saw the same apparition and instead of slamming the door shut on the fearful sight, reacted in the same matter and Hugh's mother was forced to get up and shut the door herself. She saw nothing. Make of this what you will: a super-sensitive boy who passed on his suggestiveness to the maid, or some sort of premonition of the bad news about to befall the family?

It's not the only instance of the young boy having an encounter of the supernatural kind. Once, when in the house all alone, and amusing himself by playing at the bottom of the stairs, he happened to glance up, or something caught his eye and he beheld, standing on the landing looking down at him "the form of a large, tall, very old man, attired in a light-blue greatcoat". He instinctively knew it was his great-grandfather, John Fiddes, like the way you do in dreams. I'm not suggesting that the young Hugh was dreaming, not even suggesting he imagined it, but I am suggesting he was a sensitive child. Who can tell what really happened that day? Hugh certainly believed he was there and afterwards was scared that in the dark, he would bump into him in the room from which he supposed he had emerged. It would be enough to give anyone the willies.

Despite the less-than-catchy title of his autobiography, it is, as you can see, far from dull, and what's more, Miller has a very fine prose style. In the tale of the severed arm for instance, Miller makes fine use of inversion to create suspense. But apart from being an accomplished writer, in his life he was many things: poet, essayist, newspaper reporter and editor, bank accountant (as I mentioned earlier), collector of folk tales, evangelical Christian, stonemason and quarryman – not necessarily in that order.

In fact it was his first job after leaving school, as a quarryman, that first launched him on the abiding passion of his life. In the quarry he saw two bands of red sandstone, the darker on the bottom, and the enquiring mind wondered why. Then, when that quarry became uneconomic and a new one was opened up, imagine on his very first day, when hitting a rock with his hammer, it split open and revealed a fossil! Hugh was hooked. On being told that on Eathie shore just a couple of miles away, there were some curiously-shaped stones, Miller set about splitting them open with his trusty hammer and chisel and discovered not "siller" but treasure of another sort. I can see how that would appeal as a hobby, the wondering if the next stone might contain something, the delight and the wonder when it was opened and its secrets were revealed.

There is no need for us to hammer on the door of the cottage to see what treasures lie within. It's open and free to us on production of our National Trust cards. We step into the kitchen, the heart of the house. With flagstones on the floor and its low ceiling, it looks sparse and simple, far from luxurious but not without a certain cosiness. Some hard wooden chairs are gathered about the fireplace, the focal point, with all its associated paraphernalia such as the bracket on a hinge on which the pot was hung and in which the soup, stews and porridge were made. Cooking 18th and 19th century-style.

This cottage has another fireplace with an interesting feature. It's what was known as a "hingin' lum". It had a canopy inside which fish were hung to be smoked. The National Trust has kindly cut a hole in the side and inserted a glass window so visitors can have a peek inside and see the poles. It may not seem much, but this is posh – the equivalent of having an indoor toilet, which even in the middle of the twentieth century, the first house I lived in did not have. What this means is the Millers did not have to go to an outhouse to smoke their fish, making this a very desirable residence indeed, even if they did not have an indoor toilet.

Once again we have the place to ourselves as we wander from room to room, the birth room, the writing room and the room from which the ghostly

John Fiddes apparently materialised. The dinky wee windows peeking out from under the thatch, as well as admitting some light, let us see just how thick the walls are; surprisingly thick, in fact. There are other rooms too, exhibition rooms. I'm immediately attracted to one of Miller's original manuscripts opened to display two pages of densely packed, extremely neat handwriting with hardly any scorings out or corrections. All the more remarkable when you consider these letters were created by candlelight after a day chiselling letters in stone. How strange the change from major to minor!

And here is a copy of *The Witness*, the newspaper that Miller moved to Edinburgh to take up the post of editor. He was also the main writer. It is a broadsheet consisting of regiments of densely-packed columns. It looks daunting enough even before you begin to engage with the words. They have much to do about the schism within the Church of Scotland over who had the right to appoint ministers – the parishioners or the patrons, which is to say the local landowners. As if being at their mercy in all aspects of their daily lives was not enough already without them controlling their spiritual lives also.

In a *cause célèbre* in 1839, the parishioners and Presbytery of Auchterarder rejected and refused to ordain the appointed minister. The said cleric, Robert Young, appealed to the Court of Session in Edinburgh which not only upheld his appeal but ruled that the Church was an instrument of the State and subject to Parliament. It also declared that the General Assembly of the Church of Scotland was out of order when, in 1834, it granted congregations the right to choose their own ministers. It was war: on one side the Moderates who supported the State view and on the other, the Evangelicals who supported the independence of the Kirk.

Step up to the fray, Hugh Miller. As an evangelical, he sounded a blast of the trumpet against this monstrous ruling in the form of a widely circulated pamphlet. The title recalls polemics of the past like those by Jonathan Swift: *Letter from one of the Scottish People to the Right Hon. Lord Brougham and Vaux, on the opinions expressed by his lordship on the Auchterarder case*. It was a great success, at least with those on the anti-establishment side of the fence, and that was why Miller was invited to come to Edinburgh to become the editor of *The Witness*. It did not just concern itself with the burning issue of the day but also published Miller's articles on geology which later appeared in book form as *The Old Red Sandstone* (1841).

As a matter of fact, this had nothing to do with vanity and the wielding of editorial power. There was a religious connection between the geology and the great Church debate. Miller had been an evangelical Christian for more than a decade before these events and his studies did nothing to deflect him from his beliefs. What the fossils showed, he believed, in their beauty and their intricacy, was that a benevolent Creator *must* be responsible for them. Where he differed from the fundamentalists, what his study of geology confirmed, was that the creation of the world, according to Genesis, was utterly impossible. He thought it should not be taken literally but symbolically, should be read in terms of geological ages rather than days.

He was similarly unimpressed with the new-fangled theory of evolution going the rounds. He believed that God created mankind separately from animals, uniquely giving them a soul and the ability to distinguish between right and wrong. Darwin's *On the Origin of Species* did not appear until three years after Miller's death, of which more later, but maybe it was just as well. Would it have shaken him to the roots of his evangelical soul, made him question his conclusions? Or would he have devoted the remainder of his life trying to prove Darwin wrong? I think I know which way he would have jumped.

Things went from bad to worse as far as the Church was concerned and it all ended badly when the event known as "The Disruption" took place in 1843, when 450 ministers, a sizable minority, walked out of the General Assembly and the Free Church was born. Remember Margaret Cameron in the last chapter? That was the background to the rioting that she was involved in, why she was clapped in the cells and why she was sprung by her supporters. Clearly feelings were running high. It wasn't Miller's aim, but it could be said his articles in *The Witness* fuelled the debate, inflamed passions and were a contributory factor in this schism and to this day, the Black Isle is a still a stronghold of the Free Church.

There is a famous painting by David Octavius Hill (1802-70) which hangs in the Presbytery Hall of the Free Church in Edinburgh. It is over eleven feet wide and five feet high and contains over 400 individually recognisable faces of the parsons queuing up to sign the Deed of Demission and Act of Separation whereby the Free Church of Scotland was formally established. In the foreground is the clearly recognizable figure of Miller himself in his distinctive plaid, taking notes, which as Hill said, befitted the prominent part he paid in the movement.

But how did Hill do that, after the signing, since the ministers had scattered to the four corners of the country? The answer is that recognising the historical significance of what had just taken place, a physicist at St Andrews University, David Brewster, introduced Hill to Robert Adamson (1821-48), a pioneering photographer. Photography has been around for longer than we think, since 1835 in fact, when William Henry Fox Talbot (1800-77) took a photograph of a latticed window of Lacock Abbey in Wiltshire. He went on to develop (no pun intended) the calotype or talbotype which I will not go into, but it's all to do with creating light-sensitive paper.

Anyway Adamson took group photographs of all those present and then Hill picked up his paintbrush. It took him an incredible twenty-three years to complete, by which time many of those present had gone to heaven and never saw themselves immortalised in paint.

As you might expect, here in the museum, there's a lot of information on what Miller is actually famous for: his studies in geology, his fossil collection and his discoveries, about which but I will not weary you with too much information, except to say his studies were not confined to Cromarty. At seventeen, he was apprenticed to his uncle David as a stonemason and this work took him all over the counties of Ross and Cromarty and Sutherland and which gave him the opportunity to study different rocks as well as his other interest, collecting folk tales, which he published in *Scenes and Legends of the North of Scotland* (1835).

Examples of his stonework can be seen in the churchyard, including, unfortunately, the tombstone (it's easy to spot with its scalloped top – a Miller trademark) of his first child and baby daughter, Liza, who died of a fever aged only 17 months. It was a case of history repeating itself: Miller's two older sisters died in childhood of the same thing. Tragedy never strayed far from the Miller household as you have seen – and shall see again.

The other thing was that the Old Red Sandstone did not give up its secrets so easily, were not so readily tapped into. Created during the Devonian Period, about 415-350 million years ago, when Scotland was part of a continent situated somewhere about the equator, before what is now Scotland collided with what is now England and Wales (music to the Scottish Nationalists' ears), these fossils were very much squashed and flattened and fragmented and generally knocked about a bit in their long and slow migration north to their present position. What Miller did was collect these fragments and like a jigsaw puzzle, try to make sense of what he'd found.

Later in life, he had the opportunity to travel more widely in Scotland and even to England, collecting more specimens. At this point I'd like to proffer thanks to Mrs Miller for putting up with all those pesky bits of rock cluttering up the house.

And now we have come to the most startling exhibit of all. In some ways it is for me one of the most fascinating of all: Hugh Miller's death mask. It may not be to everyone's taste, but such things fascinate me and I think it's good to see, in the days before photography, what people like Beethoven and Haydn, Keats and Cromwell actually looked like, a sort of portrait in 3D. Actually the making of death masks has a long pedigree, going back as far as Roman times at least. How else do you think they got those life-like faces on the statues of their emperors and famous citizens?

But something puzzles me. Miller posed for the camera in Calton cemetery as a stonemason as well as on a dozen other occasions. As a matter of fact, he wrote an article on the new invention for *The Witness* in 1843. So why would you go to the trouble of making a death mask when photographs already exist of the subject? And the question is particularly pertinent in the case of Miller when you take into account the circumstances of his death.

It was Christmas Eve, 1856 and Miller was alone upstairs in their house in Portobello. He did suffer from a bad chest, a legacy of his stonemason days, breathing in all those dust particles. But that wasn't it; he'd had that for a good many years. He had been overworking, under self-imposed pressure writing copy for *The Witness* and completing his *Testimony of the Rocks*. He shot himself in the chest. He left a short suicide note to his wife which was reproduced in his obituary in *The Times* of December 29th 1856 and is short enough to be repeated in its entirety here:

> *Dearest Lydia,*
> *My brain burns. I must have walked; and a fearful dream rises upon me. I cannot bear the horrible thought. God and Father of the Lord Jesus Christ, have mercy upon me. Dearest Lydia, dear children, farewell. My brain burns as the recollection grows.*
> *My dear, dear wife, farewell.*
> *Hugh Miller.*

The signing off is rather curious as if he knew it would be repeated for wider consumption. It's a bit disjointed which gives an insight into the state of his mind, as does the repetition of "my brain burns". His religious conviction is also apparent as is his love for Lydia, especially. Most striking to me however is the "fearful" dream, so "horrible" that he dare not lie down to sleep lest he saw it again. God knows what it was but we have seen how as a boy, Miller had a vivid imagination, or as he would put it, saw strange sights, and this, whatever it was, was undoubtedly very real to him.

The verdict of the medical profession was he took his life "under an impulse of insanity". I suppose that is a way to put it, but it strikes a chord with me, reminds me very much of Macbeth and the vision he had, what he called:

A dagger of the mind, a false creation,
Proceeding from the heat-oppressèd brain.

As a matter of fact, in the days before his death, Miller talked of severe headaches "as if a very fine poignard had suddenly passed through my brain."

Both Macbeth and Miller were experiencing acute mental anguish. The difference is whereas Macbeth's vision led him to kill the king, Miller's led him to destroy himself.

Chapter Ten

The Clootie Well: Taking the Waters (Part 1)

WE'RE on the road again now, turning west, on the B9163. With the Cromarty Firth on our right, we come presently to the quaintly-named Jemimaville. It's an unlikely name for a place in Scotland but your eyes do not deceive you. Keep them peeled though; blink and you'll miss it.

No greater love hath a man for his wife than he name a village after her. And quite right too. Her full name was Jemima Poyntz, also an unlikely name for these parts. She was an heiress of Dutch extraction and with her dowry, her penniless husband, who shall be nameless, though there is no shame in being poor, built a big house (in the Dutch style) as well as some more humble dwellings for the estate workers. In gratitude he named the settlement after her. He was a lucky man and he knew it, which is good to see.

A few miles later we come to the turn-off to Resolis where the unfortunate Margaret Cameron came from. At this juncture it seems appropriate to give a few more details about her arrest. It's a point well worth remembering that after the Disruption, it took no small amount of courage for the sitting minister to leave the establishment and join the Free Church. To fall out with the laird on whose patronage you depended for your living was effectively to declare yourself homeless, doubtless with a wife and family to support, and without a place to preach.

This was the situation pertaining to the Reverend Donald Sage, married with a family of eight and one on the way, now minister of the Free Kirk of Resolis. He was popular with his flock, and the laird's decision to replace him did not go down well with them to say the least. When the new man came to take up his pulpit, a large crowd had gathered in protest. This trouble had been anticipated and troops had been called out all the way from Fort George. Tempers flared, stones were thrown, shots were fired and Margaret Cameron was the one unlucky enough to be seized out of the crowd and arrested as an example to all the others. The rest you know.

The church is still there, pretty much unchanged since it was at the centre of this disturbance. So too is the now-ruined rent barn where the grain was stored in the days when rent to the laird was paid in kind, and which saw service as the Reverend Sage's new kirk. We decide against taking that slight detour to see them. That is all that remains, the rioters long since gone to their graves, every one.

And because there is nothing much to see in scenic terms and because we know precisely where we are heading next, we take a short-cut on a road so insignificant it is not even granted a name, over the hills and not so far away, towards Munlochy, where we turn right onto the A832 and head west towards Tore.

What we seek, what we have seen before, many a time and oft, is that blot on the landscape, known as the "Clootie Well". You can't help but notice it, the obscene things hanging from the branches of the trees like dead crows hung out to rot "*pour encourager les autres*", as Voltaire would put it. But fear not, should you somehow fail to spot the grisly sight, there is a handy signpost erected by the Forestry Commission which points out the car park.

It's not a car park in the supermarket sense of the word, but an unmade sort of place, rough yet ready to receive your vehicle but not, hopefully, your cloot, another un-needed contribution to the unholy mess where there are already far too many.

The well's origins lie far back in the mists of time. It's dedicated to St Boniface (c.675-754) but goes back beyond that to Celtic times, to Shamain and Beltain, especially, what we call Hallowe'en and May Day. Thus we have another example of the not-uncommon mixture of Christian and Celtic culture.

This is what the visitor in those days would have done. First of all you scoop up some water from the well (a spring actually), turn sunwise (clockwise) three times, spill some water three times, take three sips of what's left in the name of the Father, the Son and the Holy Spirit, then make a wish before tying a "cloot" – a piece of cloth – to the nearest branch you can find.

It was a place of healing. If you had an ailing part, you rubbed the affected area with your cloot, dipped it in the water then hung it up to decay. If you were too ill to get to the well yourself, a friend or relative would take the infected cloot for you instead. The idea was that as the cloot rotted, so whatever was ailing you would die away and you would be healed.

Nowadays, near the well, there is not a branch, not a twig that is not festooned with knickers, unsavoury-looking underpants, socks, tights, ties, gloves, mittens, scarves, football tops, shirts, blouses, cardigans, bras (well at least one) and even a full-length coat. Think of a garment and you'll find it here. There are even soft toys and shoes, one pair a handy receptacle for a fizzy drink can in the left and bottle of flavoured water in the right. I'm glad to see that whoever left them was publically spirited enough not to leave litter lying about.

The whole thing is a palette of brightly-coloured raiment: red, white and blue, pink and purple, yellow and green – a rainbow of dyed colours unknown to Man in the times when this well began and which will never fade away. And neither will the synthetic fibres of which they are made. But it's not all gay and bright: there is also a good smattering of greys, browns, blacks and khaki, and it is they that contribute most to the ugliness of this place. They look as if they have faded and are in the process of decaying but the truth is they are in just as good a state of preservation as their more colourful cousins. They are merely the dull and boring colours preferred by many of today's bright young things.

Pillowcases, dishcloths, dishtowels, tablecloths (you could get a thousand cloots out of one of them) and T-shirts crucified to the trunks, with writing on the front, the message being the flesh they clothed may no longer be here but the fabric is, and it's here to stay. Even the very roots of the trees that have worked their way to the surface do not escape and are lagged with rags. And way above head height, the agile have somehow managed to climb to upper branches and drape their cloots over them. And there still not being enough space, strings have been strung up between the trees like washing lines on

which clothes have been hung but will never dry.

A saltire high up, spread out, has been nailed to a tree trunk. Someone evidently is worried about the state of the country like Ross in *Macbeth* who forlornly declared, "Poor Country! Almost afraid to know itself". This flag's presence tells me the nationalists will try any desperate measure and have come here in the hope of whatever they think Scotland is ailing from will be cured. But judging from the near-perfect condition of this particular national symbol, it's not going to be anytime soon – which might give some encouragement to the Unionists.

There is also a New Zealand flag, and I don't know what whoever placed that here would like cured unless it is is to leave the Commonwealth – or nothing at all. I would bet my pension that many of the visitors who come here don't realise the reason for this place or its rituals. I can imagine a couple of Kiwi backpackers, one of whom sacrificed one of the flags which they were displaying on their rucksacks in the hope it might enhance their chance of a lift from some passing motorist. However right or wrong that may be, it does at least show people come here from far and wide. Some undoubtedly come prepared: you tend not to carry a tablecloth or a pillowcase about with you, do you?

I'm all for maintaining ancient traditions, but I wish there was some sort of by-law that said that the cloot had to be of biodegradable material (like in the olden days) and has to be of a certain size or it will be taken down. That would still leave the place looking like a rag merchant's yard but it would be much less offensive on the eye. The snag is that according to tradition, if you remove someone's cloot, you will inherit that person's maladies and misfortunes. For Highland Council, that would be like opening a whole warehouse of Pandora's Boxes. I don't see them taking this action anytime soon.

That's the only wish I make. Nor do I cast a cloot, certainly not my precious hat, though headgear of a less distinguished sort has been left behind here. We make our way back to the car leaving nothing to show we were ever here apart from our footprints in the soggy ground. Soon they will be gone. If only the cloots could disappear so easily.

Chapter Eleven

Strathpeffer: Taking the Waters (Part 2)

ORE roundabout is a major intersection where routes north and south, east and west, meet and diverge. In the days of yore, Tore was a famous meeting place for those itinerant folk, the gypsies, who came here to haggle at the horse fair and while they were at it, have a jolly good punch-up with other gypsy families.

We will be back here tomorrow taking the A9 to all points north, but in the meantime, we are heading west, back on the NC500 on the A832 which will take us in due course to Muir of Ord and which will complete our little detour of the Black Isle. It's here, at Muir of Ord, that the NC500 traveller has a decision to make – clockwise and north-west to Achnasheen, or anticlockwise and north-east to Dingwall? We have already made our decision. It's anticlockwise for us and in order to make a good start in the morning from our base in Inverness, we are making for Dingwall now – but not before we have made another little detour to Strathpeffer.

Muir of Ord does not detain us, nor does the tiny village of Contin which was the scene of an atrocity every bit as terrible as the massacre of Glencoe in 1692 where, as every schoolboy knows, the Macdonalds were treacherously put to the sword by the dastardly Campbells (and others) who beforehand had eaten them out of house and home for two weeks in accordance with Highland hospitality. But what the Macdonalds did to the Mackenzies here two centuries before that has somehow escaped the public consciousness.

Apparently, the Macdonalds on a pillaging expedition into the lands of their enemies, discovered old men, women and children taking sanctuary in the church where they thought they would be safe. Not a bit of it. Alexander Macdonald (may his name live in infamy) ordered that the door be barred and the church set on fire. Hundreds were burned alive.

There is nothing like an act of cruelty like that to inspire revenge and retribution. The Mackenzies came down like wolves on the Macdonalds and met at the battle of Blàr na Pàirce (Battle of the Park) near here. The exact date is unknown, but reckoned to be about 1485. About two thousand Macdonalds were killed or drowned in the river Conon. You might feel like saying "and served them right too" but the truth is most of them were just poor crofters doing the bidding of their lords and masters.

Actually we branch off the A835 before Contin and take its brother, the A834 to Strathpeffer. In Victorian and Edwardian times, the majority of travellers would have arrived by train, and they did, in their shoals. They came to take the sulphurous waters which had been known since the middle of the 18th century when Dr Thomas Morrison publicised their health-giving properties – his arthritis, he claimed, having been cured by the waters. The spring was fenced off by the Reverend Colin MacKenzie in 1777 to stop it being polluted by cattle, but it was when the Dingwall and Skye railway opened in 1870, followed by the Strathpeffer branch line in 1885, that the village as a spa really took off.

The minute we drive into the village it strikes me it has a vaguely Brigadoon sort of air. The clear, round globes hanging like dewdrops from the delicate iron filigree on the tall and stately lampposts that line the main street seem to transport you back to a bygone age. "Welcome", they seem to say, gracefully bowing their heads in acknowledgement of your presence.

This other-worldly sort of feeling is enhanced (and it comes as a mild surprise), to see, up to our right, sitting splendid on its mound, the spick-and-span, green-and-white Pavilion which was erected in 1880 to provide a venue for the visitors' entertainment. With its huge, arched, multi-paned window on the gable end and its wrap-around verandah and the wooden fretwork on the fascias and bargeboards, in its pristine whiteness, it looks as if it could be made of icing and marzipan, the sort of thing that Hansel and Gretel would fall upon with relish. Or if that is too fanciful, it does not require much imagination to suppose it had been transported from some alpine village somewhere. In front of it, down a grassy slope is a matching octagonal bandstand.

So this is Strathpeffer! It's quite breathtaking and there is nothing quite like it in the whole of Scotland.

And over there, on its own high ground and rising above the trees, is the Highland Hotel, just one of the grand hotels and villas that sprung up to accommodate the vast numbers of people who came here for the good of their health. This one might have been called "Many Chimneys", for there are certainly a good many of them, while the architecture, a blend of mock Tudor,

French chateau and Scots Baronial, does nothing to detract from the fairytale charm of the place.

In the square is the Old Sampling Pavilion, also very charming, looking very airy with its multitude of windows, overhanging roof and with a cupola to top it off. It stands on the site of the first Pump Room, built in 1819. It's closed now, if it is ever open for business nowadays. Alas, the baths complex was demolished in 1952 and so there is nothing for it but to make straight for the Upper Pump Room which was built in 1839, remodelled in 1909, and which now doubles as an exhibition centre and a sweet shop. An unlikely combination, you might think, and it crosses my mind to wonder if the owners were inspired by the Pavilion, thinking – like me – it a sugary sort of concoction.

In actual fact we have Anne, the Duchess of Sutherland and the Countess of Cromartie to thank for the architecture of the Pavilion and the Spa as a whole. She wanted it to resemble the spas she had seen on her travels. Well done, your ladyship, but it is the two ladies, Maureen and Shirley – the owners of the Real Sweets and Gift Company – that we have to thank for managing the Pump Room and Spa Exhibition, though it is a temptation (for some more than others) to linger in the shop. But even here, before you enter the exhibition, you take a step back into the past as you see jar upon jar of sweets, ranged row upon row on shelves, just like they used to be when I got threepence a week pocket money – if I had been a good boy.

In the exhibition, the story of the Spa is told by a series of information boards, mannequins and photographs, which is how you learn there were many types of baths and more than one type of water to drink, five different wells, four sulphurous, each with different characteristics and one of which contained iron.

Just as a malt whisky drinker may begin their education by starting off with a Speyside or Highland malt, not too peaty, and then perhaps move on to whiskies of more complexity and peatiness, so the Castle Leod Well was a well for beginners, for those suffering from indigestion and who could not take the stronger waters. The Sutherland Well, a bit more sulphurous, was a good one with which to begin the day, while the Morrison Well was stronger, best taken hot and with a dose of Epsom Salts. But beware the Cromartie Well! Take this only in small doses because of its loosening effect on the bowels. Lastly there was the Iron Well, water all the way from Ben Wyvis, and because of its concentration of iron, just the job for those suffering from anaemia or dyspepsia and taken as a tonic after the sulphur treatment. It should be taken through a straw as it is bad for the teeth (think what it does to your insides!) and never, ever, should be mixed with the chalybeate or sulphurous water as it turns black on contact. Ugh!

The Pump Room, where the waters were served, was open from 6.30 in the morning till 9. And just to make sure the sleepy heads did not miss their early morning medicine, they would be wakened by the skirl of the pipes as a piper went on a tour of the hotels. If they didn't know it already, those who had come from London on the sleeper to Inverness knew for certain they were awake and in Scotland now.

And here is a mock-up of the invalids, patients, holidaymakers – call them what you will – being served their glasses of water, tumblers actually. To help you imagine the scene, let's suppose you are a Time Traveller (actually everyone who steps over the threshold of this place is), who has just dropped into your local for a pint but have inadvertently stepped through some sort of time portal to find your favourite watering hole, familiar but strangely changed. For a start, those standing at the bar are wearing funny clothes. He is wearing a tweed suit and a brown bowler, while his lady companion is wearing an elegant long satiny dress. And the barmaid! Just look at her! She too has a long dress, a blouse and a long white apron. She looks more like an old-fashioned nurse than a barmaid. And there is not a single pump handle to be seen. Instead, behind the bar, sprouting from the tiled wall, are a series of taps just like the ones you have on your bath at home. As for the liquid that came out of the one you picked, it looks clear like water, not brown like beer. Smells funny too. You ask the barmaid if the landlord has cleaned the pipes recently. In fact, is she sure that what she has just served you is not the cleaning fluid? But no, she assures you, that is what you ordered, No. 3, and that will be threepence please, sir, unless you have a book of twelve tickets which will save you a shilling (not to be sneezed at) over the week.

Back at the turn of the century, your resident physician (run by Harley Street from 1907-27) would prescribe your water and your dosage, eight ounces or sixteen ounces. For greatest efficacy, you should drink it heated as that aids absorption, and whilst walking about, mixing with your fellow patients, as you do at a party with a glass of wine. And to enhance the general ambience of the experience, and no matter how nasty you found the taste, you drank the water to a band playing, literally. After that, you would go back to your hotel for breakfast but don't imagine you might be sitting down to a hearty plate of porridge, eggs and bacon and muffins with lashings of butter. Your kindly doctor might have ordered, for your stomach's sake, some toast and tea. And this regime was not just for breakfast either but might be for lunch and dinner too. Thanks very much, doctor. And yes, there would be none of the wine of the country either.

It wasn't all about taking the waters though. Should you have the desire, or is it the hunger, how about a nice round of golf, or a game of tennis or bowls? Or, if it is raining, a game of billiards or a hand of bridge in the Pavilion? Or you might just take a leisurely stroll in the landscaped gardens or go on an excursion in a horse-drawn charabanc, while the fitter, more energetic patients might go hill walking. You weren't just here for the good of your health after all; you were also on holiday, weren't you? You should be prepared to stay for at least three weeks, six would be better, not necessarily taken consecutively. A week at the seaside in between as a rest from the "Cure" was recommended. Yes, all very well for the leisured classes.

It was a place to be seen during the season but it was also a place where the hoi polloi could rub shoulders with the great and the good, the famous and the infamous (Aleister Crowley "the wickedest man in the world" came here, where he met his wife actually). But what was especially good about the Strathpeffer set-up is there was provision for those who could not afford the treatments as long as they were "respectable". The Nicolson Memorial Hospital was opened in 1896 with provision for fifteen patients who could stay for a month. As you can imagine, it was very much oversubscribed.

Along with the water taken internally, the "Cure" consisted of baths, where for your pleasure, different kinds awaited you: peat or sulphur, or a douche, with or without a massage. The first combined Pump Room and Bath House was built in 1861. There is a photograph of the Pump Room, a long sink enclosed in polished mahogany and on the wall, the pipes with a notice telling you which well the water was coming from.

Next to it is a very comical photograph of a douche in operation. There are a lot of serious-looking pipes on the tiled walls and a well-dressed gent in a bow tie is standing behind a curved contraption which looks like a Roman centurion's shield, and from behind the safety of which he is directing a stream of water over the back of what looks like a carver chair borrowed from the dining room of one of the hotels. More of a hose-down than a shower I would have said.

Next to it is a photograph of the Vichy Bath. Now *that* looks more like my idea of a shower. The patient apparently lay on a couch which, somewhat oddly, appears to have been made up like a bed complete with a pillow. Above it is a system of sunflower showerheads which would have given you a good drenching when the operator, who is dressed like a nurse, and who is standing well back, turns on the water.

And here is a photo of the peat bath. Now that looks positively medieval, like something from the dungeons, consisting of a winch and ropes and pulleys. You can imagine the victim taking one look at that and recanting or spilling the beans on the spot. "No! No! Anything but the peat bath!" Actually this device was for "crippled" patients, a windlass to lower and raise them from the restorative powers of the bath. But wouldn't it have been something if they came out of it and were able to throw away their walking sticks! It was supposedly very efficacious for arthritis, lumbago, sciatica and get this – obesity. Winch me down, Scotty!

I'm not so sure about the Electric Treatment though. That sounds scary, although they try to make it sound relaxing: "Just lie on the couch, grab these metal electrodes and don't worry about a thing. No, never mind the soaking floor. Now we'll just switch on the current." This treatment is reported to be beneficial (if you could first get the patient to lie on the couch), for those suffering from hysteria, anaemia and neurasthenia. Oh yes?

Another treatment, but which sounds more like torture, was Plombière's, a so-called "intestinal lavage" for chronic constipation, colitis and other problems of the bowel. No matter how much they dress it up in French, we're not that daft, we know exactly what it means and very nasty it sounds too. The patient lay on a bed, which significantly, had a hole in the middle, a tube was inserted, the water was pumped in and what was euphemistically called an "evacuation" occurred. The contents of the bucket were then inspected as to their colour, quantity and character and to see if any blood was present, or parasites. (There must be an easier way of earning a living.)

Well, you could be a masseur or a masseuse for instance, as long as you didn't mind being pelted with water along with the patient. In the Aix Douche, as well as the pressure from water jets, the pressure from the masseur was really good for easing away stiffness of the joints and making you more supple. I wouldn't mind a shot of that. Not so sure about the Scotch Douche though. That was where you were subjected to alternate drenching of hot and cold water – supposedly very good for your nerves. I suppose if you could stand the shock of that maybe you could tolerate just about any other extremes that life threw at you.

The Russian bath sounds all right though. In fact I've had a good many of them as it's really just a steam bath, but it was recommended that it should be followed by the Needle Bath which I'm sure was just as painful as it sounds – jets of ice-cold water blasted at your skin to close the pores.

I also like the sound of the Foam Bath. Some sort of foam extract, perhaps made of pine, was added to the water and gas was pumped in to make the bubbles which then gave you a gentle massage. That's what I would call a Jacuzzi and I've had a good number of them in my time too. Very relaxing.

Good for rheumatism and high blood pressure. Yes, I can see that. What I can't see, however, is how it makes you thinner, as they claimed. I would love to believe it but, for the life of me, I really can't.

Once again your physician would prescribe the amount of sulphur and the temperature of your bath and how long you should remain immersed. That would depend on the individual, what was ailing you, and how ill you were. Baths would last from ten minutes to half an hour, taken on alternate days, and you could vary the kind of bath you had.

Bathers would be advised not to take a bath if they were feeling too tired, too hot or if it was too soon after a meal or after too long a fast. It seems they regarded the bath treatment as a form of exercise. Now I am all for that. Wallowing in hot water or peat sounds a great form of exercise to me, not even getting out of breath. And after the bath you should not undertake any form of exercise but have a lie down for an hour or so. Hey, I like the sound of this more and more. It sounds like a lazy man's charter and a very handy thing indeed to be able to tell your wife when she nags you to get up and carry out some chore or other that you're afraid you can't, as you are following doctor's orders.

It comes as a bit of a surprise, on turning a corner, at the back of the museum, to find a bare, naked lady. Her name is Mrs Mitchell and the date is 14th July 1905. She is not in the first flush of youth and not firm of flesh either, but she has a great deal of it. She has evidently just had a peat bath as some of it has stuck to her in all the strategic places and her greying hair has been tied up on top of her head to keep it as clean as possible. She is being winched into the clean water bath to be rinsed off. Her doctor has prescribed six peat baths to be taken every second day and of increasing temperature and duration. She also had to take a 16 oz dose of water from No. 2 Well in the morning and 8 oz at midday. The good doctor also put her on a diet. No puddings, no sweets, no fatty foods and no stimulants. We don't know what Mrs Mitchell was suffering from, poor dear. It might have been gout, arthritis, lumbago, or sciatica or obesity. Definitely the latter. In which case why didn't the doctor recommend the foam bath? The cleaner cure.

So how much would taking the waters set you back? Well this very informative and intriguing little museum has the answer. Here are the late 1920s prices of just some of the treatments I have mentioned. Plombière's Treatment comes in top of the charts at 10/6. At equal number two on the hit-your-wallet parade is the peat bath at 9/- and the Radiant Heat with the Needle Bath. Tying for fourth place is the Aix Bath and the Vichy Douche at 7/-. In sixth

place is the medicated Foam Bath at 5/6 and, in 7th place, what probably most people came for until the doctors prescribed their regime, the Thermal Sulphur Bath at 4/6.

On the matter of the masseurs and the masseuses, it cost 11/6 per hour for the former and 10/6 per hour for the latter. An hour seems an incredibly long time to be pummelled, especially if you were having the Aix Douche. By the time you had that you would have looked distinctly pruney, not to mention feeling as if you'd been trampled all over by a Clydesdale. And it's interesting, though not altogether surprising given the times, that the masseuses cost a shilling less. Equal pay for equal work? Come off it, dear! Some women are never satisfied. Next thing they'll be asking for is that the voting age be reduced from thirty to twenty-one. It was only with the Representation of the People (Equal Franchise) Act of 1928 that all women, regardless of property ownership, were given equal voting rights with men.

So at today's prices, what would your cure cost? I offer the following guide as an approximation only, but bearing that caveat in mind, think of a shilling as being worth £2 today. I will leave you to do the sums should you wish to do so and also the more vexed question of whether it was value for money or not.

Strathpeffer's demise came about during the war years. During the First, numbers declined; during the Second, the hotels and villas, not to mention the Spa itself were requisitioned. Even when the War ended, its effects lingered on.

The Lower Pump Room was not de-requisitioned until 1948. That was late. Even rationing stopped in 1947 and I don't need to tell you when the war ended. And sadly, His Majesty's Forces did not take best care of the properties entrusted to them.

But thankfully the Strathpeffer community has done a great restoration job, and – thanks especially to the sweet, sweet ladies, Maureen and Shirley – the visitor can get a pretty good impression of the Spa in its glory days. Fortunately even without its healing waters, Strathpeffer seems to be in rude good health. Location is everything and, apart from the natural attractiveness of its setting, it happens to have the good fortune to be on the circuit for coaches taking tourists to the Highlands and Islands; a handy staging-post, providing plenty of places where they can be fed and watered and find a bed for the night.

Alas it is not on the NC500, but it's hardly anything of a detour and it's one you should certainly take. There's a lot more to do in Strathpeffer other than haul your wife out of the sweetie shop.

Chapter Twelve

Strathpeffer: Stones and Stations

L IKE the people of old, we have a pleasant stroll along the main road. It seems a street in want of a name. You would have thought with its illustrious past that the powers-that-be could have come up with a name like Morrison Street or MacKenzie Street, though I grant you the Countess of Cromartie Street would be a bit of a mouthful.

As we walk along, it gives us a chance to see the massive hotels and villas that mushroomed here thanks to the Spa. Well, it may be more accurate to say we pass the tree-lined drives leading up to them, where they lie hidden from view amongst the foliage.

We have a destination in mind: the Eagle Stone. The Gaelic Nostradamus, Kenneth Mackenzie, Coinneach Odhar, call him what you will – believe in him or not – made many prophecies, and there is one more I must mention before we leave him. He predicted that when the Eagle Stone here falls over a third time, Loch Ussie would flood the valley and Strathpeffer and Dingwall would disappear beneath the water and ships would be able to moor at the stone where it stands on the hillside. It has fallen over twice, so we are told. How the superstitious love things to come in threes!

Actually, if you don't count Baile-na-Cille, in the Parish of Uig on Lewis, where the Seer was born, this is his home turf. It's near here, on the banks of Loch Ussie, that he lived and worked. It's inconceivable he did not see this stone for himself and naturally so must we. Even without the Seer connection we would have come to see it.

It's clearly signposted so there is no difficulty in finding it. The path leads us between a line of trees on our left, and on our right, a fence that looks as if it has been erected quite recently. "Don't fence me in" as the song has it, but we are, making it impossible to give a wide berth to those pesky midges that hover like a black miasma in the air.

Fortunately it is not too far before we catch sight of what we seek, also fenced in so it can't escape. And there is definitely no chance of it toppling over for a third time either. A person or persons unknown has made perfectly sure of that. It sits in a mound ringed by boulders and may even be cemented in for good measure. Even if it weren't, I'd like to see any gale blow it over or any terrorist shove it over. I wouldn't be surprised if there was a great deal of it, perhaps just as much again, beneath the surface.

A noticeboard nearby, which has seen better days but which is still legible, gives its Gaelic name, *Clach an Tiompain* – not a literal translation from the English, but actually means "Sounding Stone". It goes on to tell us that it is a "mysterious legacy from the Picts". On it we should be able to make out the image of a horseshoe and an eagle. Hard luck, horseshoe, to the eagle goes the honour of bearing the stone's name and I have to agree, the "Horseshoe Stone" doesn't have the same ring to it. It's a symbol stone, as opposed to the cross slab we saw in the Groam museum, for the good reason it does not have a cross. Nor is it a slab, but a boulder, just as nature intended.

In Pictish art, the symbols almost invariably come in pairs, along with the enigmatic mirror and comb which has led some experts to suppose that they might commemorate the marriage of two powerful families – in this case, Eddie the Eagle to Henrietta the Horse. Others have suggested it might be a different sort of marriage, an alliance between tribes – there it is for all to see, written in stone. Still others think it might be a boundary marker between tribes – this is our land, keep out! It has also been suggested they might be grave markers. I would have thought there was one simple way of testing that theory. And maybe they did dig hereabouts and found no evidence of a body, it having turned to dust long ago, not even a single tooth remaining, that most resilient of body parts. And yet 1,300 years is but a blink of an eye in archeological terms, and you would have thought there would have been some evidence of some sort had there been a grave here. Unless, of course, the stone is not in its original position.

I'm no geologist but it looks like a glacial erratic to me and, apart from carving on it, I would have thought all the Picts needed to have done was dig a hole for it, upend it and stick it in. If that sounds easy, it wouldn't have been. It must be immensely heavy. It stands higher than my waist so it must be more than three feet and that's just what we can see of it. It's also thicker than my waist I am pleased to say. I certainly wouldn't fancy lugging it all the way up here. And yet that's what the people who know better than me think is what happened, that it came from a cemetery at Fodderty, some four miles away, and in 1411 was placed here as a memorial to the Munros who died fighting Public Enemy Number One in these parts – the Macdonalds. After all, if those four-ton bluestones at Stonehenge two millennia earlier could somehow be transported from the Presili Mountains in south Wales to Wiltshire, 150 miles away – why, this would be mere child's play. All you need are some rollers, a sledge, some ropes, some willing pullers and pushers and Bob's your uncle!

It's pretty hard to make out the designs on it because, apart from the ravages of centuries of Scottish winters, there is a great deal of lichen not only obscuring the carvings but misleading you into seeing things that aren't there. I *can* make out the eagle's beak though, and there's his back, too flat and straight in my opinion, and there's the curve of the breast and following that down, that could just be his feathery feet clinging on with crooked claw, not to a crag as in Tennyson's poem, but a stone. But perhaps he is and it's hidden beneath the ground. There are a couple of parallel lines which I suppose are meant to represent the folded wings, but I don't rate this stonemason's skill too highly. It certainly bears no comparison to the Rosemarkie artist. In fact, if I hadn't known better, I would have said the bird looks more like a pigeon. It's too squat and dumpy; doesn't look nearly majestic enough.

At the top of the stone are a couple of curved lines which could be the top of the horseshoe, or it could just be a crescent which is a common feature on symbol stones. It's very difficult to make out anything else thanks to the lichen and, not least, a big chunk somehow having been knocked off the top right-hand corner. How did that happen? Even if it were the result of ice getting into a crack and splitting it asunder, where is that chunk now? It couldn't have just got up and walked away. I hope some careless person didn't come along and think, "Hey that's a handy bit of stone!" and without looking to see if it had any carvings on it, stuck it into the circle of stones at the base. In fact, now I come to look at it more closely, this stone is just where it would have landed, is just about the right size and shape and colour...

In the distance there is a green hill not so far away. It looks a gentle sort of climb that even I could do without getting too much out of puff, and I imagine many of the fitter sort of invalids to the Spa did just that. But alas we cannot follow in their footsteps on this occasion. We simply haven't the time. The evenings are beginning to draw in and we have Dingwall on our minds. We are in mid-September.

With a darker green at the bottom and a paler green on the top, the hill is bisected by a wall of stone, running like a scar from end to end. This hill, known to the locals as "The Cat's Back", was once the site of an Iron Age fort called Knock Farril. At some stage in its life, probably when it was under attack and not the result of some domestic incident, like the catastrophic events that began in Pudding Lane in London in 1666, the wooden fortifications took fire and the heat was so intense it vitrified the rocks on which they were built.

Imagine that! That's hot. About 1000°C they think.

One of these days we will come back and see the effect of that for ourselves. Apart from a great view all around from the summit, we would also be able to see the scars in the turf, evidence of the trenches that John Williams dug in 1777 when he excavated the site. The purpose of his dig was not to uncover artifacts but to uncover the mystery of the vitrified stones – to determine if the Cat's Back was actually an extinct volcano or not. The result you know. Experts tell us that the settlement dates from about 400 BC. Within the outer defensive walls there would have been an unknown number of wooden roundhouses. You can see how a careless spark from the cooking fire might have brought not just the house down, but fused the rocks of the perimeter wall together.

There was a battle on the ridge there in 1497, the battle of Drumchatt, when the Mackenzies and possibly the Munros, who were normally enemies, took on again the mutual auld enemy, the Macdonalds. Historical records are scant, the Munro involvement not being mentioned by an earlier historian, but is by one who came along a couple of centuries later – so a reason to be cautious. If there *had* been an alliance, normal service was resumed again in this same location in 1501 when a battle took place between the Munros and Mackenzies. As in *Romeo and Juliet,* the feud between the two families came to an end when Catherine Mackenzie, the daughter of the clan chief, married Hector, the chief of the Munros. Whether they lived happily ever after I couldn't say, far less if they were even in love. It's maybe just a story anyway as there are no contemporary historical records to support it, just the word of Alexander Mackenzie in his *History of the Munros.* Indeed, there are no records of the battle either. This is the same author and historian who gave us the prophecies of the Brahan Seer, so make of that what you will.

I bring my gaze and my thoughts back to the present and the noticeboard. A map shows the Pictish Trail with dots, like a rash of measles, indicating the location of other stones. As I said before, you can't move anywhere in these parts before you trip over a Pictish stone somewhere or other. 150 of them are known to exist and new ones are being unearthed all the time. We will be back amongst the Picts again when we go to Portmahomack on the Tarbat Peninsula, but fear not, gentle reader, we do not intend to seek out each and every single Pictish stone between here and there and beyond, on or off, the NC500.

But before we run the midgie gauntlet and before this stone disappears from sight, I stop to take one last look at the Eagle Stone. Now that I know what to look for, it seems to me that from this distance, the patterns on the stone are more distinct. The horseshoe is bigger than I expected and the bird's wing looks better, conveying the impression of primary feathers with the secondary ones beneath. And then a thought strikes me. We know the ancient Greeks painted their statues and not to their enhancement either in my opinion as they chose the most gaudy of colours. We also know that the Picts painted their bodies and it wouldn't surprise me in the least if they painted their stones too. Now imagine climbing this hill and there in front of you would be the horseshoe and eagle standing out in living colour. It would have made an immediate impact. We don't know what statement it was making, but the Picts did and it was saying it loud and clear.

Smartly, through the trees we go, and back onto Mackenzie Avenue. Yes, that should be the name of the road running through the town. I've made up my mind. (Strathpeffer Community Council and Highland Regional Council please note.) Exactly which Mackenzie need not be stipulated, could remain ambiguous. It is Mackenzie country after all and there are a great number of trees on either side, so Avenue it is.

Next on our itinerary is the station which is situated further down the Avenue in the direction of Dingwall. Since that is our next destination, we decide to head back for the car in order to save retracing our steps. I am in favour of saving energy whenever I can; you just never know when you might need it. And on this point, lack-of-exercise addicts or the not-so fit may like to know that you can drive almost to the top of Knock Farril and leave your car in a car park. There is a downside though. The climb up to the top is short but steep. Still, you may think it worth your while – if you can follow the directions to the car park in the first place. However, if you are of the technological kind, an App (what's that?) is available to help you.

So we are not in the least out of puff as having collected the car, we draw into the station. It's been many years since the train last puffed out of here, not since 1951 in fact and it was closed to passengers five years before that, so for once you can't lay that at the door of Dr Beeching, Baron Beeching actually, which makes him sound more nefarious, like something out of a Victorian melodrama. He wielded his axe, and on cost and efficiency grounds, cut over 4,000 miles of railtrack in Britain in the 1960s. Now we have 44 tonne juggernauts churning up our roads, rumbling through our streets, disturbing our dreams, creating our waking nightmares. Thanks a bunch, Baron Beeching, but sleep easily in your grave. It doesn't concern you. We may be paying the price of your decision now, but how could you have foreseen the future?

Once again we have the place to ourselves. It's a sort of knack we have, aided in no small part by the time of year. It means that the Museum of Childhood which is housed here is closed to us, as is the café and the toilets.

Well worth visiting though they may be, that's not what we have come to see, though my companion may disagree with me on at least two counts. No, what I have come to see is the station itself, the place where all those visitors to the Spa arrived to take the cure. I am by no means a follower of fashion as my wife will happily tell you, but thanks to the photographs in the Pump museum, we can see exactly what they looked like and I can see their ghosts now thronging the platform in their shoals. And I have to say, they don't look in the least ill, but in the peak of perfection, chattering like a flock of starlings as they collect their luggage before being taken to their hotel.

I dismiss the ghosts and admire the station itself. It's wonderful, it really is – a symphony in maroon and white, in wood and cast iron which perfectly anticipates the Pavilion and the other buildings of the Spa. It's a splendid thing to stroll along the empty platform, to have it all to yourself, all the better to admire its light airiness and where, whatever the weather, thanks to those slim white iron pillars that support the glass roof, not a single raindrop will fall on your head. No need back then, ladies, to unfurl your fashionable accessory, your parasol, far less your umbrella, to protect the plumage on your headgear. There's even a bandstand at the end of the platform where the visitors were welcomed with the sound of music or were piped in like the guest of honour, the haggis, at a Burns supper. They thought of everything!

There are benches where you can sit and take in the stillness and ambience of the surroundings and imagine how different it must have been back in the heyday of the Spa, all the hustle and bustle. And the sound of the engines letting off steam, the slamming of the carriage doors and the guard's whistle as he blew, waved his green flag and slowly, inexorably, the massive iron wheels began to turn and the connecting rods began, slowly at first, their tireless shuttling to and fro.

Now the rails and the sleepers have gone, the tracks have turned to grass and it's like sitting in a garden with bushes on this side and a leafiness of trees on the other side. Like Paul Theroux who could never hear the whistle of a train and not wish he was on it, this track looks so inviting I have to suppress a sudden desire to o'er leap the bushes and step onto that grassy sward and see where it led me. I know it would take me towards Castle Leod, a family home for half a century, but open to visitors at certain times of the year.

Originally an L-shaped tower house of red sandstone, it has been extended over the years. And who can blame the owners? We can't expect people to go on living in the past just because of some romantic notion we'd like to cling to of seeing historical buildings go on unchanged forever as if preserved in aspic. All the same, with its battlements and towers and cute little windows, it has much of the fairy-tale castle about it, especially as the new additions are tucked out of sight behind the original building and you don't have to see them if you don't want to.

What does take my notice as I stroll to the other end of the platform however, is a poster dated July 1926 put up by the London Midland and Scotland Railway bellowing "Cheap Day Fares" in big, black bold letters like those on "Wanted" posters in the days of the Wild West, and offering a reward. What the LMSR is offering are daytrips from Strathpeffer and Achterneed, two miles to the north-east. That trip is its own reward.

Achterneed was the station for Strathpeffer until the popularity of the Spa when it was decided to run a branch line here in 1885, after which it became a station in its own right. The line still exists, taking you all the way from Dingwall to the Kyle of Lochalsh but the station itself was closed in 1965 by the British Railways Board, the same year as Dr Beeching retired from the Board. Or was he pushed?

From Strathpeffer you could also go to places like Inverness, Beauly and Tain. Achterneed destinations sound more interesting to my mind, taking in places such as Stromeferry, Kyle of Lochalsh and Kyleakin. That would set you back 5/-, 6/- and 6/9 respectively. These excursions only ran on Wednesdays and Fridays until the end of September.

It was all very organised. If you alighted at Achnasheen, Mr McIver from the Station Hotel would meet you off the 8.13 train and take you to Loch Maree and back in time to catch the evening train. That would cost you 5/- in addition to the train fare of 2/6. If there were sufficient numbers, he would also take you further on to Gairloch. Or, if you chose to go south-west rather than north-west, off the same train and for the same price, as long as there was a minimum of four passengers, Mr Paris of the Strathcarron Hotel would take you to Shieldaig.

It is some trip now and must have been something else in those days. It meant crossing the Applecross Peninsula on arguably one of the most scenic roads in Scotland, over the 2,053-foot Pass of the Cattle with gradients of 20%. I remember my father telling me how, as a boy, he would watch cars reversing up the road to the cemetery at the top of a steep hill. This was in the days of the gravity fuel system, before the invention of the mechanical fuel pump. The manufacturers of some cars even used to supply emergency handpumps to motorists. Is that what Mr Paris had to do? What an adventure for his passengers! Would they have found that more scary that the trip downhill, one wonders? It's to be hoped the ladies did not shut their eyes in terror. They would have missed some stunning scenery if they had, and as we shall see later on our trip.

On Thurdays, from here until the end of August, you could go to Inverness where you could take a cruise down Loch Ness as far as Urquhart Castle. The fare for that was 5/-, cruise included. If you wanted transport from Inverness station to the boat, a distance of about a mile, that would cost you an additional 6d each way. The cruise would last nearly four hours. What a bargain! But that's not all – the kids went free as long as they were under three, and half price if under twelve.

But better than all that, though they probably didn't appreciate it at the time, the trippers could get high on being pulled by what many go to to the ends of the earth to seek out today – the restored specimens of those mechanical dragons which ate fire and blew steam from their nostrils. No nasty, smelly diesels then, just clean black soot.

Ah, those were the days!

Chapter Thirteen

Dingwall: The Station and The Soldier

I T is back to the present and to our so-low Co$_2$-emitting diesel that it is exempt from any road tax, and it's all aboard for Dingwall. The name betrays, if that is the right word, its Viking connections. They called it *Þingvöllr* where the first syllable means "parliament" and the second means "meeting place". In other words, this was a place of some importance in the days when it used to lie at the other end of that super-highway of the seas connecting Scandinavia with Scotland. The Gaels have their own name for it. They call it *Inbhir Pheofharain*, the "mouth of the Peffery".

I doubt if it will come as much of a surprise when I tell you, apart from whatever skirmishes took place here between the local clans and pillaging parties of Norsemen, a fully-fledged battle raged on this location in 1411. It was between the Mackays and the usual suspects, the Macdonalds.

It's also the birthplace of the "real" Macbeth, exact date unknown, but at sometime during the turn of the eleventh century. There is no memorial to him but we are on the trail of one to another famous son, Sir Hector MacDonald (1853-1903). It's proving rather elusive. Although we saw it from afar on the top of a hill, a finger seeming to pierce the lowering sky, as we drive down the High Street we see no signs pointing the way and if there are none here that probably means there are none at all. After all, if you live here you wouldn't need any. Then the station appears and I pull into the forecourt and go in search of someone to ask directions.

From the front, the station is an unremarkable stone rectangle like a square bracket, with the crow-stepped gables on each of its stubby arms giving not the slightest hint of what to expect at the rear. It's a working station, and as long as you turn a blind eye to the electronic notices telling you when the next train is due, at first sight you could be forgiven for thinking it is Strathpeffer's twin. It has the same wrought iron pillars and glass roof and it is just as deserted, not a soul to be seen. That's because the LED above my head tells me a train is not due for a long time yet.

There is also another significant difference between this station and the one in Strathpeffer. Whilst that has a tearoom on the platform, it comes as something of a surprise to discover that this has a pub called *The Mallard*, named after the famous train, not the duck. Don't mock, a lot of pubs are named after birds and other members of the animal kingdom. On the wall is a noticeboard with a photo of the engine aforesaid along with some information about its illustrious past.

I remember the *Mallard*, the locomotive, and the mallard the duck, from the days when I used to collect cigarette cards and which only come second to stamps in forming a young boy's general knowledge. I was not a heavy smoker, or any kind of smoker for that matter. The cards came in packets of what we called "sweetie cigarettes" and which we consumed as it they were real, sucking them until the ends became as thin as needles at which point we bit them off.

I remember the *Mallard* especially because of its bright-blue livery and because of its streamlined shape, but most of all because it was the fastest steam locmotive in the world with its record-breaking speed of 125 mph. This feat was achieved in 1938, never equalled and never likely to be. It was taken out of service in 1963, made a few outings afterwards and now lives happily in retirement at the National Railway Museum in York and where it will see all of us out.

This is not a Wetherspoon's pub which always has some connection with the history of the locality, and which does not seem to have any connection with the *Mallard*, so why it is so named, alas I cannot tell. Nor can the barman tell me how to get to the Hector MacDonald monument.

"Who?" he asks, leaning over the bar to hear me better, but which leaves me in little doubt it was more *what* I said than an inability to hear me. He repeats the request to his colleague along the bar. Like him she is young but a good deal prettier. She pouts and shrugs her shoulders.

"Sorry, mate."

I turn to my left to where some young people are standing with glasses in their hands. "Hector who?" they repeat. I never expected this. Jesus was right when he said, "A prophet is not without honour but in his own country." What am I going to do now? Of all the beer joints in all this town, I have to walk into this one. Then to my right, a person at least as old as me pipes up, raises his pint in the direction of the station forecourt.

"Cross the road, up the hill and you're there."

"Thanks."

Well, thank God for that! But I wonder if he only knows where the memorial is and nothing at all about the bloke in whose memory it was erected in 1907. And if the residents of Dingwall don't know, then there is a fair chance you don't know either, dear reader, so before we go to view the monument it's probably a good idea for me to enlighten you.

In actual fact you might have come across him before without knowing who he was. Anyone who has ever bought, or seen a bottle of *Camp* coffee has. The label shows a gent in a kilt, sporting a very fine ginger moustache, seated in front of a couple of tall, pointed tents, more like marquees. Hence the *Camp*. From the nearest, a red pennant streaming in the wind bears the legend, "Ready Aye Ready." At his feet lie his busby and his sword. Interpret the words as you like, but the message is surely meant to be that the readiness has more to do with sitting having a nice cup of coffee rather than cutting the heads off enemy shoulders like thistles.

He has a china saucer in his left hand, a cup in his right and is being attended by an Indian servant attired in a turban and a crisp white tunic with a sash around his waist. He is bearing a tray on which stands a brown bottle, a jug and a sugarbowl. Well, no prizes for guessing which of the two is Sir Hector. Variations of this iconic label exist, though nowadays you are more likely to find the product in the baking aisle of your local supermarket than in the coffee aisle.

As the label tells you, the contents contain chicory essence which makes it not everyone's cup of tea, so to speak. In actual fact, it contains 26% chicory essence and 4% caffeine-free coffee essence. The rest is water and sugar. Add all that together and what you've got, in anybody's book, is an ersatz coffee.

Camp coffee first appeared as long ago as 1876, in Glasgow, manufactured by Paterson's & Sons. It was very easy to transport, did not deteriorate and therefore was a very handy coffee substitute for troops on the move. It was also good enough for me in my stamp-collecting, cigarette-card-collecting days, and still would be if my caffeine-addicted, ground-coffee purist wife would ever allow it in the house.

So, apart from being an anonymous Scotsman on the label of a bottle of an ersatz coffee, who was Hector MacDonald?

Born in 1853 near Dingwall to a crofter/stonemason father, he left school at fifteen, like Hugh Miller. He was apprenticed as a draper but enlisted with the Gordon Highlanders when he was seventeen, lying about his age and not telling his parents or employers. He rose through the ranks to become a major general. Nicknamed "Fighting Mac" (with good reason), he saw action in several theatres of war. (He had a minister brother known as "Preaching Mac" and three other brothers, none of whom was known as "Whisky Mac" as far as I am aware.) As well as knowing a great deal about how to deploy his troops in battle, he knew his books too, learning Hindustani, Arabic and French, all the better to do his job. To this list we can also add English, as he was born a Gaelic speaker.

During the Second Afghan War (1878-80), he distinguished himself to such an extent he was offered the choice of the Victoria Cross (which very few survive the brave deed to receive) or a commission. He chose the latter. He went on to see action in both Boer Wars. (Hands up, anyone, who knew there were two?) He was knighted in 1901 during the Second (1899-1902), having previously been awarded the DSO in the Sudan Campaign (1881-99).

After his heroics on September 2nd 1898 at the battle of Omdurman in the Sudan, he was promoted to colonel and made aide-de-camp to Queen Victoria. That was a bit of a white elephant. It did not bring in any extra salary; he had to go to the expense of buying a new uniform. He also received the thanks of a grateful nation when Parliament awarded him a cash award. In the country of his birth he was generously given a free lunch by the city of Edinburgh. It doesn't come much better than that.

His next posting was to South Africa in 1900 (see above). After that he had a brief spell as commander of the South District Army in Madras, but in 1902 he was on the move again, posted to Ceylon as Commander-in-Chief with the temporary rank of Major General.

It sounds, and was, a very glittering career but this is where it turned sour. He was not the very model of a Major General like the pantomime version in Gilbert and Sullivan. This last post, as it turned out, was not a resounding success. He did not get on with the Governor and other prominent members of the colony. His career ended in scandal when he blew his brains out in Paris on 25th March 1903, facing a court martial on allegations of homosexual acts with young boys.

After his death it came as a surprise to many to find he was married and had a son. He hardly ever saw them. No sooner was he married than he was off to the Sudan, telling his wife he would be back soon. Three years later he was. He was always the man of action, married domesticity was not his scene and that might have been part of the problem in Ceylon – there wasn't enough for a fighting man to do. Coming from his humble origins, he was not a natural mixer with the elite who had risen through being well-heeled and having all the right connections. He publicly fell out with the Governor, whom he ordered off the parade ground. Not a good choice of enemy. Rumours circulated about his penchant for young boys, and there is nothing more fearsome than the rumour mill when it grinds into gear. What they didn't know, what no-one knew until after his death, was that he was married, though that does not necessarily put him in the clear regarding the allegations. He did not tell his superior officers and never drew his married allowance, though he faithfully sent money home to support his wife and son. Another reason why he probably didn't fit in: he just didn't have the means to hobnob with the establishment, never mind the inclination.

He first fell in love with Christina Duncan when she was fifteen and he had to wait until she was older and he was earning enough before they could marry, which they did in secret in 1894. They hardly ever lived together but obviously he was home long enough to father young Hector who was born in 1899.

His body was repatriated with complete lack of pomp or ceremony. Under pressure from the War Office, the funeral took place at 6am in private, but word got out and 30,000 people turned up on the first Sunday after the funeral to pay homage at his grave in Deans Cemetery in Edinburgh. It took three hours for them to file past.

A Commission was set up into his death and reported three months after the tragedy. After taking the "most reliable and trustworthy evidence from every accessible and conceivable source" it found – "unanimously and unmistakably, absolutely no crime or reason whatsoever that would create feelings such as which would determine suicide". It also went on to say the "cruel suggestions of crime were prompted through vulgar feelings of spite and jealousy in his rising to such a high of the British Army", and he was "cruelly assassinated by vile and slandering tongues". They also described him as "brave", "fearless" and an "unparalleled hero".

Well, that seems clear enough – a complete and utter unequivocal vindication. Unfortunately mud tends to stick, and there are always those who say there is no smoke without fire. Whatever the facts of the case may be, they have built this enormous memorial to him and now we are on our way to pay our own homage to the soldier who had a glorious career but an inglorious death.

As we climb the steep hill, at a hairpin bend, we pass a young couple on the way up. We are not the only ones apparently on such a mission but when we reach the top, we find the hill is also home to the town cemetery.

The monument lies ahead of us, up a path. It's very striking. With windows puncturing the stone tower like arrowslits, it could easily form part of a castle, an impression furthered with its balustraded battlements above which rises a little crow's nest of a tower from which the saltire flaps proudly in the breeze. That's a matter of controversy actually: he was in the British army. At the base, guarding it like couched lions, is a quartet of canons, their barrels raised in salute. On one of them is stamped a badge bearing a crown with VR in the middle and around it, the motto of the Order of the Garter. *Honi Soit Qui Mal Y Pense.* How appropriate.

An inscription above the doorway tells us what we already know: to whom the tower was erected in 1907. There's another one on the B9169 in Mulbuie near Rootfield where he was born. It's good to see Hector is appreciated here in his homeland as is Hugh Miller, almost, but what a curious coincidence that the Black Isle's two most famous sons were both tortured souls who took their own lives.

With that thought, we take our leave, passing on the way the young couple whom we had passed on our way up. They have not come to see Sir Hector's memorial; they are looking for a much smaller one. They are flitting from grave to grave, obviously looking for the headstone of an ancestor. I say nothing, but wish them success in their quest, hope they find whoever they are looking for and bring his or her name back to be honoured in their own land, wherever that may be.

Chapter Fourteen

The Tarbat Peninsula: On the Trail of the Picts Again

W E are heading north on the open road, flying over the Beauly Firth on the Kessock Bridge and then over the Cromarty Firth on the A9 towards Invergordon. In another detour from the NC500, we take the B817 into the town, where, looking across the bay to Nigg and Cromarty, we can see the oilrigs which we'd seen yesterday, some of which come here for repair and maintenance. The water is very deep here which also makes it a very convenient berth for those floating hotels of the sea, the cruise ships, whose passengers can be whisked away to explore the Highlands for a day.

Actually, this harbour was once the location of an incident almost unparalleled in British Naval history; not since the Spithead and the Nore in 1797 had such scenes been witnessed. The more famous mutiny on the *Bounty* had happened eight years earlier, but the reasons for that were rather different.

The Mutiny of Invergordon took place in 1931 where ten warships of the Atlantic fleet arrived on 11th September to begin naval exercises. Five more arrived in the next two days. (It must have been a sight to behold.) The origins of the dispute lay in Ramsay MacDonald's new National Government's austerity measures brought about as a result of the Great Depression. Those in the Armed Forces were to have their pay cut by 10% in line with those in the public sector. The problem was the cuts were not to be applied equally across the board. Admirals, who of course, received the highest salary, were to lose 7% whilst at the other end of the scale, those ratings who had joined before 1925 when a reduced rate of pay came into force, would lose a whopping 23%.

Arriving in Invergordon on the afternoon of the 11th, sailors were first made aware of the cuts when they went ashore and read the newspapers, some of whom erroneously reported that the pay cut was to be a universal 25%. These measures were to be implemented in two weeks' time, not giving the sailors any opportunity to discuss this state of affairs, this body blow to their finances, with their wives. In the case of those worst affected, you could imagine despair, despondency and depression would have been much on their minds.

I will not trouble you with the details, but basically they refused to obey orders and ships were unable to go anywhere, never mind on manoeuvres. The matter was resolved when the Government backed down promising 10% would be the maximum cut anyone would have to face and with a warning that any future insurrections would be severely dealt with. They blamed Rear-Admiral Tomkinson (temporarily in charge of the fleet) for not taking a stronger line in the beginning, whereas in actual fact, he should probably have been given the credit for keeping the lid on a very volatile situation and preventing it from escalating into violence. Scapegoats needed to be found. The Big Brass doesn't make mistakes.

Despite MacDonald's promise that there would be no reprisals, about two hundred sailors were discharged from the Senior Service including their principal leader, Leonard Wincott (1907-83), who drew up their manifesto. Unable to find work afterwards, he went to fight against Franco in Spain, eventually ending up in Leningrad at the time of the Siege – hardly a masterpiece of good timing. Somehow surviving it, he became a Soviet citizen, only to fall foul of Stalin (like millions of others) and ended up in a gulag. Thanks to Khrushchev, he was released in 1958 and died in Moscow in 1983.

As for us, leaving Invergordon behind and temporarily back on the A9 (and the NC500), we come off it again to take the B1975 to Arabella. It's another intriguingly named blink-and-you-miss-it village. Formerly known as "the Bog", it was drained by Hugh Rose of Calrossie in the early part of the nineteenth century and the village was named after his wife, Arabella Phipps, whom he married in 1799. Sadly she died in 1806, aged only 27.

From Arabella, the road is clearly signed to Fearn Abbey, the so-called "Lamp of the North", one of Scotland's oldest pre-Reformation church buildings dating from 1238 when it was under the charge of the Premonstratensian order or the White Canons, so strict, so rigid, so dyed-in-the-wool were they, that their habits were not.

Nothing of those buildings remains, not surprisingly, as they were said to have been built of clay and stone. In 1372, the Abbey was rebuilt, but on Sunday October 10th 1742, during the induction of Donald Ross, lightning struck the church and the flagstone roof caved in. Thirty-six people were killed instantly; eight died of their injuries later. The preacher that day, Rev James Robertson from Lochbroom, was the hero of the day, like Samson, holding up a lintel with his shoulder to let survivors escape. Donald Ross never fully recovered from his injuries but lived on until eighty-three. You know what they say about a "hingin' gate".

Well maybe not. A new church was built to the south but in just a few short decades, by 1770, it was in a pretty ruinous state itself. Third time lucky, part of the abbey was rebuilt in 1772 using stones from the new church. Over the succeeding years and centuries, there have been several building and restoration works, which gives the building a been-through-the-wars sort of look.

If you would care to visit and see it for yourself, in the 14th century part of the church, in St Michael's aisle, you will the tomb of one of the abbots – Abbot Finlay McFaed (d. 1485). The 16th century Ross burial aisle is on the other side, and in a sunken chapel at the east end, there are a number of memorials on the wall, including an elaborate monument to Admiral Sir John Lockhart Ross (d. 1790) bearing the Ross coat-of-arms and a square-rigged ship. He it was who patronised the rebuilding of the church in 1772.

It's as straight as the crow flies on the B9165 to Portmahomack, near the tip of the Tarbat Peninsula. It sounds an outlandish sort of name for these parts, makes me think of an Indian tribe somewhere on the eastern side of the New World, like the Mohawks. Actually the name means "the port of Colm, Colman or Columba". You will remember he was here in the 6th century on an expedition to convert Bridei, King of the Picts. "Tarbat" means "portage", where boats were carried over the narrow isthmus between the Dornoch and Cromarty Firths before that triangular spit of land that exists now was created.

Our actual objective is the Tarbat Discovery Museum in the old parish church, but as we pull into the car park, my attention is drawn towards a curious sight. It's a long, smooth, white torpedo-shaped object pinned to the grass by three wooden brackets. It looks as if it is made out of concrete with a very rusty iron collar bolted around its waist. After all this time, the Picts can wait a few minutes more – I must find out what this unexpected sight is before I go any further. That's the joy of the NC500. You think you know what you are going to see but something else is always cropping up along the way, especially if you invest the time in making a little detour like this.

Mercifully, a noticeboard in front of the mysterious streamlined object explains what it is. It tells us that it is exactly what it looks like: a concrete torpedo. A practice torpedo in fact, with a ring at the end of its nose like the Piggy-Wig in *The Owl and the Pussycat*. That was so it could be hauled back to shore by the local farmers with their horses when the tide went out. A nice little sideline to tilling the fields.

These mock torpedoes were dropped into Nigg Bay from Fairey Barracuda Torpedo Bombers based at HMS Owl at Fearn. Not just famous for its abbey then. My reference to the nonsense verse above, not just a lot of nonsense then, but something of a coincidence. A photograph shows us what the plane looked like; the torpedo we can see for real. It's incredibly long, not much shorter than the plane with the propeller at the end of its nose that delivered it. It must weigh a ton. Probably calibrated to weigh as much as the real thing.

Curiosity satisfied; thankfully I'm not going to die of that anytime soon, like the Pussycat. You live and learn, and just a few yards away I learn something else. A metal plaque on a boulder has some surprising information. Everyone knows about the Highland Clearances in the 18th and 19th centuries, but who has heard of the Highland Clearance of 1943-44? Not me, for one. Actually I'm exaggerating slightly. The plaque calls it an "Evacuation". It was voluntary and temporary, for the good of the nation. It tells us that the people of Inver, Fearn and Tarbat, at short notice, left their homes in order that the 3rd Infantry Division and the Naval "S" Force could train for the D-Day landings which, as you know, took place on June 6th 1944. The happy outcome of that you don't need to be told. As for the villagers, they were told they could return to their homes in May. They had been out of them since December.

At its peak there were 3000 men and women stationed at HMS Owl, which, you understand, was not a ship, but an aerodrome. The first Wrens arrived on 1st September 1942 and one, whose name I will not mention to spare her blushes as it's just possible she is still with us, tells of the time when, off duty, as she was cycling past the perimeter, one of the Barracudas started up its engine, blasting her off her bike, blowing her skirt up over her waist and revealing all. Fortunately she was wearing her "black outs" or "passion killers", her navy-blue knickers with elastic at the knees. How the crew laughed to see such fun! Hopefully it was not their last laugh, for sadly, many never returned when practice turned to the real thing.

That was a serendipitous discovery about the recent past; now we are stepping back a few centuries to the Picts again. What new things will we discover about them?

What is special about where we are now is it used to be the site of a Pictish monastery from the 6th and 9th centuries AD and no fewer than six churches have stood on this spot since then. The story begins with the Rev. J. M. Joass, a local antiquarian, who noticed a carved rectangular stone in the garden wall of the manse which read: "In the name of Jesus Christ, the (illegible) Cross of Christ in Memory of Reo (illegible) Lius (illegible)." Actually, the inscription was in Latin but I have taken the liberty of transcribing into English, in case, like me, you have let it slip a bit since you left school.

Archaeologists, excavating between 1996 and 2006, found a cemetery dating back to the 6th century, as well as workshops, a mill, a barn and an enclosure ditch (like in Iona), all of which showed evidence of habitation in the 8th century. Then there were the artefacts, and here's the really interesting thing – there is evidence that books were made here. Under the present car park they found knives with curved blades which were used to trim hides, alkaline ash from burnt seaweed used to whiten the leather, and two bone styli or needles which would have been used to stitch the vellum pages together. Now think of the astoundingly beautiful Book of Kells and those of Lindisfarne, and that is the sort of thing that would have been produced here. Isn't that an incredible thing! (Stick that in your pipe and smoke it, Dr Johnson!)

They were also craftsmen in metal and glass and, of course, stone, and in the Christian era the symbol stones flowered into the sort of cross-slab intricacy that we had seen in Rosemarkie. Alas they did not come out of the ground fully formed like Athena from the head of Zeus. What the archaeologists found were enough fragments to keep any jigsaw puzzle enthusiast happy for years.

Like the Groam museum, there is much to see and learn about the Picts with a collection of carved stones and fragments including the stone that started it all off, the stone discovered by the Rev. Joass, and photographs of those which have been sent to the Museum of Scotland in Edinburgh. There are interactive touchscreens and a video of the Picts of Easter Ross and a (long) timeline that takes you through the story of this church from the days of St Columba to the present day when it was restored and transformed into a museum. No wonder it has won awards!

In the Middle Ages, in the days of King David I (1124-53), Pictish monuments were used for the foundations of the new church. Cultural vandalism has a long pedigree. And unfortunately, like another story we have come across before, in 1481, the church was burnt down by the Rosses with, alas, a raiding party of Mackays barricaded inside. Go down to the crypt, look closely and you will see traces of the fire. Down there you will also find, *in situ,* a fragment of a red sandstone cross-slab and if you look closely at that, you will be able to make out the outlines of animals.

From the bowels of the barrel-vaulted crypt you can climb to the heady heights of what is known as the "Laird's Loft". This is where, in the 18th century, those who lorded it over those beneath them could extend and maintain the social distance between them on the Sabbath day when they came to pray in the same building. It had its own entrance, stairs on the north side of the building, and get this, it had a fireplace! Whatever that says about the temperature inside the building, fiery words and hellfire sermons not withstanding, it is a reminder that the preaching could go on for hours, so a little fire to warm your behind instead of warming a cold, hard pew like your servants and peasants, would make the religious experience just that little bit more tolerable, especially if you could take some refreshment at the same time, even if you had to go to the tedious extent of having to serve yourself.

As I said, there is a wealth of things to see as well as do here (for there is also an activity centre), far too much to go into but I must mention the skeleton. A lot of us have them in our cupboards, but the Tarbat Discovery Centre has one under its floorboards. Such a location would normally be the sign of a suspicious act, the corpse hidden out of sight, where a person – or persons unknown – hoped it would never come to light again. But not here. This person was buried with due care and attention. He lies in a coffin of stone slabs, his skeleton partly covered in sand amongst which is a great number of shells. He was no older than thirty-five and the other things the experts found out about him is absolutely astonishing – no, astounding would be a better word.

Radio-carbon dating places him as having been born between 420-610 AD which allows for a pretty wide margin of error I grant you, but nevertheless gives you a pretty good idea of the period in which he lived. It certainly makes him the oldest Pict in this area and yet he did not come from here. By measuring the ratio of oxygen and strontium isotopes in his teeth, scientists can tell he moved to this area when he was a teenager. They also know he ate meat rather than fish (despite the shells in his grave).

From his bones they learned he was 5' 7" tall and powerfully built. His shoulders and back showed signs of heavy strain, a sign of hard work or hard work wielding a weapon, or both. He suffered from arthritis and damage to his knees from squatting – and this is the thing that gets me – they know he was left-handed! Unfortunately they can't tell us how he died. Just because the bones show no sign of a wound having been inflicted, that doesn't mean he did not die of a flesh wound, like being stabbed the stomach. Indeed, he may have lived in continual fear and danger of violent death. On the other hand, and it's maybe not much of a choice, it's entirely possible he died of natural causes through hard graft (giving lie to the adage that that never killed anyone), combined with living in a damp, cold climate. Or it might have been some nasty bug that carried him off, leaving no trace behind. At any rate, his life seems to have epitomised Thomas Hobbes' dictum that the life of Man is "nasty, brutish and short".

What's especially pleasing about this exhibit is they have been able to reconstruct his face for us. The hair, which is red, and the eyes, which are green, they can only guess at of course. The hairstyle, which is long and parted in the middle, is probably what most people would suppose is how he wore it, but as for the face, for those who have the skill and know-how, this is probably as close to what he actually looked like so that his contemporaries, if they could see him now, would recognise him as Nechtan the Leftie or whatever name he went by then.

After all I've read and learned about the Picts on this tour so far, it's good to put a face to one of them. He may have died a long, long time ago but he's doing a great job of bringing the Picts to life. And that is the image I take with me as we take our leave of the Tarbat Discovery Centre.

The trail of the Picts continues on minor roads to what is known as "The Seaboard Villages" – Shandwick, Hilton of Cadboll and Balintore and on to Nigg, where inside the Old Parish Church is a very fine stone, like a petrified page from the Book of Kells, only in monochrome.

However, since we are so near, we first go down to the harbour. It bears the hand of that man Thomas Telford again (1757-1834): road builder, bridge builder, canal builder, tunnel builder and harbour builder. Is there anything the man did not build? Well, to this list of achievements, you can certainly add a reputation for being the finest engineer of his generation. He was a Scot, born in Dumfriesshire, and I propose to say no more about him except to cite him as being another example of that fine Scottish institution, the "lad o' pairts". Like Hugh Miller, he was apprenticed to a stonemason and like him, was self-taught in the field that was to make him famous, in Telford's case, engineering.

Actually what grabs my attention most here is not the harbour with its small, moored craft, nor the lobster pots high and dry on the quay. Nor is it those distant hills of Sutherland across the water and which we will be amongst later today. No, what does interest me most is the brilliantly-white 17th century warehouse, also known as Telford House, with its enormous stepped buttress at southern end where it ajoins Chapel Street. It's like a massive wedge of Toblerone, only much whiter, the edges of which mice have nibbled away, with a fine eye for symmetry before dying and going on to chocolate heaven.

Next door is the longer and taller northern warehouse, equally white, its walls punctuated by three symmetrical rows of windows. The two buildings are linked by a narrow passage and a whitewashed flight of steps. The southern one is for sale, a very *des res*, I must say. Whatever the interior looks like, from the inside, those two tiny upstairs windows, especially, would afford a splendid view over the harbour and the Dornoch Firth to those faraway hills.

As we are leaving, we come across a cast-iron Victorian drinking fountain which dates from 1887. It was built to celebrate *Uisge Tobar Na*

Baistiad, in other words, in plain English, "Gravitation Water introduced into Portmahomack". I mentioned earlier how the Greeks painted their statues, not to their benefit in my opinion, and unfortunately the residents of Portmahomack have seen fit to rejuvinate this fountain by giving it a fresh lick of paint. Under the black and sepulcral canopy sits a golden cherub clinging onto a red oar for dear life. He is sitting sidesaddle on a turquoise water-jar which seems to have come aground on some very unlikely black rocks in the middle of the drinking bowl. It seems they had plenty of black paint left over, as the few clothes the poor chap has (seemingly only an unravelling turban), have been lovingly painted in a black that positively glistens.

Just as the little cherub is protected by a canopy, Shandwick's very fine cross-slab is protected from the elements by a glass shelter. In Gaelic it is known as *Clach a' Charridh* which means "Stone of the Grave Plots" because victims of the cholera epidemic of 1832 were interred thereabouts. They did not rest in peace, poor devils. In 1885 their poor bones were ploughed into the soil. As for the stone itself, on one side, the side facing the sea, there is a cross but the other side, to my mind, is the more interesting with amongst the usual symbols and knotwork, a panel depicting a hunt. It's a busy little scene, the artist cramming as many hunters and animals into the space as he could.

The Hilton of Cadboll stone, although the bottom part was missing, also depicts another hunting scene, arguably finer and also very crowded with a real sense of movement, horses and hounds racing out to the left in pursuit of a deer presumably, to the tune of two trumpeters with long horns. The focus is actually a woman riding sidesaddle with an iconic Celtic brooch at her breast.

That's how they know it's a woman; a man wore the brooch on the shoulder. And here's another thing: she might actually represent Mary as that is how she is often represented in Christian art, facing the viewer. The hunting scene itself might be an allegory for that elusive thing, the pursuit of the salvation of the soul.

Yes, it's very fine indeed, and I'm not sure if this is a good thing or not, but according to the very helpful notice at the beginning of the trail, the experts think the stone may well have been painted. Whilst that would make it very, very striking, I think I prefer the naked stone, as I do the Greeks' statues, but I'm pleased to see the hunch I had about the Picts painting their stones when we were visiting the Eagle Stone is vindicated by those who know about such things.

On the other side of this slab, amongst all the bosses, knotwork, writhing snakes and mythical beasts, on the upright of the cross, the main feature is a curly-headed, bearded chap clad in a robe with a snaky pattern or the real things crawling all over it. He is prising apart the jaws of a lion which I presume must be dead. This is a dead giveaway as to who the chappy must be – Daniel. This is much more like the thing, a lion with a mane and a tail that looks like a lion's, much more realistic than those on the fragment in the Groam museum.

I'm not sure which side I prefer; this side, which would be the front, or the back. Both are wonderful and thanks to local sculptor, Barry Grove, for letting us see it as those who lived a millennium and more ago would have seen it. He was commissioned to carve it in 2000. It's good to see the old skills are alive and well. As a matter of fact, the original was considered so outstanding it was taken to the British Museum and, after a brief stay, now resides in the Museum of Scotland in Edinburgh.

But long before then, in 1676, the side bearing the cross was defaced with an inscription commemorating a local laird, Alexander Duff, and his three wives which Mr Grove, for some reason, chose not to reproduce. He could pretend not to see the graffiti but could only guess at what the missing part of the stone looked like. And wouldn't you just know it – in 2001 the missing part was unearthed, as if the gods had just been waiting for Barry to put down his hammer and chisel.

In addition to seeing what the stone was like when it was new, as a sort of bonus, the visitor can also see it in its original setting. It stands beside the enclosure of what is called St Mary's chapel of which nothing now remains apart from grassy mounds. It may not have been in existence at the same time as the slab, but it may have served the village community of Catbol Fisher which has utterly disappeared too. We know it existed because fifteenth century records say it did. According to tradition and up until the end of the nineteenth century, this is where unbaptised infants and suicides were buried. In all likelihood, I am standing on them now.

From where we parked the car some half-a-mile or so in the distance, these details I have described are, of course, invisible. All we see therefore, across the scrub, is a monolith in the centre of a grassy ampitheatre surrounded by acres of empty space with the sea in the foreground. It stands tall and dark and smooth against the sun, an alien thing in an uninhabited landscape. I can't help but be reminded of the monolith in *2001: A Space Odyssey*.

That was the year, as I said above, that the missing piece was unearthed and the decision was taken not to reunite it with the main body of the slab but to keep it in the Seaboard Memorial Hall in nearby Balintore, which, apart from that fragment, does not have a Pictish stone to call its own. What it *does* have is Scotland's answer to Copenhagen's *Little Mermaid* (who is surprisingly tiny) – the *Mermaid of the North*, a bigger lass in every respect.

And while you are there, look for the plaque on the seafront which commemorates the missionary John Ross (1842-1915) who went to school at nearby Fearn and who translated the Bible into Korean.

Isn't that a remarkable thing?

Chapter Fifteen

Tain: Travelling Through Time

AT the end of the High Street, attractively bedecked with hanging baskets, must surely be one of the most striking buildings in all of Scotland – the Tain Tolbooth. With its turrets clustered around the central towering steeple, it looks as if it's about to be launched into space. That crowning glory, the steeple, was only added in 1733 to a building that was built at the turn of the century. The original tollbooth, as a stone inscribed in the turret once proclaimed: "THIS WARK BIGIT 1631 JHON MACKVLLOCH BEING PROVEST". Unfortunately it burned down in a fire that ravaged the town in 1697.

Poor Tain did not have to travel through time, backwards, its troubles to seek. Famine had hit the town that year, and the year before that. And before that, in the mid-fifties, Cromwell's troops were quartered here which led to a mass exodus from the town, the poor burghers unable to sustain the burden of having the unwelcomed guest foisted upon them, like the Macdonalds in Glencoe, so that by 1691, "a great pairt of this poor place is waist and turned ruinous" as the town records put it.

But I get ahead of myself. Our objective is "Tain Through Time", a museum, like Gaul, divided into three parts. The first of these, the visitor centre, is situated in the Pilgrimage, a converted caretaker's cottage for the collegiate church and churchyard, built in the 1880s following the restoration of the church. It houses a collection of artefacts, documents and an audio-visual display.

Once again, we are the only visitors. It seems to be a sort of knack we have picked up. A personable young man called Jason doesn't mind in the least us interrupting his researches, relieves us of our paltry entrance fee and gives us a brief guide to the museum. Upstairs, he says, a colourful display of characters and noticeboards will tell us about events in Tain's history. Outside to our left, we can visit the Collegiate Church. After that we can head across to the third part of the museum, the Clan Ross Centre, which houses amongst other artefacts, the Tain silver collection.

It's no accident that this, the first part of the museum, is called "The Pilgrimage". James IV was a regular here, coming at least once a year between 1493 and his death in 1513. A guilty conscience was weighing heavy on his mind. Being a pious sort of person, as most people were in those days, James was extremely worried about the state of his immortal soul. His father was not a popular monarch and when the young James was fifteen, a coalition of disaffected Scottish nobles gathered around him, the Duke of Rothesay as he was then, and defeated his father, James III, at the Battle of Sauchieburn in 1488. The king did not die in battle, but rather like Richard III, found himself without a horse after it threw him as he was fleeing the battlefield. He managed to find shelter in a cottage but, so the story goes, was murdered most foully by a person pretending to be a priest. He had only just celebrated his 36th birthday.

As punishment for these sins, and in an endeavour to save his immortal soul, James IV wore an iron belt around his waist, next to his skin, adding a link every year at Lent. Nor was this the only place he came on pilgrimage. In fact, he seems to have spent a great deal of his time engaged in such matters, which was also a good way of letting the public see him, rather than remaining a faceless figure holed up in Edinburgh or Stirling or wherever.

The saint he was coming here to pay homage to, and to intercede on his behalf, was Tain's very own St Duthac who was born here (maybe) in the 8th or 9th century. Sometimes you have to be very patient when you become a saint, and it was not until 1419 that that title was officially bestowed upon him. But long before that, probably not long after his death in 1065, people had been coming here to his shrine.

It was actually due to the holy man's magnetism that Tain received its Royal Charter from Malcolm III in 1066. This made it the first, or one of the first, Royal Burghs in Scotland. What this charter meant was, apart from being exempt from having to pay certain taxes, it also became a place of sanctuary where people could receive the protection of the church at the shrine of St Duthac.

However, the proof of the pudding is in the eating. In 1306, during the Scottish Wars of Independence (1296-1328), the newly crowned Robert the Bruce sent his wife, daughter and sisters here for safekeeping. They were actually en route to Orkney where he thought they would have been really out of harm's way. They never made it, were captured here by the Earl of Ross who did not give a fig for any sanctuary. He was a supporter of John Balliol, aka "Toom Tabbard", or "Empty Coat", Edward I's puppet king, and to whom he dutifully handed over the ladies.

Edward, aka the "Hammer of the Scots", split them up. The Queen was put under house arrest in a manor house in Yorkshire, which was a lot better than she might have expected. The plan had been to put the ten year-old Princess Marjorie in a cage and exhibit her to public ridicule as happened to her aunts, but for some reason Edward thought better of it, and – like Hamlet urged Ophelia to do – she was banished to a nunnery instead. In Elizabethan times a "nunnery" was slang for a brothel. What Marjorie thought of her sentence we do not know, but we can be sure she would have preferred the nunnery to the cage as the Elizabethan age was still two-and-a-half centuries in the future. After his father's death soon afterwards, Edward II continued her imprisonment. She was only released after the Battle of Bannockburn (I need not mention the date), probably as part of a hostage swap arrangement.

Unfortunately she was not to live much longer, only a couple of years as a matter of fact. One day when riding near Paisley when heavily pregnant, her horse was spooked by something, reared up and she fell off. She went into premature labour and the monks from the Abbey performed an emergency Caesarean section by the roadside, the first recorded incident of it being performed since Julius Caesar. And with no anaesthetic either. It's a wonder she did not die of shock.

The baby survived but poor Marjorie only lasted a few hours. She did know she had produced a boy however. Her last words are reputed to have been, "He's a laddie; I ken he's a laddie; he will be king". She was right, although it took fifty-five years for her words to become true. Robert II only became king in 1371 when, in a neat coincidence, he was fifty-five. The reason it took so long is very complicated so I won't take you down that road.

Robert's father was Walter Stewart, 6th Lord High Steward of Scotland and Marjorie's second cousin once removed. (That's also very complicated.) It's from Robert that the Stuart dynasty is descended, and you may remember we met his dastardly son the Wolf of Badenoch in Chapter Six. In another curious coincidence, when she died, Marjorie was only nineteen, the same age as her mother who also died in childbirth. Isn't that curious?

In 1427, the chapel was in the wars again when it was burnt down during another bit of clan warfare between the Mackays and the Rosses. As far as I know, no-one was locked up in it this time, which makes a bit of a change. At any rate, that put an end to any more so-called safe sanctuaries here. St Duthac's bones – or perhaps his uncorrupted body, depending on how it survived the conflagration – was moved to a more befitting shrine for a saint in the cathedral-like new Collegiate Church which they hastened to complete. It finally was in 1485, after the foundation stone was laid in 1370. You don't build a thing that looks like a cathedral in a day. The saint's bones are gone now and I don't mean turned to dust. They mysteriously disappeared during the Reformation in 1560.

Should you be wondering what a "Collegiate Church" is, it means it was organised along non-monastic lines by the clergy whose main purpose was to sing masses for the souls of those who, like James III, provided the cash for its upkeep. A nice little earner. If you didn't pay, or couldn't afford to – tough.

After our visit upstairs where we take in the turbulent life and times of Tain, and accompanied by Jason, we make our way down the path flanked by gravestones but not towards the church. He wants to show us something special first.

They are cylinders in stone, not unlike the concrete torpedo in Portmahomack, only rougher and thicker, not nearly so long and set into the earth which has been cut back to expose them. They remind me very much of larger versions of the graves in the cemetery at Cooling in Kent, "the five little lozenges" that Pip refers to in *Great Expectations* before his terrifying encounter with Magwitch. Those were children's graves dating from the 18th and 19th centuries; these are much more ancient. They are "hogbacks", or Viking graves. There are very few examples of them in Scotland, but we know they were normally carved with scallop shapes to create the effect of a shingled roof, a shelter for the deceased. Here, however, any carving has long since been eroded by the weather. Let's hope those within have been kept as dry as a bone. They have not been excavated, Jason tells us, much to his regret. I agree. What grave goods might be interrèd there with the bones?

Jason returns to his studies, leaving us to explore the church for ourselves. It's a shell now, but it contains some interesting memorials. Remember the little village of Arabella which we passed through not so long ago? Well this is where the poor young lady's bones lie. It's the first thing I see, the alabaster gleaming white in the half-light. No expense has been spared in the making of this memorial to her. It's neo-classical in style, with on the left, a matron dressed in the Roman manner. She is looking up forlornly at an urn which has a profile of the Dear Departed framed in a roundel, formed either by a snake or an eel devouring its own tail. In fact, from the aristocratic nose, I would say the lady looking up *is* Arabella, a fact which is borne out by the lady's right arm which languidly leads the eye down to the inscription which tells us she is "Arabella Margaret the Wife of Hugh Rose." Very good. Now if only it could tell us why she died so prematurely, it would be an admirable stone indeed!

It doesn't, but what it does tell us is that she, "in the Act of preparing Medicine for the relief of a sick and indigent Family, suddenly expired on the 9th

November 1806 aged 27 years". It doesn't explain her early death, but it does put it into context. On the face of it, it seems unlikely there is any connection between her death and whatever the poor family was ailing from. Her demise seems to have come on very suddenly with no mention of an illness. It's a complete mystery, except for a local legend that says she was murdered by Hugh's quadroon mistress. But can we trust it? We all know how tales spread like wildfire in small communities and in the telling, the truth can often be jettisoned in order not to spoil a good story.

Hugh's story is he was born in 1767, the fifth son of a minister, here in Tain. He went to the West Indies to make his fortune, where at one time his boss was the Pay Master General – Arabella's father. Having achieved his objective, Hugh returned to Tain and became a significant landowner. He bought Bayfield Cottage in Nigg which he regarded as his major domicile. Some cottage! Part of it is now available as a three-bedroomed, self-catering accommodation.

It's not unheard of and it's not a crime, but after Arabella's death, Hugh remarried. He was only forty after all. Women are accustomed to changing their name on marriage and if I were a lady, or a woman even, I would hate to have to change part of my identity like that. Thankfully I didn't have to. But not Hugh. He took his wife's name. What a progressive, forward-thinking fellow he was! Admittedly he didn't have to change it very much, only to Hugh Rose Ross, but that's beside the point. The real point is he had to if he wanted to claim his new wife's estate. And he's not the only one. There is another, as you shall see.

We have seen what a caring person Arabella was, and Hugh must surely have cared quite a lot for the alleged mistress – and she for him – to have come all the way from the warm Caribbean to Scotland's chilly climes. Did she have great expectations of being mistress of Bayfield Cottage if only first, the slight problem of Arabella could be got around? If she did think that and if she did do the dastardly deed, she was to be sorely disappointed, as you know.

But just before we take our leave of Arabella, I must mention the mourning cherub, his head in his hands, leaning against the stone. It adds to the overall effect of absolute sadness, but the most remarkable thing about this whole monument is what is written on the plinth on which it stands. It is too long to repeat here, nearly a hundred words, but in the most purple of prose and with the old-fashioned "esses" that look like "effs", and capital letters at every noun, it commands: "Reader" (full stop) stop and read about Arabella's "Purity of Manners", "Charity" and "Purity" to name but three, before her "premature Dissolution". The lady, who had at first appeared to me as kind and caring, now appears in actual fact, to have been rather saintly.

Moving along, we come to another memorial and another re-acquaintance. Nothing fancy this time. It's just a plain tablet though it contains probably just as many words, if not more, than Arabella's. It's in block capitals and dedicated to Patrick Hamilton (1504-28), the "youthful abbot" of Fearn Abbey. I'll say! He was only thirteen and not even a monk! Of course it helps to be well connected. His mother was the daughter of Alexander, Duke of Albany, the second son of James II and brother of James III. But he wasn't the only one: the act of conferring ecclesiastical benefices to patrons was not an uncommon practice in those days.

Hamilton was only the titular head of the abbey. He took the money and ran off to Paris where he was exposed to, and influenced by, the writings of Martin Luther. He had to go no further in order to see the corruption of the Catholic Church than his own experience. He also went to university in Leuven in the time of Erasmus. Although a lesser heretic in the eyes of the Catholic Church than Luther, Hamilton fell under his spell too, which – in turn – spelled the end for him.

After a trial by a council of bishops and clergy (the outcome was never in doubt), he was found guilty on thirteen counts of heresy and burnt at the stake in St Andrews on the same day, 29th February 1528, before any rescue plan could be mounted by his supporters. He was only 24. It is said he burned from noon until six as a strong easterly wind kept blowing out the flames rather than fanning them. Gunpowder was sent for but that only resulted in poor Patrick's hands and face being scorched. You might have thought that his persecutors might have begun to have had second thoughts, that it was God's will that he lived. Not a bit of it! Someone who had come along to witness the spectacle begged Hamilton to revert to Catholicism. His response was as follows: "I pray you come forward and testify the truth of *your* religion by putting your little finger into this fire, in which I am burning with my whole body". Nice one, Patrick!

Towards the end, someone in the crowd shouted out that if he still had faith in his teachings, he should give them a sign. Hamilton held up three fingers. You might have thought two would have been more appropriate. "*Ustulatus magis quam combustus* – roasted rather than burned", a spectator is reported to have said afterwards.

If you have a mind to, you can stand on the very spot where this gruesome execution took place in St Andrews. His initials have been spelled out with cobblestones in front of St Salvator's College. The tablet before our eyes tells us he was the first preacher of the Reformation in Scotland which was "sealed by a martyr's death" and his "reek infected as many as it did blow upon", while the influence of his principles was "early and decidedly manifested within these walls".

As we have seen, things tend to come in threes, and here is the third and last memorial I will trouble you with. Unlike the other two, we have not met him before. A local loon, despite his Latin-sounding name of Thomas Hoc, he was born in Tain in 1628 and this is where he worshipped in the days of his youth. Actually his name was Hog, but the tail on the capital "C" is hardly noticeable. He was minister of Kiltearn, about five miles north of Dingwall, but was "ejected" in 1662 for "loyalty to Christ's crown and covenant".

The monarchy had been restored in 1660 and it took as long as two years before Charles II reneged on the Treaty of Breda which he had signed in 1650 when in exile. In it, he promised to recognise Presybterianism as the national religion of Scotland and accept the authority of the General Assembly of the Church of Scotland. Episcopacy was restored and ministers who refused to accept the authority of the bishops were expelled. That did not stop them preaching however; they held open-air meetings known as "conventicles".

Hog held his own "conventicles" in his house at Auldern, near Nairn, and for his pains was imprisoned initially in Forres, then Edinburgh, and then the Bass Rock: the Alcatraz of its day. Eventually released in 1677, he was imprisoned again, briefly, in 1679. For the next four years he seems to have kept his nose clean or – more likely – managed to avoid being caught, but in 1683 he was charged with the same old offence, fined five thousand merks and banished from Scotland. I don't know how much a merk is in today's terms, but a thousand of anything is a lot in anybody's money.

In 1685 in London he was suspected (without foundation) of complicity in the Monmouth plot and, after his release from prison, fled to Holland where he became chaplain to William, Prince of Orange, later William III of these islands. Eventually he was reinstated to his parish in 1690 and that was where he died in 1692.

A full list of his exploits is recorded on a memorial in Evanton Parish Church, just off the A9 before Alness if you have a mind to go and see it for yourself. It's interesting because amongst them it tells us that in 1675 he was "put to the horn" and "intercommuned" in 1675. These were expressions I had never heard of before. The first means he was declared an outlaw for failing to answer a summons. The term derives from the herald giving three blasts of the trumpet at the market cross before declaring the person a rebel or an outlaw. The second means that it was forbidden for anyone to "harbour or help" him in any way. Since it came a year after his proscription, it looks as if Thomas did not want for supporters.

Well, it was an interesting life to be sure. Now after life's fitful fever, sleep peacefully Thomas Hog. It was his wish to be buried under the threshold of the church door with the following inscription on his grave: "This stone shall bear witness against the parishioners of Kiltearn if they bring ane ungodly minister in here". The inscription he got; the location he did not, not surprisingly. He is buried hard up against a wall of the church where I am sure he is having a much more restful sleep without all those feet tramping over him.

Chapter Sixteen

Dornoch: Much Ado About Burning

O N our right, as we leave the town, is the Glenmorangie distillery, whose product has been perfected for decades by the "Sixteen Men of Tain". Glenmorangie means "Glen of Tranquility", and in the 18th century there used to be a still on the farm that once stood here. How legal that was I couldn't possibly comment, but an observation I will make is that one of the reasons for the distillery's success is the rain that falls on the Hill of Tain is filtered for a century through lime and sandstone before it reaches the Tarlogie Spring, from whence the distillery draws its water.

The bridge over the Dornoch Firth, only built in 1991, cuts twenty miles or so off the road from Tain to Dornoch by bypassing Edderton, Ardgay, Bonar Bridge and Spinningdale. It is a route I have driven many, many times before on the way to see my mother who lived in Thurso until her death there in 1995. There was no-one more glad than me when that bridge was built.

The NC500 traveller with the time to spare, however, might well like to make what is now a leisurely scenic drive around the Firth, water on your right, hills on your left and with such little traffic, thanks to the bridge, you can afford to pay more time to appreciating the scenery.

Nothing need detain you in Ardgay unless you need to stop for fuel. Having said that, there *is* something that might interest you – a large white stone known as the *Clach Eitag*. It is said that in the olden days, the stone was moved from parish to parish to mark the location of the village market. Try pulling the other one! I don't know how much this thing weighs, but it looks like several tons.

Nor could you imagine anything remotely more different from Chicago than this little dot on the map, and yet I see a connection of sorts. Chicago's nickname is the "Windy City", as I am sure you know, and Ardgay, pronounced "Ardguy", sounds like one of Al Capone's friends – but that's not the connection. Translated from the Gaelic it means "high wind". Wouldn't it be a great thing if the next time I drove through Ardgay I saw a sign saying

"Twinned with Chicago!"

Not far from here is Carbisdale Castle (look for the signs to Culrain), which has an interesting story attached to it. It's a mere youngster in castle terms, a massive pile that, for all its size, took only eleven years to build before it was completed in 1917. In the Second World War it was home to the Norwegian royal family who must have rattled around in it despite all their servants and retainers.

How the mighty has fallen! Up until 2011 it was a Youth Hostel, and if there was another throughout the length and breadth of the land to compare with it then I'd like to see it. At the time of writing, plans are afoot to turn it into a luxury hotel. I can only guess what the price of a room might be but I have a feeling I have missed my chance. I should have stayed there in my youth when it was an affordable hostel.

Apart from having several ghosts and so many windows there is one for every day of the year, it has another rather curious characteristic. The square tower with the crenellated turrets has a clock on three sides but not on the fourth, the one that faces Sutherland. It's known as the "Castle of Spite", because after the 3rd Duke and the 18th Earl of Sutherland died, his Will, which favoured his wife, was contested by his son. The Duchess, Mary Caroline Mitchell, was the Duke's second wife and she spent six weeks in the clink for destroying documents. The legal battle rumbled on but at last a settlement was reached, namely that the grieving widow would drop all claims provided a house was built for her outside the Sutherland estate. This was it. Some house; some location.

Its prominent position on a hillside meant it could be seen by the Sutherlands whenever they passed by and whatever they thought of it architecturally speaking, to them it was an eyesore, a constant reminder of the emnity between them and the dowager duchess, whom I am sure, they called something else less complimentary. It is said that when the 4th Duke's train, his own *private* train if you please, passed the house, the carriage blinds would be lowered. And if this tells you anything, it tells you that despite having to build the little house, he wasn't short of a bob or two. And neither was the Duchess, for her little house has 189 rooms, one more than that massive seat of the Sutherlands, Dunrobin Castle.

Bonar Bridge used to be just "Bonar" until the bridge came along in 1812. It was that man Telford again. The present bridge is not his, however. It's the third as a matter of fact. Telford's was washed away in a winter storm in 1892, an event predicted by the Brahan Seer. The building of the bridge was precipitated by a disaster in 1809. An overladen ferry sank in midstream and ninety-nine people were drowned, almost everyone on board in fact. You can imagine the effect of this tragedy on this tiny community, scarcely a family that was not affected by it, just like the First World War a little more than a century later, as any war memorial throughout the length and breadth of the Highlands testifies.

A new bridge was opened in the summer of 1893 and you will scarcely credit this, but – by coincidence – this second bridge lasted precisely as long as Telford's, namely 80 years. The advent of heavy traffic in both senses of the word meant it was no longer fit for purpose, and the decision was taken to build a new one which was completed in 1973. Ironically, since the opening of the new bridge, the one we have just crossed, the traffic has become much lighter and the town much quieter. A bit of a mixed blessing as far as the local businesses are concerned. It's a pleasant little town and NC500 traveller, I'm sure they would love to see you, should you care to stop.

The little village of Spinningdale is just as charming as it sounds with its whitewashed cottages. It derives its name not, as you might suppose, from the former occupation of its residents but like many of the names hereabout, it comes from the Norse *spinne-dair* which means "round valley".

At Clashmore, which sounds a lot more violent than it is (and eminently sleepy), you are back on the A9. It's not long before we come off it again however, taking the B949, heading towards Dornoch. Many others seem to have had the same idea, but we manage to squeeze the car into a space in front of the castle. On the other side of the incredibly wide street is the Cathedral, and it is there we direct our steps first.

It dates from the 13th century but is much changed. The first big change came about in 1570 during a feud between the Murrays and their mortal enemies, the Mackays of Strathnaver, who set the place on fire and desecrated the grave of the founder of the Cathedral, Gilbert de Moravia (d 1245), later St Gilbert, who built the Cathedral at his own expense. His name sounds very exotic but actually could just be a poshing-up of "Moray" where his family had extensive lands and where he was most probably born.

Briefly, it all began when the Murrays snatched Alexander, the young Earl of Sutherland from his guardian, the Earl of Caithness, and delivered him to the Earl of Huntly for safekeeping until he reached his majority in 1573. Not surprisingly, this incurred the wrath of Caithness who sent his son, John, aka the Master of Caithness, with a number of men, including Mackays, to make a revenge attack upon the Murrays at Dornoch.

When he founded the Cathedral in 1214, Gilbert presciently laid a curse on anyone who might "distract and injure" it. During the sacking, William

Sutherland of Evelix burst St Gilbert's coffin open with his foot and scattered his dust all about. Sir Robert Gordon, the historian and younger brother of John, the 13th Earl of Sutherland, writing ten years after the event, tells us what happened next: "That same foot that burst St Gilbert his coffin did afterwards rot away and consume, to the great terror of all beholders, wherby, this William Sutherland grew so lothsum that no man was able to come neir with him, and so he died miserablie". And serves him right, too.

After that catastrophic event, the Cathedral was largely allowed to fall into disrepair until a partial repair was made in 1616. And that is how it stayed until the "improvements" of 1835-37, when the ruins of the medieval nave and side aisles were demolished. Only the nave was rebuilt and, to add insult to injury, the walls covered in plaster.

In 1924 the plaster was removed, restoring the Cathedral to its former glory. And maybe the demolishment of the side aisles really was an improvement after all because as soon as I enter, I am blown away by its light and airy spaciousness. And talking of light, there are twenty-eight splendid stained-glass windows, including a magnificent one of St Gilbert which was installed in 1989 to mark the 750th anniversary of the consecration of the Cathedral.

There are also three windows representing music, peace and literacy, dedicated to the memory of Andrew Carnegie who once owned nearby Skibo Castle, his "little" place in the country where he came for his summer holidays. It is yet another enormous pile that began life in the 12th century as a residence for the bishops of Caithness and which grew and grew in the early 19th and 20th centuries. It is now home to the Carnegie Club, an exclusive members-only hotel (and club). There are about 250 members. And yes, you are right, I am not one of them.

Famously this was where Madonna married Guy Ritchie in December 2000 after having their son christened in the Cathedral the day before. In my day you got married first and then had the children. Sometimes the baby was born "prematurely", but nevertheless its parents were married. How quaint the customs of yesteryear!

Dornoch Castle, funnily enough, or maybe not, has a similar sort of history to the Cathedral. It stands on the site of what was the palace for the bishops of Caithness, just across the street. Not far for them to have to go to work then. The castle dates from the late 14th or early 15th centuries and if it could see itself today it wouldn't recognise itself. Like the Cathedral, it too was set on fire by the dastardly Mackays in their revenge attack of 1570. The rebuilding saw some massive modernisations, but two hundred years later it was left derelict until the 19th century when it variously saw service as a school, a jail, a courthouse and, in 1881, a hunting lodge – a "quaint dwelling place for English sportsmen".

It underwent its most recent transformation when it became a hotel in 1947, boasting as many rooms as there are men in Tain who perfect the Glenmorangie. Like Carbisdale Castle, it has a ghost (but only one), yet with its circular stair turret and especially the tall, lean tower attached, the sole survivor of the three that the bishops' palace used to have, it looks every inch what a Scottish castle should look like and not at all a stately home.

The adjacent building seems to blend into the hotel. It's of fine red sandstone with fanciful dummy turrets with conical roofs with knobs on the top and crowstepped gables with crosses on their tops. That's the style known as "Scots Baronial". (Think of Balmoral Castle.) It was the jail from 1840-52, before becoming the Drill Hall in 1896. It's now called "Jail Dornoch". The word order is crucial. I am disappointed to find that it is not Dornoch's answer to the Cromarty Courthouse; it's merely a shop. Maybe that's why a parking space was so hard to find. It was, as the name implies, the former jail, and if Carbisdale Castle used to be the most lavish youth hostel in Britain then surely this must have been the most luxurious-looking jail in the land, at least from the outside.

As a matter of fact, its predecessor, the Castle, when it was doing time as a jail, did have a reputation for luxury. In 1818, the jailer complained that the prisoners' visitors were treating it as a public house, coming in at all times of the day and night, bearing gifts – a bottle of something to keep the prisoners' spirits up. Nice jail if you can get it. A report in the same year found the cells "commodious and neatly furnished, well lighted by three windows in each room and sufficiently aired, and are indeed the most salubrious prison room we ever had occasion to see". Actually I would expect no less from the hotel it now is. The same report states there were to be "2 stones of straw for each bed, to be changed every month". "Stones" sounds hard, but it also sounds like an awful lot of straw.

Ten years later, things were not quite so rosy. When the dungeons were condemned, normally the domain of criminals serving their sentences, they suddenly found themselves upwardly mobile, elevated to the attic with everyone else having to shove up a bit, including a number of debtors whose creditors, if you please, were responsible for their upkeep.

Someone had the cheek to make a complaint about overcrowding: a female prisoner was being kept in a cell with five men. Investigation showed the complaint was not without foundation. The reality was actually a lot worse: the ratio was one to eleven. I do not know who made the complaint. It might not be the most likely suspect. It might just as easily have been one of the men, a debtor, who was threatening to sue because he was being incarcerated with a lot of common criminals.

But it wasn't the debtors or the criminals who were the real cause of the overcrowding. The actual reason takes us back to Tain and the likes of the farm that once stood on the distillery. A government, seeing a way to raise revenue, passed the Excise Act of 1788 which made it unlawful to have a still even if it was for your own private use. Since practically every croft in the Highlands had one, this was nothing less than a blatant attack on the Highland way of life. God knows, it was a hard-enough job struggling to wrest a living from the mean soil after you'd coughed up the rent to your landlord who meanwhile lived like a king in what was a palace in all but name. And how do you suppose did the good Saint Gilbert who actually lived in a palace become so wealthy?

Now, thanks to the government's measures, after toiling all day until it was too dark to see to do any more back-breaking work, there was no wee heart-warming dram to look forward to in the evening as you eased your aching muscles and filled your lungs with smoke from the peat fire. No wonder the jail was overflowing. The records of 1828 show there were 80 prisoners – 63 males and 17 females, of whom 34 were arrested for contravening the licensing laws.

No, not such a nice place to be then – and almost two centuries later, and no offence to Jail Dornoch, but it is not where I would want to be either. Shopping is not my sort of thing, especially if my Visa card was also my get-out-of-Jail card.

I turn my back on it and have a closer look at the exterior of the Cathedral. I had been in such a hurry to get inside, I hadn't paused to look at it properly. Built of red sandstone (there's a surprise), it's cruciform in shape with a short stumpy spire like a witch's hat, rising out of a square castle-like keep. Being so squat, this crowning glory looks enormously heavy as if pressing the entire building into the ground. A nice tall steeple soaring into the sky, pointing towards heaven where the people aspire to be, I would have thought been more uplifting both for them and the building. But perhaps Gilbert couldn't raise cash enough.

And yet, having said that, if I stand just so (you have to be perfectly aligned) and look at the building straight on, the apex of the roof of one of the arms of the cross slots perfectly into the triangle of the spire. And there's something else: the bits of the turrets you can see on the "keep" look like auxilliary rockets, while the projecting roofs over the clock faces look like stubby little wings. Thus, from where I am standing, and bearing in mind what I said about the Tain Tolbooth, you might think I have space rockets on the brain, but that's exactly what it looks like – the sort of thing you used to see in comics long before space travel ever became a reality.

Coming right down to earth, the graveyard has an interesting table tombstone. It's in memory of Plaiden Ell. May she rest in peace. Poor girl, she left the planet long ago and not a single word inscribed upon her tomb to tell us when she lived. Reader, forgive me. I have been teasing you. A plaque above the "tombstone" tells us that Plaiden Ell's alter ego is "Tailors' Measure. The trading standard of its day, it was used for measuring cloth (plaiden) at the fairs and markets which were held here since medieval times. The Scottish ell was standardised at 37 inches in 1661. This stone has two metal pins in it which measure 39 inches, so probably it dates from well before that date. There are only two other surviving examples in all of Scotland.

Now if this was the stone they humphed about from market to market, despite its enormous weight, yes I could see some sense in that, but I'm sure some bright spark must have come up with the idea of having a Trading Standards-approved stone in every marketplace. Why didn't the people of Ardgay think of that?

We make our way back to the car, pausing to look at something which looks very similar to something which we had seen before – the twin of the water fountain we had seen in Portmahomack. This has the same ornate canopy, the same putto with an oar sitting astride the same earthenware vessel. Only the colours are different. This is a vision in black and red with the golden boy in the middle draped in a red cloth to protect his modesty.

It was manufactured by the Sun Foundry in Glasgow and round the arch is written: "Presented by Miss Georgina Anderson 1892". She was born in Durness in 1821 and died in 1899, here in Dornoch. It has an old-fashioned lantern on the top which must make it the most ornate lamppost in the land. That was added in 1911. As to whether that is an improvement or not, I couldn't possibly comment.

Leaving the centre of town behind, we are off towards the sea and the golf course. You may be one of those who enjoy spoiling a good walk by whacking a little white sphere ahead of you and having a good curse as you dig out a divot as you miss it completely or the ball takes an unintended trajectory into the long grass where you waste hours trying to find it. If so, you won't need to be told that there are actually two 18-hole courses in Dornoch, the Championship course and the Struie course. In 2007 it was ranked third (there's that number again) in *Golf's Digest* list of Top 100 courses in the world (outwith the USA).

But that's not what we've come to see. Definitely not. We are on the trail of something much more interesting, but on the way we are diverted by one of the noticeboards that are helpfully dotted about the town for the benefit of visitors. Well done, Dornoch's City Fathers!

We are in Littletown, actually a suburb of Dornoch, if that's not too grand a word to apply to such little places. It owes its origins to the Clearances, if that doesn't make it sound grateful. Shoved off the land in favour of sheep by the notorious 1st Duke of Sutherland (whose grand residence we are about to visit next), the crofters were forced to live on strips of land next to the sea and turn their hands to fishing for a living.

When they first came here, the poor people, in both senses of the word, built their houses of turf. In the fullness of time they were able to replace them with more permanent stone structures, the charming little whitewashed cottages (well at least some of them are) that we see today.

You can't keep a rapacious landlord down. No sooner were these more permanent residences erected than along came the Town Council in 1820 demanding rents. And here's the rub. The councillor who came along getting people to sign leases and collect the rents was none other than the Duke's factor, and the money went straight into his master's pocket. He had a mansion to keep, after all.

So now we come to what we have really come to see. You will not be unduly surprised to hear it's another stone and – like the one that marks the location of the Brahan Seer's supposed death – this marks the place of another special death. It's the "Witch's Stone", and supposedly marks the spot where the last witch in Scotland, Janet Horne, was burned to death in 1727.

Most witches were harmless old wifies who had certain remedies for the cure of certain maladies, which if they worked or if even if they didn't, laid them open to charges of witchcraft. Her fellow citizens, who either bore her a grudge, perhaps for an ineffective cure, or who merely thought she was a bit strange, saw that as a sign she was a witch. In this particular instance one woman alleged Janet was turning her daughter (who had a deformed hand) into a pony in order to ride to assignations with the Devil who shod her and that is why her hand was deformed. What an imagination!

Both Janet and her daughter were imprisoned. Luckily, the daughter mangaged to escape somehow (which seems suspicious), but alas poor Janet did not. In a hasty trial, she was tried, found guilty and sentenced to be burned to death. The very next day that's what they did. They stripped her naked, rolled her in tar, put her in a barrel and took her to this place. You can imagine the procession, the jeering that poor Janet had to endure as she made that last journey of her life.

That this horrific event took place is beyond doubt. What is less clear is if this is the real name of the poor woman or not. "Jenny Horne" is the generic name given to witches in the north of Scotland, and you can imagine the good burghers of Dornoch chanting that very name in a frenzied procession as the poor old lady was being taken to her execution. The hope is the poor soul had lost her marbles to such an extent that, in her bewilderment, she didn't have a clue what was happening to her. Another hope is when the torch was lit, death came quickly, unlike Patrick Hamilton, whose death, alas, was very protracted and who was all too aware of everything that was going on. Before he expired, his dying words were "Lord Jesus receive my spirit".

I hope he did not have a great disappointment if he found himself neither in heaven nor in hell but in the Great Black Nothingness instead. He believed he was going to meet his Maker and there must have been some comfort in that, giving him the courage to endure his gruesome death. By contrast, if her poor bewildered brain was capable of any rational thought, I would stake my life on Janet not looking forward to being reunited with her master, the Devil.

Nine years after her death, the Witchcraft Act was repealed. A more enlightened time, but alas it came too late for poor Janet.

Chapter Seventeen

Dunrobin Castle: The Duke and The Giraffe

Golspie and Dingwall have one thing in common: long before you enter the towns you can see a monument on a hill overlooking over them. By coincidence or design, both happen to be of the same height – 100 feet. Dingwall's monument, as you know, is to commemorate the life and achievements of Sir Hector MacDonald. And as many people also know, Golspie's monument on the summit of Ben Bhraggie was erected in honour of the notorious 1st Duke of Sutherland. The first you can readily understand, even if he did ruffle the feathers of the establishment; the other seems rather puzzling.

Erected in 1837, four years after his death, aged 75, a plaque on the monument is fulsome in its praise of the Duke. It's too long to go into all the details here, so I will just pick out some that may astound you. We are told the memorial was paid for by a "mourning and grateful tenantry". That may rock you back on your heels a bit, if all you've heard about the Duke would leave you to conclude that on hearing of his demise, there would have been much dancing and rejoicing in Strathnaver (if there was anybody left there after he'd cleared them all out). If it doesn't, then try this. We are are told he was a "noble and patriotic gentleman, a judicious, kind and liberal landord... a public yet unostentatious benefactor... who opened wide his hand to the distress of the widow, the sick and the traveller".

Can this really be the same man whose ill-reputation is founded upon not giving a fig for his tenants in the relentless pursuit of accumulating ever more wealth? Indeed, on the contrary, this memorial makes him sound rather saintly, like Arabella. Despite some recent attempts at sabotage by some, and by others to have it demolished or removed somewhere else such as Dunrobin Castle, it is still there and known locally as "The Mannie". That has an affectionate sort of ring to it, don't you think?

In actual fact, although the Duke's name is often regarded as being synonymous with the obnoxious Clearances, it may be he's more sinned against than sinning in this respect. As far back as 1772, Thomas Pennant (remember him from Chapter One?), when travelling in the Borders, wrote of a character "which [sic] has so little feeling as to depopulate a village of two hundred souls, and to level their houses to the ground; to destroy eight or ten farmhouses on an estate of a thousand a year; for the sake of turning almost the whole into a sheepwalk".

In the Highlands, however, you could say the Scottish diaspora began in the aftermath of the failure of the Jacobite Rebellion of 1715, when from the mid-1720s, Highlanders began emigrating to Canada. After Culloden, things only got worse as the speaking of Gaelic was proscribed, as were the bagpipes and the wearing of tartan. Just when sheep became the main cause of mass emigration is open to debate. You could say the most likely suspect is MacLeod of MacLeod, who began experimental work on Skye in 1732. At any rate, by the late 1750s and through the 60s, the process was well underway in Morvern in Lochaber. My point is that whilst it doesn't excuse what the Duke of Sutherland did, or what was done in his name, and certainly not the methods by which it was executed – it does at least place him in the bigger picture and shows he was by no means the only one involved in the Clearances, and by no means the first.

Another way of looking at it, from the other end of the telescope if you like, is the good Duke, seeing the conditions his tenants had to endure, scraping a subsistence living from the land, was appalled. Something had to be done and that is the reason he introduced the sheep and removed the crofters to the coast where they could learn new skills and cash in on the bounteous herring.

The year after he died, in 1834, a subscription was set up to raise funds for his memorial. Money came in from far and wide. Tenants were expected to stump up a shilling, an offer many dared not refuse. The following year, his widow generously donated money for the repair of Dornoch Cathedral which, as you may remember, had only been partially repaired up to this point. There was a motive behind her generosity however – she wanted a fitting place for the Duke to rest throughout eternity.

The repairs were completed in 1837, the same year as the monument on the hill was completed, so what with his statue being up there and his remains down in Dornoch, whatever his tenants really thought of him, there was no easy way of erasing the Duke's prescence from the community's consciousness. Elizabeth died two years later and was buried alongside him. She was seventy-three.

Actually he only became the Duke of Sutherland six months before his death in 1833, but since that is the name by which he is best known to history, that's how I'm going to refer to him, even though he began instigating his main claim to notoriety, the Clearances, long before he acquired that title, between 1811 and 1820 to be precise.

He was born George Granville Leveson-Gower in 1758, the Viscount Trentham. In 1786 he became Earl Gower and in 1803 the Marquess of Stafford. Collecting titles seems to have been a bit of an occupation with him, the way common people collect stamps. He collected a good many more during his career as a politician which are too many to bore you with here, except I will just mention he was the Ambassador to France from 1790-92 – not the easiest of berths given the tumultuous events which were going on in that troubled land at that time. Diplomatic relations came to an end when the royal family was imprisoned in 1791 and the ambassador and his wife were not allowed to leave until the following year.

A wealthy English landowner in his own right, the Duke had made a very good diplomatic move earlier, in 1785, when he married the twenty-year old Elizabeth, 19th Countess of Sutherland, the daughter and heiress of the Earl of Sutherland, deceased. He, along with his wife, died of the "putrid fever", which sounds rather unpleasant to say the least, when Elizabeth was only one-year old. Money attracts money. Under the terms of the marriage contract, however, the Duke had control of her lands but not ownership of them. The pertinent question however is – was he in control of *her*?

They were a fabulously wealthy couple. They owned an incredible 1.5 million acres, owned two-thirds of the entire county of Sutherland, not to mention the Duke's English estates. This made them the largest private landlords – not just in Scotland, not just in the United Kingdom, but in the whole of Europe. Indeed, at the time of his death, the Duke was probably the richest man in Europe. Meanwhile, at the other end of the spectrum, during the terrible events known as the "Clearances", what the Duke called his "improvements", it is estimated 15,000 crofters were displaced to make way for sheep. Some ended up on the coast as we have seen; others went further, took to the sea in ships and went to seek their fortunes in the New World.

In actual fact it is the terrible triumvirate of the Duchess (1765-1839), Patrick Sellar (1780-1851), and James Loch (1780-1855) who most historians agree are the real villains of the piece. After early experiments showed her the economic benefits of this new system, the Duchess enthusiastically set about promoting it throughout her empire with the gents above as her agents. In her defence, you can see where she was coming from. Between 1803 and 1817, £129,995 had been invested in the estate but only £45,932 collected in rents.

Of the two men, Sellar's name is better known. Trained as a lawyer, he was the Duchess' right-hand man, factor, or estate manager. His tactics in Strathnaver have come to typify the ruthlessness, the human tragedy and the misery of the Clearances. Sellar's lowest point was when he was charged with the death of Margaret MacKay, an old woman who refused to leave her croft and which was burned down regardless, with her still inside. He was acquitted, for lack of evidence, of direct involvement and went on to be a large landowner in his own right, making a fortune out of sheep. Whatever else you may think about him, at least he was not a hypocrite: he practiced what he preached.

Like Sellar, Loch trained as a lawyer, but it was as a hard-hearted economist that he zealously supervised clearing out the crofters to make way for the much more profitable grazing machines. Mission accomplished, he made a career move in 1827 when he became the MP for a constituency in Cornwall, standing as a Whig. This choice of party rather than the Tories seems rather surprising when you remember the term "Whig" is short for "whiggamore", a pejorative term meaning "cattle driver", used to denote those from the Western Highlands who had come south to the capital in search of corn.

And if you agree that that is surprising, you ain't heard nothing yet. At the time of the Clearances, the Duke was also a Whig and what's more, it was as long ago as 1804, seven years before he began instituting the Clearances, that he turned his back on the Tories, though as I said, he was only the titular head of the estate – and maybe the family too.

Presently we will set foot in their residence, Dunrobin. It's the sort of name that an orthographically-challenged retired burglar, after the end of a successful career, might have given to his retirement bungalow. Actually "dun" means "fort" or "hill" and "robin" probably refers to Robert, the 6th Earl who died in 1427. His wife, incidentally, was a daughter of the Wolf of Badenoch. That's some father-in-law to pick.

The castle began life in the 12th century as a fortified square keep which became surrounded and hidden from view by a number of additions from the 16th century onwards, the most extensive being in the 18th. Because the keep still stands, like a patriarch surrounded by his grandchildren, this makes Dunrobin one of the oldest continuously lived-in residences in Scotland – nine centuries of sheltering people under its roof – not family home, as it was not always inhabited by the family. In the late Sixties and early Seventies, it was a boys' boarding school and earlier than that, in the First World War, a naval hospital.

This is the way the Dukes would have come home, down an avenue as long and straight as befits the mansion at the end of it. It may be the front of the castle but it is the least familiar side, passers-by only being able to get a glimpse of the façade through the tunnel of trees. With its clock tower and oriel window and towers capped off in a variety of ways, it certainly is grand and imposing and actually, because of this very lack of uniformity, quite captivating. And thanks to this eclectic style, you can't help but see where the additions have been grafted on and how, like Topsy, the castle "just grew".

As for the more famous, the more photogenic side, it's straight out of a child's fairytale. As you gaze at it in admiration, you might wonder in which of the turreted rooms Sleeping Beauty lies awaiting the kiss from her prince. Or you might be forgiven for thinking that somehow you have been transported to the Loire. It sits regally on a terrace high above the sea, overlooking magnificent gardens, modelled after those in Versailles no less. The architect of this grand design was Sir Charles Barry who, along with Pugin, designed the Houses of Parliament or the Palace of Westminster, if you prefer.

Never mind all the attractions the castle offers; the gardens are an attraction in themselves, and there's a third thing – the museum. To be honest, give me a ruin any day rather than a swanky room with portraits and antique furniture. But that's just me. Anyway, when we step inside the castle and are told the museum closes at 4pm, half-an-hour before the castle, it's a bit of a no-brainer which we should visit first. Time is of the essence as we put on our skates and scoot down the steps towards the museum.

We are halted in our tracks however by the most amazing piece of vegetation I have ever seen. The leaves must be six foot across, the same from top to bottom and stand twice as tall as me, and for all I know, I might just be looking at a bunch of immature plants. Talk about triffids! I'd like to see Sleeping Beauty's Prince having to hack his way through this where the light struggles to penetrate the overhanging canopy.

A helpful notice tells me I'm looking at *Gunnera manicata,* or to give it its common or garden name, "Giant Rhubarb" or "Dinosaur Food". But it's not some ordinary rhubarb plant that a manic gardener has reared on steroids as an experiment. We are told it's a native of the Serro do Mar mountains of south-east Brazil. As that location suggests, it thrives on moisture so it will feel completely at home here in Scotland. In fact it finds the climate so ambient, the notice goes on to say this is only one clump of many we can find scattered around the garden.

Its nickname, "Dinosaur Food" does not come from the gigantic leaves which would have made a tasty morsel for any dinosaur as long as it was a herbivore – but from the flowers. Unfortunately it's not the flowering season at the moment, or maybe it is fortunate after all because the flowers look like coprolites – fossilised poo to you and me. There is a band of clay containing them near here so it happens to be particularly apposite. I don't know what the flowers smell like, if indeed they smell of anything, but thank God the coprolites don't.

The museum lies off to the left of the eye-catching circular, and incredibly well-manicured main parterre, which is gathered around a pool in which a jet of water playfully describes a perfect parabola. To appreciate it fully, to admire the symmetry, the artistry, the shapes and the colours, the gardens are best seen from above, a bird's eye view that you can see from the terrace before you descend.

It is a sight which the birds of prey (there is a resident falconer here) have seen many, many times as they perform their awesome flying skills for the delight of the crowds in the grassy area at the other side of the parterre. It is bordered on the seaward side by a regiment of lollipop trees and facing them, a dishevelled row of mature trees which have been left alone and allowed to grow just as nature intended. Elsewhere, wild and unruly vegetation has been tamed, hedged, clipped, trimmed and boxed-in to within an inch of its life. It may not be what Mother Nature intended but if it can ever be said that nature can be improved on, I would say this is it.

We pass through the shrubbery and arrive in front of what is now the museum but designed as a summerhouse by William, Lord Strathnaver, in 1732. It's two storeys high and must have extensive cellars as the entrance is reached by an extensive flight of steps. It's Georgian in style yet too square to be really elegant, but after all, this was just a little house at the bottom of the garden, so to speak. You can see his lordship's coat of arms and the date above the entrance. In 1878, it was improved by the 3rd Duke (of whom more later) who extended it at the rear to create the museum.

It's rather surreal to see, as soon as you enter, the lofty gaze of a giraffe meet your eye, or rather stare sightlessly somewhere over your head. It's not a real giraffe of course but a stuffed one and not the whole animal either, just the neck. Recovering from my surprise and looking past it into the room beyond, the first thing that strikes me is the enormous amount of other dead animals, or their remains, which are on display. Antlers everywhere: round the walls and on the rafters with, or without, the stuffed heads of their owners. Mainly they belonged to stags but there's a moose and one that looks as if it might be a buffalo skull. And then another surreal moment: high over our heads, a beluga whale (unless I am very much mistaken) swimming through the air towards us. Yes, well, that's the aristocracy for you: always making a killing somewhere.

The next impression is one of indescribable clutter, a veritable hotchpotch of exhibits. I wouldn't care to have had the job of itemising all the items for the inventory here: on the floor, on the rafters, in glass cases, on shelves in glass cabinets, on two crowded floors. Some contain many interesting personal items belonging to the Dukes and Duchesses, such as spectacles and various pieces of jewellery. I like things like that; they provide a real link to the person. You can imagine them once holding or wearing this or that. In the case of the stands of hair, it's actually even a bit more personal than that.

Here, however, is something I don't care for so much, though I study it with a gruesome intensity. It's a photograph of Anne, the 3rd Duke's wife lying dead in bed. She died in 1888, aged 59. The Duke lived on for four more years. Did he keep this photograph beside his bedside I wonder? Didn't he have any other photographs of her? Now she is an exhibit in the museum he built. I wonder what she makes of that. You know how women say, "I wouldn't be seen dead in that!" And now she *is* dead, and she's wearing what they chose to dress her up in for her grand exit. Death masks are one thing, but taking a *photograph* of the deceased, now that is something else.

But if you want to see something really, really gruesome (and why should you want to?), there is a diamond-shaped glass case which contains a score of little stuffed birds. It's pure Victoriana. Indeed, you could say that about the whole museum. We didn't know what to expect before we came here; certainly not this celebration of death. But what we *did* know was here, what we really came to see – is the collection of Pictish stones. Yes, we are back on the Pictish trail again.

There is a sizeable collection here, certainly more than I have ever seen gathered in one place before, containing a mixture of symbol stones and cross-slabs. Some are more complete than others; some are mere fragments. They come from along the coast from south of Golspie to north of Helmsdale, a distance of some twenty miles. Fear not gentle reader, if old stones are not your thing, even if they have exquisite carvings on them; I'm not going to give you a blow-by-blow account of every stone, let alone every fragment, but I am going to say a few words about the one that impressed me the most.

I'm not, therefore, going to say anything about the marvellous "knot-work" on the Collieburn stone; nor a word about what's known as the "Dunrobin No. 2" (no, not a coprolite), with its wonderful mad-as-hell crab (actually a pair of back-to-back decorated crescents with a couple of circles with a dot in the middle) and, at the bottom, the ubiquitous double-sided comb and mirror. Despite me not mentioning it, I would recommend you seek it out on your visit.

No, what really, really impresses me is the Golspie cross-slab. It stands eight foot high and if the front of the stone is normally reckoned to be the one with the cross on it, what is presented for us is the rear, which, like the castle, is the better side. The front is pretty-much damaged anyway but even if it weren't, this would still be the more interesting side.

Because it has been preserved from the elements in Dunrobin since 1868, the designs are much easier to make out than those on the Eagle Stone and a lot more intriguing. Permit me to give you a brief description of it.

At the top is a rectangle with three rather comical owl-like eyes as if peering over a wall like the graffiti character, Mr Chad, who appeared on walls accompanied by "Wot no...?" – supply whatever there was a shortage of in austerity-hit Britain during WWII to complete the question. Beneath that is some creature born out of the sculptor's worst nightmares. At the bottom end, so to speak, a monkey's tail is curved over its back while at the eating end there is an enormous proboscis, like an elephant's trunk but with some sort of deformity growing on its upper side. Isn't that an incredible thing! The Picts couldn't possibly have known about such animals, let alone think of putting them together in that surrealist way. What an imagination! A bit like God really, when He thought up the giraffe or his *pièce de resistance* as far as weirdness is concerned, the duck-billed platypus.

And then the penny drops as I realise I have been looking at the slab from the wrong perspecive. Tilting my head to the side, I am surprised to see, like a blurred image suddenly popping into focus, that what I had taken to be the rear end is actually the head! Having said that, it's still a weird sort of creature that never trod this earth but was born out of the sculptor's imagination.

Beneath that a dog is standing on a fish and to the left of them, a man who looks as if he has stepped straight out of the *Canterbury Tales* is pacing towards them with murderous intent – in his left hand a knife meant for the fish and in his right, a ceremonial axe which seems to be intended for man's best friend. There are some other symbols as well: the usual suspects, the double disc and a crescent and a V-rod. But what's by far more interesting, at the very bottom, are a couple of entwined snakes biting each other's tails off. Only they can't really be snakes but mythical beasts, as they have forked tails like a fish. Whatever they are, they make a very satisfactory frame for the whole picture.

There is so much still to see here, both of the weird and the wonderful, I am loath to leave. Who knows what fascinating finds I might come across if I stayed longer, but I am on a tight time-budget. We still have the interior of the castle to see.

This modest suggestion I make to my wife Iona, who cannot tear herself away from the Golspie stone. In fact, she has found so much to interest her on the bottom floor alone, she has not even gone upstairs yet to see the treasures up there. I mount the few steps up to the foyer where the custodian stands on guard to make sure we do not walk away with any trinkets (as if we would) or take any photos (which we would dearly like to have done).

I am in awe of the giraffe. I stand beneath it, looking up at it towering over me, wondering which Duke shot it (I wish he hadn't) and where and how they got it here, by which I mean back from Africa rather than through the door and up the stairs. When on Noah's ark, its ancestors must surely have had to stand out on deck exposed to the torrential rain, poor things.

"The legs are down below, in the basement," remarks the custodian, seeing my fascination.

"What! Really?" I respond in amazement.

"No, not really," he replies, laughing.

All at once I am covered in confusion. How could I have been so stupid! I feel myself blushing furiously to think I had thought, even for a nanosecond, that it was true – that they hadn't room for the entire animal and had had to cut a hole in the floor to accommodate it, and which they had put back with such loving care that you couldn't tell where the holes had been. Besides, it was plain to see there was more than enough headroom to accommodate it, legs and all – if only my brain had been engaged at the time.

I try to echo his laughter as best as I can, as if I didn't mind in the slightest being caught out as the most gullible or stupidest person in

Christendom. Thank God he doesn't know that a moment before I had been looking at the Golspie stone from the wrong end of the telescope. I am definitely now not going to ask him the question I had been about to ask about the provenance of the giraffe.

Two gaffes in two minutes are more than enough.

Chapter Eighteen

Dunrobin and Carn Liath: The Castle and The Broch

Watched dispassionately by stags' heads and the eyes of all the people in the portraits, we walk up a beautifully carved stone staircase. Not all the rooms are open to the public of course, but if they were – let's just suppose you spent just one minute in each one, not counting the time getting from one to the other – it would take you more than three hours to complete the tour.

I don't know how many rooms we are allowed to see, but I do know we have only half an hour to do so and it seems a minute is all we have in each as we rush from one room to the next. There is so much to see here that, like the museum, it's impossible to take everything in or even a part of it, so I'm not even going to try. Besides, you really need to come and see it for yourself.

There are a great number of portraits, as you would expect. It is a family home after all. Actually, it's something of an art gallery too. In the dining room, look for Alan Ramsay's *18th Earl*. Remember him, because you are going to come across his wife shortly. Separated by death, they have kept their portraits apart too. There are a whole host of other artists a giraffe-gaffe ignoramus like me has never heard of, but an educated reader like you might well have. I am sure they were famous in their day in order to have been given the commission in the first place. The castle even boasts a Tintoretto, a portrait called *Venetian Procurator* which hangs above the fireplace in the music room.

In the breakfast room is a painting more to my taste – a group of what initially appears to be three figures but actually there are four – a shadowy person is all but swallowed up by the inky background. It's *The Breakfast* by Sir David Wilkie. On the right of the painting, a man wearing what looks like a Santa Claus hat is having a cup of tea with a woman who looks as if she could be his mother. They are being served by a younger woman who might be the maid or who could be the festive person's wife. Same thing in those days, probably. As a matter of fact, the older woman is believed to be the artist's mother.

In the same room are two more Ramsays: *Lady Margaret Wemyss, Countess of Moray* and below it *Mary Maxwell,* the wife of the 18th Earl whom you saw in the dining room.

As for the furniture, I will say even less. If you are interested in that, the drawing room is the best place to see that sort of thing: Louis XV settees and *fauteils,* complete with draught screens. Really, who could ask for anything more? Except actually you could. This may be a family home, but it is also a museum and every museum has a star. I'm not sure what the star of the entire castle is, that might be a matter of taste, but the star of this room is the Louis XVI French table with the Florentine *pietra dura* top. So now you know.

You will remember that Barry was responsible for the outside of the castle, and what a legacy that is! The Scottish architect, Sir Robert Lorimer, designed the interior and that's his. There was a fire in 1915 at which time the castle was serving as a naval hospital. Luckily the fleet was in and the sailors were deputised as firefighters. Also by good fortune, there were enough buckets to form a human chain and the fire, which might have burned down the entire building, was extinguished – but not before it had done a great deal of damage.

Lorimer, seeing the damage, had a light-bulb moment. What the castle needed, he decided, was a bright and spacious room, a *salon,* in the French style, which would give grand views over the gardens and which would replace the pokey Victorian rooms that had been there before. Anyone who is remotely familiar with Victorian interior design knows just how claustrophobic their rooms can be with their gloomy wallpaper, dark furniture, antimacassars on every armchair and an aspidistra in every room, not forgetting a stuffed ferret or bird just to complete the tone. Yes, it takes an 18th century royal who lost his head to show a 20th century Scots aristocrat a little bit of taste and refinement.

The library is another Lorimer creation. A bedroom and a dressing room were combined and lined with sycamore wood and then most of it hidden behind 10,000 books. You would be disappointed if many of them were not rare editions, so I am happy to tell you they are. But if you are more interested in furniture than books (and may God have mercy on your soul) then you will certainly want to admire the Chippendale mahogany pedestal library table and the Regency mahogany circular rent table behind which the factor sat to collect the Duke's dues. And don't forget to clock the grandfather timepiece by Hanley and the globe by W. & A.K. Johnstone. To be honest, *te absolvo* from being more interested in the furniture than the books – many of them are about Scots Law. Yawn. Prescribed reading for an insomniac. Sweet dreams.

From the dream to the nightmare: the seamstress's room is said to be the source of the castle's ghost (any self-respecting castle has one). This is where the 4th Earl (or possibly the 5th) abducted a beautiful Mackay lady after a battle and so much in love was he that he wanted to marry her. With that aim in mind, he incarcerated her in a tower. Obviously he had never read *How to Influence People* and certainly never *How to Pick up and Impress a Lady*. Of course you can read between the lines as to what he was really after.

Anyway, the lady refused his modest proposal of marriage and one night, the Earl, losing patience, burst into her room only to catch her in the act of trying to escape, as in the best escape stories, by climbing down a rope made of knotted sheets. Taking out his sword, he slashed the sheet right through and she fell to her death. And this is the room where it happened.

She seems to be a ghost in search of a room, as ghostly footsteps have been heard in various parts of the castle. You can blame Lorimer for that, with his penchant for knocking rooms together and thus making some of them disappear. It sounds to me as if the lady could be looking for the room where her earthly life ended and the afterlife began. If only she could find her way back to where that awful event happened, perhaps she could reverse time, or so she hopes. So, when you visit this little room, remember this is the story behind it and make sure you pay particular attention to the window.

And as you walk along the Queen's Corridor, keep a lookout for the watercolour by Eugene Lami which dates from 1849. To help you find it, look for the bust of a lady (you know what I mean, not just the pointy bits – the entire head and shoulders) – it hangs above her. It's worth your attention because it shows you how to have a good time, Victorian style. The scene depicts what was known as a "Crush", which was all the rage back then. Hundreds of people got gussied up in their best party clothes and stood packed tightly together, chatting for two hours or more without so much as a drink or a canapé to sustain them. Such simple pleasures. Our well-heeled ancestors certainly knew how to have a good time without spending a penny. Which, come to think of it, must have been a bit of a problem for the ladies if they needed to do such a thing at these receptions; the plumbing in those days not being what it is today, not to mention all those petticoats and hoops and bustles to have to fight your way through.

It's also worth keeping your eye open for a glimpse of the original part of the building, the keep, which you'll see on your way out if you keep your eyes peeled. The red sandstone and tiny windows make it look incredibly ancient, which of course it is. The circular tower in the same material is an addition perfectly in keeping with the original square building, but which can't be said for the much younger whitewashed buildings squeezing it tightly on either side. For all the world it looks as if an ancient and weathered grandma is being propped up by the fresh-faced grandkids, who to her surprise have grown so incredibly tall – almost as tall as her.

Although the drive by which we arrived is extremely wide and straight, wider and straighter than many of the roads we will be driving on tomorrow as we head across the top of the country, it's a one-way system and we are made to leave a different way, through the trees. We turn right at the end of the drive and this time passing the imposing driveway, we continue the NC500 and head north. It may be goodbye to Dunrobin but not the Duke. As we proceed, we will not fail to find evidence of his legacy.

A couple of miles later, just before a wide sweeping bend on the A9, we have another stately home to explore (if that's indeed what it is) from at least two millennia before the Duke's time. It's the broch of Carn Liath, which – despite its ruinous condition – is one of the best-preserved brochs in mainland Scotland and extremely accessible.

We pull into a car park on the other side of the road, aware all the while that our movements are being watched unsmilingly by the Duke, up there on his pedestal so high, on top of the Ben. Don't worry, your Dukeship, we're not about to rustle any of your precious sheep. But then, you wouldn't expect to see any here. This is the unlikely-named Strathsteven, the coastal strip, more hospitable to people, less suitable for sheep.

Brochs are the skyscrapers of the Iron Age and uniquely Scottish, the best surviving example anywhere being Mousa in Shetland which still soars an incredible 43 feet into the sky – and that's just what's left of it. It would have been a good deal higher than that originally. I know that is puny by Manhattan standards but in its day it must have been the marvel of its age, and still is today, when you consider the methods available to the builders back then.

There are two hundred or more brochs scattered around the north, the west and the islands, to which you can add another three hundred possibles, only in such ruinous conditions they can't be positively identified as such. The greatest concentration by far in all the country is in Sutherland and Caithness. Radiocarbon dating shows they were built between 100 BC and 100 AD.

So just why were the brochs built? Some have suggested they might have been a status symbol, a sort of manor house where the head honcho with his extended family could lord it over the folk of the common sort, and/or they could have been a place of refuge for all the community in times of emergency. And just who was enemy Number One in the first century AD? The Romans, that's who!

In 78 AD, Agricola, the new governor of Britannia arrived, and the following year ordered a fleet to circumnavigate the island. In actual fact, the ancient Greeks had engaged on such an expedition as long ago as the late third century BC and in his *De Situ Orbis* (43 AD), the Roman geographer, Pomponeius Mela, gave a pretty accurate description of the Orkneys.

By 83 AD, the process of Romanisation of the southern tribes was well underway. But in the north it was a different story. There is nothing like a common enemy to make the warring tribes forget their differences, bury the hatchet and unite against a common foe, the likes of which they had never seen before. Unity is strength and there is strength in numbers but, despite that, it didn't go well against the well-disciplined Roman military machine. The Caledonian confederation was routed at the Battle of Mons Graupius in 84 AD. The exact location is disputed: it could be in the north-east, that is to say in present-day Aberdeenshire, or it could be in Perthshire, or it could be somewhere completely different. For what it's worth, from what I've read, my money is on Perthshire.

Despite this massive victory, the Romans did not pursue their advantage. Agricola was recalled to Rome and it seems his successors had little stomach for a prolonged fight against people who wouldn't stand and fight you face-to-face like proper soldiers. Besides, what was this gods-forsaken land good for anyway? (It seems sheep did not occur to them.) And in any case it was not as if they posed any threat to the empire. That came from elsewhere. In the third century, finding them on the back foot, the Picts did take the fight to the enemy, breaching Hadrian's Wall several times. By 410 the Romans had had enough and left Britannia for good.

If they looked impressive from the outside, what you've got to realise is the brochs are twice as impressive as they appear. That's because they are double-skinned. Mousa had an external circumference of fifty feet while the interior was a mere twenty. That's what I would call pretty thick-skinned. There was a course of stone steps between the inner and outer walls which would also serve to bind them together. Blessed are the ties that bind, for they didn't rely just on the stairs alone; they also used dedicated stone ties to keep home and hearth together. They knew what they were doing, these Frank Lloyd Wrights of yesteryear, taking no chances these towering structures would collapse in a heap of rubble upon their heads – as they might just have a tendency to do in a high gale for instance – since they were drystone constructions. These skilled craftsmen had no need of any poncy mortar. They were carpenters too. The floors would have been made of wood, as would the roof, most probably.

The double walls were a pretty good defence against all the slings and arrows any enemy could hurl at them. But of course each stronghold has its weak point. If the people can get in, so can the invaders. Carn Liath is within stone-throwing distance from the sea: attackers could more-or-less sail right up to the front door. They would have been visible on a clear day from miles away, which would have given the people living in the round houses huddled around the broch plenty of time to get inside and bar the door, where, once inside, they must have felt reasonably secure.

To gain entry to the broch, if at first you did succeed in knocking down the front door, attackers would have been faced with a second door at the end of a narrow passage. One attacker at a time if you please. A bit like the Pass at Thermopylae in the battle of the same name, where famously in 480 BC the Greeks kept the numerically superior Persian forces at bay for days. And that's not all. At the side of the passage is a guardroom, a feature adopted by its descendant, the castle.

But Carn Liath wasn't just a place of security. It was also a home for the extended family or several families even. A noticeboard shows what it would have been like on the inside. And very cosy it looks too.

The men are gathered around the fire telling stories while the women are doing all the work. (Where did it all go wrong, oh Lord?) Well, to be fair, one of the men has exerted himself enough to lazily stir a pot on the fire. Meanwhile a woman is doing a bit of weaving whilst another, on an upper storey, reached by a wooden ladder, is hanging up yet more fish to be smoked. And there could be no better place for such an activity. There is no chimney, no windows, and the only entrance as described. Most of the light would have come from the fire which never would have been allowed to go out. It seems to me these broch-dwellers were in greater danger of dying of carcinogens from the woodsmoke than from the enemy, only they didn't know then that smoking was injurious to your health. I don't know if there is such a thing as dying of a surfeit of fish, but they must have been utterly sick of it. Fish with everything and they didn't even have chips.

As time passed, the Picts must have felt increasingly secure. The Romans did make repeated incursions into north-east Pictland by means of skirting the mountainous centre and establishing marching camps around the coast. All that came to an end with the death of Septimius Severus in 211 AD, after which, apart from a few skirmishes by his son, Caracalla, who knew when he was beaten, the Romans never tried to mount another invasion. As a matter of fact, it could be said as far as the Picts were concerned, the threat ended, ironically enough, with the Romans' massive victory over them at Mons Graupius – only they didn't know that of course. Foresight is a wonderful thing. Well, sometimes it is. Ask the Brahan Seer.

If it is accurate, the radio carbon-dating would suggest the great age of broch building came to an end at about the same time as the Romans' evacuation, though it seems to have continued for another century in the north of Shetland. Either the islanders didn't get to hear about the Roman retreat or suspected a trap, or they had their own reasons for continuing to build the brochs. After all, they had been around long before the threat of a Roman invasion.

There was a cluster of dwellings huddled around the broch as I mentioned earlier; you can see the stones and the depressions in the ground where they once stood. However experts disagree about whether they came later or were contemporaneous with the broch. They might have been built after there was no longer any need for such a mighty structure, a sort of Pax Romana persisting after the departure of the mutual enemy. If so, it would have been a very handy source of building material, those builders showing scant consideration for the archaeologists and historians of the future. Vandalising and cannibalising existing buildings for present needs has a long pedigree.

The experts reckon these humble homes were still in use up until 400 AD, three centuries after the broch was built. Meanwhile, a long, long time in the past, archaeologists found a bronze-age grave complete with goods, evidence that people had been living (and dying) here, who had chosen to live in this place three millennia or more before the Duke of Sutherland forced them to.

He is still on his pedestal, master of all he surveys, as we head back up the track towards the car.

Chapter Nineteen

Helmsdale: Murder, Treason and Plot

I T'S not long before we pass the sign to Doll off to our left. It's a scattered community which almost certainly owes its unusual name to the Norse *daer* for valley, modern Norwegian, Swedish and Danish *dal* and the modern English "dale".

After that it's on the switchback road to Brora which straddles the river of that name and which is fed by the loch of that ilk. There is a sort of irrefutable logic to all that, and indeed the town's name comes from the Norse meaning "river with a bridge". We are not going to be stopping here but, NC500 traveller, as you pass through, please note the 1922 magnificent Scots Baronial-style clock tower which doubles as a war memorial. You can't miss it, but what you may not realise is this peaceful little town, which looks as if nothing interesting has ever happened here, has, in fact, a history which is not only interesting but holds some details which might surprise you.

Who would have thought for instance, with a population of just over a thousand souls, it was once known as "Electric City" – the very first place in the north of Scotland to be powered by that source of energy? It was thanks to the sheep actually. Electricity was needed for the woollen industry. And another distinction belonging to Brora is, despite this extremely rural setting, it once boasted the most northerly coalmine in the UK. It only closed in 1974.

It won't surprise you in the least to learn that in the past, fishcuring and boat-building were occupations here, but the major one was salt-panning which was vital for the herring industry. Its picturesque little harbour was never big enough to compete with the herring fleets of its competitors around the Moray Firth but it was big enough to export salt, the pans being heated by an unending supply of local coal. At its peak in 1818, four hundred tons of salt were exported from its harbour. And it was from here too, the coal left until the coming of the railway in 1871. And who do you suppose it was who improved the harbour to make it fit for these purposes? The Duke of Sutherland, that's who.

And there's one more thing, I've kept the best till last – Clynelish Distillery. It was opened in 1968 and is still operating, but there was an earlier distillery on the same site built in 1819 by the Duke of Sutherland at a cost of £750. Which just goes to show you he wasn't all bad. In fact, the previous year he had set up a brick works. The two distilleries operated side by side from 1969 until 1983, when the Duke's was mothballed. Who knows, one of these days it may blow off the cobwebs and arise from its sleep like Rip Van Winkle, although it's already well past his wake-up call and no sign of the spirit stirring yet.

Miles and miles of golden sand are on our right, the Sutherland Rivieria, as we breeze out of Brora towards our next stop of Helmsdale. At Portgower, the hills squeeze in on our left, whilst on our right the sea licks at the shore and the road, which had been wide and broad a moment ago, is now pinched into a narrow thread. Portgower is an unsuitable place for sheep but people are able to live here, if not thrive exactly. And that's how it came into being, part and parcel of the Duke's new and improved agricultural policy.

On a mound to your left as you come into Helmsdale, you will see, fluttering in the breeze, or standing out straight and stiff, depending on the vagaries of the weather, high on their poles, some national flags which you will recognise as coming from New Zealand, Australia and Canada, as well as the homegrown sort. You should allow them to flag you down and take you up the little road to where there is ample car parking.

From here there is a good view of the harbour, the town, the bridge over the river, the clocktower and, beyond it, the Strath of Kildonan. Actually, if the NC500 tourist should find himself short of time, the A897 just across the bridge provides both a detour and a shortcut up the straths of Kildonan and Halladale to Melvich on the Pentland Firth, cutting off the whole NE corner of the country. But here, right in front of us, is something rather special.

Gerald Laing's *Emigrants Statue* is a composition in bronze of a group of windswept figures standing on a high stone plinth. It was only unveiled in 2007. His plaid billowing out behind him like a sail, a bare-breasted and kilted man, his long hair streaming back from his head, is staring with jutting chin and an air of indefatigable determination, straight ahead into the distance. He is facing the sea and an uncertain future. At his side, his son – with more waves in his hair than Marcel ever dreamt of – is looking up at him. He's not sure what's going on but he's searching his father's face for a sign that whatever is happening, it's going to be all right. His mother, wrapped in a shawl and with her back to the wind, has a baby in her arms. She is facing the Strath of Kildonan, back the way they have come and where she imagined her children would grow up, and where she would be buried with her ancestors when she died. But now, suddenly, her world has collapsed about her. She does not know what the future holds, but the fear of the unknown is probably the biggest fear of all.

A plaque in English and Gaelic tells us they "went forth and explored continents, built great countries and cities and gave their enterprise and culture to the world". It was not an honour they sought, but something thrust upon them. Incredibly, within the space of twenty years, four-fifths of the population of the Strath had gone.

A bitter, hard, crossing they had of it, and on the other side, faced famine, flood, disease and harsh winters. They settled in the Red River district of present-day Manitoba and, in the fullness of time, founded the city of Winnipeg. As a matter of fact, a copy of this very statue is situated in Waterfront Drive, Winnipeg. They call it the "Selkirk Settlers Monument" after Thomas Douglas, a director of the Hudson Bay Company and the 5th Earl of Selkirk, who recruited them. They brought with them bushels of wheat which not only survived the salty sea crossing, but the harsh winter. In that rich earth, those seeds that Scotland nurtured, grew and ripened. That foreign field is now a prairie of golden wheat stretching as far as the eye can see.

The first tranche of about 100 left in June 1813, with a second following two years later. They brought with them letters and parcels. You can imagine how joyfully these were received by the first settlers. If, in the end, the new land turned out to be a land of opportunity for the emigrants and their descendants, it was also good for the new territories, for the newcomers' influence on their adopted land was profound. I don't intend to create a roll-call of all the Scottish emigrants or descendants of emigrants who hugely affected the course of their new country's history, yet they were many and we've already met some as a matter of fact – but I will just mention the first Prime Minister of Canada, John A. MacDonald, who was born in Glasgow and emigrated to Canada in 1820 when he was five. More pertinent to our present story, that babe in the woman's arms (if she weren't just a symbolic figure) could turn out to be George Bannerman, the great-grandfather of Canada's 13th Prime Minister, John Diefenbaker (1895-1979) – for this is where he came from, somewhere up that valley where his mother is taking one last, lingering look.

That is past history and the babe in arms the future, but beneath our feet an older history lies concealed. It was on this site that Helmsdale Castle used to stand. It was built in the second half of the fifteenth century by Elizabeth Baillie, the 7th Countess of Sutherland. It had been a ruin centuries before it was demolished in 1972 as part of the road improvement scheme that took us here, so nothing remains now but the ghosts of those who once lived and died here.

And three did in 1567, in rather tragic circumstances.

It was here, at this, the Sutherland's hunting lodge, just a little bit up the road from Dunrobin, that Isobel Sinclair tried to poison her nephew, the 11th Earl of Sutherland, his wife the Countess, and their fifteen year-old son. She was the daughter of Alexander Sinclair, the laird of Dunbeath Castle and the wife of Gordon of Garty, the 4th son of the Earl of Sutherland. They're all very complicated, these inter-family marriages and relationships, enough to tie your head in as many knots as on a Pictish cross-slab, but all you need to know is her son, John, was but one step away from becoming the 12th Earl of Sutherland. Like Macbeth, that was a step which she must "o'erleap" in order for him to secure the glittering prize. Hence the poison plan.

Murder is a filthy business and, through circumstances beyond her control, she made a right mess of it. She succeeded in poisoning the Earl and the Countess – so far so good – but Alexander their son, whom all these shenanigans were meant to dispatch, missed his early demise by rudely arriving late for his tea, having been out enjoying himself hunting with John. Like a good guest, Alexander went to make his apologies. Meanwhile, complaining of thirst, John went off to get something to drink and an unwitting servant passed him the poisoned chalice.

By this time, however, the effects of the poison were beginning to show on Alexander's parents. His father, realising what had happened, and naturally not wishing his son and heir to suffer the same fate, gathered up the tablecloth, swept everything to the floor declaring "the bitch" had poisoned them. It's not recorded if those were his last words or not, but they might have been.

Thus it was that John died and Alexander was spared. I suppose you could say it was rough justice and it served her right, but it is a bit of a shame for the innocents. As for the Lady, she committed suicide the night before her execution in Edinburgh. Better to die by your own hand than your feet dance at the end of a rope.

This multiple poisoning might remind you of the attempt in 1643 at Cromarty Castle to poison the "mad young laird of Calder", who was married to Sir Thomas Cromarty's sister and which also ended up with the deaths of three dinner guests whilst the intended victim escaped unscathed. It's all very *Hamlet*esque, where you will remember the last act of the Danish play, written about 1599, has much ado about people being poisoned, with unintended consequences.

But to our tale. George Sinclair, the 4th Earl of Caithness, selflessly appointed himself as Alexander's guardian, whipped him off to the Sinclairs' stronghold of Girnigoe Castle near Wick and lost no time in marrying him to his eldest daughter, Barbara, who at 32, was more than twice as old as the lad. Clearly he was looking to the future and hoping the experienced older woman would take the boy in hand, make a man of him and set up a dynasty.

In 1569, Alexander was sprung by the Murrays, as I related in Chapter Sixteen, which subsequently led to the sacking of Dornoch in a revenge attack by the Mackays. As soon as he attained his majority in 1573, the first thing Alexander did was divorce Barbara. He then set about implementing his own revenge, waging war against his former father-in-law and guardian and eventually winning a decisive victory at the battle of Wick in 1588.

Alexander married again, his choice this time. In the merry-go-round of political marriages that were not uncommon in those days, she was Lady Jean Gordon of Huntly, the ex-wife of the Earl of Bothwell whom he divorced to marry Mary, Queen of Scots.

Bothwell had married Jean in February 1566. A year later, Mary became a merry widow when her husband, Darnley, was murdered. While the Queen was attending a wedding, leaving Darnley behind, an amazing thing happened – the house they were living in at the time blew up. But that's not what killed Darnley. He was found in his nightshirt in the orchard, unharmed by the explosion. Beside the body was a cloak and a dagger. He had been strangled. But whodunit? It is a cloak and dagger mystery, literally.

In April 1567, Bothwell was accused of being one of those involved. In a trial lasting as long as seven hours, he was acquitted. The following month, he divorced Jean after admitting adultery with one of her servants. Eight days later, on 15th May 1567, he and Mary, Queen of Scots were married.

As everyone knows, they did not live happily ever after. And maybe that served them right too.

Chapter Twenty

Helmsdale: Spending Some Time in the Timespan

Once upon a time there were two warring Viking chiefs called Swein and Olvir. They fought a great battle here in which Swein emerges victorious. That decisive event is recalled in the name "Helmsdale" from the Old Norse *Hjulmundal,* or "Valley of the Helmet".

The bridge over the river of the same name was completed in 1812 at a cost of £2,200. No prizes for guessing it was engineered by that man Telford again. There was also a tollhouse. The Duke was looking for a return on his investment. He wasn't *that* altruistic.

Crossing the river for free, we enter the award-winning Timespan Museum for a modest fee. It's an art gallery, shop, café and archive centre where you can trace your roots – as well as being a story-telling centre which features five animated films on the myths, legends and superstitions of the area. Arguably the greatest of all these is the splendid Caen Virtual World. It sounds very French, but actually this Caen is a little settlement in the Kildonan valley (after St Donan and the Pictish word *kil* which means "cell") and where you can get a good idea of what life was like on the eve of the Clearances, where you can peer into the past through the peaty smoke of a longhouse and see people up one end, cattle at the other.

The oldest part of the museum is housed in what used to be part of the fish-curing yard that was here formerly. We'll come to that part later, but to begin our visit we are transported along a timeline with illustrations and texts which put Helmsdale into not just a global setting but from a time when not just our planet was formed, but the universe.

You would expect to find information on the Clearances here and there is. You can follow a colour-coded story seen through the eyes of some of the key players and compare and contrast their different lots in life with regard to dress, diet, dwellings and education. Some we have already met: the Countess, Patrick

Sellar and James Loch. New characters on this real-life stage are Major William Clunes, sheep farmer with an appalling sense of dress; Catherine Macpherson, one of the emigrants who went to Canada with the Earl of Selkirk; and the Cheviot sheep whom I will call "Dolly", though the museum does not call her anything.

Dolly was born in 1811 and came to Kildonan with a lot of her peers in 1813. Thanks to the Napoleonic wars, wool was a very valuable commodity, something sheep farmers could, and did, make a killing from – wool being much in demand for soldiers' tunics, the making of. By 1820, there were 118,400 of Dolly's race in Sutherland. Alas Dolly herself died in 1824, in a snowstorm, but she never knew the storm she whipped up just by being in that particular place at that particular time.

Another major character is the Rev. Donald Sage. You may remember meeting him earlier when he was minister at Resolis, in Cromarty – one of the ministers involved in the Disruption of 1843. That was in the future. In 1813 he was minister at Achness and Ach'na H-uai in Strathnaver, a valley which was to become infamous in the story of the Clearances and which the Reverend was to write about in his memoirs. In them, in January of that year, he writes that on both sides of the river, from Kildonan to Caen on the left and Dalcharn to Marrel on the right, were, "at one fell sweep, cleared of their inhabitants". The cleared land was leased to the Major William Clunes of Crakaig, Loth, aforesaid, and to a Mr Reid from Northumberland.

Incidentally, Glen Loth lies midway between Brora and Helmsdale and, if Dornoch can lay claim to having the distinction of being where the last witch was executed, Loth is said to be where the last wolf in Sutherland was shot, around 1700, by a certain Peter Polson. A stone by the side of the road commemorates the event, supposedly, but in all the times I've driven up and down this road, I've never seen it, not once.

It may interest the reader to know that wolves were once such plentiful pests in Sutherland that in 1577 James VI made it compulsory to hunt them three times a year. The last wolf in Britain is said to have been killed by a Mr MacQueen of Findhorn in 1745. At the time of writing, they are talking about reintroducing them to keep the deer down – a proposal which is not greeted with singing and dancing by the sheep farmers in the straths.

But back to the Rev. Sage's tale. He goes on to say the evictions were "so suddenly and brutally carried out, as to excite a tumult among the people". To the Sheriff-Depute of the County, this looked like an uprising. He panicked and sent for a detachment of troops from Fort George. However the Chief Magistrate intervened, sent back the troops and instituted an enquiry into the crofters' grievances.

They signed a petition pleading to be allowed to stay, agreeing to pay as much rent as the sheep farmers but refused to rule out violence if their demands were not listened to. Negotiations continued – and broke down. More petitions were sent, even to the Prince Regent. The Duke and the Duchess offered certain concessions, such as generous prices for the crofters' cattle and, in addition, they would be given six months' notice before having to leave and not before their new houses were built. These measures defused the situation somewhat. Furthermore, some lairds in Caithness offered to take some families, whilst the Earl of Selkirk, as I said above, offered a new beginning in Canada at £10 per head, per passage. By April 1813, 580 people had expressed an interest in his offer, though in the event, considerably less than half actually undertook the first voyage, as I mentioned earlier.

In 1819 it was the turn of the minister and his congregation to be turfed out. In the October of 1818, the tenants were told their leases would not be renewed the following May. The month before the fateful day, the Reverend preached his valedictory sermon in the open air at Achness. He writes: "All lifted up their voices, and wept, mingling their tears together. It was indeed the place of parting, and the hour. The greater number parted never again to behold each other in the land of the living". The following Sunday he preached his last sermon at Ach'na H-uai.

That same week, the Clearances began, beginning at Grunmore, with Patrick Sellar in charge of operations, supported by the Fiscal and a strong body of constables, sheriff-officers and others. The cottagers were given half-an-hour to get their belongings out of the building and then the roof was torched. A soldier's widow, who didn't have the strength to remove her belongings by herself, was refused permission to wait until her neighbours could come and help her. A shepherd offered to help but permission was refused. She dragged out what she could in the half-hour allocated to her and then the cottage was set alight. Naturally, she couldn't drag the furniture very far. The wind carried sparks from the roof and the meagre possessions she had managed to drag outside caught fire and were burned to ashes.

At the next little community of Ceann-na-coille, there was another widow in an even worse state than the previous one. She was so crippled she could not walk, could not even lie in a bed but had to sit in a chair day and night. Her family asked for two days' grace until a means of transport could be organised to take her to the coast. This was refused on the grounds they should have thought of that beforehand. She was carried out in a blanket, in great pain, and her humble home set on fire.

Another story concerns Robert MacKay whose family was ill. He carried one daughter on his back for a certain distance then laid her down while he went back for the other. And so he continued for twenty-five miles.

The following week, our chronicler had occasion to pass through the Strath on his way to Tongue and he describes the utter scene of devastation he saw before him. Not a cottage that had a roof remaining, the rafters still smoking; a gable wall here and a long wall there which had collapsed and everywhere, the acrid smell of smoke.

For her part, the Countess, who was evangelical in her espousal of these agrarian reforms, was uncomprehending as to why the crofters just could not see what was good for them; why they could not see the benefits of the new life being offered on the coastal strips – the opportunity to turn their hands to new skills such as fishing or coal mining or making bricks and living in nice new houses which they did not have to share with their cattle, even if they had to build them themselves, at their own expense. Maybe she had a point: it's not as if they were already living off the fat of the land. They had experienced near-famine in 1807 and 1808. Some people need to be dragged screaming into the nineteenth century for their own good. And they were.

Kildonan is not only infamous for the Clearances: it was also the site of Scotland's goldrush. In 1818, a nugget of gold was found in the River Helmsdale. Nothing happened for half a century. Then a local man, Robert Gilchrist by name, a Klondiker who had also worked in the Australian gold fields, was given permission by the Duke to go a-prospecting. He found significant quantities of gold in the tributaries of the Helmsdale river. Somehow the press got hold of the story and the rush was on. By the spring of the following year, 600 prospectors had come to seek their fortune. A photograph shows the shantytown where they lived and if you didn't know any better, you could be looking at somewhere in California in the early days of their Gold Rush. A speck of the gold that was found there you can see through a magnifying glass.

No-one was going to make their fortune except the 3rd Duke himself, if he had anything to do with it. He started charging £1 for a licence plus 10% on every find (if he got wind of it). This was a big turn-off as far as the prospectors were concerned; after all there was no guarantee of finding anything, let alone the nugget of the century. As finds began to tail off and the lure of the silver darlings, the herring, offered more certain and immediate rewards, the prospectors voted with their feet. By the autumn, those 600 had died down to 50.

The New Year is a time for resolutions. On January 1st, 1870, the Duke unveiled his. From henceforward there would be no more prospecting. As ever, with the Sutherlands, it was profit-motivated. Once the Duke found out he could make more from the rootin'-tootin'-fishin' set, he turfed the prospectors off his land.

If you have a mind to, you can try your hand at panning for gold today at Baile an Or, or Place of Gold, on the Kildonan Burn. Read the notice about the rules and regulations first. The rights are owned by the Suisgill estate.

The museum has recreated a shop of those times, and here's the irony – the providers of provisions to the prospectors made more money than they ever did, not an uncommon phenomenon amongst those with the gold-lust in their eye. For some locals, the shop might be a day's walk away so it might be a case of the weekly shop. As well as catching up on all the latest gossip in the Strath, the crofters' wives could barter their eggs and cheese for other goods. Try that today and see where it gets you.

The last main exhibit is a mock-up of the interior of one of the new croft houses, proudly boasting a dresser and fireplace. There is even a clock on the wall. The real thing would have consisted of two rooms: a living room, dining room and bedroom as well as a small scullery with a separate byre. The floor would have been of packed earth and less cosy and comfy than this appears, I suspect. This was the sort of thing the first Duchess had in mind when she wanted her tenants to abandon their semi-detached existence with their cattle and chickens at the other end of the building. They were, however, expected to build these desirable residences themselves, although they were given assistance with the purchase of timber and lime and the Duchess even offered cash prizes for the winners of the who-can-build-the-best-new-croft competition.

The new industry of fishing naturally played a big part in the community, both the sea-fishing sort and salmon-netting in the river. The linear farming lots attached to the new crofts, no more than two acres maximum, were too small for the crofters to live on what they could grow on that rocky ground alone. Begun in 1814, the same year as the new town of Helmsdale, the harbour was completed in 1818 at a cost of £1,800 and extended in 1823 to cope with the herring boom, and yet again in 1892. In 1814 there were only 20 fishing boats in Helmsdale; by 1819 there were 204! At the peak of the herring boom, between 1839 and 1841, an incredible 700 women were employed in the gutting and the packing of the herring which were sent far and wide – to Germany, the Baltic and Russia. In addition, there were the ancilliary occupations of coopers, curers and blacksmiths.

The harbour is quiet now, a picturesque sort of place, but back in its heyday you can imagine it as a hive of industry as the fish were landed and gutted and packed in barrels, on the first layer, the tails pointing to the centre, heads on the second, tails on the next and so on. This was women's work back then. They worked in threes, two to gut and one to pack. And they worked with amazing rapidity; gutting between thirty and fifty herring a minute with a knife called a *cutag*. That's practically one a second. Imagine that! And when they did cut their fingers, as was inevitable, given the speed with which they worked – it must have stung like hell when it came into contact with the salt.

To take their minds off the repetitive tedium of the job, they gossiped or sang as they worked, which they did from 6am until there was no more herring to gut – which could often be twelve hours later. The adage goes that the Devil finds work for idle hands to do. Well, he didn't waste his time coming to Helmsdale.

There used to be an icehouse for the preservation of white fish but it was demolished in the 1990s. Another still exists, up by the clocktower, which also serves as the war memorial. (Forty people from this little place lost their lives in the First World War. Compare that with sixteen in the Second.) Believe it or not, the icehouse is a protected building under the care of Historic Scotland. It was built for the packing and storing of the salmon before they were sent south to Glasgow and Edinburgh. Built into the brae and constructed of stone, it was roofed with turf and insulated so well that the ice would last through the summer. When there was a mild winter, ice was imported from Norway.

On the top floor of the museum, in a temporary exhibition, some sturdy, purpose-built tables have been laid out bearing all manner of objects under headings such as "Catching", "Caring", "Clothing", "Looking", "Eating" and "Making". Most intriguing of all is the one labelled "?". They are a living testimony to my maxim that you should never throw out today's everyday object, as it's only a matter of time before it becomes the historical curiosity of tomorrow.

There's an outdoor museum too which is open all the time, come rain or shine. It's a rock garden, but not like any rock garden you have ever seen before, or at least I haven't. It's a geologist's dream, enough to warm the cockles of poor dead Hugh Miller's heart. Like an open-air sculpture gallery, it features boulders of varying textures and hues – green, grey, red, pink and brown, each one set in its own little patch of pebbles with a plate at the base telling you its name and age, like a tombstone does the dear departed. It's a memorial all right, a reminder of just how incredibly ancient this landcape is.

The Timespan Museum. Yes indeed. It doesn't just span centuries; it spans aeons. If you take my advice, NC500 traveller, you should spend a little money and a lot of time here, as Shirley Bassey didn't quite put it.

Chapter Twenty-One

Badbea and Dunbeath: Life on the Edge

NOW we are leaving the coast behind, heading for the hills, as we leave Sutherland behind and pass through the Ord of Caithness. A brown sign pointing to the right indicates the historic town of Badbea. There is plenty of space to park.

A path through the heather leads to a cairn at the top of the cliff. It was erected in 1911 by David M. Sutherland in memory of his father, Alexander Robert Sutherland, who was born here in 1806 and who emigrated to New Zealand in 1839. Alexander seems to have been the son of William Sutherland, the fifth of nine children. First came the six boys followed by the three girls. Funny how things pan out. A similar sort of thing happened in my father's family and in another's, as you shall shortly see.

On the other side of the memorial, the ground slopes steeply away to the sea. Good God, to be made to come to such a place! No-one would ever willingly choose to live here. There is no natural protection from the biting wind as it blows in across the grey North Sea all the way from Siberia. It catches in your throat, takes your breath away and tosses it away into the distance somewhere. The only shelter from the blast is the wee bit housie that you had to build yourself with the stones you found lying about, which fortunately were plentiful. It's living on the edge, in both senses of the word, where one stumble or one capricious gust of wind could send you spiraling into the void below. In fact a noticeboard tells us that whilst the people worked, the children and livestock were tethered to the ground precisely to prevent that catastrophe.

And just how hard to scratch a living, to clear land of the heather and the stones and dig into the topsoil with your *chas-crohm* or foot-plough! And then how did you persuade your oats and potatoes to grow in the teeth of that relentless wind and that mean soil? And how could you feed your animals, let alone yourself and nine children for God's sake? (Did William Sutherland not know what was causing them?) No wonder they had to leave: there had to be a better life somewhere over the seas. I hope there was, but as we saw with the settlers in Manitoba, it was not all plain sailing.

As early as 1792, the so-called "Year of the Sheep", they came here, eighty people and twelve families shoved off the Langwell estate to scrape a living in this God-forsaken place. That was the first tranche. The second came in 1804 when the crofters from Ousdale were evicted. The villain of the piece was Sir John Sinclair of Ulbster (1754-1835) who revolutionised the crofting way of life when he introduced the black-faced Cheviot to Scotland in 1792. He probably knew not what he did – that his methods would be emulated the length and breadth of the land.

And if it was a bad thing he did, full of unintended consequences, *he* wasn't all bad. He was the creator and first president of the Board of Agriculture and the compiler of the *Statistical Account of Scotland*, where ministers contributed a description of their parishes as well as certain facts about them. It's a great mirror into the past for historians. He also had the ear of Pitt the Younger, and had a good many other accomplishments to his name besides. I will not mention them apart from he established a society for the improvement of wool in which, of course, he had a vested interest.

There was another villain, if that's the right word – James Anderson, 1st of Rispond (1746-1828) on Loch Eribol on the north coast, where we will be tomorrow. Apart from his part in the Clearances, his claim to distinction in my view is that he was married three times, separated from his spouses by death not divorce, poor chap. Actually that's not it – it's the number of children he had that is remarkable.

By his first wife he had five sons; by his second, four sons and a daughter, the daughter coming second-last in the hierarchy. Now here's the really interesting thing – by his third wife (whom he married in 1793 when he was forty-seven), he had six daughters on the trot. The seventh child was a boy who was followed by two more girls before yet another boy was born. The last child, a daughter, was born in 1808. Although he lived for another twenty years after she was born, it seems James had finally twigged what was causing all these children. Or it might have had something to do with his wife, Barbara Gordon, who was forty-three by the time the last was born. Although nineteen years younger than James, she died two years before him, aged 61. Worn out probably.

And that, his part in the Clearances not withstanding, as far as I am concerned, is James Anderson's claim to fame: twenty-one children fathered and three wives buried. It's worth mentioning in the passing that child number nineteen, Georgina (b 1799), was an ancestor of Robert Louis Stevenson, the precise details of which I need not trouble you with. I also will not worry you with the finer details, but Barbara, the third wife, was distantly related in time to Jean Gordon, the second-hand wife of Alexander, the 12th Earl of Sutherland, having previously been married to the notorious Earl of Bothwell.

Here beneath my feet, the heather is scattered with stones, and here and there, some parts of walls still stand a few feet above the ground. These are the remains of the longhouses where these people lived, if you can call it "living". When they died, they were taken to Berriedale where you can see the stones they never saw, the ones that mark their final resting place. After such a life it must have seemed rich to die.

Chief amongst these was John Sutherland (1789-1864), Mr Badbea himself. That's what they called him, "John Badbea", rather than his real name. Self-appointed preacher and doctor to the community, he was said to have owned the only watch in the village which must have made him a man of distinction amongst these people who had next to nothing apart from the clothes they stood up in and the spinning wheel from which they could make new ones.

He had a brother, who died at Waterloo, and several sisters. His father died young and he took on the responsibility of caring for his siblings. Who would want to marry a man with a ready-made family like that? Marry me; marry my sisters. He never did receive an offer. He did, however, offer his house as a sort of church since a purpose-built establishment was miles and miles away. It was a hard-enough life without, on your day off, having to tramp miles through the heather to give thanks to the Lord for all your blessings. He had a full house. Mind you, it wouldn't take many to fill it.

He died at 75, which just goes to show you hard work never killed anyone. Not a bad age for those days, considering the circumstances. He was buried at Berriedale where several hundred mourners came from all over to pay their last respects. He is also commemorated on the memorial stone, along with some others.

To enhance your visit, several noticeboards combine an artist's impression with photographs of some of the people who lived here. The one at the start shows a woman with her head in her hands, a study of despair. Another shows a photograph of the village taken in 1903, and pretty bleak it looks too. Beneath it is another photograph of some well-fed women in a fishing boat who appear to be loading creels with the catch, the main source of sustenance. There were thirteen boats (they look little bigger than rowing boats) at the nearest landing place along the coast to the north at Berriedale. What little the ground yielded, no-one was going to starve with that harvest from the sea on the doorstep.

And then in the 1850s along came the new laird, Donald Horne, who put an end to that in favour of the more profitable salmon fishing in the river. It was a bad day for Badbea. With even fewer jobs available, emigration was the only answer.

And so we take our leave of Badbea too. For drivers from across the seas who are used to wide, flat and open roads with scarcely a bend to be negotiated, the Berriedale Braes might provoke something in the manner of a slight challenge when first they see it, their fears possibly increased rather than allayed by the sight of an emergency escape lane, where, in the event of brake failure, your vehicle will grind to a halt in feet of gravel. Past that, the road descends steeply towards a hairpin bend at the bottom before immediately rising again, even more steeply, at another hairpin bend and then another before it continues to the top.

And as you do that, please try and spare a thought for the women of Badbea who had to walk all the way down here, but which was as nothing to the trek back uphill laden with a full creel of herring on their backs. Dear God, to be born for that!

You will probably be too busy thinking about that or negotiating the Braes, but – if you dare – spare a glimpse over to your right where you might be able to catch sight of a couple of towers. These were built by the new laird, the eccentic and reclusive the 5th Duke of Portland (1800-79) who bought the estate from Donald Horne for £90,000 in 1856. In his estate at Welbeck Abbey in Nottinghamshire, the Duke constructed a vast underground complex, while up above, he had the rooms stripped of furniture, paintings and tapestries that he put into storage while he rattled around in a suite of five rooms which, like the rooms below ground, were all painted pink. And contrary to what you may think, the towers on the headland are not the remains of his castle in the north. Locally, they are known as the "Duke's Candelsticks", lighthouses actually, built to guide fishermen into the mouth of the river. On a projecting spur you might just be able to make out the remains of the actual castle which has been around since the beginning of the 14th century, if not before.

Having safely negotiated the Braes, we need the brakes again as we sweep down, gathering speed, towards Dunbeath, from the Gaelic "fort of the birches" or "fort of the chief called Beth", but not the same one immortalised by Shakespeare. Take your pick. It is an ancient landscape well steeped in history with the remains of a monastery, a castle, chambered cairns, hut circles and brochs – and if that weren't quite enough already, it has a river running through it.

It's the birthplace of that prolific author Neil M. Gunn (1891-1973) and the setting for many of his books, although he left these parts when he was only twelve. The primary school he attended is now the heritage centre and museum. From the front door you can see his boyhood home, now grown taller, just as boys tend to do, with another storey added to the cottage he knew as a boy.

The river, actually Dunbeath Water, is the source of inspiration for the way the museum is presented to the visitor. From the harbour to its source, you are given a buzzard's eye view of its serpentine course which has been painted on the floor. Along the "banks" are quotes from *Highland River* as well as images inspired by the places described, giving the visitor an overview of the landscape and its inhabitants.

For Kenn, the main protagonist in the novel, his physical journey up river to its source is also a symbolic journey, not just back to his childhood but to a simpler time, to a more innocent time, to a time when Man was more in touch with nature. It's a deliberate contrast to the First World War from the carnage of which the adult Kenn has just returned, and where the narrative is not linear but, like the river, twists and turns between childhood memories (by no means always idyllic) and adult horrors of the recent past.

Each museum has its star and the star of this museum, arguably, is the 7th century Ballachly Stone which was found in 1996 near the aptly-named Chapel Hill, the site of the former monastery. It is given a place of honour in a dedicated room, "The Shrine Room", which has a specially tiled floor.

The design on the broken stone has a cross with curly arms which some experts think looks like the Greek letter "Rho". This, with the cross itself, forms the first two letters of "Christ" in Greek. What's more, they argue, you can just about make out the faint outline of a salmon in the top-right corner, swimming towards those enveloping arms. As I need scarcely point out, for the early and persecuted Christians, the sign of the fish meant they were among like-minded dissident thinkers. Others suggest the curly ends might represent the sun and the moon. Who knows? But if you would like to know what I think (and you probably don't), the second I clapped eyes on it, I thought straight away of a pair of ovaries and a uterus. Wouldn't it be a laugh if some future scholars said that's exactly what it was – a fertility symbol?

In a glass case are some artefacts from a plane crash on August 25th 1942 which involved the Duke of Kent, the first member of the royal family to be killed on active service for five hundred years. Isn't that an incredible thing! He was only 39 and on a mission to Iceland. There were fifteen aboard the Sunderland Flying Boat when it crashed at Eagle's Rock near here, and ironically only the tail gunner, who normally occupied the seat of death, survived. There are more conspiracy theories surrounding this crash than you can shake a joystick at, and probably that's just exactly what they are.

What is beyond dispute is he was the younger brother of Edward VIII and George VI, and before his untimely death led a very colourful life. A cocaine user, if not addict, he had a string of (alleged) lovers, male or female, he wasn't fussy – Barbara Cartland, Jessie Mathews, Noel Coward and Antony Blunt, the Soviet spy, to name just a few. And they made such a fuss when Prince Charles had a wee cherry brandy when he was at boarding school at Gordonstoun!

Here you can find information on the history of Dunbeath Castle, of which more presently, and the Neolithic sites of Camster Cairns and the Hill o' Many Stanes which we'll be visiting later. You can also see Neil Gunn's typewriter and some of his books, but if you go down to the harbour you will see a statue of the boy Kenn, bent double under the weight of an enormous salmon on his back. It reminds me of Wilfrid Owen's simile from *Dulce et Decorum Est,* "bent double, like old beggars under sacks" – very apposite considering what the adult Kenn would face before he was very much older.

From here there is a good view, across the water, to where the splendid Dunbeath Castle sits like an eagle in its eyrie above the precipitous cliffs. It's worth coming down here just to admire it, even if you have no interest at all in a statue of a fictional character from a book you've never read.

A fortified building was known to have existed on the site since 1428. In 1633, Sir John Sinclair built a four-storey tower house which, in 1650, played a minor part in Scottish history when James Graham, Marquess of Montrose, Lieutenant-Governor of Scotland and Commander-in-Chief of the Army, landed in Orkney with troops from the continent, bent on restoring the exiled Charles II to the throne. Strengthened by recruits, his army crossed the Pentland Firth to John o' Groats and marched south, hoping to gain more on the way. Getting wind of this, Sir John, not being a fan of the Stuarts, galloped south to Edinburgh to spread the alarm, leaving his wife in charge of the castle. No greater love hath a man for Cromwell and his country than he abandon his home and castle, leaving his wife to cope with the enemy threat.

After a siege lasting several days, she and her loyal servants were forced to surrender to Montrose's deputy, General Hurry. That done, the general rushed off to rendezvous with his commander at the Ord of Caithness, leaving the castle under the command of Major Whiteford. After Montrose was defeated at Carbisdale on April 27th 1650, David Leslie, the Cromwellian general, dispatched troops, which included the 14th Earl of Sutherland's regiments, to retake the castle. At this time it had a moat and like something out of Enid Blyton, a spiral staircase, now blocked up, that leads to a cave which, at certain times and tides, is flooded by the sea. In the event, the castle was retaken by cutting off the water supply. It's easy when you know how.

Sir John died the following year, and I will not trouble you with his descendants and the rest of the history of the castle except to say that more modifictions followed in 1853 and 1881 until it is as we see it today, another masterpiece of the Scots Baronial style. Then after more than three centuries of Sinclair ownership, Admiral Sir Edwyn Alexander-Sinclair sold the castle in 1945. It changed hands a few more times after that before becoming the property of R. Stanton Avery, an American millionaire who made a fortune by inventing the sticky label in 1935. He died in 1997 just a month short of his ninetieth birthday. Pity he couldn't have stuck around for just a month longer.

The next and present owner of this very desirable residence was and is Stuart Wyndham Murray-Threipland. It is not open to the public, but once a year in August, on Garden Day, you can visit the two walled gardens, which also gives you a chance to see the castle from an unusual perspective – its façade.

The Murray-Threiplands were staunch Jacobite sympathisers. The Old Pretender, during his unsuccessful uprising in 1715, stayed with the Murray-Threiplands at Fingask Castle in Perthshire. As a token of his gratitude, he showered them with gifts. Thirty years later, another Stuart Murray-Threipland was Bonnie Prince Charlie's physician during *his* unsuccessful uprising, and who also emulated his father in the matter of bestowing gifts.

It's nice to be appreciated, so I am told.

Chapter Twenty-Two

Laidhay and Latheron: The Longhouse and The Jawbone

ONLY a few miles further on we stop at the Laidhay Croft museum. Although there are a number of cars in the car park, we have the longhouse all to ourselves. The owners must be in the nearby tearoom. There is no entry fee, only an honesty box with a suggested amount.

It looks very attractive from the outside with its whitewashed walls, pillarbox red doors and windows as well as its thatched roof, weighed down with slabs of slate to keep its hair on so to speak. It appeals to the sense of the romantic within us and of a bygone age; but what would it have actually been like to have lived in such a house? We are just about to find out.

Astonishingly, the croft was still occupied until 1968 when William Biel, the last occupant, died. In 1974 it re-opened as a museum. It's not an attempt to recreate the longhouse at any particular period, more an exhibition of the sort of everyday objects the people who lived in this area used in the past. I hope they kept an inventory as the exhibits came in. I wouldn't care to be given the job of starting one now for its range really is staggering, a real potpourri of items.

Here is a wind-up gramophone for instance, and at the other end of the spectrum, so to speak, a porcelain slipper bedpan. It is shaped just like the sort of thing Cinderella might have worn to the ball, only much larger. I hope the day never dawns when I have need of such a thing, regardless of how comfortable it looks. Apart from the loss of dignity, it looks extremely cold to the touch. But here is something which did give me a great deal of comfort in the winter nights of my boyhood when the frost was so thick on the *inside* of my bedroom window that I had to scrape it off with my penknife (an indispensible item in every schoolboy's pocket in those days), to see outside. It is a stone pig, or hot water bottle, so called because of its carrying handle or snout. You know you are getting old when you see things from your past in a museum.

The longhouse construction is most probably a legacy from those neighbours from hell, the Vikings, who dwelt in such houses a matter of a few hundred miles across the North Sea highway. And the Laidhay Croft *is* long, without any exaggeration. 105 feet and 5 inches to be precise. It is also two hundred years old, so it gives us a pretty good idea of what the houses in Badbea would have looked like when the Bethune family came here in 1842. It had sixteen arable acres attached, and rights to graze on a further fifteen. It's the two chimneys that tell you this is a very desirable residence, a much-improved dwelling from its predecessors, the blackhouses, or further back still, the brochs, which, as I am sure you will remember, had a peat fire in the middle of the room – and no chimney.

Nor did they have any windows, in the early days. Well, why would you, if you didn't have any glass? And, as we had seen at the cottage on Culloden battlefield, at the gable ends, the stone walls were not continued to the rafters. After a height of only a few feet, they were built up with divots of turf while the roof was made of the same material and covered with straw or rushes, held in place with ropes made of twisted straw with boulders at the end to weigh them down.

Cupboards, called "aumries", made of stone, were set into the wall and sideboards, or dressers, were made of slate, as were the beds, with heather or straw to lie on. Should a resident from the 3000 BC Neolithic village of Skara Brae on Orkney, just on the other side of the Pentland Firth, somehow be transported here through time and space, he would have found himself quite at home. Welcome to early 18th century life in the Highlands.

By the end of the century, however, things were beginning to look up. There still were no windows, but they did have a skylight of sorts; in other words, a hole in the roof which doubled as a kind of chimney, although its efficacy as a flue was rather reduced by its being offset from the fire. It just wouldn't do if the dearly-wrought fire was put out by the rain. In really inclement weather, when all you wanted to do was huddle round the fire, the hole in the roof would be plugged with heather. Given the northerly location of Caithness and its exposure to the bitter, biting winds from the north and east, it's no wonder the walls were soon black with smoke.

They all lived happily together, in a long stone house, the people and the animals, entering by the same door and with no wall to divide them. Once you got used to the smell, and actually you probably no longer noticed it, the animals would have been an additional source of heat. And for extra cosiness, they cleverly built one gable end to face the prevailing wind and if possible, the animals' quarters were built at the downward end of a slope for reasons that you can easily imagine.

By the time the Bethune family came here, things were getting better, but it still would also have been very dark because there were no windows at the back of the house, only the front, and they weren't very big either. To help prevent the residents from bumping into each other in the gloom, they gave the interior walls a wash of lime every so often, and it helped to give a little cough to let people know you were near so they didn't trample you underfoot, especially if you were just a little person.

There were two fireplaces with chimneys and a designated kitchen and scullery, with a separate door for the animals and two multi-purpose rooms for eating and sleeping. Privacy would have been at a premium at night, but once you had clambered into your boxbed and pulled the curtain behind you, that would have given you a certain amount of that rare and precious commodity, even if it would have been no defence against snoring. It certainly would have been cosy sleeping with your siblings in such a bed, a double in name only.

The floor is, and was, of flagstones, and if there is one thing there is not a shortage of in Caithness, then it is flagstones. The streets of London as everyone knows, and as Dick Whittington found out, are not paved with gold, but a good number of them are with Caithness slate. And here's a tip, Londoners: if you want the patch of pavement outside your house to look nice, wash your slates with buttermilk to bring up the blue sheen. That's what Mrs Bethune did and she should know; she and her descendants lived here long enough.

At the west end (normally considered the up-market end of a city, and it may tell us something about the pecking order of the livestock), the horse or horses were stabled and at the east end, the cattle. As for the chickens, they had to make do with perching on the rafters. Since none was house-trained, there was a handy drainage trough in the middle of the floor, which was cobbled lest you slipped, and cunningly positioned to catch the deposits. And at the gable end, not a tiny window, but a hatch through which the manure was shovelled outside to form a midden heap until it was ready to be used as fertiliser. Great idea: a lot better than carting it out through the house.

The byre also served as a smiddy and carpenter's workshop. Versatile. It was in the workshop that a piece of furniture peculiar to Caithness was made – the Caithness chair. As anyone who has travelled through this landscape knows, trees are rather thin on the ground: no forests and no woods apart from the odd squadron of soldier pines which are a recent addition. Unfortunately wood *does* grow on trees, which means it is rather difficult to find any to make things out of that material. Which is why so many are made out of driftwood, and the seat has a gap at the front so no more wood is used than is strictly necessary. They were also very low, so the occupants – arthritic joints permitting – could sit around the fire beneath the smoke. It also made a very handy rail to hang clothes on to dry in front of the fire. Children were not allowed such a luxury. They either sat on the floor or stools called "creepies".

Their diet was sparse and Spartan, and it would have come to no surprise to Dr Johnson that it was based upon that versatile cereal – oats. It was kept dry in a chest called a "girnel" and, when ground into meal, just look at the sort of things you could do with it! Oatmeal with everything, any time of day. For breakfast or lunch – brose when mixed with water; or gruel, a watered-down version of the same; or porridge when made with milk. For supper, "sowans" when mixed with sour milk (though why would you want to, except not to waste anything), and which you would eat with a spoon made of wood or horn. You could have a bannock or oatcake along with your kail, or curly cabbage, which you would eat off a plate of slate (crockery did not appear in Caithness, as far as the poor were concerned, until the 19th century). And thanks to Sir John Sinclair, who introduced the potato and swedes in the latter part of the 18th century, there was "clapshot"; a mash of tatties and neeps. To wash it down, there was a plentiful supply of Adam's ale or the one you brewed yourself.

For those who lived in houses like this, but near the coast, fish was a ready source of protein – herring, coalfish and shellfish. You couldn't afford to kill your cow until her calf had grown up, but you might bleed her neck and catch the blood to mix with your oatmeal, and anyone who is partial to a bit of black pudding would be a hypocrite if the sound of that makes you turn up your nose. By the 19th century, the herring was finding its way, fresh(ish) to the inland crofts, where if it wasn't eaten then, it was dried for later.

Here, at Laidhay, in the 20th century, a detached barn was built with a cruck roof (so much more attractive than a straight A frame, and more roomy – and from which we get our word "crooked"), and also a cart shed. You can see farm implements such as a threshing machine and a carriage and some other pieces of machinery scattered about outside if that sort of stuff interests you, if you have a particular interest in crofting, as it used to be done in the past.

The next place of interest along the way is the intriguingly named Latheronwheel. It comes from the Gaelic *Latharn a' Phuil*, meaning "muddy place of the pool", which just goes to show you certain words are best not translated at all. Originally, the owner of the land, a certain Captain Dunbar, wanted to call the tiny settlement "Janetstown" after his wife, which might have got him a certain amount of brownie points with her, but "Latheronwheel" has a far better ring to it as long as you don't know what it means. Actually you will see both names mentioned on the maps. It was begun in 1835 and the harbour was built in 1840 with a lighthouse, and was once home to, incredibly, fifty boats.

A little further on is the altogether larger metropolis of Latheron (*Làthair Ròin,* "place of the seals"), not that it is of any size, just a few houses and a Post Office and a church, home to the Clan Gunn Heritage Society which, unless you are a Gunn or a son of a Gunn, you may choose to skip as there is so much else awaiting you on the NC500. The Gunns claim their descent from the Norse Jarls of Orkney, so if you are a Gunn or merely interested in the Viking heritage of this area, you will almost certainly want to stop and spend a little time with the past.

Here's an interesting thing you will learn there, if it weren't for me just about to tell you. It is claimed the 1st Earl of Orkney, Henry Sinclair, and Sir James Gunn sailed to the Americas as long ago as 1398, nearly a century before Columbus "discovered" it in the *Santa María.* In any case, his first landfall was in the Bahamas and Hispaniola (Cuba) anyway, and what's more, he never actually ever set foot on the North American continent in any of his four voyages. And Columbus and his men, in their turn, as everyone knows, were three centuries behind the Vikings in their longships.

In another first, and a dubious honour, the Gunns claim Sir James was the first European to be buried on (and in) the new continent at a place now called Westford, Massachusetts. This proud boast is based on a headstone depicting a medieval knight in full armour, armed with a sword and shield bearing the Clan Gunn crest – a hand wielding a sword framed by a buckled belt, on which is written the motto *Aut Pax Aut Bellum* (Either Peace or War).

Far be it for me to spoil the party, but I have looked into this matter and my researches would seem to show that that distinction should really be awarded to Thorvald Eriksson, son of Erik the Red and less famous brother of Leif, who was killed by an arrow in Vinland (probably Newfoundland and Labrador) in 1004. We don't know what happened to his body, alas. His brother, Thorstein, set out to repatriate it but he died in Greenland before his mission could be accomplished. Even so, there must have been lots of Norsemen who died there in the years following Thorvald's death and, even if they were cremated as was the Viking custom, they sometimes buried the ashes rather than scattered them. That surely counts as a burial, doesn't it?

Once upon a time, here in Caithness, there must have been a body of gargantuan dimensions, if what remains of it is anything to go by, but what happened to it and where the rest of its bones lie I do not know. However, I can tell you, if you keep your eyes open – on your right, before you come to the former church, now the museum – you will see the jawbone of a whale. It would make a fitting lych gate for a church and indeed there is a gate beneath this pointed arch, but it's only of the traditional five-barred sort and it doesn't lead to a church but a field. But after the Disruption, barns and other buildings, as in Resolis, served as places of worship – yet often it was just the open air that served as the dissident ministers' house of God.

Perhaps this was a gateway to a church after all.

Chapter Twenty-Three

Camster Cairns to Cairn o' Get: Stepping into the Past

HAVING come off the A99 to Wick, we're now following the single-track road to the Grey Cairns of Camster, as straight as any road the Romans built, though this is a mere youngster, dating only from the 19th century, to connect Lybster with Wick.

We make good speed as there are few other road users, just a few pedestrians who obligingly move their fat posteriors into the side to let us pass, whilst those who are devouring the delicious grass at the side of the road don't even bother to look up. If there's one thing you can trust them not to do, it's to suddenly dart across the road in front of you where they think the grass is greener. They may never win *Mastermind,* but generations of exposure to the internal combustion engine means these sheep have at least learned road sense, which is more than can be said for some of our children.

The road widens out at the cairns to afford some parking for visitors and from where you can see your objective in the near distance – two enormous mounds of stones. One is round, the other is elongated like a petrified grey slug caught in the act of rippling its way along the ridge. There is a third pile some distance off to the left but not considered to be part of the complex, and thus it is dismissed, although it is the first we visit by means of a boardwalk over extremely boggy ground. It gives me an uneasy feeling that if I were to fall in by inadvertently tripping over my shoelace (which has a habit of coming undone), I would never be seen again.

It's quite breathtaking to see so many stones gathered together in one place, but of course that's not the really awesome thing at all – it's the sheer skill of the people who built these monuments to honour their dead 5,000 years ago. They are actually chambered cairns with corbelled roofs. To get inside you have to crouch or crawl along a narrow passage. If you have a tendency towards claustrophobia, you will try not to think about the enormous weight of stones above your head without an iota of cement to bind them together. As a matter of fact, a French governess got stuck in a passageway here in the 19th century and they had to dismantle the stones from the top and lift her out.

The round cairn on the left is 60 feet in diameter and 12 feet high. Once it was surrounded by kerb stones which have now gone. Inside, divided into three chambers, archaelogists found the floor covered in a one-foot deep layer of black earth, ash, flint tools, and human and animal bones. But to my mind, here's the most interesting thing; the dead had been buried in an upright position – and their legs were missing. I suppose it makes sense: there was only a limited amount of room and so many people queuing up to join them, which in those days was probably not too long in the future.

The "slug" is 200 feet long, with horns at either end and tapers towards the tail. It is encircled by a low, narrow, platform, while between the horns at the "head" there was another, much wider platform which has been grassed over. There would have been another at the "tail" end which has disappeared. Two passageways give access into the chambers which, the experts tell us, would once have been two separate, round chambers. Indeed, there might well be a third. The north chamber, when excavated, revealed a pottery shard and some bone fragments; the southern, some ash and bone.

And there's something else: people had been coming here long before the cairn builders. Archaelogists found, beneath the southern end of the long cairn, a number of burnt areas containing pottery and flint which they reckon predate the cairns by a couple of millenia. Isn't that incredible! It seems an inhospitable place now but, we are told, the climate was warmer then and the present peat bog was scrubland. It would have to have been.

You can hardly move in these parts before coming across one Neolithic site or another, and that's exactly what we are about to do. It's back the way we came to the A99 for our next destination, the Hill o' Many Stanes, where, like cockleshells laid out in a row, hundreds of stones peek over the heather and gorse.

It's though these stones have been here for almost as long as the Camster Cairns – about 4,000 years. It has been suggested they are some sort of astronomical calculator, or a Pictish graveyard or some sort of form of ancestor worship. Which just goes to show you no-one really has a clue. It's an enigma, and – in my view – all the more intriguing for that.

Today there are 192 stones left standing, in 22 rows, laid out in a fan shape, like a necklace draping the side of the hill which slopes down towards the glittering sea. If you look along the lines you will see not all of them are perfectly straight, and to which I do not think we should read any arcane purpose. But what do I know?

Caithness has many more sites such as these but this is the biggest, the best preserved, not only in Caithness but in the entire British Isles. It reminds me of Carnac in Brittany, a sort of miniature replica, a stone Legoland. They are small, many only knee high, which, unless you are a grasshopper, is not very high at all. A writer who visited at the end of the 19th century counted over 400 stones, while the experts, working it out from the existing pattern, think there were possibly three times as many as there are now. Impressive now, it would have been even more impressive then.

How many primitive people does it take to erect a knee-high standing stone? Fortunately a noticeboard supplies the answer. Three. One man to dig a hole with a spade made from the shoulderbone of an ox or an ass, another to manoeuvre the stone into place, and another man to stand over them to make sure they are doing it right. He's probably the head honcho, because he is wearing a fur cloak and a necklace composed of several strings. He is leaning on a spear which is planted on the ground. Catch him getting his hands dirty: he didn't get where he got today by planting stones that never grew any taller. Nearby is a pile of little stones with which to pack the base, just as at the Eagle Stone in Strathpeffer, only they used boulders there to prevent the predicted calamity by the Brahan Seer.

Step we gaily, on we go. We are heading for the Whaligoe Steps. There are 365 of them (or there used to be), one for every day of the year as I am sure I don't need to tell you. They were created about 1792 by the laird, David Brodie, at a cost of £8 and the name comes from "whale" and "goe", the latter

betraying its Viking roots. A "goe" means a rocky inlet, and there must have been a whale washed up here at some time in the past, as at Latheron which is how they came by the jawbone.

The locals keep the whereabouts of the Steps a closely guarded secret. There is no sign, but there is, fortunately, one to Cairn o' Get, and that is how you get to the Steps – by following the road on the other side of the crossroads. And a very impressive sight they are too as they snake down the precipitous cliff face with at times no more that a foot between you and the rocks so very, very far below. You really ought to go to the steps of Whaligoe – unless you suffer from vertigo.

The height from top to bottom is 250 feet, and at the bottom you can still see the rusty winch that was used to haul the boats high and dry onto the beach. You can also see what the fishermen called the "barking kettle". It's a round, stone-built tank where they used to preserve their nets from the corrosive effects of the salt water by immersing them in a heated solution of water and conifer bark and cones.

Higher up is the "bink", a flat grassy area which reminds me very much of a miniature Inca terrace. At the end of it are the ruins of a building – the former salt store for the curing of the herring. At its height, twenty boats would have come here dropping off the catch, salt, and empty barrels and taking away the full ones. By 1920 there were five boats; by 1960 there were none. Amazing to me there were any.

Before you leave the steps, just stop a minute, look back down the way you have come and this *will* knock the breath out of you, even if you are fitter than the proverbial fiddle and you are not breathing any harder than usual. As you take in the steepness of steps, think this: think of the hardy women who carried the creels laden with herring on their backs, like Kenn and the salmon, all the way up those steps. These creels could weigh up to a hundredweight – eight stones, or to put it another way, for those of you who are too young to know about such things, fifty kilos. But that was just the beginning. After that there was the seven-mile walk to Wick to try and sell them. And you would hope you would, as it would mean a lighter load on the way back before you got down to cooking the evening meal (of herring) for your husband and the kids. They don't make them like that any more.

Whilst I get my breath back, I stop and take in the scenery, but given that they had seen it so many times before, it wouldn't surprise me in the slightest if they just kept their heads down and plodded on and on and up and up under their heavy loads, like donkeys in places like Santorini today. Remind me, who is meant to be the weaker sex?

Still puffing, carrying no load at all, we cross the main road to the Cairn o' Get.

It's a bit of a hike to where it sits at the top of the hill, though nothing like as steep, and if you've visited the Camster Cairns beforehand, and you are not much given to exercise for its own sake, you might well find it something of a disappointment. It's built to the same design as those at Camster, but reduced now to a roofless, grassy mound. However, you can still see the stone passageway with its circular stone core. At the time it was in use, scholars think it would have been fifteen feet high. Sometime later, horns were added to form a U shape at either end of the passageway (think of an H with a curvy crossbar), and on stone platforms between the horns, ceremonies would have been performed.

At some time much later, the roof collapsed, which, in a way, was a good thing for us, as it sealed in what lay below – the unburnt bones of seven individuals and – beneath them – burnt and unburnt human bones, some pottery and flint arrowheads. According to the noticeboard, a very pretty pink flint arrowhead is attributed to coming from here, although there is no firm evidence to say it actually did.

Later still, so the noticeboard informs us, stones were removed to build a nearby dam to feed a watermill. That's progress and we are moving on too, finished with Neolithic stones – for the present.

Chapter Twenty-Four

Wick: The Inventor, The Photographers, and The Edible Object

AND so, leaving the past behind, we arrive in Wick in time for lunch. And where better to go for people like us on the historical trail than Wetherspoon's?

As I mentioned earlier, the chain likes to reflect local history in its choice of name – in this instance, the "Alexander Bain". The said gentleman was born in Watten, a little village near here, in 1811. (My mother used to live there, in Bain Place, as it happens.) He left school with little prospects and, more by good luck than good management, found himself apprenticed to a clockmaker, not far from this very pub as a matter of fact. His claim to fame is he invented the electric clock in 1841. Not a lot of people know that, I suspect.

As well as that, Bain also invented a whole range of electrical instruments which I won't try your patience with by bothering to name. Suffice it to say he lodged twenty-one patents in the UK and eleven in the US. Despite this, he became bankrupt in 1852 and depended on charity for the last twenty-five years of his life. He died at Kirkintilloch in 1877 in the ghastly-named "Home for Incurables". The sad truth is, unless we meet our demise by some sort of calamity such as being run over by a bus, we all die of something incurable sooner or later. We call them "hospices" now which, although it sounds kinder, doesn't fool anybody.

In addition to claiming one of Scotland's most prolific inventors, the "Weekers" – as they are called by their rivals in Thurso – also claim to have the shortest street in Britain. Now that is very interesting indeed, as Falkirk (my home town) claims *it* has the honour and it must be true because there is a plaque on the street that says so.

This "street" is really just a front door, the entrance to the Bistro in Mackay's Hotel, the premier hotel in Wick. If you would care to picture it, think of the Flatiron Building in New York, only not half so impressive. With

Union Street to the right and River Street to left, that doorway is just wide enough to display a brass plaque on either side proclaiming it to be No. 1. Near the top of the Dutch-style gable end is written "Ebenezer Place" and, below that, on the lintel over the window, a date – 1883. And there you have it.

What happened was when Alexander Sinclair built the hotel, the Town Council – as such institutions are prone to do – stuck its nose in and said he had to give this little frontage a name. I don't know who Ebeneezer was, and maybe Alexander was dyslexic or maybe it was a form of protest, but that's how Ebenezer Place came about and in 1887 the Council officially declared it a street. In 2006 the *Guinness Book of Records* awarded it the title.

Now we are in the award-winning Wick Heritage Museum at 18-27 Bank Row, which celebrates the life and times of what they quite rightly and without exaggeration call the "herring capital of Europe". The harbour, actually Pulteney Harbour, and yet another Thomas Telford creation, was built in 1808.

Pulteney, originally consisting of an upper and lower town, was incorporated into the burgh of Wick in 1902 and is still home to the Old Pulteney distillery and once also was the home of Caithness Glass which famously made the *Mastermind* trophy. The name "Pulteney", which needs no introduction to those who know their Bath and their Jane Austen, comes from Sir William Pulteney (1725-1805) a contender, along with the Duke of Sutherland, for the title of the richest man in Britain. He was born William Johnstone but changed his name in 1767 after his wife, Frances Pulteney, inherited firstly, the 1st Earl of Bath's estates in 1764 and then those of his younger brother's in 1767. No greater love hath a man for his heiress wife that he change his name to hers. In 1794, he was known as the 5th Baronet Pulteney after the death of his older brother, James.

Ten years after its creation, there were 822 boats plying their trade from Pulteney Harbour. That was just the beginning. By 1860 there were 1,100. The biggest ever catch was on 23rd August 1864 when 976 boats landed 24,000 crans of herring which, in a neat mathematical arrangement, amounted to 24 million herring. In 1867, it's claimed that in two days, 3,500 women gutted 50 million herring. They must have seen fish guts in their sleep – or, should I say, nightmares. But by the 1930s it was all over. Incredible, given the enormity of that scale of death, the industry lasted as long as it did.

The season began in July and lasted for three months. The shoals began their migration from Norway and were tracked by thousands of migratory workers as the poor, benighted fish made their way down the east coast of Scotland and as far south as Norfolk. In a not very clever move on their part, some species of herring hatch in the spring, others in summer and yet others in autumn. A herring for all seasons.

During the Wick season, the population would be swollen by as many as 6,000. Even now, the population stands at a little over 7,000 souls. This huge influx of population needed to be accommodated somewhere. The fishermen would sleep on their boats, the gutters, wherever they could find – in people's houses, in their attics, cellars, even their sheds. Most, however, slept in dormitories above the fish-curing buildings. Their belongings – their change of clothes, practically all their worldly goods – travelled in a box called a "kist" by boat. The owners, however, had to find another way. Sailors are a superstitious lot, and it was considered bad luck for women in that world of men to be aboard.

Arguably, the jewel in the crown of the museum, the thing that makes it really special, is all facets of local life, not just of Wick's past, but also the past of rural Caithness, have been documented and preserved for posterity by three generations of Johnstons – the brothers Alex and James; Alex's son, William, and his son, Alexander. Photographing pioneers, on glass-plate negatives, they took nearly 100,000 photographs of which 50,000 survive, a good many of which are displayed in the museum.

Probably the most interesting subject of all, the herring industry, has been documented from first to last: preparing the boats, hoisting the sails, landing the catch, the gutting and packing into barrels. It also records those associated with the trade – the coopers, the rope makers, the basket weavers and so on. In fact, you are given a mouth-watering taste of the Johnstons' work before you even enter the museum, with huge reproductions on the wall outside. It really is beyond astonishing. I would have said "belief", but seeing is believing. At first glance, one scene reminds me of the Tunguska event in Siberia in 1908. I'm sure you'll know the photograph I am thinking about – a scene of utter devastation, trees flattened for miles around as if someone had tipped a box of matchsticks onto the floor, with some, bizarrely, still standing upright, rooted to the spot. This apocalyptic scene was probably the result of a meteor exploding in the atmosphere above it.

This photograph, taken in 1865, also looks as if a hurricane had blown in and denuded an entire forest of its leaves. In actual fact it's a blur of masts stripped of sails and so many boats you can hardly see the water, moored as they are, three deep around the perimeter of the harbour walls. It's hard to say if it's that or the barrels that grab your attention more. Barrels everywhere. More barrels than you thought could ever exist. Barrels standing on any part of the quay wherever there is an inch of space to accommodate their bulging girth, but most piled three tiers high or more on their sides, from end on looking like some gigantic honeycomb made by monstrous bees. In fact, pressure for space was so intense that barrels were stored as far upriver as the bridge – which, no prizes for guessing, was built by Telford. And when you realise each barrel contained between 800 and 1,000 fish, it's utterly staggering the seas should contain so many herring.

There is much else to see in the museum, which claims to be the largest in northern Scotland, and which I don't doubt for a moment despite what I think of the town's claim to have the smallest street. I have already pointed out the address needs nine numbers, and there are buildings out the back too. It has twenty-five rooms, some with period furniture spanning the first quarter of the 20th century, a lighthouse that works, a printing works (that looks as if it might), a schoolroom, a smiddy, a cooperage, a kippering kiln, a harbour display with real boats, a radio station (which began in 1908 and played a vital role during the First World War when it provided a link between the Grand Fleet in Scapa Flow and the Admiralty), a coastguard station, an art gallery, two gardens, displays of 19th century clothes including military uniforms, Caithness glass, and another speciality of the region – a Caithness "gansey", or fisherman's jersey.

One photograph shows a row of women knitting as they walked abreast on their way to work – as if they hadn't enough to do already. But there's something special about their knitting that can't be detected from this image. They designed their own patterns, and here's the vital thing – if a body was washed ashore, the face eaten by fishes, the poor soul could be identified by his woolly jumper.

There's more; much more than we have time to see properly, that's for sure. But what goes without saying is with all this and the Johnston collection as a sort of icing on the cake, Wick's past is well and truly documented.

Wick Castle, however, will not be winning any awards, not now or anytime soon. It stands on a windy and rocky spit of land well to the south of the town. So far out of town in fact, and the only way to get there by foot and through a Ministry of Defence rifle range to boot, we decide it is not worth the candle. In this wind it would certainly be snuffed out long before we got there anyway, if our lives were not. Just for the record, all that remains is a lonely broken finger of a tower, from this distance at least, looking like the remains of a broch, only squarer.

That's all that remains of the 12th century keep, known affectionately by the locals as "The Old Man of Wick". It's another record for the town, for the former castle has the distinction of being one of the first castles built in Scotland, dating from 1100 or thereabouts. It was probably built by the Earl of

Orkney, Harald Maddadson [[sic]] (c. 1136-1206), and if it sounds a trifle Scandinavian, you would be right. In Harald's days, Caithness, along with Orkney, was a southern province of the Vikings.

Harald, born in Orkney, was half-Gaelic through his father, Matad of Atholl, and half-Norse through his mother, Margaret, daughter of Earl Hakkon Pausson of Orkney. From 1158, Harald was the undisputed master of all Caithness, where neither the king of Norway or Scotland dare challenge his demesne.

If we considered the walk to the "Old Man" not really the best use of our time, it was well worth coming here just to see the rocks. This is Scotland's coast at its most ragged and craggy, the spits of land reaching for the sea like the toes of a dinosaur. It's on one of these that the castle stands. Impregnable from the sea, it was protected on the landward side by a double moat. Records of the castle are scant but, in 1569, it was captured by John Sinclair, the Master of Caithness, the same individual who was mentioned in dispatches for his part in the burning of Dornoch, you may remember. Like Dunbeath Castle, due to the besiegeds' lack of any water to drink, it fell after only eight days. Simple.

At my feet, a long way down, the precipitous rocks drop sheer to a flat shelf that slopes gradually to the north. The tide is out at the moment as I can tell from the stranded rockpools. It's as if the whole cliff face has been sliced through and then turned over on its side like a slice of cake. At high tide, it would be treacherous for any sailor unfamiliar with this coast: it could give the bottom of his vessel a very nasty scrape indeed.

Chapter Twenty-Five

Girnigoe Castle: Murder, Torture and Feud

B Y Papigoe and Staxigoe, we are on our way to Girnigoe Castle – or Castle Sinclair Girnigoe, to give it its full name – via Noss Head (where the lighthouse lamp we saw in the museum came from). Its name comes from the Old Norse *snos* meaning "nose". With a distance of twenty-five nautical miles, it first began flashing out its red or white light every twenty seconds in 1849. And if Thomas Telford's fingerprints are on practically every bridge and harbour in the Highlands, then the same can be said of the Stevenson family whose lighthouses are dotted all around the coast, some even far out at sea like the famous Bell Rock and Skerryvore lighthouses.

This particular one was built by Alan, the son of Robert, the brother of David and Thomas, lighthouse engineers every one. Thomas was the father of Robert Louis who disappointed his father enormously by not following him into the business, but as we know, the lad "done good" in the end. Near here, in the present car park in fact, there was a radio station during the Second World War, with nine masts like pylons listening in to, and intercepting messages from, the Nazis. They are gone now, as are the lighthouse keepers, but the cottages are home to the Clan Sinclair library.

As for the castle, it was the setting for at least two murders. We are not told if King Duncan in *Macbeth* saw any ravens as he made his way to his appointment with death, but on our way to Girnigoe we see lots – or are they crows? For if you aren't a bit of a birdman, it's hard to tell a carrion crow from a raven unless you see them together. The collective name for ravens is an "unkindness", whereas it's a "murder" of crows which would be more apposite for the castle we are about to visit. Perched on either side of the paling posts, they form a guard of honour as we drive down this narrow road in this treeless, featureless landscape. It's quite an unnerving sight and, having seen *The Birds*, I wouldn't care to walk down here without the protective umbrella of the car's steel and glass. But most sinister of all, they do not fly off at our approach, merely swivel their heads to follow our progress. Very, very spooky.

The castle has undergone many stages of development over the centuries, which you can readily understand thanks to a series of illustrated noticeboards. Pardon the history lesson, and I'll try to be brief, but you could say the castle's story begins with William Sinclair, 3rd Earl of Orkney and Shetland and also, from 1455, the 1st Earl of Caithness, a title bestowed upon him by James II. On the king's death in 1460, Margaret of Denmark, daughter of Christian 1st of Norway and Denmark, aged a tender four years, was betrothed to the new king, James III. They were married in 1469 when Margaret was thirteen and James was about nineteen. Christian had pledged Orkney and Shetland as her dowry, but it was never paid. The islands were forfeited; then two years later, in 1472, James forced Caithness to give up his castle in Kirkwall as well as his lands in Orkney. Not so much a king in the making but a king on the make. (Incidentally, the Earl's main seat was at Roslin Castle near Edinburgh and his lasting legacy, the wonderful Rosslyn chapel which all the world has heard of thanks to Dan Brown's *The Da Vinci Code*.)

The person really responsible for building this castle, in the years between 1475 and the end of the century, was the 2nd Earl, also called William Sinclair. He did not get much time to enjoy it: he was one of the 10,000 "Flowers of the Forest that wede away" at the battle of Flodden in 1513, where the new king, James IV, also perished.

It was here, at Girnigoe, you may be excused for having forgotten, the orphaned Alexander, the future 12th Earl of Sutherland, was made to marry Barbara, the daughter of George Sinclair, the 4th Earl of Caithness. After Alexander was rescued, the Earl dispatched his son, John, the Master, on a punitive raid to Dornoch. The Murrays surrendered the castle on condition they were allowed to leave peacefully, which they were, apart from three hostages whom Alexander Sutherland, the 8th Laird of Duffus, promptly beheaded in contravention of the agreement. Immediately after his act of treachery, Duffus sickened and later died, haunted by terrible visions. The curse of St Gilbert strikes again.

As far as the Earl was concerned, the Master's leniency towards the Murrays convinced him that he and MacKay of Strathnaver were plotting against him. He therefore inveigled John to Girnigoe and silenced the Master's voice by throwing him in the dungeons for seven years. After a plot to free him was foiled by his own brother, William of Mey, John, despite his fetters and malnourishment, managed to kill him when he came to gloat, by crushing him to death. He was supposed to have possessed a strength of legendary proportions.

Naturally this did nothing to restore him to favour in the eyes of his dear papa. Indeed, his death was expedited by being put on a diet of salt beef with not a drop to drink. He died, mad of thirst, in 1577.

His loving father died in 1582 and John's son, George, succeeded to the title as 5th Earl. He was known as the "Wicked", which is a bit rich considering what his grandfather got up to, but – apart from his perpetual feud with the Sutherlands – he amassed a great many others by his tyrannical actions. His first act was to personally put his father's jailers to death, running one through with his sword and shooting the other.

In 1588, he successfully withheld a 12-day siege from Alexander, the 12th Earl of Sutherland, aforesaid. It's ironic in a way that Alexander did not think of cutting off the water supply so that George, like his father, died of thirst. Maybe he did, only it just wasn't possible or the well was too deep.

Anyway, George went on from strength to strength and did a bit of home improvement to Girnigoe such as adding an ornate oriel window, private chambers and a banqueting hall. In 1606, by an Act of Parliament, Girnigoe's name was changed to Castle Sinclair. In actual fact, it is known by both names today in the best double-barrelled aristocratic tradition. George also repaired Keiss Castle along the bay a bit, and which had been attacked by Alexander at the same time as his unsuccessful conquest of Girnigoe.

Naturally such building works don't come cheap. However deep his well might have been, his pockets were not. To cover his debts, George literally began making a mint, coining it, going into the forging business. In 1623 he was declared a rebel by James VI and forced to flee the country. He died in 1643 and his son and grandson, Lord Berriedale and the Master of Berriedale respectively, having predeceased him, his debts and title were passed on to his great-grandson, also named George. No greater love hath a fond great-grandfather for a great-grandson than he pass on his name, his title and debts to him, but the greatest of these are his debts.

Saddled with this inheritance, this George, the 6th Earl, had a different, but not entirely original method of clearing them. Reader, in 1657 he married Mary Campbell, a daughter of one of his chief creditors, Archibald Campbell, the Marquess of Argyll. It wasn't enough. In 1661 and 1672 he made two dispositions in favour of Archibald's son, Sir John Campbell of Glenorchy, under the terms of which he mortgaged his lands and title. He died in 1677 without producing an heir and his estate and title passed to Glenorchy, who, for good measure, also claimed the hand of George's merry widow the following year.

The Privy Council, acting on a ruling by four of the foremost lawyers of the day, and despite one of them being a Sinclair – Sir Robert Sinclair of Longformacus – it confirmed that Glenorchy was entitled to both the lands and the title. This did not go down well at all with a first cousin of George deceased, George Sinclair of Keiss, who claimed to be the rightful heir since he was a descendant of the 5th Earl's second son, Francis Sinclair, and that the title was hereditary, passed down through the male line.

Glenorchy marched north to make an appearance in his new lands and, in 1680, the Sinclairs and the Campbells faced each other at what turned out to be the last major clan battle in Scotland at Altimarlach near Wick. The Sinclairs were routed. It was said so many were slain the Campbells stepped dry-shod over their bodies in the river in pursuit of the fleeing Sinclairs.

Failing to regain what he saw as his stolen inheritance by arms, in 1681 George turned to the law. This time, thanks to the influence of the Duke of York, the future James VII, in a judgement that seems to fall far short of the sort Solomon might have made, the Privy Council restored Keiss and the title to George but ruled that the land belonged to Glenorchy. And, as some sort of compensation for his loss of the title, he was created the Earl of Breadalbane and the Baron of Wick.

Thus George became the 7th Earl, but of not very much. He didn't give up the struggle to regain his estates, however. In 1690, he attacked and regained Girnigoe again, ironically damaging his own property, or at least, that's the way he saw it. It was never repaired and allowed to fall into decay.

So that's a potted history of Girnigoe Castle, apart from when, in 1651, during the Civil War, it served as Cromwell's northern headquarters. The ravages of time and battle are not the main cause for its present ruinous state however, but rather, as I have mentioned before, that not-uncommon phenomenon of recycling. There is nothing left of the western barbican at all but the eastern part of the castle has fared rather better, which is not to say it's in good condition. Far from it, in fact.

A footbridge gives access to the ruins which seem to grow out of the cliff face. At the end of it, the remains of the gatehouse stick up like a sore finger and thumb, while out in the bay, a stack with a punky topknot of turf could just as easily be the chopped-off digit of a prisoner which some torturer has tossed into the sea and which happened to land upright. And now, as I turn my gaze from the sea to the sky, I notice that this pancake pile of stones has the same crazy grassy hairstyle.

Actually, the severed finger in the sea looks incredibly like a stack of pancakes too. As well as the castle, the rocks are incredibly interesting and worth coming to see on their own account. Hard to believe now, but the ground beneath my feet was once a tropical lake known as Lake Orcadie and the rocks were laid down about 370 million years ago. In the much more recent past, a mere 20,000 years ago, all this was covered by a vast sheet of ice. What we see now are thin layers of shale built up and hardened into flags, just begging to be taken away and used as a garden path or fencing.

Out at sea, a good bit out, I can see a swirling eddy of water and nearby a dark shape in the water. A skerry, opines Iona; a collapsed stack. But I'm not so sure. In fact I'm as sure as I can be it's a whale, which, as you know from Whaligoe and Latheron, are not unknown in these waters. Oh, for the binoculars languishing on the back seat of the car!

As a matter of fact, this wild place happens to be a good place to observe the flora and fauna of Caithness. Believe it or not, this northern heathland comes under the description of sub-Arctic tundra. At 58 degrees north, Wick is on the same degree of latitude as Linkoping, Sweden; Perm, Siberia; Juneau, Alaska and Churchill, Manitoba. God bless the Gulf Stream! The average winter temperature in Churchill is a chilly -27 degrees whilst in Wick, it is a balmy 4 degrees plus.

In Churchill, you would expect to see lichen on rocks. Here, however, you can see plants – the usual suspects of heather and gorse, but amongst others, orchids, bog cotton and the delicate butterwort, each in its season of course. Not only that, but in place of reindeer, little animals such as shrews, stoats and otters, albeit your chances of actually seeing them are about as much as the proverbial snowball's chance in hell. And birds too, lots of different species: lapwings, linnets, skylarks, curlews, oystercatchers, snipe, and here we have it, the proof, that guard of honour who kindly welcomed us to the castle – ravens! We can see a photograph of three youngsters in a very untidy nest, their beaks open, hoarsely croaking to mum if she doesn't get a move on, "dusty death" will be soon be at hand.

All this I know thanks to a noticeboard which not only tells us about those who take to the air, but also about the denizens of the deep. Since you have even less chance of catching a glimpse of them than the birds, you will surely pardon me for not mentioning them here.

These are very useful and interesting noticeboards indeed but better, in my view, are the ones that show what the castle looked like from the outside and inside when it was inhabited. You can see the stairs, the windlass that worked the drawbridge and the portcullis, the chambers and the service rooms (of which there were a great many), the storerooms and the bakery, the buttery and the pantry. In addition to that, and arguably the most important room of all, the littlest room in the castle – the latrines. Then there were the lords' and ladies' day rooms, the chapel and the priest's lodging, the guests' lodgings and chambers. And finally, the best of all, through the fancy oriel window – a view of the Great Chamber and the Great Hall beneath.

I can also see, what I hadn't appreciated before, there was a drawbridge between the west and the east parts of the castle. At that end was a barbican with a sally port and steps leading down to the goe. Finally, in what I think is a very attractive feature, there is a covered hanging wooden gallery on the northern side, the side facing the sea, which led from the Great Hall to my lord and lady's chambers.

It's rather striking the way the doors, windows and quoins have been finished off with red sandstone. On the northern side they have been very much worn away but still remain on the more sheltered south, giving a better idea of how magnificent this castle once was.

After years of being allowed to fall into decay, steps are being taken to preserve it. In 2002 it was put on the World Monument Fund's list of one hundred of the most endangered sites in the world. The problem is that its spectacular location is also its soft underbelly. Whilst puny Man is shoring up the ruins above, down below, Mother Nature in the form of the mighty sea is gnawing away at its foundations.

You really should go to this castle sometime in the next millennium or so, before the land it stands on becomes a goe, before it tumbles into the sea, before it becomes a skerry, before it disappears from sight below the grinding sea forever.

Chapter Twenty-Six

To John o' Groats: Feuds and Family Problems

N O ravens, those acolytes of the Grim Reaper, see us off the premises. Like leaves from a burnt manuscript, they must have fluttered into the grey skies, gone to convey their grim message elsewhere.

Back to Wick we must go before rejoining the A99. On the way around the bay, we pass the end of the road to Ackergill Tower. Actually a castle, unlike Dunbeath to which it has a passing resemblance, you *can* stay in this one if you wish to impress the love of your life by spending a couple of hundred pounds for the night. It's now a five-star, last-word-in-luxury hotel.

The Castle or Tower, call it what you will, was built sometime in the 14th century, possibly by the son of John Keith of Inverugie. It has an interesting history, and a ghost story which goes like this. Dugald, chief of Clan Keith, being smitten with a certain Helen Gunn, snatched her on the eve of her wedding to her kinsman, Alexander Gunn. During the attack, Alexander was killed and Helen was abducted and locked up in the tower of Ackergill. Preferring death to being possessed by Dugald, she committed suicide by jumping out a window. (Sounds familiar?) Today she haunts the castle as a green lady or a lady in red with her long, black hair piled up on top of her head.

Thus began the five hundred-year-old feud between the Gunns and the Keiths. In an attempt to settle their differences, it was agreed there should be a trial by combat at the chapel of St Tayre's or St Tears near Girnigoe, both sides to arrive at the field of battle on twelve horses. It took place in either 1464 or 1478 and is known to history as the "Battle of Champions".

The Gunns arrived early and went to pray – as well you might, considering the fight to the death which was about to begin – and so a little support from up above would not come amiss. According to an account written two centuries after the event, the Keiths turned up with twenty-four men, claiming no breach of the rules as they had arrived on twelve horses as agreed.

They fell upon the Gunns whom, you would have thought, hadn't a prayer of winning this combat. But in actual fact perhaps there was divine intervention after all, as the Gunns carried the day with four of them surviving. It was such a blood bath that it was said the gore was still visible on the walls two hundred years later.

There was a tit-for-tat sequel in skullduggery when the grandson of the Crowner, as the chieftain of the Gunns was called, a certain Willam Mackames, (son of James) and some others, ambushed George Keith of Ackergill, his son, and twelve others and slew them all.

And so the feud rumbled on, no love lost between the rival clans. Then, in 1978, at the instigation of their North American descendants and to mark five hundred years after the events at St Tears, a "Bond and Covenant of Friendship" was signed between the chiefs of the warring clans. It took place at the site where their ancestors met, to settle it once and for all, supposedly, half a millennium previously.

The Keiths did not have their enemies to seek. The colourful history of Ackergill Castle continued when their neighbours, the Sinclairs, led by the 4th Earl of Caithness, attacked and seized it in 1547 and again in 1556. He wanted it for his number two son, in order of appearance only – William. Yes, the very one in the last chapter who betrayed his brother and was given the deathly bear hug by his older brother, John, who died of thirst in the dungeons of Girnigoe.

But there was an enemy even closer to hand than the Sinclairs, and like them it came from within the family. In 1593, William Keith, the Earl Marischal, complained to the Privy Council that his brother Robert had seized Ackergill. At some time in the intervening six years, it must have been returned to him as it was in his possession again in 1598 when it was attacked yet again – this time by Thomas Keith of Sumster – and taken from him. And so it passed from one person to the next like some I'm-the-king-of-the-castle until the Sinclairs finally did the honest thing and bought it from the Keiths in 1612.

But that was not the end of Ackergill's troubles. Eleven short years later, in 1623, on the orders of the Privy Council, it was besieged by Sir Robert Gordon, the historian and fourth son of Alexander, the 12th Earl of Sutherland and long-standing enemy of the 5th Earl of Caithness, aka "the Wicked". The castle surrendered without a shot being fired, as did Keiss Castle, the Earl having fled to Orkney, and therefore without damage to the fabric of the building, unlike Girnigoe. Finally, along came Cromwell in 1651.

After that, it got a bit more peaceful for Ackergill and I will not trouble you with any more. But stop, traveller, as you pass by, or as you catch sight of it just up the coast from Girnigoe and reflect on its troublesome past. Or even better, if you are lucky enough to be able to stay there, even for just one night, as you lap up your luxurious surroundings, you will be all the better placed to appreciate it, now you know something of its troublesome past.

We pass through Reiss where the broad, sandy beach starts and continues all the way up to Keiss, surely the equal of any on the French Riviera only a lot less crowded and unfortunately a lot less smitten with sunshine too. Keiss Castle, whose fate is closely linked to that of Girnigoe and Ackergill as you have seen, is, if anything, in an even more ruinous state than Girnigoe. But sharing an equally dramatic location and, in its day – with its four storeys and turrets – it could easily have appeared in any fairy tale book you would care to mention. It hadn't been completed long before the "wicked" 5th Earl had to flee in 1623. His heir, his great-grandson, George Sinclair, built himself a new castle in Thurso East, now in ruins.

After life's fitful fever, the 7th Earl died in 1698 without issue, as the saying goes, and Keiss passed on to a second cousin, Sir John Sinclair of Mirkle. Despite all the shenanigans, the fighting and the disputes between the 7th Earl and Sir John Campbell of Glenorchy, it seems – at some stage after that – the latter somehow did regain ownership of Keiss, even if it was a bit of a ruin. It is recorded as having been sold to William Sinclair, 2nd Baronet of Dunbeath who founded the first Baptist Church in Scotland, at Keiss, as well as the dynasty which still holds the baronetcy today.

Leaving Keiss, we come in a few minutes to a viewpoint called Warth Hill (from the old Norse *vartha* meaning "to watch"). From this high vantage point, John O' Groats lies below the brow of the hill and further out, you can see the Pentland Firth and all of Stroma, surprisingly near, and a little further out, the tiny pimple of Swona, one mile long by half-a-mile wide, home only to a herd of feral cattle who were left behind when the last inhabitants left in 1974.

Bigger Stroma, two miles long by one wide, once had some more interesting inhabitants – the Kennedy mummies. That family built a mausoleum in 1677 and due to the constant spray of salty water, the very air itself being suffused with it, not to mention the drinking water, some of the bodies became mummified – and something of a tourist attraction.

Although he did not manage to come here personally, falling victim to foul weather, not to mention the difficult terrain, Thomas Pennant wrote about the mummies, in particular their amazing flexibility. A certain disrespectful son, Murdoch Kennedy, used his father's corpse to put on a show for visitors. Without telling them what he was going to do, he would get them to stand at the foot of the body, then he would bend one of his father's arms and place the hand next to his temple. Next, pressing down on his father's feet with one of his own, to the amazement, if not the horror of his audience, his father's body would bend at the waist and rise up to salute his audience.

But he wasn't finished yet. Laying the body out flat again, he would bang on his father's stomach, making it sound like a drum. I don't know how many performances he gave of his amazing saluting corpse with a tum like a drum, but he did it just once too often. One day his father's head fell off. Imagine the shock, the horror on the countenances of the watchers as they saw that decapitation. Murdoch, however, was not deterred. He did not let his father retire and rest in peace but kept working him in death, to death, until other bits dropped off too. I suppose that's a severe example of a repetitive strain injury.

By 1786 the show was over for everyone. Some thanatourist vandals broke down the door of the mausoleum, presumably losing patience because no-one inside had sprung up quickly enough to answer their knock. Then the cattle and sheep got in and trampled the mummies and bodies to dust, to which we must all be reduced, unless it's to ashes. Which, you might say, is a darned sight better than being a working corpse long after you are dead.

The last five native inhabitants left Stroma in 1962, and in 1997 the lighthouse keepers and their families also abandoned it. When the original lighthouse was built in 1890, some islanders were actually opposed to it, shipwrecks being a source of income as well as that rare and valuable commodity – timber. In 1896 it was replaced by another lighthouse, designed by David Stevenson. He, with his brother, Charles, were responsible for more than ninety lighthouses, including one of cast iron on Swona (1906), and the Flannan Isles where, in 1900, the three lighthouse keepers mysteriously disappeared leaving behind a *Mary Celeste* sort of situation, celebrated in W.W. Gibson's poem *Flannan Isle*.

The Pentland Firth is a hazardous place for shipping with tidal races and reefs, skerries and shoals, eddies and whirlpools, to say nothing of winter storms. One such storm in 1862 even deposited wreckage and debris at the top of Stroma's 100 foot-high cliffs. To date, more than sixty vessels have perished on its rocks, with many more coming to grief on Swona, the mainland, and Orkney.

In 1931, the 6,000-ton Danish freighter *Pennsylvania* ran aground on Swona with a cargo of practically everything but the kitchen sink. It was an event that foreshadowed, ten years later, the wreck of the *SS Politician* on Eriskay and which inspired the book and film *Whisky Galore*. According to an eyewitness at the time, the islanders of Swona, Stroma and South Ronaldsay liberated the cargo and hid it all over the islands: in the fields and in the haystacks, in the caves and in the goes.

Largely the islanders were self-sufficient, building their own houses and growing their own food. There was a school and a church, and three shops supplemented by a floating shop where the islanders could buy such things as flour, clothes and paraffin. Now there's only some sheep and cattle of the non-feral kind.

Lifting my eyes I can see the bigger, black bulk of the Orkneys, with, if you know precisely where to look and on a clear day, off to the left, you might just be able to make out the head of the Old Man of Hoy peeking coyly over the shoulder of the island that bears his name. But not today. The sky is low and grey and, out in the firth, it appears to be raining. Over to the right lies Duncansby Head and beyond that, far out to sea, the Pentland Skerries.

And so we arrive at John o' Groats which, as no-one needs to be told, is famous for being the beginning (or the end) of many, many journeys, many for charitable causes, to or from Land's End, 876 miles away. On that indisputable fact rests its fame even if it is not the most northerly point on the mainland, just as Land's End is not the most southerly. They are a couple of imposters both, but at least John o' Groats is not a tourist trap; that is its triumph and Land's End's disaster.

Some people, when they are being asked to believe something which stretches their credulity rather a lot, come out with the line, "Oh yeah? And my father was a Dutchman". As most people probably know, John o' Groats *was* a Dutchman, Jan de Groot, as his parents named him, who was given permission in 1496 by James IV to operate a ferry business to Orkney. *Groot* is the Dutch for "great", while the groat was neither large nor worth a great deal of money – hence the expression "not worth a groat", but which has rather dropped out of currency these days. Coincidentally, a groat is what Jan charged for the six-mile crossing to Orkney. Made of silver, it was worth fourpence.

If there is one recurring theme in this book, it is the trouble with families and Jan seems to have suffered more than others in that respect. He had seven sons, all of whom were very jealous of each other. To maintain no hint of favouritism amongst them, he went to the enormous lengths of building an octagonal house with eight doors and eight windows. And in the house that Jan built, he had an octagonal table so no-one could say he was at the head of it and no-one could be miffed for being seated at the bottom. So runs the story, although it has more than a whiff of a fairy tale about it if you ask me.

I am glad to see that since I was last here, the hotel, which was shut and had a very dilapidated air about it and which gave the entire place a very sad and neglected appearance, has now been refurbished and has reopened. The façade has been given a gleaming-white coat of paint which makes it look much younger than its 150 years (nearly), but even better than that, five, three-bedroomed, self-catering lodges, brightly-and-variously painted in the Norwegian manner, have been built to one side of the hotel – and very attractive they look, too. It adds a very welcome splash of colour to what can be a very dreich place especially on a winter's day – or one like today, for that matter.

The octagonal nature of Jan's original house is reflected in a part of the hotel, and also in the two "First and Last" gift and souvenir kiosks painted the same maroon as the *Bryggen* in Bergen. Yes, this place has cheered up considerably since it earned the unenviable "Carbuncle Award" from a magazine in 2010.

The foot-passenger ferry, the *Pentland Venture,* and well named – so it seems to me, considering the perils of the Firth – lies moored in the harbour. For £17 it will transport you to Orkney in forty minutes. At this time of year, September, there are two sailings a day. In June, July and August, there are as many as three.

Piled up on the quayside are masses of lobster creels, yards of rope, orange floats and white, plastic fish boxes. A noticeboard tells the visitor about the denizens of the Pentland Firth and it is satisfying, at least in my eyes, to see that it is home to not just seals and dolphins but whales – killers and minkes. It could well, therefore, have been a minke I saw out in the sea at Girnigoe. They are seen here between June and October; killers from June to September.

The killer, the noticeboard informs us, is not really a whale at all but an orca, the world's largest dolphin, but killers they most certainly are. They kill seals, birds and fish, and have even been known to form pods to hunt minkes. They, by contrast, are the gentle giants of the deep who can weigh up to ten tonnes and grow to twenty feet or more in length. They swim along with their mouths open, catching sprats, squid and krill in their baleen, a sort of hairy filter in which their prey is trapped.

Now, here's something else interesting – a sign like a Cross of Lorraine on the wall of the ferry-waiting area. At the very top it tells me I am at John o' Groats – longtitude 58° north and latitude 3° west. Between the two arms on the upright of the cross, an arrow points to Stroma only two-and-a-half miles away. The top arm tells the distance in miles to the North Pole (2,200) and Land's End (876), while the slightly shorter one below says it is 6 miles to Orkney and 690 to London.

But here is the really interesting part – on the upright of the post is a silhouette of New Zealand with a red dot at the bottom of South Island and an arrow pointing downwards with "Bluff, New Zealand" written as a column.

And at the very bottom, the distance: 12,875 miles. Straight down, right beneath my feet, I am standing on someone's head in New Zealand!

Or would that be their feet?

Chapter Twenty-Seven

The Castle of Mey: A Thoroughly Modern Castle

I N what marks a turning point on the NC500 trail, we're no longer heading north but west towards the Castle of Mey. However it's not long before we make a slight detour, the A836, to tiny Canisbay. The Church of Scotland here is pretty impressive with its tall white tower which doesn't look as if it belongs to it at all. In the vestibule is Jan de Groot's headstone, which is made of red sandstone. It has a faintly inscribed cross as the main feature, with ornate medieval lettering arranged around the border. It was discovered under the floorboards, embedded in the south wall, during restoration works in 1898.

The site itself has been a place for Christian worship for 1,500 years. St Drostan founded a chapel here, or had one named after him, in the 6th century. Of royal birth, but not the first in line to the throne, he chose the kingdom of heaven instead and became a follower of St Columba, literally.

In the present immaculately-kept church, the north aisle is known as the "Stroma" aisle, traditionally where those islanders sat when they came here to worship. (You can see the island quite easily across the Firth from the churchyard.) And this is where the Queen Mother came to worship after she bought what was Barrogill Castle in 1952 and began restoring it, also giving it back its original name of the Castle of Mey. William, the blue-eyed boy of the 4th Earl of Caithness, was the 1st Laird of Mey, after his doting father built the castle for him between 1566 and 1572. He did not enjoy it for very long – he was strangled by his brother in the dungeon of Girnigoe, as you know.

His former home (and the Queen Mother's) is where we are going now, the most northerly castle in mainland Scotland. It was based on the traditional Z-style – a central tower with two offset towers – and has seen many alterations since.

An extension was added in 1700 which seems to be the same time its name was changed to Barrogill Castle. Further changes took place in 1819 when the 12th Earl added the dining room and the grand entrance. Seventy years after that, and after three hundred years, the Sinclair occupancy came to an end when the 15th Earl died aged only thirty, unmarried and without issue. He bequeathed the castle to his friend P.G. Heathcote on condition he changed his name to Sinclair, which he did. Well, what would you do? As for the title, it was passed on to a relation descended from Sir James Sinclair, 1st Baronet of Mey. In 1928, Mr Heathcote's widow sold the castle to Captain F.B. Imbert-Terry, who in his turn sold it to the Queen Mother.

She found out it was for sale almost by accident when, grieving at the loss of her husband, George VI, she was being comforted by her friends, Commander and Lady Vyner, at their little place in nearby Dunnet, the House of the Northern Gate. Out on a drive one day, they happened to pass by the castle and one of the Vyners happened to mention it was on the market. Although her friends thought it probably wouldn't be a suitable place for an ex-Queen who was used to palatial palaces, nevertheless the Queen Mother went to see it. The rest you know.

The new owner immediately began making extensive alterations to her recently acquired property. It had no electricity and no bathrooms. Imagine that, in the middle of the twentieth century! A programme of modernisation began and, once it was completed in 1955 and until her death in March 2002 aged 101, the Queen Mother visited her home (the only one she ever owned), twice a year in August and October. Now it is owned by the Castle of Mey Trust which the Queen Mother had drawn up in 1996.

The wind that blows us southerly towards the Visitor Centre has also chased the storm clouds away and you would scarcely credit it, but overhead now are white, woolly sheep scudding across the sky as if chased by an invisible sheep dog. NC500 travellers from overseas should not be surprised at this phenomenon, where in Scotland you can sometimes experience all four seasons in a day.

The Visitor Centre opened in 2007 after five years' fierce debate as to what form it should take. It's good to hear the winning architects came from Tain and the construction contract was awarded to a local firm. And a very good job they have made of it too, using the local stone for the walls and Caithness slate for the roof and floor. And if the original Castle of Mey was built on a Z-style plan, I would call this a "Thermometer-style" plan – a bulb where the entrance and gift shop are, with an oblong extension which houses the tearoom. It serves local produce, as you would expect. With the mighty wooden rafters and the larch cladding on the ceiling, it has been done very tastefully indeed and I'm sure the food is just as tasty. What the visitor can't see is the insulation is made of wool. Another use for another local product.

After buying our tickets we are directed to the front of the castle where we are told a tour will be departing in ten minutes. On either side of the big arched doorway are carriage lamps bearing the Queen Mother's cypher, the entwined E&R, just one of the little touches which she made to put her own stamp on the place. Another thing she did, apart from the gardens which we will come to later, was to install on the lawn some 18th century cannons from a nearby battery whose original purpose was to blow Boney out of the water, in the unlikely event the master strategist should launch an invasion from the North.

Along with half-a-dozen others we are herded into what is called the "front hall", where our guide begins his exposition. And right from the very beginning I can see this is going to be a tour with a difference; not so much a castle, more of a family home, even if the family consisted of only one. That's because beside me are some walking sticks which I was very used to seeing, as the dear old lady had practically a symbiotic relationship with them in her later years. Nearer still, so near I could actually rub shoulders with it if it were not for the fact that a scruff like me should even dare to *think* about rubbing shoulders with royalty – the Queen Mum's trademark raincoat (and hat).

Bidding us follow him, we pursue our guide up the stairs. Just think, even in her hundredth year, the great old lady climbed these very stairs, aided by one of her faithful sticks. Of that I am certain. No poncy lifts in this place.

Now we are standing beneath the portrait of the 14th Earl of Caithness, who looks down on us in full-kilted ease. He inherited the title from his father in 1855. Apart from being a Lord-in-Waiting to Queen Victoria, he was also Lord-in-Waiting, what we call a "Government Whip" nowadays, in the House of Lords during the Liberal administrations of Lords Palmerston and Russell. And if that were not portfolio enough, he was also tutor to the future Edward VII and a Vice-Admiral of Caithness.

He had been Lord-Lieutenant of Caithness from 1856 and, a decade later, Queen Victoria created him Baron Barogill which has a nice ring to it if nothing else. And there was something else too. In 1862, he was invested as a Fellow of the Royal Society and, if Mr Chadband in *Bleak House* had a "great deal of train oil in his system", then the Earl had a great deal of steam in his. He fancied himself as a bit of an inventor, though – like Alexander Bain – it would be more accurate to say he improved and refined existing inventions.

Most notably there was his "steam car" and his "steam plough", which he used on his farm at Mey. Amongst his other inventions were an automatic rail-carriage washer for the American market, a tape loom, and a gravitational compass – whatever they were. His crowning achievement, if that's the right term, was his artificial leg which won a prize in the French Exhibition of 1866. Furthermore, if the 5th Earl was the "Wicked Earl" then James Sinclair should be known as the "Good Earl". He opened up a good many flagstone quarries, thereby creating employment for a good number of people. He died aged 59 at the Fifth Avenue Hotel in New York in 1881 and his body was shipped home.

We're in the drawing room. It looks very homely with lots of squidgy armchairs and some occasional chairs and tables, one made by Viscount Linley, the Queen Mother's grandson. It's not my purpose to give you a blow-by-blow account of each and every room and thus spare you the price of an entrance ticket. You really need to come and experience it for yourself, but I will point out some things that captured my attention.

The collection of little soft-toy animals on the pelmets, for example. The daddy of them all is the rather amusing tartan Nessie wearing a tam o' shanter at a jaunty angle. It was put there by one of the Equerries, probably whilst in merry mood, and was intended to be removed before the QM saw it. As it happens it wasn't and, far from being outraged, she was amused, which is more than can be said for her daughter's sometime predecessor. Out of such trifles a tradition is born, and now Nessie has accumulated a family of companions, though not of the same species.

This is where the Queen Mother would receive her guests, where they would drink afternoon tea or, before dinner, have something a little stronger. Most of us know what her favourite tipple was and if you don't, it doesn't matter, but I will give you a hint – it wasn't Scotland's most famous product, despite her being a daughter of that fair land.

Back in the 18th century, this room was the great hall, and can be again, more or less, when the double doors that now give entry to the Equerry's room are left open, as they are now. A pleasant room, the thing that catches my eye most is the portrait of the Lady Herself above the fireplace. It was commissioned for her 90th birthday, the only painting to feature her with her beloved castle. As a matter of fact, it is playing a discreet role in the background. Much more prominent, sitting by her side, is Ranger, one of her beloved corgis, looking as large as a baby Shetland pony.

Arguably the most interesting room of all is the library. Banish acres of wall-to-wall dry and dusty books from your mind; this is the most homely of all the rooms so far and where the Queen Mother's personality has left its most obvious mark behind. I think you can always tell a lot about a person by looking at their bookshelves. Here are to be found books on horseracing (there's a surprise), gardening, and natural history, as well as others on Caithness of which she became rather fond.

This is where the pensioner lady, either on her own, or with others, like those who could play the upright piano, spent her time relaxing when she was off duty and, God knows, she kept on working long after most of us put up our slippered feet in front of the telly. Despite her workload, however, she did have some time in front of the goggle box. This actual one in fact; a rather ancient-looking model beneath which are box sets of *Yes Minister, Fawlty Towers* and *Dad's Army.* Which tells you not only did she like a laugh (who doesn't?), but the old jokes are the best.

As well as some knick-knacks, there are a lot of family photographs dotted about the room. Amongst the most notable is one on the piano of her two daughters taken in their younger years and signed by both. That makes it even more special (and collectable). It was taken by Norman Parkinson as an eightieth birthday present, and a very good job he has made of it too; they look much younger than a quick mental calculation tells me they must have been at the time when it was taken.

Up the spiral stairs we go to the QM's bedroom. (Don't step on the ghosts of the corgis – that's where they slept.) Imagine her at 101, climbing these stairs. I didn't count how many there are, but not nearly as many as that. We are allowed to peek in, but – like the corgis – we may not enter. It's a very light and airy room with windows to the north, south and east. Nearby is her Clothes Room – not wardrobe, please note. Imagine that; a whole room just for your clothes!

The next room of interest is what's known as "Princess Margaret's Bedroom" because, one afternoon, Princess Margaret had a lie-down on the bed. When she came here, she preferred to sleep on the Royal Yacht, *Britannnia.* But it may not have had anything to do with the bed – the room is said to be haunted.

The source of the tale has to be laid at the door of that otherwise good egg, the 14th Earl, the inventor. He had a daughter whom he named "Fanny" which is an unforgivable thing to do, even if he may not have known any American English at the time. But that's not it, not the really bad thing he did. When the poor girl fell in love with one of the grooms, he threw a hairy fit and banished the pleb, not just from the premises, but sent him south – out of sight and, he hoped, out of mind.

Fanny was heartbroken and spent a lot of time pining on what later became known by the locals as "Lady Fanny's Seat", which to North American readers will sound rather tautological. In actual fact the original was a memorial to her grandfather's friend, Charles Canning (1770-1827), who later became Britain's shortest-serving prime minister – 119 days. When she wasn't there, Fanny was moping on a window seat in her bedroom from which she probably hoped against hope that one day she might catch sight of her suitor coming to carry her away. He never did and she died of a broken heart in 1883, unmarried, aged only twenty-nine. Others say, and it's a familiar story, she threw herself out the window. Others still, with absolutely no regard for what makes a good story, maintain she died of tuberculosis.

It may not have been a very nice death for poor Fanny, but I'm placing my bets on the suicide version. How else do you explain the Green Lady that has been seen haunting the upper floors, and doors shutting and lights going off and on for no apparent reason? Some people have reported feeling a chill in the air. No wonder Princess Margaret preferred to sleep on the *Britannia*.

Should you go to Carisbay to visit the church and see Jan de Groot's headstone, why not spare a moment to visit Lady Fanny's grave too? Next to one of the church walls, it's a very simple affair, a small cross with scalloped edges embedded in a mound of stones.

The guest bathroom dates from 1954, when the castle's restorations were completed. It certainly looks of its time, particularly the stripy curtain round the wash-hand basin which artistically matches the window curtains. Guests nowadays would probably complain about it not being en-suite, but the only one of that sort in the entire castle is in the QM's bedroom.

Next are the Vyner's bedrooms. This is posh. A spacious, tastefully-decorated big bedroom for her with a Louis XVI-style bed which Goldilocks might have supposed was for Mummy Bear, with Baby Bear's poky little bedroom beyond. Only she would have been wrong, because the tiny little bedroom is for Lady Vyner's husband as the Louis XVI bed is only a single.

And so we come to possibly what's regarded as the highlight of the tour – the dining room extension which was added in 1819. The architect was William Burn and, in what I regard as a masterstroke, he not only gave it crenellations but added them to the turrets too, making it much more like a castle. The sandstone panel above the triple windows is by Huw Lorrimer and was added in 1960. I think it's a worthy improvement too, alleviating the austereness of the rectangular block.

I will not tell you about the Regency mahogany table or the ironstone dinner service or the Caithness crystal, but I would recommend the pair of paintings by Prince Phillip. I can see where Prince Charles gets his talent from.

It's a few steps down to the butler's pantry where all the plates, glasses and cutlery are stored, and it's also a step back half-a-century with its stainless steel sinks, plain white cupboards with chrome D-handles and antediluvian refrigerator. It is also where the dumb waiter hangs out and who, despite his name, protested so much at having any work to do that those below stairs allowed him to remain as silent as the job description, preferring to carry the food upstairs themselves.

Sacking the waiter was not the only measure that was taken to keep the noise down. The ceiling is thickly padded with green felt so those who sit and dine above will not hear a sound from those below who only wait to serve.

The adjacent kitchen is very spacious and fitted out in the same style as the butler's pantry. Huge steel sinks line the wall beneath the windows, while an enormous table in the middle displays a range of vegetables and cooking utensils. Wait a minute; there's a potato masher just like the one my mother used to have! An ingenious little gadget, you popped your boiled potatoes in at the top, added some milk and and a knob of butter, pulled down the handle and out came instant creamed potatoes. And if I'm not much mistaken, on the dresser over there, that's a Kenwood Chef like she used to have, next to the tin bin with "Bread" on it, ditto.

And with that we are done. We are free to go, but no matter how pressing time is or how far we have to go today, we must at least poke our heads into the gardens. We could not see Dunbeath's but have seen Dunrobin's and this, as you would expect, poses the same challenges of wind and sea spray, not to mention the water that comes from the heavens above and the sun which is more of a casual visitor than a permanent guest in these parts.

The answer to a hostile environment, as the Romans knew, is walls, and those in Mey are of a good height, aided by hedges which give shelter and succour to the flowers and the vegetables which are destined for death in the castle kitchens. I don't care much for vegetables, not on my plate, far less serried rows of them growing in the ground, so we give them a miss and restrict ourselves to the flowers.

Bearing in mind this is the ninth month, it's amazingly colourful. This is provided by roses in beds as well as others climbing the walls in an effort to get away from nasturtiums growing so incredibly high at their feet. Most spectacular is the avenue of sweetpeas – red, white and lilac, with at their feet, an untamed carpet of shamelessly blue cornflowers and brassy marigolds. We are flanked on the other side of the path by regiments of tall hollyhocks and lupins.

That's what we saw. Come another time, another season, and you are sure to see something different, but I bet it will be just as impressive.

Chapter Twenty-Eight

Thurso: From Dunnet Head to Dounreay

FROM the castle we saw it darkly in the distance, a pimple or – as we Scots say – a "plook", sticking out into the Pentland Firth, and now we are on the B855 heading towards it: Dunnet Head, the most northerly point on mainland Britain. For that reason alone, the NC500 tourist may consider it a short detour well worth the making, particularly if birds are your thing and seabirds your speciality: guillemots, razorbills, kittiwakes, fulmars, skuas, shags, gannets, gulls and the clown-faced puffins, to name but a few. And that's not all – there are the groundbirds, so to speak, such species as rock pipits, skylarks, twites, peregrines and ravens. Or if you prefer wild flowers, you can see, for example, sea campion, Scots lovage, ragged-robin, Spring quill and thrift.

The wildness and the remoteness of the scene is spoiled somewhat by a cluster of disused military buildings. They are the scars of war. During WWII, this was a radar station which was tracking enemy shipping, submarines and aircraft. Over the sea and not far away was the strategic naval base of Scapa Flow in Orkney, a target for enemy bombers.

It goes without saying this is the perfect location for a lighthouse. The only question is, which Stevenson built it? A noticeboard in front of it tells us it was Robert, in 1831. It's 66 feet high, to which you can add 344 feet of cliff. It has a range of 23 nautical miles. It's automated now, but originally it had a lighthouse keeper as well as two assistants who lived in the cottages clustered around the base. You would wonder the Northern Lighthouse Board thought it needed as many as three men to keep the lamp trimmed but, not to worry, they found other things for them to do like maintaining the properties which now make very handy holiday retreats for those who want to get away from it all – apart from the flocks of tourists who come here, augumented now, possibly, by NC500 travellers.

If you do not suffer from vertigo, and if you can put your faith in a capricious gust of wind not to come along and sweep you off your feet, you can look down over your toes to where, 416 feet below, the water hungrily gnaws away at the bottom of the cliff – not that there's any immediate cause for concern of it collapsing into the sea. And while there, you might like to ponder on the fact there are 64 million people who inhabit this crowded little island and here you are, the most northerly person on the British mainland.

When you return to the junction with the A836, at the crook of the bay, you will find a splendid two-mile beach with sand dunes. It is here birdwatchers come to twitch, dog owners to exercise their pooches, beachcombers to seek the serendipitous find and windsurfers to ride the waves – as long as they are in possession of a wetsuit. In fact the waves are so high and mighty, possibly the best in Britain for this pursuit, it's a venue for surfing championships.

We drive through Castletown, which, as the name suggests, must have had a castle once but of which no trace now remains, likewise the air base which was here to protect Scapa Flow. A century ago it employed five hundred men in the flagstone quarries which paved the streets of many cities both at home and abroad, until someone came up with the bright idea that concrete beneath our feet was better and that was the end of that.

And so we come to Thurso. No prizes for spotting its Viking roots – *Thorsá*, meaning Thor's river. It may surprise you to learn however that such was the sway of Norway in these parts that it was not until 1196 that Caithness came under Scots rule.

Of Thurso East Castle built by the 6th Earl of Caithness in the mid 17th century, not a thing now remains, and only a shell of the 1878 Scots Baronial mansion that Sir Tollemache Sinclair built which incorporated the original tower house. It caught fire and was partly demolished in 1952. Which is a shame as a photograph shows it to be very splendid, the equal of Dunrobin. You can catch a glimpse of what's left as you come into town.

At the heart of Thurso is Sir John's Square presided over by a statue of the man himself, Sir John Sinclair of Ulbster. Behind him is St Peter's and St Andrew's Church which was completed in 1832. The architect was William Burn (1789-1870), who designed the dining room at the Castle of Mey and gave the castle its crenellations. He has a good many other churches to his name as well as country houses, hospitals and hotels. But that's by no means all.

How many people I wonder, as they post their letters in Glasgow General Post Office or admire a piece of art in the Scottish Gallery of Modern Art, realise they were both designed by William Burn? In fact, how many people have even heard of him until now? In fact it is he, along with his pupil, David Bryce, we have to thank for creating the Scots Baronial style.

Sir John Sinclair (1754-1835) needs no introduction, but I wouldn't blame you if you have forgotten who he was amongst the plethora of Sinclairs I've subjected you to recently. I mentioned him in Chapter Twenty-one as being the instigator of the Statistical Account. He was also responsible for introducing the black-faced Cheviot to Scotland in 1792 for which a great many people, now dead, would not give him any thanks at all.

He was born in Thurso Castle and it is thanks to him that the splendidly named Tollemache Sinclair, above, got his name. His first wife was Lady Catherine Camilla Tollemache, a handle befitting the daughter of Lord Huntingtower. Actually some sources say his first wife was Sarah Maitland, but the Tollemache has to come from somewhere so I am sticking with Lady Catherine. Sir John had two children by her and thirteen by his second wife, Diana MacDonald, the lucky lady.

They are gone now, like the people displaced by Sir John's sheep, but the streets of Thurso are still here, devised in a grid plan in 1798 by Sir John.

If you want to know more about the town itself, or if you wish to pick up the Pictish trail again, then the recently-opened Caithness Horizons is the place for you. It houses, under one roof, a collection of artefacts formerly in the care of Highland Council, Thurso Heritage Society and Dounreay Visitor Centre, which is very good news indeed for the NC500 traveller as it saves a good deal of gadding about. However, if you can resist the lure of two massive standing stones to the left of the entrance, it might be an idea to begin at the top floor and allow the splendid and aptly-named film of the same name as the museum to set the scene for you. And like the best things in life, it and the museum are free – or rather, entry is by donation. Please give generously. You will get your money's worth. Trust me.

The Pictish stones aforesaid are the Skinnet Stone and the Ulbster Stone. The former is tall and skinny; the other, like me, is shorter and stockier, but they have an unusual feature in common. Each has a cross on both sides.

The seven-foot tall Skinnet Stone, reckoned to date from 800 AD, was discovered, or recognised for what it was, by the Rev. T. S. Muir in the wall of a ruined chapel near Halkirk in 1861, but somehow it was dropped and broke into six pieces. Not a challenge of Humpty Dumpty proportions to put together again, or so you would have thought, yet somehow they messed it up, putting bits in the wrong places, with gaps all over the place. There are still gaps, but at least it has now been reassembled in the right order.

What you should pay particular attention to, near the bottom of the stone, is the pair of horses which must be drawing a carriage or chariot of some kind, but only the hands holding the reins are faintly visible. Out of all the hundreds of Pictish stones and fragments discovered to date, there are only two other examples of horses being used as draft animals.

And there's something else. The cross on the other side, the one that has been designated the B-side – like a 45 record in the Sixties, though slightly smaller – is beautifully carved which, scholars speculate, may represent the Second Coming. The cross on the other side, of course, represents the Crucifixion. But that's not all. What you're actually looking at is a medieval book! If you look carefully, you will see one of the thin edges is carved, like the spine of a book, while the other side is blank. It's as if the *Lindisfarne Gospels* has been turned to stone.

Finally, as I said before, in connection with the Eagle Stone at Strathpeffer, the whole thing was probably coloured. Not only that, but covered in plaster with metal fittings attached or items of glass jewellery. If true, not an improvement in my view.

In 1770, the five-foot high Ulbster Stone was unearthed from St Martin's Chapel. Each Pictish stone is unique and, as well as having crosses on both sides, it is said to contain more varieties of symbols than any other known stone. As well as the usual suspects, such as the crescent and V-rods, this has a hippocamp or seahorse and the so-called Pictish beast. No-one can say for certain what it's meant to be, but I can't see why it can't just be mythical. As a matter of fact, no-one knows what the whole stone is meant to represent. While it would be nice to know, maybe the mystery makes it even more intriguing.

What no-one could fail to know is the name of the stone. Some vandal has inscribed "The Ulbster Stone" on the back. No random act of graffiti this. It has been lovingly carved in a Gothic script. Did no-one raise a finger to prevent this act of desecration to stop the hand that hit the hammer that smote the chisel?

Much less complicated and much smaller, by definition, are the stone fragments: the very plain Cannisbay Cross, looking for all the world like a child's first jigsaw puzzle, and the oldest stone in the exhibition, the broken 6th century Watenan Stone, of which all that remains are the tip of a V-rod and the horns of a crescent. The fragments are of different colours as, at some time or other, one part was subjected to fire. An artist has supplied her impression of the missing piece to let us see what it would have looked like in its entirety.

Another interesting stone is a thousand-year-old runic grave-marker. Someone who can read the runes tells us it is dedicated by his children to their dead father, Ingölf. It was found in the graveyard of Old St Peter's here in Thurso.

Old St Peter's dates back to 1125 with 16th century additions. It is in ruins now, though fortunately the south wall window with its Gothic tracery still remains. It closed its doors for the last time in 1832, when St Peter's and St Andrew's first opened its doors. I couldn't possibly comment on what St Peter may have said about sharing his church with his brother and fellow disciple, but there are some interesting remarks to be read in Old St Peter's kirk session minutes.

In 1701 a lady was found guilty by those good, pious gentlemen of being "intimate" with a Dutch sailor and, *pour encourager les autres*, was sentenced to have her head shaved before being paraded through the town by the hangman. As anyone who has read *Tam O' Shanter* knows, the kirk sessions were full of self-righteous hypocrites. However, this next tale stretches one's credulity not a little. Apparently boys, so eager to hear the sermon, used to perch on the rafters and one day in 1726, the inevitable happened. One or more fell onto the unprotected craniums of the worshippers below. I can believe that part: I would bet my pension the sermon was so boring they just dropped off.

In 1786 there was a complaint about dung and rubbish being dumped on the graves which is a dreadful way to treat the dead but, I regret to say, not as bad as in our own times, in 2013 to be precise, when in a deliberate act of vandalism, five headstones were toppled over and broken. Now if they had shaved the heads of those culprits and paraded *them* through the town, that would be more like the thing.

And lastly, on the subject of stones, there is one more possibly worth your attention, the so-called "Ye Auld Fish Stane", around which the fishwives used to congregate to sell their wares. I say "possibly" because it could really just be any old stone, only this has a brass plaque on it telling you what it is. It stood in the market place from 1850 until it was removed in the Seventies.

Cromarty has Hugh Miller, Wick has Alexander Bain, amongst others, like William Barclay (1907-78) the theologian, and James Bremner (1784-1856) the naval architect, harbour-builder and ship-raiser. But Thurso, with a population of less than 8,000 souls, has a good many famous sons to its credit, even although they may not be household names. You will pardon me for not mentioning them as it is a rather extensive list.

Out of those many, the museum has chosen, with good reason, to honour Robert Dick (1811-66). Another "lad o' pairts", he was born in Clackmannanshire and left school at thirteen to become an apprentice baker. Just as Hugh Miller went about with his hammer collecting rocks, Dick went about with his trowel collecting wildflowers and other plants. His father was a customs and excise officer and, when he was posted to Thurso in 1825, he advised his son he could do worse than come to Thurso and set up a bakery business, which he did, and which provided his bread and butter for the rest of his short life.

Although he did not give up the day job, he continued his interest in plants in his spare time. In fact, he broadened his sphere of interest to include molluscs and insects. After he read Miller's *Old Red Sandstone*, he also became interested in rocks and fossils. He was a retiring sort of man who kept himself to himself, never publishing his findings, although he did correspond with Hugh Miller and sent him specimens.

Arguably his greatest achievement was to have a primitive fish named after him. It lived about 385 million years ago and was three inches long. It was discovered in a Scottish loch, though of course it wasn't Scotland when it died. It is known as *Microbrachius dicki*, and what's really special about it is it's the earliest example of a creature possessing sexual organs. They would have "done it" side by side, holding hands so to speak, their lobster-like claws locking them together, which is rather touching I think. The male had a special L-shaped appendage which he inserted into the bottom part of the female. It was God's first experiment into an alternative method of reproduction – and it didn't catch on. Which just goes to show you if not even He got it right the first time, everyone should be given a second chance. It took another million years before sharks and rays took up copulation as a method of reproduction instead of spawning and, thank God, this time it did catch on.

His fossil collection became a lifeline in 1863 when the *SS Prince Consort* sank with a consignment of flour outside Aberdeen harbour and left him practically bankrupt. Only by selling his fossils was he able to keep his head above water. The end came when he collapsed while collecting fossils in a quarry and never recovered. I don't suppose many people die happy, but at least he was doing what made him happy before this tragedy struck.

Some of his fossils are on display in the museum. To see the rest you would have to go to the National Museum of Scotland or the British Museum. Caithness Horizons, however, has his herbarium, an amazing collection of over 3,000 mosses, ferns and flowering plants.

From Dick to Dounreay. An entire room is dedicated to that major provider of employment in Caithness, reflecting its importance. It's being decommissioned at present, a process which is going to keep people gainfully employed for a long, long time. Its story is told through a series of wall displays and photographs as well as the actual control panel from one of the reactors and a cutaway model of a reactor to let you see the workings inside. Whether you understand it is another matter entirely, but perhaps I only speak for myself.

It's a fitting end to our visit and a fitting introduction, as that is where we are going next.

Chapter Twenty-Nine

Dounreay: Acronyms and Accidents

L EAVING Thurso, we see the sign to Scrabster, where the A9 begins and ends. However, if you have a mind to go to Orkney, then this provides an alternative to the Gills Bay or the John o' Groats terminals, the gargantuan *MV Hamnavoe* whisking you and your car to Stromness in ninety minutes. If you do choose this route, you will be rewarded by a fine view of the Old Man of Hoy as you pass by. The best way to see it actually, from the sea.

The harbour in Scrabster was built in 1820 by – that's right – Thomas Telford. Before that era, the boats used to tie up at high tide to rings embedded into the cliffs, giving rise to Scrabster being known as "The Rings". This is where the *Britannia* moored when the Queen and her sister and other royals came to visit the Queen Mother at Mey. Nowadays the *Britannia* has retired to become a tourist attraction in Leith, while by contrast, the harbour, busier than ever, has expanded out of all proportion to its location. Meanwhile, on Holborn Head, at the western extremity of the bay, is a lighthouse which is, of course, another Stevenson erection, if I may put it that way.

A little further on, at the Crosskirk/Bridge of Forss crossroads, an Ancient Monument sign points to the right, to the 12th century Saint Mary's Chapel. The road leads you through a farm to a little car park, where another sign points you in the direction of the chapel, though truth to tell, it is not needed as you can see it in the distance through the grassy sward. It's roofless now and windowless, which is not surprising as the experts reckon it was thatched originally and it never had any windows in the first place. And if that is a bit surprising, as the candles must have struggled to shed a tiny light against the gloom, it's more of a surprise to see tombstones growing like mushrooms in the nave. In 1871, a chancel was rebuilt or added by the Gunns to commemorate their dead, whilst outside the building, the green, green grass of the graveyard is well patronised, having being in use until about the same date.

A little further on, but off to the left this time, another historic monument is signed, the unexcavated Cnoc Freicadain chambered cairns. This involves a bit of a detour by road and a bit of a hike to the cairns, which the neolithic builders 5,000 years ago inconveniently built for us on top of a hill. But not half as inconvenient for those who had to lug thousands upon thousands of stones and boulders up there.

To be honest, the cairns (there are two of them) might be a bit of a disappointment, particularly if you have been to Camster Cairns, as the whole site is pretty much grassed over. But what does makes the climb worthwhile, in my view, is from the top, the fine appreciation you get of time in the landcape. There, at your feet, is a construction from 3000 BC built to honour the dead, whilst if you lift your eyes to the hills, you will see the bright and shining future, a host of windmills semaphoring this is clean energy. Meanwhile down there on the coast, the sun has set on that dirty big sphere that once was heralded as the bright new dawn in man's insatiable desire for energy ever since he got so smart and needed power to drive his machines.

In the layby that serves as a car park, that's exactly what a series of noticeboards does – takes you through this landscape from when the ice retreated and it began to be settled, from Neolithic times to the post-medieval period. Thanks to LiDAR (Light Detecting and Ranging), the land is giving up its secrets. Over three hundred new settlements have been discovered by its all-seeing, all-encompassing, penetrating eyes – not a hump, not a bump, not a lump that it does not see and which can be photographed and rotated and turned into a 3D image.

Actually I would argue the LiDAR image of Cnoc Freicadain is better than the real thing. Resembling a couple of bones that a dog has gnawed, you can see, perfectly clearly, the rounded cairns at the ends and the horns projecting from them like open pincers. Also, unusually, the two cairns are set at right-angles to each other. The roundhouses of the Bronze Age people have long since disappeared, but LiDAR picks out the circular indentations which they left behind.

As Caithness Horizons will tell you, Caithness is the Broch capital of Scotland. You can scarcely avoid stumbling over one, not to mention a chambered cairn, and here a LiDAR photograph of one makes me think of the crater created by the boiling mud in a geyser when its bubble has burst. During the medieval period, it's the layout of the field systems that has been laid bare, as it is in the post-medieval period, where you can see where the grand houses of the estates once were, the farmhouse and the crofts – even the dovecotes. There is just no hiding from LiDAR. If you live in a house or, like Voltaire, "cultivate your garden", LiDAR will find the footprint you left behind.

There's no need to feel guilty in the way some people do about leaving their carbon footprint on the planet. It's part and parcel of living in the 21st century and, with the best will in the world, you can't eliminate it entirely – even in death, the disposal of your body comes at some cost to the environment. However, on the hill on the other side of the road, Baillie Wind Farm – with more windmills than Don Quixote could possibly tilt his lance at – is an attempt to cut down on all our carbon footprints. Operational since 2013, its 21 wind turbines, measuring 360 feet from tip to toe, produce 52.5 megawatts (MW) of energy annually, enough to power an estimated 42,800 homes. Whilst that may be impressive, what impresses me less is that this new technology will have a life span of only twenty-five years.

We retrace our route to the main road and despite the time of day, like a harvest moon climbing into the sky, the iconic 135-foot high steel sphere of Dounreay gradually grows larger as we draw nearer. We pull into the car park. This far we can go, and no further. It's a fair way down a long, straight road to where, beyond the barrier, the sphere now looks like a golfball, teed up, waiting for some native of Brobdingnag on a golfing holiday to come along and hit it out of sight somewhere. It may only be sixty years old, but we are looking at the past.

Dounreay has more acronyms than you can shake a fuel rod at. In 1955, the Dounreay Nuclear Power Establishment (DNPE) decided that fast breeder reactors (FBRs) should be built and operated here by the United Kingdom Atomic Energy Authority (UKAEA). Four years later (fast to build and fast by nature), the Dounreay Fast Reactor (DFR) went "critical" in 1959. A significant choice of word you might think for "began working", but it was not until 1962 before it supplied electricity to the national grid whilst it underwent safety checks. It was shut down in 1977, and if you think £15 million was a lot to pay for that short lifespan, hang on to your hat.

The phenomenal speed with which the complex was built and became operative had much to do with it being a child of its time, and little thought was given to the problem of waste. In those Cold War days, stocks of uranium were limited, and those that were available were needed for the nuclear deterrent. However, new discoveries in Canada and Australia meant that the heat was off, so to speak.

The DFR was followed by the Prototype Fast Reactor (PFR), capable of producing 250 MW compared to the DFR's meagre 14 MW – enough output to keep the lights of a city the size of Aberdeen burning. It was constructed between 1967 and 1975 and was shut down in 1994, the last of the three reactors to come to the end of its useful life.

You may be relieved to know I propose to say nothing at all about the first reactor to achieve criticality in 1958, the DMTR – which, of course, stands for the Dounreay Means Test Reactor. It was shut down in 1969. Nor am I going to say anything about the Vulcan NRTE (Naval Reactor Test Establishment), which puts the reactors of the submarines through their paces on dry land thus hopefully avoiding any problems under the sea. When the current tests are complete, it too will be decommissioned at an estimated eye-watering £2.1 billion.

Nor am I going to say anything about LAIRD (Loss of Coolant Anti-Accident Rig Dounreay), the only one in the world and which does exactly what it says on the tin. I will, however, just say a little more about the STF (Shore Test Facility) because in 2012 it discovered a microscopic leak in the cooling system of the PWR2 (Pressurised Water Reactor), and *HMS Vulcan* was earmarked for attention next time it was in Faslane on the Clyde for refuelling. This tiny leak will take three-and-a-half years to fix at a cost of £120 million. And that's just for *Vulcan.* The rest will need to be done too. As the anti-nuclear brigade never tire of telling us – that's an awful lot of hospitals.

In 2009, with all the world's oceans to hide in, *Vulcan* somehow managed to collide with the French submarine *Triomphant.* Isn't that an incredible thing! But we must remember they are like the worst sort of fart: silent but deadly.

As things turned out, the two fast breeder reactors were the only ones ever built in the UK. The idea behind them (in case you don't know) was to test the theory that it was possible to generate electricity at the same time as breed new material. It was, but don't ask me how. And when they were looking for a place to build them, Dounreay was given the nod over Winfrith in Dorset, a real feather in the cap for Scotland – or so you might think.

Actually Caithness was chosen because, in the event of an explosion, it was over the hill and far away from major centres of population, not to mention the seat of Government. Which just goes to show you that away back then, when I was in short trousers, long before Chernobyl ever came to pass, a far-sighted and benevolent government was concerned for our safety. Good news for most of us; not so good for those living under the shadow of the dome in Caithness, Sutherland and Orkney. Not that they had much say in the matter. Nor, do I suspect, did those in the front line mind too much either, not because – in the event of an accident – the dome is designed to implode, but because it brought 700 construction jobs and much-needed employment to the area and still does today, in its dying days. At its height, it employed 3,000 scientists and others, more than doubling the population of Caithness to over 8,000.

The name "Dounreay" derives from the Gaelic for "fort on the mound". The present castle, or what remains of it, is only a stone's throw from the dome. It was built in the 1560s by the 3rd Earl of Caithness and knocked about a bit by Cromwell in 1651, but was repaired and inhabited until 1883 when it was allowed to fall into neglect. In February 2015, during a storm, the north wall collapsed leaving it in a more ruinous state than ever.

During the Second World War there was an aerodrome here, yet another prong in the Scapa Flow defences. It was known as *HMS Tern II* which sounds like an odd name for an aerodrome, but that's because it was operated by the Admiralty until it was transferred to the Air Ministry in 1949. Whenever a plane took off, they had to close the access road to Dounreay as it bisected the runway. (Talk about beware of low-flying aircraft!) The last plane took off in 1990, and the aerodrome finally closed in 1993. During the construction of the reactors, the ancillary buildings were used as accommodation for 2,000 construction workers and the UKAEA staff, but the aerodrome remained on standby, ready to be used in the event of hostilities. It was during the Cold War after all.

Now the whole site is being decommissioned and demolished by Dounreay Site Restoration Ltd. (DSRL) under contract from the UK Nuclear Decommissioning Agency (NDA), who owns it. The latest estimate for completion is 2033 at a cost of £3 billion; that's £4.6 billion including waste management. All of which makes the £15 million cost of the original DFR seem like a bargain.

And so the Caithness job bonanza continues. 1,500 people are employed in the decommissioning, half as many as it took to build it. Nice work if you can get it. But is it?

80% of the waste at Dounreay is low-level waste (LLW), less than 0.1% radioactive. For the higher-activity waste (HAW), workers operate behind thick lead sheets, putting the really toxic stuff into steel drums mixed with cement. They might well imagine themselves in a tale of horror by Edgar Allan Poe called *The Shaft and the Silo*. The Shaft, 215 feet deep and fifteen feet in diameter, was built to remove spoil from a tunnel which was being built to take radioactive effluent out to a diffuser 2,000 feet out to sea and 150 feet below the seabed. After the tunnel was built, they plugged the bottom of the shaft which allowed it to become a very handy waste receptacle. As for the Silo, it is a 720 cubic metre concrete "swimming pool" into which they threw all the rubbish of the day and where an explosion took place in 1977.

No-one was hurt in that accident, but that's by no means the only one there has been. In 1983, a two-kilometre stretch of beach was closed off when it was found to be contaminated with particles of spent fuel rods which had been discharged into the sea. No bigger than a grain of sand, each one is capable of killing someone if ingested. They contain caesium-136 which has a half-life of thirty years but, if they contain plutonium-239, that has a half-life of 24,000 years. Isn't that astonishing? We all know that half a loaf is better than no bread but, in radioactive terms, a "half-life" means the time it takes for half the material to decay. If you get one of those particles in your sandwich on your Sunday afternoon picnic on the beach, you are likely to have no life at all.

In what seemed a very leisurely approach to the leak, a two-kilometre ban on fishing was introduced in 1997, and in 2008 a remotely operated vehicle (ROV) was sent in to clean up the seabed, together with divers equipped with something resembling a carpet sweeper. Over 2,300 particles were recovered from the seabed in addition to nearly 500 from local beaches and the Dounreay foreshore.

In 2011 the Scottish Environment Protection Agency (SEPA) reckoned this clean-up was counter-productive, causing more harm to the ecosystem by stirring up the seabed than protecting the public from a hazard it described as "insignificant". It had to admit that looking for, and finding, every lost particle was the equivalent of looking for a particular grain of sand on the beach and gave up its aim of restoring both the seabed and foreshore at Dounreay to their former pristine selves. To this day it still is a restricted area, even although SEPA says that of all the particles washed ashore, only one was found to be of a "significant" level of danger.

Most recently and despite UKAEA's motto "Safety First – Always", as a result of human error a fire broke out on October 7th 2015 leading to an "unauthorised" release of radioactivity. (I have no idea what an "authorised" release of radioactivity is.) The Office for Nuclear Regulation (ONR) found the staff to blame, but served the bosses of DSRL with an "improvement notice". They were probably well pleased with that. Earlier, in 2007, the UKAEA was fined £140,000 at Wick Sheriff Court for using a landfill site to dispose of radioactive materials which leaked particles into the sea. For twelve years. You might consider the fine too little, too late, but I couldn't possibly comment.

During the decommissioning, 300,000 tonnes of waste will have to be dealt with and disposed of. Only 1% will remain on site, at present stored in two £20 million, purpose-built vaults thirty-six feet below the ground. Four more are to be built. The liquid waste, known as "raffinate", is dealt with by the Dounreay Cementation Plant (DCP). It is neutralised with sodium hydroxide, then mixed with cement powder before being put into 500 litre drums each weighing 1.25 tonnes. Now it is ready for storage.

So much for the waste, but then there is the little matter of what to do with the unspent fuel; that is to say the stuff that can be reprocessed and used again. I am very pleased to hear it. I hate waste.

On 1st April 2016 it was announced that 1,540 lbs of highly-enriched uranium (HEU) from Georgia would be sent from here to Savannah River, South Carolina. The reason we have it in the first place is because in 1998, it was sent for safekeeping lest it fell into the hands of Chechen terrorists or the Iranian government following the period of uncertainty after the referendum in favour of the restoration of Georgian independence on the last day of March 1991 and the collapse of the Soviet Union on Boxing Day of the same year.

When you look at the date when the uranium transfer story broke, you might have been forgiven for thinking it was an April Fool's Day joke devised by the newspaper editors to test the nation's gullibility. In actual fact, however, the Government regards this as very good news indeed as, in return, a different type of uranium will be sent to the European Atomic Agency (Euratom) in France. This will be converted to isotopes and used to diagnose and treat cancer. It's a 7,000 mile round trip in what has been called "transatlantic nuclear ping-pong", but first it has to get by road to Wick airport, which any terrorist might think would be a pretty soft spot to launch an attack. Though I'm sure the powers-that-be have thought of that. I hope and trust.

Then there is the small matter of the 44 tonnes of what is quaintly known as the "exotics"; the "breeder material" from the PRR. In 2012, the first shipment by rail from Dounreay to Sellafield in Cumbria was made under armed escort. It will be stored there until such time as it can be reprocessed – or just stored there forever more. It's a lot closer than the USA, only a mere 400 miles, and it will take at least sixty rail journeys before the job is done.

A simpler and safer solution, you might have thought, would be to store it at source, at Dounreay, but we are told the £60 million cost of transporting it is by far the cheaper option. It would cost billions to build a facility to house it and, what's more, it's a bit like an albatross around the neck. If the fuel is everlasting (which to all intents and purposes it is), then so is the security cost.

In order to transport it, the fuel is put into stainless steel drums which are then compressed to a fifth of their size. They call them "pucks" – six inches high and about one-and-a-half in diameter. Economy-packed uranium. Fourteen are stacked end-to-end and put into a cylinder before they are put into what's called a "flask". Now they are ready to go. Safe as houses.

As I said earlier, it's going to take the best part of twenty years from now before the decommissioning will be completed and another three centuries, ten generations after that, before the site will cease to be a restricted area.

At one point it was intended to leave the dome on the landscape as a reminder of what once was here instead of a fence saying "Keep Out!", but that proposal has been shelved on grounds of cost: £0.5 million every decade or so, just to give it a coat of paint. Surely with all the technology that has gone into the building and decommissioning of this place, you would have thought someone could have come up with some sort of paint that had more than a half-life of five years, to put it in nuclear terms.

A notice tells us armed guards patrol the premises and we are not to be alarmed should they suddenly appear wanting to know what we are doing in the car park which they have so thoughtfully provided for us. After all, there's no reason to come here now that the visitor centre – which used to be housed in the control room of the aerodrome – has been torn down, and the display removed to Caithness Horizons.

I hang about as my official snapper takes photographs to her heart's content of the complex with and without her zoom lens – and, as far as I know, no-one saw us, or if they did through their high-powered binoculars, cared not a whit what she was doing. Certainly no vehicles, heavily-armoured or otherwise, screech up bearing cops bristling with Kalashnikovs or even revolvers, demanding to know what we want all those photographs for.

In an unhurried way, we escort ourselves out of the car park and head for the hills which are already starting to rumple up the western horizon. The most scenic part of the NC500 is about to begin.

It's an exciting prospect.

Chapter Thirty

Bettyhill: Boats and Buoys

I F you are interested in church architecture, you might like to stop and have a look at Reay's rather unusual T-shaped church, whose bell tower is reached by an external staircase. It was built in 1739.

The village itself nestles behind the dunes of the appropriately-named Sandside Bay (another renowned windsurfing site) at the west end of which is Cnoc Stanger, a prehistoric mound. But that's not all Reay has to offer by any means. It boasts the remains of a stone circle, a Bronze Age settlement and Viking roundhouses, all of which have left their mark on the landscape in a series of mounds which you don't need LiDAR to see.

According to legend, the 1st Lord Reay, Donald Mackay (1591-1649), aka the Wizard of Reay, won a tizzy of fairies in a contest with a witch. Under his instruction, they began digging, looking for hidden treasure, hence the goodly number of mounds hereabout. Donald soon wearied of their littering the landscape with monstrous molehills with nothing to show for it and ordered them to stop. But it was no good – they would not listen, such was their zeal for digging. For a while Donald scratched his head, then he had a light bulb moment. His bright idea was to order them to build a causeway of sand across the Pentland Firth. There is a tide in the affairs of fairies which takes up all their time and leads to futility. They are at it still, to this very day, but we need not shed a tear for them: digging is what they love to do and they are as happy as sandboys.

Like the fairies, my tale is not over yet with Donald Mackay, magician of this parish, but I will keep that to another time and place.

In 1437, there was a battle here between the Mackays from Strathnaver, bent on attacking Thurso, and the men of Dounreay bent on preventing them from going one step further. At first the Mackays appeared to have the upper hand and drove the Caithness men back towards Forss Water, but at that point reinforcements appeared and it was the turn of the Dounreay men to drive the Mackays back towards the Cnoc. Foreseeing this eventuality, the Mackays had placed a rearguard on the mound and, when they joined the fray, the tide of battle turned yet again as they descended upon the Dounreay men who turned tail and fled. That is why the battle is known as the "Battle of Sandside Chase". The slaughter on both sides was terrible.

Melvich, which is next, boasts yet another very fine surfing beach beyond the dunes and a rather unusual early 19th century icehouse with a conical roof. If you turn right at the Strathy Inn, in a short while you will come to Strathy Point where you will see another unusual sight – a lighthouse which for once was not built by one of the Stevensons. Isn't that an incredible thing! That's because they were a' deid by then. It was only built in 1958 – Scotland's first all-electric lighthouse. Looking more like a fortress than a saver of sailors' lives, it has a square tower protected by rectangular buildings. After it was automated in 1997, the complex was converted into private homes.

Our NC500 route, the A836, has now become a single carriageway with passing places but there is so little traffic it does not hinder us much. With hills to the left of us, hills to the right of us, hills ahead of us and hills behind us, we are feeling a sense of another Scotland, a far cry from the bustling metropolises of Glasgow and Edinburgh, or even Thurso for that matter. We are literally in the Highlands now, where a different, wilder, more untamed sort of Scotland begins. And if one of your primary reasons for exploring the NC500 is to enjoy the scenery – the mountains, the rugged coastline, the sea and one splendid sandy bay after another – then you are in for a treat.

We have left Caithness behind now and are back in Sutherland. Despite its northerly location, it was the southern lands as far as the Vikings were concerned. And if there are two words that are associated with the place, one is "Duke" and the other is "Clearances". I don't propose to say much more about either here, having dealt with them in the Helmsdale chapter, and I only mention them again now because we are getting very close to Strathnaver where the worst excesses took place. As I have already pointed out, it was the Duke's wife, Elizabeth, aided and abetted by her factor, Patrick Sellar, who was the more ruthless of the two, more committed to the new-fangled agricultural "improvements". For her foresightedness, for the misery she caused, she has a place named after her – Bettyhill – where, driven north out of the river valley, a good many ended up and were forced to call "home".

It's a bumpfly sort of landscape, a few dwellings scattered amongst a rock-strewn landscape at the mouth of the Naver. If the idea was the crofters should try their hand at fishing rather than farming and thereby improve their standard of living (whilst the Duke improved his fortune), it might have been helpful if he had first provided a harbour.

Before Bettyhill the village, not too distant from the even smaller place called Farr, we come to the former church of St Columba, built in 1774 on the site of an earlier church dating back to the early 13th century. It sits imposingly on its grassy knoll a little distance from the road. Like a pioneer's covered wagon under attack from hostile Native Americans, it is surrounded on every side by a massive number of gravestones, amongst them – on the western side – a Pictish stone dating from the early 9th century and called the "Farr Stone".

According to legend, it just appeared suddenly overnight at the same time as a mysterious foreign ship had been seen anchored in the bay and, according to an entry in the *Old Statistical Account* of 1791 by the Rev. James Dingwall, he claims it commemorates a "Dane of distinction". Make of that what you will, but to the locals it is the *Clach Erchar* or stone of Farquhar, sometime physician to Robert II of Scotland and said to mark his resting place, but clearly the stone predates the good doctor by several centuries.

We've seen quite a few Pictish stones on this trip, and this has to be one of the finest. In fact, it is so beautifully carved you might have thought they would have protected it from the elements so it can be appreciated by future generations. It depicts a very fine Celtic cross with the panels around the cross filled in with intricate knot work. The centre has a swirl which has a certain mesmeric, hypnotic sort of quality to it as if drawing you in like the snake's eyes in Disney's version of *The Jungle Book*. The ends of the arms have a Greek keys pattern, and it stands on a hemispherical base as if designed to be the centrepiece of an altar.

It may, or may not, double as a headstone but – immediately to the right of the church's entrance – there is a Bronze Age grave. Workmen found it when repairing a road at Chealamy in Strathnaver and it has been removed here for our interest. Known as a "short cist burial", it is not very roomy, not very deep and lined with slabs. When the workmen found it by accidentally drilling through the lid, it contained only a few bones but enough for the experts to tell he was male, aged between 25-30, and had been buried lying on his side in a crouched position. In a much better condition was a beaker which had been buried with him and which, although cracked, was still in one piece. It would have provided the nourishment, probably mead or honey, for his journey to the afterlife. He must have drunk deeply thereof because not a drop of that precious elixir remained. Whoever he was, I hope he made it safely and nothing too nasty was waiting for him on the other side. As for the beaker, it has made it safely inside the museum.

Finally on the subject of graves, on the same side of the church as the Bronze Age cist, near the boundary wall, is that of Dr Ian Grimble, writer, historian and broadcaster who had as many close shaves with death as the proverbial cat. Eventually, however, the Grim Reaper did catch up with him in 1995. Apart from the achievements above, as well as the stone beneath which he lies, he has yet another memorial – for it is largely due to his sterling efforts that when the church ceased to be as a place of worship in 1935, it was resurrected in 1976 as the Strathnaver Museum.

It's hard to say what the main attraction of that is – not a nook, not a cranny that has not something that reflects the twin facets of this area's heritage of farming and fishing. Upstairs is dedicated to Clan Mackay, for this is their territory. The highlights there, for me, is a very amusing Mackay prayer (unless you are Irish) pinned to the wall and a ledger which, amongst other things, details Dr Grimble's dices with death.

Downstairs in the crowded body of the kirk, the eye is caught by the interior of a croft which has been reconstructed, complete with box bed. In something that recalls the Peggotys' upturned boat house in *David Copperfield,* the roof is partly formed from the timbers of the hull of the 262-ton Norwegian barque *Thorwaldsen* out of Cardiff with a cargo of coal and fourteen souls aboard, bound for Trondhjem. On March 9th 1858, it was shipwrecked in a storm off Strathy Point with the loss of ten lives including the captain, Hans Berg, and his English wife, Eleanor. They are buried in Strathy. It's a tragic tale indeed, but life goes on – and waste not, want not, especially in a place where trees and therefore timber is at a premium.

In a corner on the other side of the room is the figurehead of the ill-fated vessel, carved by Hans Michelsen (1789-1859). You can see he was a fine figure of a man once upon a time but he is looking a bit bashed about now, not surprisingly, considering what he went through. Whoever he is, he does not look in the least bashful but rather astonished and poppy-eyed, as if to say, "How come I ended up here?" and "Where's my boat? I was very attached to it".

There's another boat here too, and a very interesting one. It could be the sort of thing a small boy such as me might have played with in the bath or sailed in a pond, but actually it's much more interesting than that – it's one of St Kilda's mailboats which was washed up near Hope, along the coast to the west. It bears a notice which reads: "St Kilda Mailboat. Please open tin". It has been securely lashed to the deck by means of wire. It has come a very long way indeed. Now a UNESCO World Heritage Site, St Kilda is an archipelago some forty miles west of South Uist, itself a long way from the Scottish mainland and an even longer distance from the NC500 – and not one of the easiest places in the world to get to, either.

This is actually a very modern specimen, sent by some soldiers who were stationed on the island in 1974 to look after the radar station, but the origins of the mailboat date back just over a century to 1877 when nine Austrian sailors (!) were marooned after a shipwreck. John Sands (1826-1900), journalist, artist and amateur archaeologist was living on St Kilda at the time and as he records in his autobiography, he came up with the bright idea of attaching a message to a lifebuoy from the stricken vessel and casting the sailors' fate, and theirs, to the wind and the waves. The islanders could ill afford to feed nine extra mouths.

By good luck, only nine days later the lifebuoy was washed ashore on Orkney and the sailors were eventually rescued. Imagine the wait, not knowing what would happen to their message; imagine the suspense, imagine the jubilation as some days later, the rescue boat appeared on the horizon. After that, the St Kildans, whenever they wanted to communicate with the outside world, when starving for example, they would fashion a boat out of wood like the one in the museum, attach the bladder of a sheep to it and, when the wind was blowing from the north-west, cast it into the sea. Then they waited...

Whilst the oldest exhibit in the museum is the Bronze Age beaker aforesaid, arguably its most unusual exhibit is a buoy for fishing nets made of dogskin. The idea was that as the nets filled with fish, the floats kept them from sinking to the bottom. It's rather a grisly object to be honest: the stumps of the legs and neck making it all too easy to imagine poor Rover romping about full of waggy-tailed life. Unusual though it may be, apparently it's not unique. It seems many of man's best friends were actually born and bred to be buoys. No wonder we have the expression "It's a dog's life".

I imagine the recipe for making such a buoy; as Hannah Glasse, the Georgian cookery writer, might have put it: "First catch your dog, kill him and gut him and hang him up to dry. When he is ready, put his inside to the outside and make of him a sack with wooden bungs where his head and legs were. Pour in a mixture of archangel tar and linseed oil and shake him thoroughly until he is waterproof. Now he is done".

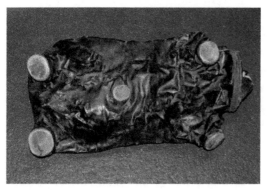

Archangel tar is variously known as "pine tar" and "Stockholm tar". Pine because that is the source material, and Stockholm because a single company had the monopoly in shipping it out of the Swedish capital. And incidentally, to be fair to Mrs Grasse, in her *The Art of Cookery Made Plain and Easy*, she didn't actually say "First catch your hare". What she actually wrote was "Take your hare when it be cas'd", in other words when it has been skinned. The *Oxford Book of Quotations* is full of instances where the speaker or writer's words have been "improved" by others, and maybe they have been – as in the case of Mrs Grasse.

Almost as interesting as the buoy is the Melness shoe – a lady's boot, actually. Both it and the dogskin were found concealed within the walls of a house along with a whisky bottle which the owner had been careful to empty first. The thinking is they were placed there as good-luck charms or to ward off witches and evil spirits, though usually they were placed in chimneys which were considered the weak part of a house for letting in ghosties and ghoulies and long-leggedy beasties.

However strange a practice it may seem, the shoe thing is actually a more widespread and common practice than many might suppose. Shoes have traditionally been associated with good luck and fertility. It's a tradition which seems to have been largely discontinued nowadays but in my boyhood I remember seeing old boots and shoes being tied to the rear bumpers of the car that bore the newlyweds away to begin their new lives together. Nowadays it's as likely as not it's the kids you'll see trailing behind them as they jet off somewhere sunny for the honeymoon. As for the whisky bottle, my guess is the man of the house was hiding it from his loving wife, aka the drinks police.

Another thing that catches my eye, in a glass case, is a knitting belt; a contraption with perforations, stuffed with horse hair, which was worn around the knitter's waist, and – as the notice that goes with it explains – an extra pair of hands. Not being an expert knitter, or indeed a knitter of any description, I don't quite see how it works, but what it did allow women to do was knit as they walked. (You may remember the photograph of the herring gutters knitting on their way to work in Wick.) Upstairs, in the Mackay museum, is a photograph that trumps that. It shows a woman, not in the first flush of youth either, with a wicker basket full of peat, higher than her head, knitting a pair of socks. Which just goes to show you what a remarkable piece of work a woman is. A donkey might be able to carry as much peat but I'd like to see it knit a pair of socks at the same time.

In the same case is a related object, something the knitter above may have used as her raw material – human hair, twisted into a thread. To me it's a grisly sight, the skeins of grizzled hair, and I for one would not care to wear a shirt made out of it. We're in the land of sheep after all, so what's the point – unless it's an unusual way of keeping close to grandma after she's gone.

The original pulpit dominates, as it should, this being a church let us not forget, the very one where the Reverend David Mackenzie read out the eviction notices to his flock, where he told them they had to move out so those belonging to the Countess could move in. At its rear, framed by a white arch, in big block capitals, also in white, is written "MGM 1774". The date of course, tells us this is long before the silver screen and Metro-Goldwyn-Mayer productions. The letters celebrate Master George Munro, first minister of this church and, by all accounts, much respected by his parishioners despite his youth – and as was the custom before the Disruption, appointed not by the people but their lord and master, the laird.

Pinned to a board on your right, as you go in, is an account of how the crofters lived a subsistence existence, as well as some brief eyewitness testimonies from those grim times. You might only notice them as you are leaving since there is so much ahead of you that draws you in, like the pulpit and the figurehead, but it's really worth stopping a moment and reading them (they are very brief) and reflecting on the poor people of Strathnaver who happened to have the misfortune to live in that particular place at that particular time. You are already familiar with some of these stories from a previous chapter, but these are fresh horrors. I will leave you to read them for yourself and, having done so, to reflect on this universal truth: it is a terribly dangerous thing to be born. You have absolutely no control over when or where or to whom.

With that sobering thought in mind, we are going to make another detour from the NC500 and follow the Strathnaver Trail – if not into the valley of death exactly, at least the scene for some of the worst excesses in the whole sorry business.

Chapter Thirty-One

Strathnaver to Tongue: The Deserted Villages

THE A836 and the NC500 sweeps south down the Naver valley a little way before swinging west towards Tongue. The Strathnaver Trail, however, lies straight ahead on the B871. Along the way, as well as the traces of the villages that were cleared, are chambered cairns from Neolithic times from about 6,000 years ago, Bronze Age standing stones and stone circles from about 4,400 years ago, and Iron Age brochs from about 2,600 years ago. This is a road through the past if ever there was one.

We pass through Chealamy (blink and you'll miss it) where the beaker in the museum was found, but our first stop is at the memorial to the 93rd Sutherland Highlanders which is to the side of the corrugated-iron Strathnaver Public Hall. In 1799, six hundred men responded to an appeal by the 16 year-old Countess of Sutherland for the able-bodied sons of her tenants to enlist for king and country against the Napoleonic threat. In September of the following year, they mustered at Syre where the memorial was originally placed.

One of them was Sergeant Sam MacDonald (1760-1802), whose height has been greatly exaggerated but who actually stood six-foot-ten in his socks and who had a chest measurement of forty-eight inches. He once appeared as Hercules in *Cymon and Imphigenia* in a Drury Lane production. When the Countess saw him, she spontaneously awarded him an extra allowance of 2/6 a day as he must "require more sustenance than his military pay can afford".

The regiment went on to distinguish itself all over the globe, most famously in 1845 at the Battle of Balaklava in the Crimea where they formed the "Thin Red Line" against the Russian cavalry, and at the Relief of Lucknow in 1857 where no less than seven men distinguished themselves by being awarded VCs, six of them on one day – the 16th November. Incidentally, an incredible total of twenty-four medals were awarded that day, a record.

But long before these deeds of derring do, the Sutherlanders were much less inclined to answer the country's need for cannon fodder, having become disenchanted with their landowning masters after the Clearances especially, retorting since they "preferred sheep to men, let the sheep defend them!" As a matter of fact, it was as a result of firstly, the American Wars of Independence, then the threat posed by the Revolution across the Channel, followed by full-blown war with France, that made sheep farming the profitable business it was, their wool required for the soldiers' uniforms, their mutton for their stomachs.

Just a little further on is Skail, the site of an ancient cemetery and a pre-Reformation chapel. There's nothing to be seen now, the stones having been used to shore up the bank of the river in the early 19th century, but in a grassy field is what's called the "Red Priest's stone", said to mark the grave of St Maelrubha who founded Applecross Abbey and a lot of other churches besides. It's an unremarkable stone, apart from the cross that has been carved into one of the sides. "Side", please note; not one of the faces.

The "Red Priest" travelled widely around Scotland, spreading the Word. Historians seem to agree he died in 722 AD, but not where exactly and who killed him, if indeed a third party was involved at all. He certainly did come to the Naver valley, but the year seems rather early for his death here at the hands of the Vikings as some allege, since they did not begin raiding these shores for another seventy years or so. Anyway, we shall leave him there for the present. We will return to him later, but in the meantime we are moving on just a little way to Syre.

At its heart is a rather quaint church, another corrugated-iron building, this time with white walls and a red roof. It was commissioned by the Free Church in 1891 and prefabricated by Frederick Braby & Co in Glasgow. In the series of schisms and divisions that the Church went through from 1842 onwards, there was a burgeoning need for new churches and in the Highlands, the quickest and simplest solution was to make them of tin, so to speak. And if it looks utilitarian from the outside, its interior is the complete antithesis, cosy and charming.

If the church is the centre of the village, you could call Syre the epicentre of the Clearances, for this is where Patrick Sellar, who is widely regarded as the villain of the piece, chose to settle, surrounded by his sheep. You can see his cottage just up the hill from the church, with the same red roof and white walls, though the roof wouldn't have been like that in Sellar's day.

And while on the subject of the sheep supremo, it's worth mentioning in the passing, that he thought he was doing nothing wrong in evicting all those tenants. In fact, in his own words, he saw the "improvements" as "a most benevolent action, to put these barbarous Highlanders into a position where they could better associate together, apply themselves to industry, educate their children, and advance in civilisation". That's one way of looking at it I suppose, but there are ways and means too. In the final analysis, as many as 15,000 people were cleared from the Countess's 1.5 million acre estates.

It was here, as I said, the 93rd Regiment mustered, and to the left of the church entrance is a war memorial, which – like so many small places the length and breadth of the Highlands – bears testimony to the sacrifice made in the two World Wars. In this tiny community, twelve lost their lives in the First and four in the Second. And there's something else that's striking. In the Great War, the one that was going to end all wars, more than half of the surnames are either Gunn, MacKay or Sutherland.

The next settlement is Rosal, one of the larger villages, of which the remains of fifteen to eighteen longhouses (one 108 feet long) along with barns and other outhouses can be seen among the humps and bumps in the grass. You have to follow a trail marked by poles which begins with a walk through the forest. Once you arrive at the site, there is also evidence of much older human habitation such as souterrains, cairns, and hut circles.

Rosal has gained a certain notoriety thanks to the polemics published in the Edinburgh Weekly Chronicle by Donald McLeod [sic] and reprinted in book form in 1841 under the title *Gloomy Memories.* It's an appropriate title considering what he saw and experienced: the evictions from Rosal between 1814 and 1818; then in 1830, the eviction of his family and furniture from his cottage in Bettyhill while he was working in Wick as a stonemason, dire threats of eviction being levelled against anyone who sheltered him or his family. Hounded out of the county as an agitator, he went initially to Edinburgh before finally ending up in Ontario where a third edition of his recollections was published in Toronto in 1857.

It was a vitriolic response to Harriet Beecher Stowe's "Sunny Memories of Foreign Lands" (1854), which extolled the virtues of the Countess and her improvements. She may have known something about *Uncle Tom's Cabin* but when it came to talking about a longhouse in the Scottish Highlands during the Clearances, Donald thought Harriet was speaking through a hole in her hat. Given her abolitionist stance against slavery, it's surprising she came down on the side of the fence she did.

Donald left her in no doubt that he was not a member of her fan club. You don't have to read any further than the title page to get a flavour of the contents: *Gloomy Memories of the Highlands of Scotland versus Mrs Harriet Beecher Stowe's Sunny Memories in (England) a foreign land, or, A faithful picture of the extirpation of the Celtic race from the Highlands of Scotland.* You can also see, just from that, why Donald has been accused of over-egging the pudding. Nevertheless, I wonder: did it make Harriet pause and reflect that she might have got it horribly wrong?

A cairn commemorates Donald and his book. Across the river, where crofters would once have scratched a living and where sheep would have grazed after they had gone, all you can see now is a phalanx of firs across the river – though, like the crofters before them, it looks as if their days are numbered as those nearest the river have been felled.

If you are interested, and you don't mind a hike of two-and-a-half miles from the car park and the same back, the next point of interest is a Bronze Age stone circle. What's intriguing about this one is, although small, it has a cairn in the middle. Very unusual. It's called *Clach an Righ* if you want to seek it out.

Since the ninth century, the Norse Earls of Orkney had ruled over Strathnaver, but in the twelfth century that came to an end near here at the head of the loch where the Scots sent the Norsemen home never to return, at the Battle of Dalharrold. It was the turn of the Mackays now to hold sway until, in their turn, their hegemony was chipped away by the Gordons.

And so, on the banks of the loch, we come to what were the twin settlements of Grumbeg and Grummore. In 1813 there were thirty-two families between them. In 1814, there were fifteen. In 1819, sixteen houses were set alight and that was the end of them altogether.

Grummore has the remains of a broch, while Grumbeg – not to be outdone – has a Neolithic chambered cairn and an ancient cemetery, the walls of which are still of a good height. A cross-slab and a carved stone were found near here and in the ancient burial ground of the Aberach MacKays, two more cross-slabs and a cup-marked stone. They were last seen in 1961. Where they are now, someone knows. You can, however see the first two in the Strathnaver museum. Look for them on the left as you go upstairs to the Mackay museum.

A noticeboard repeats the story, as told by the Rev. Donald Sage in his *Memorablia Domestica*, of Hetty Munro – a widow who had followed her husband through his campaigns in Sicily and Spain, for which thanks she was evicted in 1819. Sellar's men gave her half-an-hour to drag her "trumpery" outside, then the roof was torched. Unfortunately the wind blew sparks onto her furniture and it was burned to ashes, not the first instance of this happening you may remember. Hetty was left with what she stood up in.

And so at the end of the loch and the Strathnaver valley, the B873 also comes to an end. To our left is Altnaharra, which means "Stream of the Watching". It is well named because it stands at a crossroads: the A836 leads south to Loch Shin and Lairg (21 miles); north to Tongue (16 miles); east to Bettyhill (24 miles), the way we have just come, and north-west to Hope (21 miles). The village, consisting of less than a dozen houses and with a population of about fifty, stands on an old Drove Road where cattle, sheep and horses were driven south to the famous Falkirk Tryst or to Crieff, to be sold with thousands of others from every corner of Scotland.

The village has a fame far beyond its size because it often features in weather forecasts because of its extreme low temperatures. It has the dubious honour, on December 30th 1995, of achieving the UK's coldest-ever recorded temperature of -27.2°C. In December 2009, the snow started on the 17th December and it snowed right through until March. It is also well known for its luxury hotel, the successor to the inn that stood on the same site in order to cater for the drovers, and now where deerstalkers, gameshooters and trout and salmon fishermen can be cosseted after a hard day plying their deadly sport in the area.

Turning to the right, it's a scenic drive along the banks of Loch Loyal to Tongue, where – like a sleeping stegosaurus – on our left rises the impressive massif of Ben Loyal, then little Loch Craggie. And shortly after that, we come to the junction of the A838, back on the NC500 again. Tongue is one mile away to the left and Bettyhill just twelve to the right.

Tongue's unusual name comes from the Norse *tunga* which means a spit of land (or tongue) projecting into water. Overlooking the Kyle, from the Gaelic *caol* meaning a strait, is *Caisteal Bharraich* or Castle Varrich, whose origins are disputed. Some say it's Viking, the stronghold of Kali Hunadson, one of those Norsemen who in 1033 tried to conquer Scotland during the reign of Malcolm II (the grandfather of the historical Duncan I and Macbeth); others say it was built by Bishop Bar of Caithness, while yet others claim it was the Mackays. What the Mackays are certainly responsible for is, or was, a tower house on the other side of the Rhian burn estuary, built around 1500 and which sustained some damage during the Civil War a century-and-a-half later. Out of the ruins, in 1678, arose the present-day House of Tongue, extended in 1750 and diminished in 1830 when what remained of the original tower house was demolished.

What can't be seen, but what is of historical interest, is the slight part Tongue played in the history of these Isles. It happened in May 1746 when the French sloop, *Le Prince Charles* ran aground in the Kyle. Originally called *Hazard* (imagine inviting disaster by calling a ship that!), the previous November it had been captured in Montrose harbour by the Jacobites. It was bound for Inverness with a cargo of £12,000 in gold coins as well as arms and other supplies to support Bonnie Prince Charlie. It was being pursued by *HMS Sheerness* which is why it ran into the Kyle, hoping to give it the slip. The new plan forced upon them was to take the gold overland to Inverness, no mean undertaking, but desperate times call for desperate measures.

The gold party didn't get very far at all, just a few miles south to Lochan Hakel, intercepted by the royalist Mackays whose intervention at this point might just conceivably have changed the course of not just Scottish, but British history too. Under attack from the Mackays, the crew and Jacobite soldiers began dumping the gold in the lochan. Most of the gold was seized by the Mackays and sent south in the *Sheerness* along with 156 prisoners, most of them Frenchmen. But if scuba diving or snorkelling is your thing, you could do worse than try your luck here. As for *Le Prince Charles*, recaptured again, it resorted to its original (and risky) name of *Hazard.*

It certainly was bad luck for the Young Pretender – perhaps a double disaster because, on hearing the news but not that the gold had been recovered, Charlie dispatched 1,500 men to recover the treasure, men off on a wild gold-chase whose strong sword-arms might have been used to better effect at Culloden. Probably they would have slain quite a few before being cut down themselves, but it's doubtful if their presence would have been enough to turn the tide of battle. The Prince's pig-headedness, his refusal to listen to his advisors and the aborted attack on Nairn (which *could* have made a difference, had it been successful), not to mention the exhausted and ill-fed state of the Highlanders, were what turned the tide of British history – not what happened here. Against Cumberland's well-fed and disciplined army, there was only going to be one winner all along.

In those days, Tongue was much more isolated than it is today. Telford is to blame, if that's the right word, for opening it up to the outside world. His road south to Lairg, now the A836, was completed in 1828, followed by the road east to Thurso in 1863 from which ran a daily coach. It was later followed by the road west to Durness. Actually, it was quicker by far to get there by taking three ferries across the Kyle, the River Hope and Loch Eriboll respectively – the Pentland Firth having very much gnawed away at the coastline in this part of the country.

The Kyle ferry stopped operating in 1953, and since 1971 a causeway and bridge has curved gracefully across the Kyle, cutting off eight miles or so. After that you can carry on west towards Durness on the NC500 or take another small detour, if you will, by heading north on the west side of the Kyle through several scattered communities such as Melness (where the shoe and dogskin buoy came from) and Talmine, from where you get a good view of the three

Rabbit Islands (where the *Hazard* ran aground), which are uninhabited by humans but very much overrun with those proverbially prolific breeders as the sandy soil makes it easy for them to burrow into.

You probably won't set foot on the islands, but if you have an irresistible desire to feel sand between your toes, there are some very fine beaches along the shore. The original settlers did not come here to be beside the seaside however; they came because they were forced to find somewhere else to live. Yes, you've guessed it – they are Clearance villages.

Before we leave them, let me tell you the islands were originally known as "Eilean nan Gall", or "Islands of the Strangers", because this is where the Vikings landed in the 9th century.

If it's not one damned pest it's another.

Chapter Thirty-Two

Loch Eriboll to Smoo Cave: When Worlds Collide

W E'RE crossing the Moine, from the Gaelic *A' Mhòine*, towards Loch Eriboll. It's a boggy, peaty place pitted by *dubh lochans*, dark pools, where the heather grows, the deer roam and birds nest. The hamlet of Hope stands at the head of the loch of the same name, and this is where the St Kilda lifeboat we had seen in the Strathnaver museum was washed ashore. At the head of the loch, towering over the landscape, is the lowering bulk of Ben Hope, Scotland's most northerly Munro which just makes the right to be called so by a slender forty-one feet. It is also a Marilyn, which some wit coined to describe a bump in the landscape of over 150 metres or 492 feet. For your information, there are 1,217 Marilyns in Scotland but only 282 Munros.

Soon, straight ahead of us, we catch our first sight of Loch Eriboll and the land beyond. It marks a change in the landscape: a wild sort of place, more rugged, treeless, untamed, largely uninhabited. The difference between one side of the loch and the other is quite remarkable, but the reason for the change is even more so.

Once upon a time, long, long ago (540 million years ago in fact), in a distant continent south of the equator, layers of sandstone quartz, later to be metamorphosed into quartzite, began to be laid down in the warm tropical waters. And so it continued over the aeons, this landmass, a part of which would come to be called "Scotland" inexorably and imperceptibly drifting north, a thick layer of limestone being deposited on top of the quartzite over the millennia. The limestone has its own story to tell too, as does the quartzite for that matter, for the fossils embedded in them are very similar to those found in North America. That's how we know Scotland was once part of the same continent as that of our transatlantic cousins.

Then came a series of tectonic events during the Late Proterozoic and Early Paleozoic periods, and then – round about 430 million years ago – the continent, of which England and Wales were a part, collided with Scotland's. The rocks were metamorphosed, tilted and rumpled up like a tablecloth, to form mountains as high as the Himalayas but which have since weathered down to their present height. So you see, Scotland and England really are different countries, once were worlds apart, literally, and also differ in many other fundamental respects, so many would contend. All of which might be music to the ears of the Scottish nationalists – if they are not already aware of it.

This is where the North West Highlands Geopark begins, in its own words, to "Explore Deep Time, Evoke a Sense of Place and Encourage Stewardship". We are on the NC500, we know that, but we are also on what the NWHG calls the "Pebble Route". For geographers and geologists, it is a place of unparalleled interest, for here are to be found the oldest rocks in the United Kingdom – or in the world for that matter. For them this place "rocks", if you forgive the expression (their words, not mine), but for the NC500 traveller who knows nothing about, or cares even less for rocks and stones and only sees mountains, silver sands and seas – the truth is that the beauty is all they need to know, as Keats didn't quite put it.

Topping the rise and heading down the side of the loch, almost immediately we come to Ard Neakie. It has two back-to-back curved white beaches like a labrys or double-headed axe, separated by a narrow strip of land which connects it to the shore. Half close your eyes and you could imagine it is some Ionian *presque-isle*, if only the water were more blue. There are four large lime kilns, and a pier from which the lime was shipped out. There is a plentiful supply of limestone here, none nearer if you don't count Ard Neakie itself, than the island of Eilean Choraidh (Horse Island) just down the loch a bit. As gardeners know, lime is used to treat acidic peaty soil, which is particularly prevalent hereabouts.

It is also from here the Heilham ferry used to leave for Portnancon on the western side of the loch. The pier and ferry house are still standing, but when the road around the loch was completed towards the end of the 19th century, the ferry was discontinued.

Of all the sea lochs that indent this ragged coast, at ten miles long and one mile wide for most of its length, Loch Eriboll is the biggest. It's two hundred feet deep in places and that is why, sheltered by the hills on either side, it was used by the navy in World War II as a safe harbour from the stormy Pentland Firth. But before then, in 1937, the world's largest battleship and the supposedly invincible *HMS Hood* berthed here. It was sunk by the *Bismarck* at the Battle of Denmark Strait in May 1941 with the loss of 1,415 lives. There were only three survivors. It still holds the record for the Royal Navy's largest loss of life from a single vessel. When they were here, the sailors emulated the tradition, begun a decade earlier, of leaving their mark on the hillside above Laid by spelling out the name of their vessel in white stones. You will need binoculars to see them from the road.

Probably because of its remoteness and dismal winter climate, some wit dubbed the loch "Loch 'Orrible", and the name stuck with the servicemen who saw duty here. In actual fact, however, the name derives from the Norse *Eyrr-bol* which means "farm on the beach" and, yes, looking to the south there is still a croft there today.

Nearly seven hundred years earlier, King Haakon of Norway's massive fleet sheltered here on its way to the Battle of Largs in 1263 – not that he knew that at the time, of course. What happened was that a storm drove some of the fleet ashore at Largs, and the Scots took the chance to launch an attack. After a whole day of skirmishing and with the weather worsening, the Norwegians turned tail and set sail for home. It was the beginning of the end for Norwegian rule in Scotland. Three years later, at the Treaty of Perth, the new king, Magnus, gave up the Norse territories in the west of Scotland to Alexander III and the two countries have been friends ever since.

Loch Eriboll was more than just a harbor, however. The Fleet Air Arm pretended Eilean Choraidh was the *Tirpitz* and practiced bombing it. Eventually the real *Tirpitz* was sunk on 12th November 1944, and it was here in 1945 that the German U-Boats came to surrender. Peace and tranquility came back to Loch Eriboll, and sheep could safely graze on the island again without being terrified out of their fleeces by low-flying aircraft. In 2011, however, Loch Eriboll was in the wars again. This time it was the setting for deadly serious war games, the largest ever staged in the UK – "Exercise Joint Warrior".

From Ard Neackie and all the way to Durness – and beyond, for that matter – the road becomes single track, a sure sign we are about to enter the remotest and most sparsely populated part of the country. Not that the area around Loch Eriboll is exactly crawling with people either. There are only two little settlements to speak of on the loch, facing each other across the water with Eilean Choraidh between them. In fact, Laid only came about in 1832 when the inhabitants of the village of Eriboll were cleared out. There is a Farm Park here which boasts more than forty different breeds of animals as well as a tearoom with homebaking and, if you haven't already done so, there is another chance to see what life was like for the crofters and be thankful you were not born then, back in the days of the Clearances, breaking your back from dawn to dusk, scratching a subsistence out of the weary soil.

At the head of the loch is Rispond, which you may remember I mentioned earlier in connection with James Anderson (1746-1828), the so-called 1st of Rispond, whose claim to fame is he was married three times and had twenty-one children. In 1814 he left to take up sheep farming in Ousdale in Caithness, where he ousted the people. He was succeeded as Lord Reay's factor or tacksman by his son, also James, who was not quite as prolific in producing children as his father: he only had one son, William, and eight daughters, in that order. Poor William died in a riding accident in Australia, aged 42.

During the Napoleonic Wars, James made a killing by processing and shipping to the south and even to the Baltic countries, salted fish, crab and lobster which he bought from his tenants, paying them not with cash but with tokens which they exchanged for goods in his shop. With the peace came an end to the profits. James looked for another way to make money, and – like his father before him – turfed out the people, only not in favour of sheep, but cattle. We will return to him a little later but suffice it to say in the meantime that today the Rispond estate plays host to the fishin' 'n' shootin' set.

At this point we've turned a corner, so to speak, now heading north-west along the top of the country towards Durness. Before very long we come to a broad expanse of beach which goes under the unpronounceable name of Tràigh Allt Chailgeag. Behind it is the six-hundred-foot high Ceannabeinne which means the "head or end of the mountains", a chain of tops stretching south-west as far as the eye can see. The beach, for those who don't have the Gaelic, means "the beach of the burn of bereavement and death". In its English translation, it's a fine example of accidental alliteration, but its name dervives from the time when an elderly woman accidentally fell into the burn when it was in spate and this is where her body ended up.

At the other side of the beach, the rocks are particularly interesting for a geologist especially, because they are Lewisian gneiss – amongst the oldest of rocks on our rocky planet. They were subjected to vast forces of heat and pressure which melted and squeezed them into fascinating swirls and patterns.

The village of Ceannabeinne, a little further along, is well worth visiting, especially if you did not take the Strathnaver detour. It will only take about half-an-hour to complete the circuit along a path which has noticeboards along the way telling of this settlement's turbulent past. Incredible to think, looking at it now, that this settlement of fourteen houses once was a thriving community. At one time it was the largest on the Rispond Estate, in fact, despite the boggy and peaty soil strewn with boulders, the glacial erratics left effortlessly behind by the ice as it retreated but a devil of a job for man to move so he could till the soil. By 1841 the writing was on the wall for the community.

The census returns for that year show that four cottages were unoccupied and there were forty-nine people in all, of whom twenty-eight were children and infants, enough to require a school, one room serving as the classroom while the other was the schoolhouse. It's still there today, having been transmogrified into a holiday cottage. The community was employed in a mixture of crofting and fishing, with one person being a ship's carpenter. It is a snapshot of a village on the cusp of extinction. In fact, some residents had already been displaced here from elsewhere and now they were just about to experience, late in the day, their second Clearance and they were not prepared to go without protest. Enter the villain of the piece: James Anderson, 2nd of Rispond.

He chose his time well – or he thought he did – to serve his eviction notice, giving the crofters only 48 hours notice to be gone. The men were at Balnakeil about four miles away, gathering marram grass for thatch, and only the women and children were at home. He did not reckon with one doughty woman, however, who grabbed the writ and burned it. (Writ? What writ?)

A few days later, the top brass – Police Superintendent Philip MacKay of the Dornoch Constabulary – arrived with a new writ. He was set upon and in a hail of stones was chased out of the village to the echo of curses, laughter and the skirl of the pipes, having lost his coat, his pride and the new writ in the process. Ceanneabeinne 2 - Anderson 0.

Licking his wounds, the Superintendent was ordered to raise a "trusty party" and try again. It should be no surprise to anyone that, in what had become a *cause célèbre*, all MacKay could muster were three old men who, once they got to the Hope Ferry, on hearing that the men of Durness were waiting for them, decided discretion was the better part of valour and went home. Ceanneabeinne 3 - Anderson 0.

But then on September 17th 1841, a Saturday (the day is important), matters came to a head when Superintendent MacKay, third time lucky as he might have seen it, and accompanied by a party of fourteen constables, the Procurator Fiscal and a sheriff substitute, arrived at the Durine Inn in the evening with the intention of serving the eviction notices the following day. They were met by a deputation of fifty men from Durness who asked the sheriff officer not to serve the eviction order on the Sabbath day but to keep it holy, just as they were accustomed to doing. When this modest proposal was refused, the men of Durness attacked the inn at 10pm with an estimated crowd of three hundred spectators cheering them on. It was no contest. The constables fled and tried to hide in the fields nearby, but were rounded up and they and their superiors were turfed out on their collective ear – or escorted to the boundaries of the parish, to put it more literally. Ceanneabeinne 4 - Anderson 0.

Enter stage left, the Sheriff of Sutherland, who threatened to call in the troops, the 53rd Regiment from Edinburgh, and enter stage right, the Rev. William Findlater who appealed for help from an unlikely source, the Duke of Sutherland. Apparently, although he was horrified at these events, the Duke's hands were tied. Although he had bought the Rispond estate from the bankrupt Lord Reay in 1829, according to the terms of the lease James Anderson was entitled to run the estate as he pleased and was well within his rights to treat his tenants with contempt.

By this time the weight of public opinion had swung behind the crofters in the newspapers, although this had not been the case to begin with. Oddly enough, the "local" paper – the *Inverness Courier* – was less sympathetic to the crofters than the more prestigious *Scotsman* in the capital. These latest events prompted a government enquiry, the upshot of which was that the threat of troop involvement was withdrawn, as was the eviction notice. It seemed like a 5-0 victory for the crofters, except Solomon's judgement reaffirmed Anderson's right to evict the tenants. The crofters were told they could leave "voluntarily" as long as they did so by the following May, which gave them six months to get used to the idea. And so that is what they had to do, taking themselves to either the even more barren and rocky land at Sangobeg just a few hundred yards along the coast to the west, or to the other extreme, thousands of miles across the seas.

All this goes to show that the only battle that counts in the end is the last one. And maybe the last one was not the one Anderson eventually won, but the Crofting Act of 1886 which came about as a result of all these goings on and which gave the crofters the right of tenure. Many would say it was just about a century too late. But better late than never, as the adage has it.

The island which can be seen from here and which looks like within swimming distance, is the 69-acre Eilean Hoan, a hybrid from the Old Norse and the Gaelic, meaning "haven island". How ironic. In 1842 it too was cleared of its four families. The dead, however, were allowed to sleep on. In medieval times, the good citizens of Durness buried their dead here to prevent them from being dug up and eaten by wolves, so it is said.

Before Durness, that metropolis of the far north-west territory, there is Smoo Cave to explore, Britain's largest limestone cave. This name is not to be confused with Smee, the amiable pirate in *Peter Pan*, but not inappropriately because there could be no better place for pirates to hide their ill-gotten gains than Smoo Cave. "Smoo" comes from the Old Norse *smjuga*, which means a narrow opening and which has resonances with our word "smuggler". Who knows where Barrie got the name "Smee"? Not me.

There is a well-constructed path from the car park leading down to the cave. Archaeological evidence suggests, thanks to the shell midden (look for it on the left as you go in – masses of them), that it was occupied 5,000 years ago, give or take a couple of millennia. From the seaward side, the cave entrance lies at the end of a narrow inlet not easily noticeable by passing pirates and others intent on doing you harm and therefore a very good place to hide. And let us not forget in this terrain, in those times, travelling by sea was far easier than travelling overland.

Smoo is actually a cave complex with three chambers, the second of which contains a waterfall and the third is only accessible by a small boat. The first is 200 feet long, 130 feet high but only 50 feet high at the entrance. Room enough to accommodate lots of Neolithic families, a sort of linear skyscraper – as long as you didn't mind the little matter of the tide and the drips from the roof.

A covered walkway protects you from raindrops falling on your head as you walk to the second chamber, where you will see a spectacular fall of water as the Allt Smoo tumbles 60 feet from its sinkhole to form a pool on the floor of the cavern. And there you have it; this is what makes this place extra-special. The first cave, or chamber, was created by the sea. This one has been caused by

freshwater. From the car park, a path leads to where, from a wooden bridge, you can see the architect of this creation at close range and look down into the sinkhole. You may be surprised to see, not a raging river as you might have expected, but a tinkling burn. You might gaze and still your wonder grow that that small trickle of water could hole out such a cavity.

Whether or not you visit the third chamber, accessible by boat, is completely out of your hands as it depends on the level of water in the second. It needs to be low, so if you want to go, you need to pray for a dry spell – which you probably would do anyway. We were not able to, if you would like to know.

What I *do* know, however, are three stories connected with the cave, two of which I'm going to tell now and the third I will keep to a little later. In the years following Culloden and the attempt to snuff out Highland culture, there was a crackdown on illicit stills. The excise officers had heard there was one in the third cavern and bribed a certain Donald Mackay to row them into it, little realising Donald was one of the guilty. Donald rowed them into the waterfall where the boat capsized and the "gaugers", as they were called, were drowned. Meanwhile Donald swam to safety. The body of one was never recovered and it is said his ghost haunts the place to this day.

According to the other story, set in those far-off superstitious times – in the days of the lairds of Reay – the bodies of those who fell foul of a certain unsavoury character whom you will meet in the next chapter, were dumped down the sinkhole and where no-one dared retrieve them as it was said to be the home of the Devil. Which brings me to to another story, one I promised you earlier about the first Lord Reay, aka Donald Mackay, aka the "Wizard of Reay", soldier, scholar and traveller and who happened to bump into the Devil in Padua. His Ungodly Highness of the Underworld happened to be there at the time where he was running an academy in the black arts. Naturally Donald signed up.

The deal was that at the end of the course, as payment, the Devil could claim the soul of the last person to leave the class. You can imagine a mad *sauve qui peut* for the exit door. Someone had to be last and it so happened it was Donald. But the quick-witted Scotsman pointed to his shadow on the wall behind his teacher and uttering the words which have been much imitated since, "De'il tak' the hindmost," he took to his heels. The Devil fell for it and it was said, after he came back to Sutherland, Donald never cast a shadow.

The Devil wasn't satisfied with chasing shadows. He pursued Donald to Scotland, made Smoo Cave his lair and lay in wait for him, biding his time. He was the Devil after all, with infinite time on his hands, unlike Donald, whose days were numbered. I wouldn't have thought there was much doubt about his ultimate destination, so I wonder why the Devil didn't just wait for Donald to come to him instead. Maybe he didn't have infinite patience.

At last, one night, when Donald was visiting the cave (probably checking his still was doing nicely), his dog scampered on ahead and came back hairless, terrified out of its skin. From this Donald deduced his *ancien mentor* was lying in wait to claim his debt. What would have happened next had the Devil come out to get him, unless Donald had another trick up his sleeve, we will never know. Fortunately for Donald, just at that moment, a cock crew, and the Devil, urgently requiring to get back to his kingdom before dawn, blasted his way through the roof of the cave accompanied by three of his hellish female consorts.

That's what caused the holes and you can understand why the locals were not very keen on coming here to reclaim the bodies of their loved ones. They might just as well have been in hell as far as they were concerned. And maybe they were anyway, depending.

Chapter Thirty-Three

Durness to Keoldale: Graves, Guns and a Little Geography

S O this is Durness! Scotland's most north-westerly town – if that's the right word for a scatter of white houses dotted about the landscape like the sheep, innocently grazing, minding their own business, never suspecting that one of these days not only will they lose the wool off their backs but their lives too.

At the end of the road, to the north-west, is the quiet backwater of Balnakeil Bay, where in 1991 a tourist out for stroll on the splendid mile-long, westerly-facing, crescent-shaped beach, made a grim discovery – the Grim Reaper had been there before him. A storm had blown away the sand and exposed a body. What! In this little community, where everyone knows everybody else and where they probably don't bother to lock their doors at night? Surely someone must have missed the deceased and started asking questions?

Arriving on the scene, the local GP and constabulary both confirmed the tourist had indeed stumbled upon a dead body. Actually "skeleton" would be more semantically accurate, and was a pretty good clue that the person was not only very much deceased but had shuffled off the mortal coil some time ago. But whodunnit and when? Was there a possibility the killer was still alive and could be brought to justice?

Not the time to call in Miss Marple with her intuitive insight into the darker goings-on of village life, but rather the time to call in other experts who examined the clues – objects which had been buried with the body, most notably an iron sword which had been placed beneath the corpse. In what had been the grave, archaeologists, those antiquarian detectives of the past, also uncovered the boss of a shield. Obviously the deceased had been a warrior of some sort – but who wasn't in those days? It was part and parcel of the pillaging and the other things that came with being a Viking in what was, for them, the Southern lands.

Along with these masculine items of warfare were some items of jewellery, so the unknown warrior had his feminine side too – though I for one would not have pointed that out to him, had I happened to meet him face to face. The experts reckoned he had died sometime between 850 and 900 AD. His death may or may not have been violent, but he was certainly laid to rest with the utmost reverence until that storm disturbed his rest.

He is not unique in this area, this unknown warrior. In Sangobeg for instance, a little to the east – and just to balance things up a bit – archaeologists found the skeletal remains of one of the natives, a Pict from the pre-Christian era. In fact this area is so full of history, who knows how much has yet to be uncovered and discovered? When you walk along many of the splendid beaches here, be careful where you walk: it may be the bleached bones rather than the dreams of the dead that you tread upon.

In more recent times, in the aftermath of World War II, during the so-called "Cold War", an early warning station was built at Balnakeil, part of a network along the north and west coast. The buildings consisted of a barracks, canteen, vehicle maintenance sheds, a guardhouse, even a hospital. They had no electricity and weren't even connected to the water mains. As things turned out, the buildings were never commissioned and, in 1964, the County Council offered to let the units as business premises. Most of those who responded to the adverts were artists and arty-crafty folk in general, so that is how Balnakeil Craft Village came into being. In a further development, in 1980, Highland Regional Council sold the properties to the tenants. There are more than twenty establishments selling all manner of things and offering a variety of services.

You would probably far rather go there than to where we are headed now, but the fact is I am a bit of a thanatourist and I am on the trail of a couple of graves. The first is that of Rob Donn (1714-77), an illiterate Gaelic-speaking cowherd and poet, dubbed the "Burns of the North". He was a contemporary of Burns (1759-96) and, like him, his verse could be bawdy at times. But while the Lowland poet went on to fame, if not fortune, the Highlander was condemned to obscurity. Who knows, his day may yet come, though I have to say the Gaelic is against him. As it is, schoolchildren today struggle with Burns, and – in what is an added layer of obscurity – Donn "wrote" in his Strathnaver version of Gaelic which, I'm told, loses something when transcribed even into Scottish Gaelic, so you can imagine even more nuances would be lost when translated into English. As a matter of fact, "Donn" is more of a descriptor than a surname and means "brown-haired". His real surname was Mackay. His mentor was the minister of Durness, Murdoch MacDonald, who read him Alexander Pope in Gaelic translation.

You can't fail to spot Donn's tombstone – an obelisk erected in 1827 with inscriptions in Gaelic, English, Latin and Greek. He was a Jacobite supporter, his life happening to span both rebellions, albeit he was only a baby at the time of the first. He showed his quick wits one day when, hauled before the authorities in Tongue because of the seditious contents of one of his songs, he told them it was incomplete, added two more verses on the spot in praise of the government and walked away a free man.

The other grave I have come to see is inside the ruined church which was abandoned in the mid-nineteenth century and is now very much covered in ivy. It is that of the highwayman, Donald McMurdo, aka Donald Macmurchow or Domhnull MacMhurchaid, who – it is said – murdered eighteen people and threw some of his victims down a sinkhole at Smoo Cave. And that is the third tale I alluded to earlier in connection with the cave.

Whatever name he was known by, "highwayman" seems an odd word to describe his occupation which, to me at least, conjures up images of Dick Turpin with a brace of cocked pistols ordering stagecoaches to "Stand and deliver!" For a start, the "highways" would have been more like grassy tracks through the heather. "Thief, robber and murderer", I would have thought was a more apposite job description. To which you can probably add "hired assassin", as these were lawless times and it suited some people to have their dirty work done for them whilst they kept their own hands lily-white. In any event, although well known for his dirty deeds, Donald was allowed to go about unhindered. One day, the Rev. Alexander Munro, accompanied by an armed bodyguard, called upon him in his old age and urged him to repent before it was too late. Donald took mighty umbrage at the insult and – had it not been for his old age and infirmities, to say nothing of the bodyguard's musket – he would have added to his murder tally then and there.

When the minister had gone, Donald sent two of his strapping sons after him with instructions they were not to return unless it was with the heart of the dastardly man of God. The sons were prevented from carrying out their task either by the sight of the matchlock aforesaid or a crisis of conscience. Too frightened of dear papa, they killed a sheep on the way home and offered that as a quid pro quo. Donald studied it for a few moments then said, "I always thought the Munros were cowards but I never knew until now that they had the heart of a sheep".

Well, Donald did die, in 1623 as it happens. In another story, four years previously when Donald was looking to the future, he paid £1,000 of his ill-gotten gains to finance the building of the church that was being built at the time, on condition his remains were interred inside. By these measures he hoped to save his immortal soul. You can imagine many people were looking forward to the day of Donald's demise when he was under the sod and they could dance upon his grave.

This gave Donald some food for thought and he devised a cunning plan. That is why his remains are housed in a little recess, like a little house complete with a slate roof though I am not sure how old that is. The tombstone has a rather interesting inscription which reads: *DONALD MAKMVRCHOV HIER LNS LO: VAS IL TO HIS FRIEND VAR TO HIS FO: TRUE TO HIS MAISTER IN VEIRD AND VO 1623.* There is also a skull and crossbones with *MEMENTO MORI* carved around the top, as well as another panel unfortunately so worn away it's impossible to make out what was there.

According to another story, the Presbtery of Durness took the money but had the last laugh on Donald, or so they hoped, by fulfilling the contract by burying him half-in and half-out of the church, where the Devil would be able to get a hold of him and drag him off to where he belonged. In which case they would have had to bury him at right angles to the wall. And maybe they did. And where is Donald now? Who knows?

Sadly there is also a mass grave in the cemetery, though you may not realise it. There is no marker; only a grassy mound. In 1849 an emigrant ship sank with the loss of all on board off nearby Faraid Head. You can walk there if you like, across one of the most splendid and deserted beaches you are ever likely to see, with – on your right – dunes tufted with marram grass. It's only a couple of miles and, from there, you can see Cape Wrath to the west and Whitten Head, a bird colony, to the east. It is private farmland actually, so please observe the country code.

On the other hand, if you are a devotee of that sport whose detractors describe as being "a good walk spoiled", you can always play nine holes in Scotland's most northerly golf course – though it doubles as eighteen, hitting off from different tees on the way back. On the ninth and eighteenth you face a water hazard, a drive of more than 260 feet over an inlet of the sea. Another peculiarity of this course is that on the sixth and fifteenth, a local rule states golfers must give way to anglers. And quite right too, because before God created golfers, he created anglers – well, fishermen, at least.

So that was Durness, but mainly Balnakeil. Now the A838 is taking us south-west towards Ullapool, though it's not long before another opportunity for a detour presents itself. It's the little road to where the ferry leaves from Keoldale on the Kyle of Durness – not much of a detour in itself, but the gateway to a much longer one if you have the time, and if the time is right too. It's the departure point for the ferry to Cape Wrath, which – as everyone knows – is Scotland's and the UK's most north-westerly point on the mainland.

If "ferry" conjures up some sort of image of a ship large enough to accommodate your car, then think again. It's what I would call a "motor boat", and it's all you need for the ten-minute hop across the water to where a minibus will pick you up for the eleven-mile drive across the heath or Parph to the Cape. It only operates between May and September, when the tide is in and when the Ministry of Defence is not making the moor resound to the sound of gunfire. Despite this sound of fury, enough to scare any bird out of its feathers, paradoxically it's also a place of Special Scientific Interest, a Special Protection Area (for birds), a Special Area of Conservation, and a Special Landscape Area. It is eighty square miles in area, and if there is an area more special in the whole of the United Kingdom then I don't know where it is.

The Ministry of Defence has had a naval and aerial bombardment range here since 1933, seemingly somewhat at odds with its "Special" status. If you are lucky enough to be here when the Army is practicing, blowing the range to crockination, you will certainly know about it as red flags will be flying. You might also see Air Force planes bombing Garvie Island, but you will only hear, not see, the navy shelling the range as their battleships are twelve miles out to sea.

The Cape's name has nothing to do with anger as you might suppose from the stormy state of the seas hereabouts and the gales that swirl about the cliffs (the highest cliffs in the land are just to the east). Rather it comes from the Old Norse *hvarf*, which means "turning point": the point at which the Norsemen either turned south to wreak havoc, or – after a raping, robbing and pillaging expedition – headed east along the Pentland Firth towards home with their booty, some of it in the form of women. Gone but not forgotten, the threat of their return was a constant concern, the sighting of their longships on the horizon enough to provoke panic. This reign of terror began with Lindisfarne in 793 and ended with Largs, as I already said. During that time, not all turned for home: some stayed, some settled, some intermarried.

As for the road, the only one in and the only one out to the Cape, it was built in 1828 to give access to the lighthouse. Having read this far, you will know by now you would be pretty safe on putting your pension on it being built by one of the Stevensons who had cornered the market in the construction of such things. This one is no exception. But which Stevenson was it?

The answer is Robert (1772-1830), the daddy of them all and with many more letters after his name than the one he was christened with. He was the brains behind the lighthouse on the infamous Bell Rock, off the coast of the Tay estuary – so named because before the lighthouse, a bell, operated by some sort of float system, was installed on the reef by the Abbot of Aberbrothok in order to warn mariners of the danger. It is immortalised by the then Poet Laureate, Robert Southey (1774-1843), in his *The Inchcape Rock*. According to the poem, the bell was stolen out of pure badness by a pirate who rejoiced under the unlikely name of "Ralph the Rover", and who later perished on the reef himself. And served him right, too. It's a moral tale, the sort of thing that Stevenson's grandson, Robert Louis, might have dreamt up, he being no stranger to composing tales about pirates. I'm sorry to inform those who like such tales there is no evidence of the bell ever having existed.

The Cape Wrath lighthouse was a much easier project than the Bell Rock, the main difficulty being its remoteness and the roads, or rather the lack of one. But built it was, and it was manned until 1998. The semi-circular base has now been converted into a three-bedroomed house whose owners have created what is to said to be the UK's most remote refreshment station, the Ozone Café, which seats eight. Be warned: if you are one of those who can't undertake a journey of any kind without the need for an injection of caffeine to revive you afterwards, and there are more than that number on your ferry, be prepared to queue or get off the vessel PDQ.

During the off-season, there are only two ferries a day – at 11am and 1.30pm – but from 1st June to mid-September, they run from 9am onwards unless it is a Sunday, when the first one leaves at 11.

Where we are now, back on the A838, it's what's called *Rubha an Tigh Shaille* which means "Point at the Salt House" which bears no resemblance at all to its English name which is "Keoldale Green" and which suits it very well as we definitely are in Keoldale and it certainly is green thanks to the limestone bedrock which vegetation rather likes. Rather different to the landscape we've been accustomed to since Loch Eriboll.

At the side of the road is Cnoc na Cnaham or Hill of Bones, a 4,000 year-old Bronze Age settlement, while on a grassy knoll in front of the car park is something a lot more modern. It's a standing stone, tall and slender, with a Celtic design near the top. Do not be deceived. It only dates from 2000 and, apart from being a reminder of the Picts who once lived here, I must say it does give the landscape a sort of romantic ambience in much the same way as arguably the epitome of all castles in Scotland, if the number of times it features in calendars is any guide – Eilean Donan on Loch Duich. Many tourists may be

staggered to learn it only dates from 1932, the original castle being blown to smithereens in 1719 by the English in the aftermath of the first Jacobite rebellion.

Behind it, the broad sweep of the Kyle of Durness stretches ahead of us towards the distant hills. On the map, with its forked tips, it looks like a serpent's tongue. And here's another thing. "Kyle" comes from the Gaelic *caol*, meaning "narrow"; but if there is one thing this inlet of the sea is not, in all its length until you get to the two tips, it is narrow. The tide is out at the moment, leaving what water there is to carve a meandering channel through a vast swathe of sand, leaving marooned islets of sand. And in a process that has been going on for thousands of years, when the sand is dry, the wind whips it up and carries it away to the east, and that is why the sand dunes are so incredibly high at Balnakeil Beach and Faraid Head, as you may have noticed if you went for a walk there or just happened to peep over the cemetery wall.

And the reason the water is so incredibly clear, so a noticeboard informs us, is because when the rainwater comes down from the hills on the other side of the Kyle, it carries very little sediment as the rocks it flows over are the extremely hard Lewisian gneiss and Cambrian quartzite on which it makes no impression, running like the water off the proverbial duck's back. On this side of the Kyle, the limestone, we are told, does not erode into little grains like sand.

So that's two very good reasons why the water in the Kyle is so pure.
Until of course, the sea comes in and gives it a good dose of salt.

Chapter Thirty-Four

From Unapool to Ullapool: A Trip Around Assynt

WE continue south along the banks of the Kyle until at last we reach the River Dionard which flows into it. In the hills, to left and right, are cairns and the remains of a broch – evidence that long, long ago this thinly-populated landscape was once more inhabited than it is now. It's a single-track road and runs straight as a die towards Loch Inchard and it might as well be a motorway for all the traffic we meet. Nor are we delayed much because, as often as not, we happen to reach a passing place at just about the same time as the oncoming traffic. Driving under these conditions is easy. Such a pleasant change from city driving. And the scenery is much easier on the eye, too.

When we reach the bottom of the loch, at Rhiconich, another little diversion offers itself – the B801 along the loch through a series of little settlements to Kinlochbervie. It's an ancient landscape where, everywhere you look, stones protrude from the hillside. You don't have to glance twice to know they are as old as the hills, as the saying has it. What is much newer is the harbour at Kinlochbervie – not one of the prettiest it has to be admitted – with its vast fish-handling facilities which were set up in 1988. It is the most north-westerly fishing port in the country, where the catch is sent by refrigerated lorries to all points south.

Despite its tiny size, Kinlochbervie has produced a famous son, Robert McBeath VC (1898-1922). He was a mere lance corporal when he won the highest military honour a grateful nation can bestow on November 20th 1917, during the Battle of Cambrai, when he single-handedly knocked out a nest of German machine-gunners and captured three officers and thirty men. Real *Boys Own Paper* stuff which, if you read in a novel, you would dismiss as being too far-fetched.

You may have noticed he was very young when he died – before his twenty-fourth birthday as a matter of fact. After the war he emigrated to Canada and joined the British Columbia Provincial Police before making what turned out to be a fatal move to the Vancouver Police Department. Fourteen months later he was dead, shot by a person whom he had arrested for a driving offence. The police department gave him a massive funeral, only it's a pity they didn't spell his name on the tombstone correctly, inserting an "a" in "Mc".

A couple of miles further on is the delightfully named Oldshoremore, which has a splendid beach presided over by a massive frog. Actually it's a naturally shaped rock, and from the distance that's exactly what it looks like – a big hulking amphibian.

At Rhiconach and back on the A838 (which has now become a fast two-lane highway), in a short time, we come to Laxford Bridge which spans the river of that name, funnily enough. Not one of General Wade's, the road was begun in 1834 and not completed until 1851. It's a very fine-looking bridge but hardly the widest or the longest in the world, though it seems to have taken an inordinate amount of time to build.

Time well worth spending when you realise just what a timesaver and a vital link it is. This truth was seen in October 2009 when an army lorry on its way to play war games as part of "Exercise Joint Warrior" (but carrying nothing more deadly than a digger) plunged thirty feet into the river below. Thankfully no-one was hurt but, for the residents of Durness, the bridge's closure meant an inconvenient detour of a hundred miles if they wanted to go to Scourie (where we are going next) via Lairg. For those pupils of Kinlochbervie High School who lived to the south of the river and who were thus cut off from their seat of learning, I wouldn't be surprised at all to learn they thought the Christmas holidays had come early.

Crossing the bridge, and now on the A894 which is also a two-lane road, we speed on towards Scourie. Never was a place so well named, because these ancient hills are as striated as an elephant's hide. Elephants always seem to me to have an immense weariness about them and this landscape, just like it did in Kinlochbervie, looks ineffably weary as if worn down by old age. Which of course these humps of stone are, the ground-down molars of what once were incisors, peaks once as high as Everest.

At Claisfearn there is a burnt mound where it is supposed the ancients heated stones in order to boil water for cooking, only there is no trace of where they lived or any other impact on the landscape. The road takes a U-bend round Loch a' Bhagh Ghainmhich and, halfway round, we are seduced by a little five-mile circular tour which takes in Tarbet, Fanagmore and Foindle.

From Tarbet you can see Handa Island, about a mile-and-a-half long and a mile wide. It was home, according to the census of 1841, to 63 souls who held a parliament which met daily to discuss the day's chores: real democracy in action, the like of which has not been seen since ancient Athens. Traditionally the oldest widow was crowned the "Queen of Handa", which I assume was an honorary title and therefore she was only a constitutional monarch. Even so, it was amazingly progressive for those days that they chose a queen and not a king. It was 1918 before women were given the vote in the UK and, even then, only to some.

This majesty's subjects were crofters and fishermen who supplemented their diet with seabirds and their eggs. Well, needs must. Personally, if I had to, I'd prefer to eat the birds in the embryo stage. Nevertheless, despite that ready source of protein and salt being surplus to their breakfast fry-up, the islanders were unable to support themselves. The beginning of the end came in 1846, the year of the Highland Potato Famine which affected even this rocky outcrop. Two years later, the islanders threw in the towel and emigrated to Canada, like so many Scots before them.

Now, during the breeding season, the cliffs echo to the sound of 100,000 guillemots, not to mention over 150 other species of birds, including razorbills and puffins. It would be some sort of bird paradise except for another predator, the deadly and aggressive skua, which preys on the chicks and eggs of other birds but will dive-bomb anyone unwittingly going near one of *their* nests, which are on the ground. This, you might think is, a very silly place to build a nest, until you realise trees are not exactly thick on the ground.

The island is a Site of Special Scientific Interest, managed by the Scottish Wildlife Trust, and it's not just because of the birds either that it's a SSSI. There are more than 200 species of plants and 100 types of moss as well. Isn't that an astonishing thing? And if you are lucky, out at sea, you may see porpoises, dolphins, basking sharks and three different types of whales.

Back on the NC500 again, at Scourie, this little dot on the landscape, like Kinlochbervie, also produced a famous son: Hugh Mackay (1640-92), Major-General and Commander-in-Chief of William of Orange's forces in Scotland during the so-called "Glorious Revolution". Ungloriously, he is credited with losing the Battle of Killiecrankie in 1689, despite superior numbers, to John Graham of Claverhouse, aka Bonnie Dundee. It was nothing short of a massacre. About 2,000 were slain on Prince William's side and 600 on the Jacobites'. And that is Hugh Mackay's claim to fame, though he probably would have preferred if I hadn't mentioned it. Having said that, it's the last battle that wins the war (as in the case of James Alexander 2nd of Rispond), and in this case there were two more, Dunkeld (1689) and Cromdale (1690) – both Orange victories – to which you can possibly add the shameful events at Glencoe in 1692 which was carried out in the name of King William.

Skirting the shores of Loch an Daimh Mor, the road threads its way through Lower Badcall on the left and Upper Badcall on the right before we come to the graceful sweeping curve of the Kylesku Bridge which allows us to soar as effortlessly as an eagle over the narrow channel that separates Loch a' Chàirn Bhàin on the seaward side and Lochs Gleann Dubh and Glencoul on the landward. It was not always so easy. The bridge was only built in 1984 and, before that, cattle on the Drove Road – on their way to the market in the south – had to swim across the channel. The cattle drovers fared better. There was a ferry, a rowing boat actually, which meant they did not get their feet wet, let alone their skins.

And if my memory serves me well, or so it seems to me, once upon a boyhood, when camping with my parents in the Highlands, we took the *Maid of Kylesku* which could accommodate as many as two cars at a time. Such a thing transforms a holiday into an adventure for a small boy. And here's another wondrous thing – it was free. But now, sadly, surplus to requirements, the *Maid*, like a discarded lover, lies abandoned and neglected on the beach.

The bridge is free too. A memorial plaque on the north side commemorates its opening by the Queen as well as a reminder that despite how peaceful and quiet this place is now, it was once in the theatre of war – even if it took a back seat. Here, we are told, is where the XIIth Submarine Flotilla was formed, a unit of "X-craft" and "Chariot" miniature submarines. This was their training ground; the North Sea off Norway their battleground.

In the distance, to the south, the impressive bulk of the Quinag range shoulders into the sky. Composed of three Corbetts (mountains over 2,500 feet): Sàil Ghorm, Sàil Gharbh and Spidean Conich, the greatest of these is the middle one at 2,650 feet. At the bottom end of Loch Beag, an extension of Loch Glencoul, is another impressive sight – the highest waterfall in Britain, Eas a' Choul Aluinn. It means "waterfall of the beautiful tresses". I wouldn't mind betting a lot of people have never heard of it, and yet who hasn't of Niagara? But here's the thing – Niagara is a mere 167 feet while this has a single sheer drop of nearly four times as much – an impressive 658 feet. Unfortunately for the NC500 traveller on a time budget, it is a bit of a hike to get there, but – if you do have the time but not the legs for it – a boat trip from the Kylesku Hotel will take you to the end of the loch, and there you can see it, a silver gash dashing itself to death down the hillside.

Just after the bridge is Unapool, from *Uni'bolstadr*, the farm belonging to Uni, whoever he was. The former school has been transformed into a café, but no ordinary café this. It's called the "Rock Stop", very appropriately, because here, like something out of *The Flintstones*, you can stop and have a rock bun or a softer sandwich. However, if you really want to understand why geologists get so high on this landscape, there is an exhibition which does an excellent job in helping the layman get to grips with how North-west Scotland came to be formed and why it is so different, geologically speaking, from the conjoined land to the south and east in much more detail than I gave you earlier. Having said that, if you are like those who feel no need to understand the workings of the internal combustion engine in order to be able to drive, you can just accept that that's the way it is and admire the scenery for its own sake.

It's at this point the NC500 follows the single-track B869 to Lochinver through a landscape peppered with settlements with houses as white as sheep, beaches of white sand with bays of blue, and lochs and lochans that pit the landscape like lace. Arguably this is the best scenery the NC500 has served up so far.

This is Assynt, where once upon a time there were two brothers, Unt and Ass-Unt. As has often been the case since Cain and Abel's time, no love was lost between them. Unt was a man of peace while his brother was a man of discord (the meaning of their names actually), and Assynt got its name when Ass-Unt emerged the victor in this sibling rivalry and modestly called the land after himself.

Amongst the highlights of this scenic circuit, Clashnessie – at the eastern end of the Stoer peninsula – has a beautiful sandy beach and a trail that takes you to a fifty-foot waterfall. And indeed, that's where its name comes from – *clais an easaidh*, "the ditch of the small waterfall". It's a lot better than it sounds.

About halfway round the bottom of the peninsula, at Rienachait, an even more minor road off to the right to Totag will take you eventually to Raffin and, at the end of the road, the lighthouse built in 1870 by the Stevenson brothers, David and Thomas, in 1870. It was automated in 1978. If you are looking for a holiday home with a difference where you can get away from it all, you can't get much further away than here.

You *can* go further however, on foot, to the Point of Stoer where you will be rewarded with some spectacular coastal scenery, the highlight of which has to be the 200-foot-high stack of the Old Man of Stoer. And if, at the end of your hike, you fancy a swim and a bit of rock climbing, you can swim across the thirty-foot gap and scale the heights.

Back on the B869 is Stoer itself which boasts an 1829 Telford church and manse, now grandly known as "Stoer House". Just to the south of the sandy white bay is something much older, a broch, though – truth to tell – it is so tumbledown it looks more like a heap of a rubble than the majestic structure it once was. You can, however, still see a doorway with a massive triangular lintel and marvel how muscle-power alone managed to get it up there.

Finally, before joining the A837, and turning left to Lochinver, it's really worth making a detour to Achmelvich Bay. With its silver sands and blue waters, half close your eyes, imagine the palm trees, feel the heat on your skin and you could believe yourself to be somewhere on the Caribbean. But if lying on a beach and soaking up the sun or building sandcastles for the kids is not your thing (though if the masses of residential caravans are anything to judge by, there are lots for whom it is), there is something nearby which might pique your interest.

To get to it, you need to turn your back on the beach and head towards the hummock of An Pharaid Beag, and presently you will come to what is known as "The Hermit's Castle". It is reputedly the smallest castle, not only in Scotland, but in Europe – to which you can certainly add, the most ugly. Made entirely of concrete (never the most attractive of building materials and much beloved by architects in the Sixties, of which the Carbuncle of Cumbernauld is the most notorious), it was built in 1950 by an eccentric English architect who allegedly only spent one night in it and then left, never to return. Curious, certainly. Charming, certainly not.

There is something else the beach can offer, something that none of the others can – the sight of Suilven keeping an eye on things from the south-east. Although not a Munro, not even a Corbett, it looks a lot higher than its 2,389 feet and surely must be one of Scotland's most iconic mountains. The Vikings called it "Pillar Mountain" and, from the direction they saw it, they were quite right. The really fascinating thing about Suilven is it has many different faces, so it looks quite different depending on the direction from which you approach it.

Lochinver has an excellent visitor centre which, from the outside, has much of a Swiss chalet about it. A huddle of boulders at the entrance gives a clue as to what you can expect to see inside – much ado do about stones. Just as the sight of a certain bird may be a non-event to lots of people but can drive certain others to twitch with delight, so these mute stones may just be dumb rocks to many people but to a geologist they are not mute at all, but speak volumes about the creation of this landscape. Here, after the Rock Café, is a second chance to try and understand how this part of the land we know as Scotland was formed and how it has changed over the aeons.

Apart from that, there is a lot more to see and learn about such as the wildlife of the area, but the thing that appeals to me most, tucked away at the back of the museum, is a stone with runes carved upon it. It was found in 1987 at Inverkirkcaig, just a few miles to the south. The runes turned out to be an Icelandic form of Old Norse and, when deciphered, read: "Angela carved these runes in memory of her father. May Thor consecrate these runes."

Talk about stones speaking! It doesn't take a scholar to work out this stone is as recent as sliced bread, Angelas not being thick on the ground in Iceland, not today, never mind the *Icelandic Sagas*. It does, however, give rise to certain questions: who is this Angela who knows Old Norse and, unless she had an accomplice, is pretty handy with a chisel too? And why did she carve it in such an out-of-the way place, where it might never have been discovered? No greater love hath a daughter for her deceased father than she carve her name with pride, chipping away at an old block in the wilderness.

Not far after the junction with the A894, at Skiag Bridge, is another castle, the perfect antidote to the hermit's castle at Achmelvich, the most definitely charming and romantic Ardvreck. It was built towards the end of the 16th century by the Macleods and has fallen into a pretty ruinous state, but which does not detract from its appeal one little bit. In fact, I would say it actually enhances it. In its way it is as iconic as Suilven, a pin-up, calendar castle where it is sometimes seen in silhouette against a sunset. Scotland for the romantics.

Behind the romantic image, however, lies a dark story which should not come as a surprise to anyone who knows anything at all about Scottish history. You may remember I mentioned earlier, in connection with Dunbeath Castle, the Marquess of Montrose (1612-50) at the start of his mission to avenge the execution of Charles I and to restore the Stuarts to the throne. Ardvreck Castle was where the beginning of the end for Montrose began. It's a gory tale, worthy of *Macbeth*.

After the battle of Carbisdale where he was defeated, "routed" perhaps may be more the *mot juste*, the wounded Montrose made his way here, so weary and ravenous it is said he was driven to eat his own gloves. He expected to be given help and succour by MacLeod, whom he regarded as an ally. There was a goodly sum on his head however, and MacLeod gave into temptation and in contravention of the tradition of Highland hospitality, betrayed him. Or, according to another version, he was away from home and it was his wife whodunit. She was the daughter of Munro of Lemlair who, with Colonel Archibald Strachan, was a commander of the Covenanters at Carbisdale. She locked him up and sent for Cromwell's men.

Montrose was taken to Edinburgh for execution. He met his death stoically, wearing his finest clothes for the occasion. Dressed to be killed. He was hanged and his body left hanging for three hours before his limbs were cut off and sent to Stirling, Perth, Aberdeen and Glasgow. The torso was buried in unconsecrated ground in the Burgh Muir to the south of the city. The head was displayed on a spike in the Tolbooth in Edinburgh where, incredibly, it stayed for eleven years.

Times change. King Charles II's posterior being securely ensconced on the throne of the United Kingdom, in 1661 Montrose was successfully reunited with his disparate body parts, unlike poor Humpty Dumpty. Furthermore, he was given a hero's burial in St Giles Cathedral for the part he played in trying to restore the Stuarts.

As for the MacLeods, retribution was to follow shortly after. Inter-clan wars were alive and well and, in 1672, Ardvreck was attacked and conquered by the Mackenzies and with that, their rule over the lands of Assynt came to an end. The castle fell as the result of a siege, and its present ruinous condition came about in 1726 as the Mackenzies plundered it for stone for their new stately pile of Calda House which was being built just a stone's throw away further along the loch. It too is in ruins – all there is left to see being the M-shaped gable ends, an innovative style for its day; very posh and later emulated elsewhere throughout the Highlands.

In 1737, it was struck by lightning and caught fire; divine retribution, the killjoys said, for merry-making on a Saturday that carried on to the Sabbath day. Everyone perished in the flames apart from one man, a lone piper, a God-fearing Christian man who refused to play a note after the stroke of midnight and thus was saved, while on the other hand, you suppose, the conflagration above was only a foretaste of the everlasting bonfire below, the just desserts of the merry-makers for their misdeeds.

According to another story, the Mackenzies led an extravagant lifestyle beyond their means, for which the lady of the mansion gets most of the blame (probably quite rightly), and were forced to sell the castle to their other deadly enemy, the Sutherlands. Rather than see Sutherlands occupy the house, faithful retainers, it is said, put it to the torch.

Whatever the truth may be, it mattered not. Just eight short years later, after Culloden, the Mackenzies – being on the losing side in that conflict – found their lands forfeited to the Crown and the house was never rebuilt.

There are no ghostly legends attached to Calda House – it hardly had time to have any – but there are to Ardvreck. It is said a chieftain's daughter married the Devil in a pact to save the castle and when that didn't happen and with her reputation, as well as the castle, in ruins, she drowned herself in the loch. Now her ghost walks along the beach, weeping. Others say this is not quite the truth – what really happened was her dastardly father made a pact with the Devil, that in return for his help in building the castle, he could have the hand of his daughter in marriage. The castle was duly built but, when the fair maid found out who her husband was, she threw herself out the window (it was a traditional tower house) and drowned in the loch. Whatever version you prefer to believe, the outcome, sadly, was the same: she did drown and she does haunt the beach, weeping.

It's only a few miles further to Inchnadamph at the end of the loch. It seems a strange name but here, at least, there's no mystery. Translated from the Gaelic it means "Meadow of the Stags". I am by no means a geologist, but for anyone whose passion is rocks, this is the place for them. Near the hotel is a monument which bears the following legend: *To Ben N Peach and John Horne who played the foremost part in unravelling the geological structure of the North West Highlands 1883-1897. An international tribute. Erected 1930.*

As I have already explained, it has all to do with the Moine Thrust, a theory formed in 1907 after the normal order of layers of rock, with the oldest at the bottom, was seen to be reversed near here at Knockan Crag. Normally, Lewisian gneiss, about 3,100 million years old, would be beneath Hugh Miller's beloved Torridonian sandstone, about 1,700 million years old, while on top of that, the white Cambrian quartzite about 540 million years old, would the icing on the cake, so to speak. What Peach and Horne were able to show here was that the older Moine rocks were lying on *top* of the younger Cambrian rocks and therefore something must have happened to bring this extraordinary state of affairs about.

Some years later, the theory of Plate Tectonics was postulated – and very controversial at the time it was, too. Even in my time, sitting in geography classes, it was not being taught in schools. But now that it has been proved beyond doubt, it's staggering to think the earth beneath my feet was once part of the Appalachian Mountains before it was thrust eastwards, crushing and submerging other rocks beneath it. The Scottish emigrants, setting out for a new beginning in the New World, whether or not they were victims of the Clearances, when they travelled across the ocean that now divides us, when they eventually made landfall were, in one sense, setting foot on the same old soil.

There are some famous caves here, the Bone Caves of Inchnadamph, where in 1927 the skull of a polar bear was found, the only one ever discovered in Britain. They also found the bones of an Arctic fox and the northern lynx, as well as reindeer – and if that's not a sign of life in a cold climate then I don't know what is. Indeed, radiocarbon dating showed the bear was alive and well and living in Assynt during the last ice age about 11,500 years ago. Probably it was hibernating and never woke up from the deep freeze. That's a good way to die, to slip without pain into the biggest sleep of all. They also found the bones of four humans which the experts reckoned were a mere 4,500 years old. That's the merest blink of an eye in geological terms. Nothing at all. Scarcely worth mentioning in fact, so I won't.

A few miles to the south we come to a parting of the ways. Beauly is straight ahead on the A837, but that is not the NC500 way and therefore not ours. We take the A835 towards Ullapool and just a couple of miles after Elphin (population about 70) is the aforementioned Knockan Crag, high on the hill to our left. Most people probably hardly spare it a glance, but for geologists, or geography teachers for that matter (like my better half), this is Mecca.

There is a visitor centre with a very comely turfed roof from where you can take a number of trails to the top of the crag and as well as studying the rocks, admire a variety of sculptures, most notably Joe Smith's "Globe" which makes me think of poor Sisyphus and the boulder he was condemned to roll to the top of the mountain, only for it to roll all the way to the bottom again.

One good legend deserves another and, according to a local one, the reason for this outcrop of rock is it was the site of a battle between two giants whose titanic struggle was so intense that the very ground beneath their feet shook, causing the earth to rise up. While it's interesting the ancients felt a need to explain this feature of their landscape that they instinctively knew was out of the ordinary, it's remarkable to think just how close they were to the truth – long before geography teachers were instructed to teach tectonic plate theory.

Chapter Thirty-Five

Ullapool to Inverewe: Klondykers, Convoys, Germs and Gardens

WE'VE crossed the border. We're in Wester Ross now, Ullapool (*Ulli bolstadr*, or Ulli's farm) to be precise, white and neat, nestling around the harbour on Loch Broom, hemmed in by hills. It was conceived by the British Fisheries Society in 1788 as a planned fishing village for the herring industry. It was built on a grid plan drawn up by David Aitken with a certain Robert Melville, who more or less appointed himself as the person in charge of overseeing its construction.

Melville was a man on the make, however. He went into the fish-processing business himself, in opposition to the Society, and deviated from Aitken's plans by building warehouses where it suited him best. To the rescue came that tried and tested man, Thomas Telford, whom the Society appointed as Surveyor of Buildings. He improved on Aitken's plan, the sanitation and water supply in particular, not to mention the harbour.

Only ten years later, the herring were showing some signs of declining numbers and by 1820 were gone altogether. Fortunately the settlers had not put all their eggs in one creel, so to speak, and Aitken's design included large gardens which the cottagers could cultivate. They were also able to rent land on which they could graze a cow and grow crops. Self-sufficiency was the order of the day. Then along came the Clearances and, far from declining, the population of Ullapool actually grew as a result.

Then, in the 1970s, the "Klondykers" came along. The loch was crammed with scores of Russian and Eastern Bloc factory ships, rusting hulks come to buy and process, not herring, but mackerel. *Plus ça change, plus c'est la même chose.* In appalling conditions below deck, workers stood ankle-deep in freezing water, gutting, gutting, gutting. Like their namesakes, although they came in their shoals, few, if any, made a fortune. In the museum you can see a wonderful wooden model of a traditional Romanian house which one Klondyker sold for some little extra comforts away from home.

They left in the Nineties and, although some fishing boats are to be seen in Ullapool, like the Disciples the town has turned instead to being fishers of men – catering for the needs of tourists such as us. The town is hoaching with coach parties as well as independent travellers. We've not seen so many people gathered together in one place for a long time. Indeed, we've grown unaccustomed to the sight of faces other than those of sheep, and very often their backsides too, as they grazed the juicy grass by the side of the single-track roads, not even bothering to raise their heads, trusting us to avoid them. As for us, if we trusted to our ears alone, we could imagine ourselves on Sauchiehall Street on a Saturday afternoon.

From the harbour, the *Isle of Lewis* shuttles across the North Minch to Stornaway; a little bit off the NC500 track, admittedly. Much nearer are the Summer Isles which the *M.V Shearwater* will take you to on a three-hour cruise, or one half as long if you prefer. If you are interested in wildlife, it is something you may well consider doing. You have a very good chance of spotting colonies of seals, porpoises, dolphins and, if you are lucky, minke whales or even the rarer humpbacked variety. On a casual glance, one seal may look very much like another, but in actual fact no two have exactly the same spots. I suppose you could say it's a case of spotting the difference. You are certain to see countless numbers of seabirds so, if you can't tell your gull from your gannet, you had better take your *Observer's Book of Birds* with you.

On the longer tour, you are taken to Cathedral Cave where you may be amazed to learn that the "common cormorant (or shag) does not lay its eggs in a paper bag", as Christopher Isherwood (1904-86) unreliably informed us, but rather here. Well, at least one of their nesting places. On this tour too, you visit the only inhabited island in the archipelago, Tanera Mhor. In the 18th century it was a herring station, gone long ago of course, but it has something of interest for philatelists. It has a Post Office with a licence to produce its own stamps with its own postmark, though they are actually franked on the mainland. Collectors' items. There are also a number of holiday cottages available for rent.

The museum, formerly a church, closed its doors as a place of worship in 1935. It's another Thomas Telford creation, built in 1829 and shaped like a T. It's tempting to see Thomas being inspired for the design by his initials, leaving *his* stamp all over the Highlands. And if you have ever wondered how come he built so many churches, thirty-two to be precise, as well as forty-three manses, the reason was partly a knock-on effect from the Clearances.

So many people were at such a distance from a place of worship that the *Additional Places of Worship* Act (1823) provided funding for the building of churches in remote areas, as well as an annual stipend of £120 for the minister. They were called "Parliamentary" or "Government Churches" because there were stories of itinerant Jesuit priests going around the Western Islands particularly, converting poor "ignorant Highlanders". Three generations after Culloden, Catholicism was still regarded with suspicion, and one might be forgiven for suspecting that this was the real motivating factor behind the establishment of these churches. Apart from a few missing pews, this church is as close as you can get to a Telford original, the only one still retaining its gallery (where you can see a multi-lingual film on the history of Ullapool) and with the original décor and fittings.

The church took on its new role in 1995 and it reprises the old, old story of the Scottish diaspora, crofting and the Clearances – but with a local twist, as you would expect. Particularly poignant is the voyage of the eighty-five foot-short, three-masted *Hector*, built in the Netherlands which, in July 1773, called in at Loch Broom from the Clyde, bound for the Americas. In addition to the passengers it was already carrying from Greenock, it took on another 189 – twenty-five single men and twenty-three families. It was vastly overcrowded. Had they all decided to go on deck at the same time, someone has calculated that each passenger would only have had two square-feet of deck space.

They were in search of a new life post-Culloden. The winter of 1771-72 was particularly harsh, the snow lasting until April. And if things were not already bad enough, a cattle plague swept through Loch Broom in 1772. Writing in Assynt in 1774, Thomas Pennant describes the terrible plight of the people: "They wandered in a state of desperation; too poor to pay, they madly sell themselves for their passage, preferring a temporary bondage in a strange land to starving for life on their native soil".

In addition to the free passage, they were lured by the promise of a year's provisions and land to cultivate along a bay. What had they to lose? Nothing but their lives. Eighteen didn't make it, falling victim to smallpox and dysentery during the eleven weeks' crossing which was only supposed to have taken six. Cruelly, with Newfoundland in sight, a storm blew them off course, delaying them by two weeks. By this time, food was running so low they had to resort to eating mouldy bread and water had to be rationed.

You will probably not be surprised to learn that when they did eventually make landfall, their troubles were not over by any means, that things did not turn out as they had been promised. Apart from there being no provisions, there was precious little in the form of tools to cultivate the land and thirdly, the promised land was, in most cases, well inland and therefore the settlers had no fishing rights. Worst of all, there was no shelter and this was

September, too late to plant their seed corn. In any case, the land was very heavily forested and had to be cleared first. It all seems very reminiscent of the *Mayflower* and the Pilgrim Fathers in 1620. In this case it was the native Mi'kmaq who came to the settlers' rescue.

Of the 180 people who arrived in Pictou (from a native word *piktuk* meaning "explosive place" – a reference to a nearby seam of coal), there were only seventy-eight heads to be counted the following year. The others had moved on to more settled parts of the colony. Despite this unpromising start, Pictou flourished and grew, largely thanks to the trees which, ironically, had dismayed the settlers so much when they first caught sight of their new home. They built ships and began exporting the seemingly endless supply of timber. And when that did run out after thirty years or so, there was that handy coal seam to turn to instead.

Over the next hundred years, more than 120 ships with a cargo of settlers arrived in Pictou. By 1879, 93% of the land-owning settlers could claim Scottish blood and today it is estimated there are 140,000 descendants of the *Hector* living in Canada and the United States. One of their ancestors was a piper, John MacKay from Sutherland, who had been turned away by the ship's master, John Spiers. However, the passengers pleaded for him to be allowed aboard, saying they would share their rations with him in return for his entertaining them on the voyage. They were Gaelic speakers and, to this day, Gaelic culture is alive and doing very well in Nova Scotia, thank you very much. The Hanoverians may have tried to wipe out Highland culture; all they did was displace it.

A model of the *Hector* is displayed in the museum but, if you go down to Pictou harbour, you will see a life-size replica. And that, I think, is a very fitting tribute to that bunch of hardy men and women who toughed it out in 1773 and stayed.

We, however, are on our way again and – not far after the end of Loch Broom – we come to Corrieshalloch Gorge, 197 feet deep with the 150-foot Falls of Measach tumbling into it. Ours is the only vehicle in the car park as we walk down the path through the trees to the very fine suspension bridge, from where we get a dizzying view of the gorge beneath our feet and – by doing nothing more strenuous than merely lifting our eyes – the falls. The bridge was built in 1874 and designed by Sir John Fowler, one of the designers of the iconic Forth Rail Bridge.

"Shalloch" means "ugly" and "corrie", as you probably know, means a pot or cauldron, a relative of the Welsh "cwm", that seemingly unpronounceable word which is actually pronounced "coom". I can see where the "corrie" comes from, but who first thought of tacking "shalloch" on to it or why, I really can't explain. It's what's known as a "slot gorge", and it has all to do with the power of water. Not the River Broom, however – it's too puny. No, the gorge was formed between 10,000 and 13,000 years ago by melting ice water from a glacier which once covered this landscape under hundreds of feet of ice.

There are two walks, both very short. The first, which we are on at the moment, carries on to a viewing platform at the other side of the gorge. The other, which is only over half-a-mile long, runs along the near side of the gorge from the car park, to another viewing platform.

From here it's only an hour or less, depending on how slowly you drive, across Scotland's narrow neck to Inverness via the A835. It will be our destination eventually, but not yet. We take the A832, heading north-west. The first part, the section from Braemore Junction to Dundonnell at the head of Little Loch Broom (the baby brother of the one on which Ullapool stands), is known as "Destitution Road". It was built in 1846-47, during the Highland potato famine, to give employment to crofters who were starving because of the failure of the crop due to blight. It was the brainchild of *The Central Board for the Destitute Highlands* and this road, alas, was only one of many in Wester Ross. They were not paid with money – what use was that? – but with oatmeal. The famine was a lot more severe in Ireland, of course.

Dundonnell House can be found off to the right up an avenue of beeches. It was built in 1769 by the 3rd Laird of Dundonnell, Kenneth Mackenzie. The 5th Laird, also named Kenneth, accrued so many debts he was forced to flee to France. Much of the estate was sold off and the childless Kenneth bequeathed what was left to his brother-in-law, a smooth-talking lawyer in the south, named Robert Roy. This did not go down well with Kenneth's brother, Thomas, who expected to inherit. Nor did it go down well with the tenants. In what came to be known as the "Dundonnell Atrocities" of 1826-28, terrorists – who were never identified – fired shots at the house, set fire to buildings, maimed cattle and killed Roy's carriage horses, the poor innocent creatures.

In a more legitimate effort to gain what he saw was his rightful inheritance, Thomas appealed to the due process of law. Having no money of his own, a fighting fund was set up by the "country Gentlemen of Ross-shire". Five years of legal litigation followed before, finally, the will was overturned on the grounds that Kenneth was a "simpleton" and had been manipulated by his avaricious wife and Roy himself.

Actually, while Kenneth may not have been over-endowed in the brains department, he was certainly a tad eccentric, having a great passion for all sorts of hens, the company of "wandering idiots", beef steaks and his favourite tipple

– cream, which made him rather obese. Alas, poor Thomas, the overturned ruling did him no good whatsoever, apart from, perhaps, providing him with a certain moral satisfaction, as by this time the legal suit had completely and utterly ruined him.

And that, you might think was that. Not a bit of it. It was only the start. To meet his debts, Thomas sold the estate to Murdoch Munro-MacKenzie who, no doubt inspired by what had happened to Thomas, entailed it. This meant the estate could only be passed on through a certain stipulated line of descent. Murdoch's son, Hugh, died in 1869, leaving a daughter, Mary. Unfortunately, because she was illegitimate, she was barred from inheriting and the estate passed to her uncle Kenneth, a sheep farmer in Australia. Mary contested what she saw was *her* rightful inheritance, and the legal wrangling went all the way to the House of Lords – who threw out Mary's claim. In order to pay her legal bills, Mary had to sell the two estates of Mungasdale and Strathnasheallag which she *had* been allowed to inherit. All that dearly wrought worry and stress for nought. Poor Mary.

The current owner, since 1998, is the lyricist Sir Tim Rice. The gardens have been restored thanks to the painstaking efforts and hard work of his wife, Jane, and the gardener Will Soos. It contains a 2,000 year-old yew tree and a holly tree, a mere stripling of 500. Imagine! Incidentally, the holly leaf is the emblem of Clan Mackenzie.

It's a pleasant drive along the shores of the loch then, presently, rounding a corner, we come across a place which has associations with something rather sinister. It's Gruinard Bay, and there – within swimming distance if you are so inclined – is Gruinard Island. It's an unremarkable sort of place, one mile long by half-a-mile wide with nothing special to distinguish it from any other island, just a hump emerging from the water. You can imagine it's the sort of place that the Famous Five would row out to on their holidays, the prelude to yet another jolly exciting adventure. But they didn't, and just as well for them too as it could have been an "awfully big adventure" as Peter Pan imagined what dying would be like.

The 1881 census shows that six people were living on the island then, dead and gone, long ago. It is uninhabited now and has been since the Second World War, if not before, and with good reason. In 1942, the British, worried the Germans would use chemical or biological weapons, as they did in WWI, began looking into methods of producing their own nasty stuff, either as a means of retaliation or as a deterrent. In Porton Down, Wiltshire, the boffins created a deadly strain of anthrax known as Vollum 14578, named after its creator. Having created it, experiments needed to be done to see just how deadly it was. They needed a place remote enough so that if something went wrong, such as a whimsical wind blowing it the wrong way, casualties would be kept to a minimum.

Gruinard Island had the doubtful honour of being selected. It was requisitioned by the government and eighty sheep were chosen for the sacrifice. Most were not free to roam the island but were kept in pens while a 30-pound anthrax bomb at the top of a tall pole was detonated above their poor, unsuspecting heads. The following year they experimented with a 4-pounder designed to be part of a cluster of a hundred such bombs. And that, fortunately, was the end of the experiments as the tide of war began to turn in favour of the Allies and mercifully these vile weapons of mass destruction were never deployed.

A film in "glorious technicolor", and which was declassified in 1997, is testimony to the whole ghastly process. A brown spray can be seen drifting towards the helpless sheep. Nothing seemed to happen at first, but three days later, they were all dead, bleeding from their mouths, a sign of internal haemorrhaging. Soldiers suitably and eerily dressed in masks and protective clothing came to dispose of the carcasses. In their wisdom, the military decided the easiest way to do this would be to dump them at the bottom of a cliff, blow it up, and they would be buried beneath tons of rock. Only it didn't quite work out like that. Some sheep were blown out to sea and soon stories began circulating of sheep mysteriously dying on the mainland. In an effort to stop the spread of any panic, the government found a convenient scapegoat – a Greek freighter, which conveniently had been seen in the area. They accused the sailors of throwing infected carcasses overboard. In an unprecedented gesture of altruism and generosity, the UK Government went so far as to compensate the farmers for the loss of their very-much-dead stock on behalf of the Greek Government.

After that, the island was quarantined. A notice in block capitals read: "This island is Government property under experiment. The ground is contaminated with anthrax and is dangerous. Landing is prohibited. By Order". And then there was a space where an interchangeable date could be placed after the latest examination. Despite this grave warning, some locals admitted to visiting the island – even staying long enough to picnic on it.

During the next two decades, microbiologists returned to take soil samples and pronounced it as contaminated as ever. However, more detailed studies in the Seventies and early Eighties found the contaminated area was actually confined to only a few acres around the detonation site. And then, in 1981, there was a development. Operation Dark Harvest. Some might call them terrorists; others would call them environmentalists. They described themselves as "microbiologists", their aim being to bring the contaminated island to the attention of the public with a view to getting it cleaned up.

They contacted the newspapers, claiming they had taken three hundred pounds of contaminated soil from the island and threatening to leave parcels of it in strategic places until the government took some action to decontaminate it. They began with leaving a package on the doorstep of Porton Down. Tests showed it was indeed contaminated with anthrax. A few days later, a second package was discovered in Blackpool where the Conservatives were having their annual conference, the one where the Lady announced she was not for turning. The soil was analysed and pronounced to be harmless.

It takes a long time for the wheels of government to grind to a halt, never mind execute a U-turn, and it was not until 1986 and at a cost of £500,000 that the decontamination of Gruinard began in earnest. First came the spraying with a herbicide, then the burning, then the worst of the contaminated soil was removed before the entire island was sprayed with 280 tonnes of formaldehyde diluted in 2,000 tonnes of seawater. After that, twin core samples were taken, two feet deep, down to the very bedrock in some cases, before being sent to two different centres for analysis. Except for one or two places, no anthrax spores were detected, and those that were would be found to be miniscule. These places were treated afresh, tested again in 1987, and this time given a clean bill of health.

Despite all these painstaking measures, to make doubly sure a flock of forty sheep were reintroduced to the island, where they happily grazed for six months before being shipped back to the mainland in perfect health to die another day. And so, forty-eight years after it was first contaminated, in April 1990 the island was pronounced to be perfectly safe and the descendants of the owners were allowed to buy the island back for the original requisitioned price of £500. I suppose you could say that was some compensation for not being able to use it during all that time.

In a twist to the tale, in 2001 an archaeologist, Dr Brian Moffat, directing a dig at a medieval hospital near Edinburgh, said his team had found anthrax spores which had survived all those years and he for one wouldn't like to set foot on Gruinard. So take your pick. Who do you put your trust in – the microbiologist or the archaeologist? What would the Famous Five do? Can you imagine ever reading *Five Go to Anthrax Island?* No, neither can I, somehow.

We've come now to Loch Ewe and, for all its idyllic setting and tranquillity, this loch, like Gruinard Island, has a darker past – you might even say a secret past. It wouldn't surprise me if the hordes of tourists who come to visit the world-famous Inverewe Gardens on its sleepy shores don't realise that, like Loch Eriboll, it too once played a vital role in WWII.

Loch Ewe is relatively narrow at its mouth, which made it easier to protect from German U-boats. It is also deep and faces north, which made it an ideal meeting place for the Arctic convoys that supplied the Russians in Murmansk on the Barents Sea and Archangel on its inlet of the White Sea. Winston Churchill, borrowing from the title of Apsley Cherry-Garrard's autobiographical account of Robert Falcon Scott's ill-fated journey to the South Pole, famously described it as the "Worst Journey in the World". In summer, the convoys sailed north of Iceland outwith the range of German aircraft. In winter, because of the ice, they were obliged to take a route closer to shore. Three thousand sailors lost their lives, mainly merchant seamen. They are the forgotten heroes. They didn't set out to be; they just did what they had to do. The tempestuous seas were bad, an icy grave an even worse prospect, whilst the unseen threat below of suddenly being blown to smithereens by submarines must have been worst of all. Winston was right.

Once upon a time, both shores of the loch bristled with anti-aircraft guns while boom nets and mines were strung across the entrance. There was also a barrage balloon in the bay where the merchant ships and the navy's main force in European waters, the Home Fleet, were anchored, just to the north of where the present-day Inverewe Garden is.

So well protected was the loch that, although air-raid warnings were many, the guns were rarely fired in anger and even then mainly at reconnaissance aircraft. This was indeed a haven: the real threat was out there on the high seas. In the course of the war a total of nineteen convoys, composed of 481 merchant ships, escorted by more than a hundred navy ships left from here. The last one was on 30th December 1944.

Having said that, danger was never far away – and not very long into the war, either. Just before Christmas, on 23rd December 1939, two trawlers – the *Promotive* and the *Glen Albyn,* requisitioned by the Admiralty – were sunk by U-Boat 31, the *Johannes Jacobost,* which had laid mines as early as October 27th. War had only been declared on September 3rd.

They were not the only mine victims. The flagship of the fleet, *HMS Nelson,* hit a mine near the entrance to the loch and was put out of action for eight months. She never returned to Loch Ewe, but was in the thick of it elsewhere during the Normandy landings where she was hit again by two mines. She lived to fight on to the end of the war but, long before all that, for two days in September 1931 she was one of the vessels involved in the Invergordon Mutiny which, you may remember, I mentioned when we were in those parts.

Mines, torpedoes and enemy fire were not the only dangers, though God knows that was plenty. In another incident and close to safety, on 26th February 1944 in gale-force winds and driving snow, the Liberty Ship, the *William H. Welch*, flying the American flag, ran aground on Eilean Furadh Mohr near the entrance to Loch Ewe and was split in two. "Liberty ships" were so-called because they were carrying arms to the American troops and the Allies. The real William H. Welch (1850-1934) was an eminent pathologist and bacteriologist. He was also one of the four founding members of the world-famous John Hopkins teaching hospital in Baltimore, Maryland, where he died. I suppose there is a certain appropriateness in that.

As far as the ship that was named after him is concerned, unfortunately it wasn't possible to deploy the lifeboats which might have saved several lives. After the break-up of the vessel, clinging to the wreckage, the sailors made their own way ashore as best they could. Having made it that far, unfortunately some were dashed against the rocks. Only a dozen survived out of a complement of seventy-seven.

Enter local heroes and housewives, Katrina Kennedy, Mary Maclean and Jean Mackenzie who, alerted by the coastguards, brewed up kettles of tea and took food, blankets and cigarettes (let us not forget rationing was in force), and trudged through the frozen wasteland to the scene of the disaster. How hot the tea was by the time they got there I couldn't say, but I am sure it was welcomed warmly by those washed ashore, freezing to death and covered in oil.

Eventually ambulances arrived and took the survivors to the naval hospital in Gairloch, apart from one whom Alfred MacLennan carried on his back – over trough terrain and in dreadful conditions – the best part of a mile to Cove on the western side of the loch. What a hero! But why was he forced to resort to such a desperate measure? Perhaps the ambulances were full and his passenger seemed the least likely to die imminently.

For these great acts of kindness their names should be remembered. But in addition to them there were others: the lighthouse keepers, the coastguards, crofters and soldiers who came to that rock-strewn beach. They came, I imagine, hoping to rescue survivors but more in the horrible expectation of finding bodies after the sailors' long immersion in those bone-chilling waters and boiling seas. And indeed, it was a grim harvest they reaped on the shore.

You can find out more about this tragedy if you take the single-track B8057 up the western side of the loch to the strung-out community of Inverasdale where, in the old school, an exhibition known as the "RACM Project" has been organised by a small group of hardworking volunteers. The acronym stands for the Russian Arctic Convoy Museum, if you haven't already worked it out. When funds permit, the plan is to move the museum to the more accessible Aultbea on the other side of the loch. If you carry on through Cove to the point of Rubha nan Sasan, as well as the remains of the battery, you will find a memorial to those who lost their lives in the Arctic convoys.

But I am getting ahead of myself. We are at the world-famous Inverewe Garden and Estate, just a little to the north of Poolewe at the head of the loch. The plants and trees that grow here in such profusion really shouldn't – not at this latitude, the same as Moscow's. Bizarrely, plants, shrubs and trees from exotic locations from the southern hemisphere, such as Tasmania, New Zealand, South Africa and Chile – to name but a few – grow very well here in these northern climes. As many people know, there's a simple explanation for this phenomenon. It's all thanks to the Gulf Stream, which comes particularly close to shore here. Without it, the hairy Highland cattle we know and love would be reindeer and the grass the cattle love to ruminate would be the lichen the reindeer like to lick.

The Garden was founded by Osgood Mackenzie in 1862. He had the misfortune to be born the third son of the laird, Sir Francis Mackenzie of Gairloch. The first inherits all. That is the way it was and still is when it comes to the aristocratic way of life. But with the financial help of his good old mum, Osgood became a landowner in his own right at the tender age of twenty by buying the neighbouring estate of Inverewe. Part of it included a peninsula jutting into the loch, which he began fencing off in a bid to keep out the deer and the rabbits. No small task: one has a habit of jumping and the other has a habit of burrowing, so he needed to build it high and dig it deep. And that wasn't all, not by a long chalk. They must have thought he was mad. The ground was poor and rocky, and soil was imported by the cartload from Ireland and then carried to the site in baskets. Back-breaking work to be sure, but that was only the start – as anyone who tends a garden knows only too well.

There is a saying, with a number of minor differences, and attributed to the Talmud as well as the Cuban revolutionary, José Martí, amongst others, that in order to achieve a "measure of immortality, every man should plant a tree, write a book and father a child". Osgood took heed, particularly with regard to the first. Before he started laying out his fifty-acre garden, he planted more than a hundred acres of trees to provide the screen he knew would be needed to shelter the tender plants from the winds that came swirling about from all the airts.

The job was still not completed at his death in 1922, but the spade was taken up, so to speak, by his daughter, Mairi, and her second husband, Ronald

Sawyer. As well as fulfilling her father's dreams as far as the garden was concerned, in 1937 she and Ronald also built Inverewe House on the site of the original baronial lodge which had remained derelict ever since a fire in 1914. In 1952, the year before her death, and with no children surviving her, Mairi generously gave the gardens to the National Trust of Scotland, as well as an endowment to pay for its upkeep. Known as "The Oasis of the North", it is also financed by the visitors' entrance fees, as well as the subscriptions of NTS members, such as us.

As for the book, Osgood's *A Hundred Years in the Highlands*, first published in 1921 a year before his death (phew, just made it!), despite its less than riveting opening sentence – "I was born on the 13th of May, 1842, at the Chateau de Talhouet, not far from the little town of Quimperle, in the Morbihan, Brittany" – is a best-seller today, and I suppose if you are going to tell the story of your life, you may as well take a leaf out of Julie Andrews' songbook and "start at the very beginning".

A maze of paths with mysterious and inviting names such as Fictolacteum and Cinnabarinum lead the visitor to intriguing places such as Bambooselem and Coronation Knoll and the Devil's Elbow. There are a good number of viewpoints too where you can stop and admire your surroundings, not just within the garden but to the loch and hills beyond. Furthest away from here, at the tip of the peninsula, is Cuddy's Rock. Had we but time enough, we would go there and pass the livelong day, but at my back I hear "time's wingèd chariot hurrying near". Therefore, instead of going as far as that, and although it doesn't sound like it, we take the shorter route through South Africa, the Walled Garden and the Rock Garden to Japan, returning to the visitor centre via America.

Pausing to take a last look over the palm trees and across the shimmering loch to where the hills clamber into the sky, I could be in some other Eden. I don't remember dying but I suppose I must have, like the polar bear in the last chapter. After all, I have tried to be good all my life.

This must be my reward.

Chapter Thirty-Six

Poolewe to Kinlochewe: The Legend of the Loch and Other Tales

POOLEWE, tidy and white, you would hardly believe, was once an industrial centre. At the beginning of the 17th century it had an iron-smelting furnace, until the supply of wood that was needed to make the charcoal ran out. In the 18th century it was the point of disembarkation for the cattle from Lewis and Harris, which had to swim ashore before being driven south to market along the banks of Loch Maree.

In the old cemetery you will find a Class-1 Pictish stone, very much worn, depicting a crescent and V-rod. It's not standing but lying flat on its back, recycled as a graveslab. No wonder it wasn't recognised for what it was until 1992, assumed to mark the grave of just another anonymous dead person whose name the sands of time had worn away. Now it has a little six-inch fence around it, which doesn't do much to keep people out but does a grand job in helping you locate it should you wish to do so.

Now let me direct you to the stone-built St Maelrubha's Church, which looks for all the world like a crofter's humble cottage with a smaller building attached. If you didn't know any better, you might assume that's where the facilities were – but of course such luxuries were unheard of then. You may remember we last came across the Irish monk St Maelrubha in Strathnaver, where he was allegedly buried in 722. This church was only built in 1965 and has the distinction of being the first Episcopalian Church built in Scotland since the Jacobite rebellion of 1745 – more than two hundred years later. Isn't that astonishing? It has a sort of link with the saint in the form of a stone fragment which has been set into the wall to the left of the altar. From that small piece, experts have been able to deduce, from the style of the carving, that it dates within a century or two of the saint's time.

We follow the cattle route out of town, at least to begin with, along the banks of the River Ewe – which, at only four miles long, is one of the shortest rivers in Scotland. A little later we reach the point where the A832 takes a dogleg just before Loch Maree, taking us west along the banks of Loch Tollaidh to Gairloch after the Gaelic *gearrloch*, meaning "short loch". This area has been inhabited from time immemorial, evidence of a Bronze Age settlement having been found, and at the end of the beach is the Iron Age vitrified fort of An Dùn.

And then, of course, along came the Vikings whose rule ended after their defeat at Largs in 1263, as you know. After that, the local clans, the Mackenzies and the Macleods, slugged it out for dominance with the former finally getting the upper hand when they received the support of James IV in 1493.

You will remember Osgood Mackenzie's father was the owner of the Gairloch estate, lands he had inherited from his ancestor, Hector Roy Mackenzie, who had benefited from the royal patronage. Skip forward a few centuries. During the Clearances, neither Osgood's father, Sir Francis, nor his good son, John, evicted their tenants, not a single one. As a result, the population of Gairloch grew as those who were evicted from other communities made their way here. Not that the village is a big place, even today – home only to about 800 souls.

A big dent was made in the population, however, on 15th July 1842 when 215 people turned their backs on Gairloch forever and emigrated to Cape Breton Island in Nova Scotia which had been founded in 1805. No prizes for guessing they called their new settlement "New Gairloch". And they were just the first tranche. In the mid-1840s, the potato blight, which had such a devasting effect in Ireland, affected Scotland too – to a lesser extent thankfully. But nevertheless it resulted in another exodus from the Highlands, as we saw in the microcosm of Handa Island.

There is a car park in the little retail centre which includes a multi-tasking café, giftshop and information centre, and we walk the few hundred yards to the Gairloch Heritage Museum which stands right at the junction with the B8021, where you become acquainted with the past long before you enter the building. Outside are some fishing boats including the gloriously-named *Queen Mary*, which bears no resemblance in any shape or form to its illustrious and twenty-three-year younger namesake which was launched in 1934 and since 1967 has been enjoying retirement in Long Beach, California.

The attention is drawn not so much to the boats lying about but more towards a lighthouse lamp and foghorn. Just the Fresnel lens actually. Both come from Rubha Reidh where, in 1944, the lighthouse keepers, Duncan Mackenzie and Alex Combe set off across bog and mire in biting gale-force winds to do what they could to help the stricken sailors of the *William H*

Welch with the result you already know. The lighthouse was another Stevenson creation, conceived by David Stevenson as long ago as 1853, but the Board of Trade grumbled at the £5000 price-tag and it was not built until 1912 by Stevenson's son, also named David, at a cost of £14,900. It is automated now, the last keepers having left in 1986 and, like so many which are surplus to requirement, the keepers' accommodation has been turned into a self-catering apartment or a guesthouse. The choice is yours.

The foghorn's clockwork mechanism can be seen just inside the entrance, along with a brief explanation of how it works. Having read it, it's no criticism of the notes, but I am not a great deal wiser.

Inside the museum proper is another explanation which is rather easier to understand. It's of an illicit still with a cut-away barrel, so you can see the metal "worm" inside. In fact it is a very handy recipe for anyone who is thinking of building one to put in their garage or garden shed. Thank you, Gairloch Heritage Museum.

The making of the water-of-life was of course a widespread practice throughout the Highlands, and the museum – as you would expect – also reflects many other aspects of life in the area from farming and fishing to spinning and weaving, as well as a section on geology and wildlife.

The inside of a crofter's house as it was a century ago has been created with a row of buttons which the visitor can press to illuminate particular points of interest such as the box bed. And there is also a model of a 17th century watermill which actually works at the press of a button with an explanation next to it, not about how it works, but how the system worked. The laird had the poor crofters over a barrel. They had no option but to have their corn ground there for which service the laird took a "multure". If the crofter tried to grind it himself on the quiet, if discovered, his quern would be broken.

From Melvaig, at the end of the B8021 some ten miles to the north, and from the more recent past – from more or less my own times in fact – is Mr Macrae's shop as it was in the 1940s. It's the sort of place where you could buy anything from a safety pin to an anchor. And if you wanted coffin trimmings, well, Mr Macrae could supply them too.

If that display depicts the most recent past, then the Pictish stone which has a very fine salmon carving near the top is by far the most ancient. It's only one of two ever found in Wester Ross. The other you know. It's Torridian sandstone and known as the "Achtercain Symbol Stone" because, funnily enough, that's where it came from – the proverbial stone's throw away from here. It's now in its permanent home after having been moved about a bit. Unfortunately at some stage it was broken at the top, where the feet and tail feathers of a bird can be seen. At first it was thought it might be a goose but the experts, by comparing it with a similar stone in Orkney, think it's an eagle. I would have thought that was far more likely. And because the stone doesn't have a cross, it can be dated to sometime between 500-700 AD.

I've kept till last what, for me, is the most interesting exhibit of all – though it may not be much to look at, truth be told. Think of a *Punch and Judy* show that you used to see on beaches in the summer to entertain the children and which, for all I know, maybe some still survive. This stands about nine feet tall with a front flap that opens outwards to create a sort of sounding board just like the pulpits in the churches. It's what was known as a "Preacher's Ark".

It was a self-assembly unit, designed to be taken apart so it could be put on a wagon and reassembled at the place of the next gathering. The reason for all this palaver has its origins in the Disruption of 1843, when the Free Church broke away from the established church over the issue of congregations being forced to accept the minister the laird foisted upon them. Fifty years later it split again to form the Free Presbyterian Church of Scotland, over reasons I will not delve into, but the point was there were no churches for the disaffected to go to. As a result, the open air became their church, the Preacher's Ark, the minister's pulpit, with the precentor standing below leading the chanting of the psalms. This ark comes from Shieldaig in Torridon, not the one nearby at the head of loch. Gairloch had a similar one which saw a great deal of use, as it was not until 1920 that it had its own bricks-and-mortar church.

But the thing that really gets me is the photograph of the ark in action, so to speak, just like a *Punch and Judy* show, on the beach. The area around it is thick with people, masses and masses of people, many who may have walked as far as twenty miles or more to be here on the Sabbath, their day off, and having set out the previous evening. The sermon might last for at least an hour, so I suppose you could say they got their money's worth. Many ministers in these more secular times would give their eyeteeth to have as many bums on pews as that. But of course, back then it was more than just a church service; it was a great day out, a gathering of the community with a picnic to follow after the service.

Some other photographs are on display, featuring a plane called *Sleepy Time Gal*. It was, and is, a tradition to give planes a nickname and paint it on the fuselage next to the nose cone, and the curious name for this comes from the title of a 1926 jazz song and since 2001, a film. Surprisingly, there were at least ten others which adopted the same name.

I'm sorry to say it's a sad tale concerning the mysterious crash of the B-24 H Liberator Bomber on June 13th 1945 in an area known as the "Fairy Lochs", just behind Shieldaig. It had a crew of nine and six passengers, all of whom were killed. It seems cruelly ironic that the crew, after having come safely through eleven combat missions, and having told their friends and families they were on their way home, had to die in such awful circumstances. It's not been proved, but suggested that the most likely cause was a fire in one of the engines and, crucially, they had deviated slightly off course. The pilot may have thought he was over the sea, not mountains, when he went into a steep dive in an attempt to extinguish the flames.

The crash site is still littered with the debris and it may just be a story but it is said bad luck will befall you if you take anything away – as one woman is alleged to have done, removing the parachute silk to make her wedding dress. Maybe the marriage ended up badly and that's what gave rise to the superstition. Anyway, for that reason, or purely out of respect, locals and visitors leave it alone and take nothing from the site.

Leaving Gairloch, the A832 swings east following the River Kerry and, just after the power station, there is a place to park and take in a waterfall, though you might prefer to carry on until the car park at Slatterdale not many miles further on, through the forest. You can have a bite to eat there if the time is right and admire the 3,281 foot-high massive molar of Slioch taking a bite out of the sky. Or, if you really have waterfalls on your mind, you can drive on just a few more miles to where you can admire the Victoria Falls, just as long as you are not expecting anything like the one David Livingstone "discovered".

Slioch is probably one of Scotland's most recognisable mountains, whilst Loch Maree that it dominates is certainly amongst the most scenic lochs. At twelve miles long and two-and-a-half at its widest, Maree is the fourth largest freshwater loch in Scotland with more than sixty islands, and – like any self-respecting Scottish loch – it is said to have a monster known as *Muc-sheilce*.

It possibly takes its name from *Eilean mo Righ* or even *Eilean a Mohr Righ*, the "Island of my King" or the "Island of the Great King", where the ceremony of choosing the next king beside a holy well and tree took place. Or it might possibly come from Mourie, a Celtic god who was associated with bulls and other animals with curved horns. In that mythology, as with other cultures, curved horns are associated with the moon, while our own word, "lunatic", as I don't need to remind you, comes from the Latin *luna* for "moon".

Now let's get a bit more up to date. Step up to the plate the Irish Saint aforesaid, St Maelrubha, also known as St Mourie. His base was in Applecross, but since this was a heathen stronghold, he set up a hermitage here on this island, about halfway down the loch on the eastern side. The connection between the two names is no accident. As is common with the Christianising process, the saint's name had been grafted onto the pagan deity just as many pagan festivals were grafted onto the Christian calendar. Another instance of *plus ça change, plus c'est la même chose*. They knew they couldn't erase centuries of pagan culture and worship overnight.

One of the practices the Celts indulged in was bull sacrifice, something so deep-rooted in their culture the saint was powerless to prevent it. The best he could do was move the date of the Celtic festival of Lughansa to his own birthday. The reason for the sacrifice was to make sure that the sun god, Lugh, would triumph over the forces of chaos. You may scoff as much as you like, but it was vitally important to them.

Bizarrely, the practice was still regarded by the locals as a cure for insanity until the end of the 17th century. The Presbytery of Dingwall took action against four offenders in 1678 but it did nothing to halt the practice. The last recorded instance was in 1698 when Hector MacKenzie, his son and grandson, sacrificed a bull to cure the madness of Christine MacKenzie. Alas it does not say what the poor lady's relationship was to them, far less if it worked or not.

The remains of the hermitage can still be seen next to where the holy tree once stood rooted. The present tree, which may or may not be a descendant – the so-called "money tree" – is a blasted oak into which people have hammered a coin and made a wish. Or it might be the other way about. As with ceremonies of this nature, the order in which they are performed is vital. Whatever you do, make sure you make a good job of hammering your coin home – for if it falls out, your wish will not be granted.

The oldest coin dates from 1828 so it's actually a pretty recent practice, and it is said that in 1877, when Queen Victoria was staying at the Loch Maree Hotel in Talladale for a week, she visited the island and asked, or should that be commanded, that someone put a coin in the tree for her. Being a monarch she would not have had any cash on her, of course. No wonder our monarchs are so rich if they never have to spend a penny.

She was grateful and had a good holiday here. We know because it is written in stone, a stone which still stands in front of the hotel. It is in Gaelic and, translated, reads: *The Queen in her gracious condescension willed that this stone should be a remembrance of the pleasure she found in coming to this part of Ross-Shire.* I like the oxymoron of the "condescension" and the "willed".

The stone is there still, but the sacred well has disappeared. There is a depression in the ground near the tree, however. Its waters were said to cure madness if certain procedures were followed. (You just can't get away from associations of madness in this place.)

This is was what they did. First of all the afflicted one was rowed three times round the island clockwise. On each circuit the victim was ducked under the water before being taken to the well. After that a cloth was tied to a tree, like at the Clootie Well in the Black Isle, or else a coin was driven into the bark. However, an account of 1772 says that first of all the patient should drink the water and then be ducked into it three times. The process was repeated daily for several weeks until a cure was effected, or not. But which of these methods was the right one? As you know well from the instructions on a medicine bottle, you must follow the instructions precisely if you expect them to work.

The most efficacious day to undergo the cure, apparently, was on August 25th, the Saint's Day. Well, what do you know! The last recorded occurrence of the practice was in 1858. This time we know the cure was ineffective as the poor sufferer, a young lady, was committed to Inverness Lunatic Asylum.

Those are recent activities, with no bulls being harmed in the process. But there were other practices that were extremely harmful to the health of old women, particularly if their behaviour was deemed to be a bit out of the ordinary. At one point in the loch there is a spit of shingle jutting far out into it. It is known as *Rudha Chailleach*, or "witches' point", and the water is particularly deep there. To test if the old women were witches or not, they were marched along here with their hands tied behind their backs and thrown in. The perceived wisdom was if they were witches, the De'il would protect his own by making them float. If they did, they tried to fish them out so they could be burnt at the stake. If they failed, no matter – they'd soon be toasting their toes before the everlasting bonfire anyway. If they sank and drowned, that's just too bad; the price for being a bit odd, no smoke without fire anyway, as they saw it. However, John H. Dixon FSA Scot, in his comprehensive study of the subject in *Gairloch in North-West Ross-shire* (1886), reports no existing tales of this happening. Which is not quite the same thing as it never having happened previously.

The most impressive structure on the island is what's called the "Druid Circle", which archaeologists have dated to 100 BC. One visitor was that indefatigable pioneer traveller, Thomas Pennant, who came here in 1772 and who, as well as mentioning the well, if you pardon the pun, reports the island was still being used as a cemetery, as it still is today. It's not any Tom, Dick and Harry who can be buried here, however; it's a privilege given only to a few, like the local MacLeods for instance. In 1922 it also became the last resting place of the manager of the Loch Maree Hotel, who took his own life after he unwittingly killed eight of his guests by serving them liver pâté infected with botulism.

There are also a couple of interesting Viking graves, said to belong to a royal married couple whose bodies, as befitting their status, would normally have been burnt in a ship. The reason that didn't happen is because they both committed suicide. It's a story which bears many similarities to *Romeo and Juliet* as written by a certain William Shakespeare. The Prince's name was Olaf and a warrior bold was he, who loved his men and his wife almost equally. The couple lived happily in a wooden tower on the island, from the top of which he could see his beloved galleys where his men slept. But came the day came when Olaf had to set sail and do what a Viking has to do. Naturally it was a bit of a wrench to leave his wench behind, not knowing when he would return, but knowing full well he might not come back alive, given the nature of his profession. Accordingly, the pair hatched a plan so the minute she espied her lordship in his longship at the far end of the loch, she could be prepared. If it flew a white flag, he was alive and well. If black, he was dead and gone to Valhalla.

And so off he went. Time passed; time which hung heavy on the hands of the lady, during which she not only worried if her husband was alive but increasingly came to wonder if he actually preferred making war with his mates than making love to her – or some other woman for that matter. "Frailty, thy name is woman", but in mitigation, we all know what sailors are meant to have in every port, and especially what being on a Viking raid entailed. Happily Olaf survived his expedition and was able to fly the white flag. The princess was mightily relieved but decided to test how deep was his love. She set out to meet him in her barge, raised a black flag, swathed herself in a shroud and laid down on the bier.

The moment the vessels came within touching distance of each other, Olaf leapt on board her barge and seeing what he took to be the corpse of his only true love laid out before him, gave vent to a cry of utter despair and grief, and without hesitation, drew forth his dagger and plunged it into his breast. Well, the lady had her answer. She leapt up, now convinced of the sincerity of her husband's passion, but it was too late. He had made a clean job of it. Stricken with grief and remorse, she pulled out the dagger and plunged it into her own heart. And that is why they were not consumed by fire in a ship but buried here on this island, not side by side, but toe to toe.

Leaving Loch Maree behind, we head towards the oddly-named Kinlochewe at the bottom of the loch. I say "oddly-named" only because it is miles away from Loch Ewe, even as the eagle flies. It should really be called "Kinlochmaree" which I think has a very fine ring to it. The reason it doesn't is because until 1700, Loch Maree was known as "Loch Ewe", the two Ewes connected by the river of the same name, which incidentally, was not navigable by the Viking longships and which had to be hauled over the four miles between them. The reason why they called the loch "Maree" you already know.

Near the end of the loch is the visitor centre for the 18 square-mile Benn Eighe National Nature Reserve – Britain's first, incidentally, established in 1951. All time pales into insignificance when you realise the mind-boggling time it took to form this landscape. It all began some 800 million years ago when massive amounts of sand and gravel nearly four miles high were dumped by gargantuan rivers upon the even more ancient bedrock. This was the Torridonian sandstone that poor old tormented Hugh Miller was so fond of. Just imagine that – four miles high! Then about 400 hundred million years ago, as I said before, the earth moved and thrust some of this sandstone on top of much younger rocks made of quartzite, like granny getting a piggy-back from one of her grandchildren.

Talking of grannies, there are quite a few here actually, the so-called "grannies of the grey slope" – pine trees over 350 years old, descendants of the ones who first arrived here over 8,000 years ago when the ice had retreated. Which, of course, makes the present trees merely babies. The "grey slope" is the Glas-Leitir on Benn Eighe, which, if you ignore the trees at the base, you could easily imagine as being somewhere on the moon.

The majority of people who come here, whether or not they know anything about the history of the ground beneath their feet, come to go on walks. There are three trails: the Mountain (4 miles), the Woodland (1 mile) and a plooter around the Visitor Centre. This is not from where you make the ascent of Benn Eighe; that's from the car park at the Coille na Glas-Leitir, just a little before this. And for those who don't already know, Benn Eighe is not a single mountain but a massif, of which the highest peak is Ruadh Stac-Mohr – which, at 3,300 feet, is a Munro with plenty of feet to spare. Its long, grey, humped back looks extremely like that massive mammal, that poor hunted-to-death Moby Dick, seemingly raised from the depths of the ocean to heights he never dreamed of, as if transported to whale Valhalla.

All this and more you can learn in the visitor centre, such as the sort of wildlife you can expect to see on the trails, like buzzards or a golden eagle or a pine marten, or – if you are exceptionally lucky – a glimpse of the indigenous, rare and extremely shy wildcat. What you are certain to see in profusion is Noah's Mistake, aka the midge, Scotland's not-so-secret weapon against invaders. The Romans knew them well. Unfortunately their little brains can't distinguish between hostile invaders and friendly tourists.

And let us not forget the flora, which is rather special; what the botanists call the "dwarf shrub heath", the like of which you would have to travel to the arctic to see and here it is right at your ankles – but please keep to the path.

At Kinlochewe, like Poolewe, there was an iron smelting industry near here in the 17th century. There was also another at Letterewe at the north-east end of the loch, and which similarly denuded the landscape of trees. They were replanted, as it happens, but then along came the Second World War and once again you couldn't see the trees for the wood that was requisitioned for the war effort, the making of ammunition boxes thereof.

The hotel dates from 1800, built to serve the Drove Road, which – funnily enough – ran down the eastern side of the loch where no road ventures today. As for us, it's westward ho we go on the A896 towards Loch Torridon.

Chapter Thirty-Seven

Torridon and the Applecross Peninsula: The Monk and The Body Snatcher

I T'S not what you are going through that makes the difference; it's what lies ahead. It may not be a metaphor for life but I think it may well be a maxim for the motorist, in particular the NC500 motorist.

As we thread our way through Glen Torridon on the single-track road, with frequent stops to let oncoming traffic pass, as far as I am able to tell from the letterbox view provided by the rear-view mirror it looks just as splendid this way as that. This is good news for the NC500 traveller who might wonder which is the better way to go round it – clockwise or anticlockwise. I would unquestionably recommend the latter, the way we are doing it, and I will tell you why at the end of the chapter.

All of a sudden, the mountains that have been hemming us in vanish, and out we pop into the open, allowing us to get our first view of beautiful Upper Loch Torridon. Yes, so good they named it twice, as someone famously sang about a certain city. Lower Loch Torridon is a sea loch and there is also a village of Torridon, although it only changed its name from Fasag in the 1950s. One of the things that makes it so special is the way the 3,000 foot-high mountain of Liatach rears sheer out of the sea behind it, transforming the houses beneath into dolls' houses.

In the 17th century this is where the pig iron that was produced on Loch Maree was converted into wrought iron before being shipped to England. Pardon me for mentioning this if you already know, but lest you were wondering why "pig" iron is so called, it's because after smelting, the molten metal was poured into a channel with rectangular blocks branching off it. It reminded someone of a litter of pigs feeding from a sow and so the name stuck. "Wrought" iron, of course, simply means iron that has been worked or "wrought" by a blacksmith.

I have already explained why the iron industry in this quiet rural backwater came to an end. It would have had an impact on the economy, but even tougher times were to come a couple of centuries later. In 1831, the estate was bought by the dastardly Colonel McBarnet, a former plantation owner in the West Indies. Given his previous credentials, the crofters could expect no mercy and they received none. They were unceremoniously and mercilessly cleared off the land with only a small patch left upon which to grow potatoes. Hard times but, believe it or not, they were to get even harder. In 1859 they were removed from that overworked little plot to the even less fertile land at Annat on the other side of the loch.

Things improved, however, when Duncan Darroch 4th of Gourock (1836-1910) bought the estate in 1873. He was one of the first landlords to begin reforestation of the Highlands. He wanted to farm deer, not sheep, so now it was *their* turn to be cleared. He resettled the crofters, fenced off their land so the deer couldn't eat their crops, allowed the crofters to let their cattle share the upper grazing land with the deer, and loaned them money with which they could purchase cattle or boats. A goodly man was he. Look out for a stone by the road erected by his widow, Ann, on which is written:

> *In memory of the devotion and affection shown by one hundred men on the estate of Torridon, who, at their request, carried his body from the house here on its way to interment in the family burial place at Gourock.*

Since 1967, the landlord of the Torridon estate has been the NTS. At the junction with the A896 and the little road to Torridon village, so small they never named it at all, you will find the Countryside Centre. Inside, along with information about the geology of the estate and its wildlife, you can get an eagle's view of it from a 3-D topographical map. A hell of a place to lose a cow, but heaven for hill walkers.

A few hundred yards along the track is what has to be one of the most unusual museums you ever will see – a deer museum. It boasts more skulls and antlers than an entire millinery would ever need to hang its wares, while further along the track are even more prospective hat stands. They are still attached to their owners who, for the present, are living on a deer farm. And should you be looking for somewhere to hang *your* hat, carry on and you will come to some NTS self-catering cottages.

On the other hand, you could stay at the award-winning hotel in Torridon, simply known as *The Torridon*. It has won the AA Hotel of the Year (Scotland) twice, whilst its *1887 Restaurant* has been awarded three AA rosettes. It offers three courses, or five if that's not enough, or – if you are still hungry after that – a magnificent seven. But that's not why I mention it. I do so because the restaurant's name comes from the year the shooting lodge was built for the first Earl of Lovelace, aka William King, the 7th Baron (1805-1893). Some lodge! No wonder it took twenty years to build.

If the name "Lovelace" rings a bell it's because in 1835 the baron married Ada Lovelace (1815-1852), Lord Byron's only legitimate daughter, mathematical genius and now credited as being the world's first computer programmer. Through her mother she was a descendant of the Barons Lovelace, a title which became extinct on the death of the 6th Baron in 1736. In 1838 however, her husband was created Viscount Ockham of Surrey and the 1st Earl of Lovelace. Thus Ada, as well as being a good counter, became a countess as well as mistress of Ockham Park and Torridon.

It's worth continuing through the village round the north side of the loch to Inverallegin. This out-of-the-way place was once the centre of a thriving illicit whisky industry thanks to a cleft in the rock known as "Smuggler's Cave". It was a bit like Smoo, which those killjoys – the excisemen in Shieldaig, just along the coast a bit from here – knew not of. This was the distillery; the problem and the danger was smuggling it out to the consumers. I'm sure it tasted all the better for that little bit of danger, and the whisky tradition in this area is reflected in the malt whisky bar in *The Torridon*. In 2013 it was awarded gold status by *Whisky Magazine*. But with more than 350 on offer, which to choose? Well, for £30 you can have a nosing and tasting assisted by the knowledgeable staff.

If you are a film buff who likes to visit film locations, carry on a little further and you will come to Diabaig which most people probably do not realise is the village which featured in the 1996 movie *Loch Ness*, but obviously is nowhere near the loch. The things that you're liable to see in the movies, they ain't necessarily true. The camera is forever telling lies. Monster movies are not my thing, but Diabaig is worth coming to see because of its superb location.

We have come back round the loch to Shieldaig now and, although it looks very much like a Clearance village, in fact it owes its origins to a rather unlikely person. We have to go back to 1810 when war was raging all over Europe and, however surprising it may seem, the Admiralty chose this remote place as a base to build boats and train men for the navy against Napoleon. Though as every schoolboy knows, but which the Admirality couldn't possibly have foreseen, victory and Waterloo were just five years away. In the event, as far as we know, the men of Shieldaig never went to war.

The government had a second string to its bow, however. People were attracted by generous grants for the building of boats to create a fishing industry. Indeed, Shieldaig derives its name from the Old Norse meaning "loch of the herring", shoals of the silver darlings out there simply dying to make the incomers' fortunes. They were also able to buy salt at duty-free prices with which to cure the catch before sending it south, and at a guaranteed a price to boot. It was an offer not to be refused. And for a while things went swimmingly, but then disaster struck.

Although not conceived as a Clearance village, as I said, Shieldaig became a victim of the Clearances all the same. In 1857, the Mackenzies sold the Applecross estate to the Duke of Leeds who began turfing out the smaller tenants and replacing them with sheep. This policy was continued by Sir John Stewart and his sons who, in 1864, bought the Lochcarron estate from Leeds when he broke up the Applecross estate into seven lots. Hard times were here again.

The ubiquitous herring are gone now, but have been replaced by mussels and prawns and tourists – whether or not they are on the NC500 trail. Opposite the hotel, the Tigh an Eilean, out there in the loch, is Shieldaig Island where the Scots pines grow incredibly thickly. But do not be deceived – these are not the descendants of the *silva Caledonia,* the ones Pliny the Elder wrote about after the Roman invasion of Britain, nor are they the "grannies of the grey slope" that I referred to earlier. No, seemingly these were planted in the middle of the 19th century to replace those that were felled for the building of ships, grown from seeds taken from Speyside.

However, these trees are not the same as the native Highland pine – not that you could tell from this distance, or most people could even when standing right next to one, the differences being rather subtle. For arborists though, these little differences are extremely important and they are mightily worried that these incomers will cross-polinate, in the promiscuous way trees do, with Pliny's pines, if I may call them that, in Glen Shieldaig forest. In order to protect and conserve them, the plan is – over the centuries – to replace the Speysiders with the rarer Highlanders. In the meantime, the island, in the care of the NTS, is now a place of Special Scientific Interest, particularly to anyone who is interested in birds.

The shape of the Applecross peninsula has been compared to the blade of an axe, and one that has seen a great deal of service if the indentations on it are anything to go by. We're circumnavigating it now, skimming the seashore on a road so narrow, like the one to Torridon, it's not even been credited with a name – at least not on the map. *A Horse With No Name* by "America" pops into my head. Apart from the little matter of there being no desert, we have plenty of horsepower under the bonnet of our car which shall be nameless, and our journey has had much to do with plants and birds and sand and hills and (Pictish) rings.

It's astonishing to think this part of the road we're on now, from Shieldaig to Kenmore, was only completed in 1970. A "Parliamentary Road", built in 1822, did link Applecross with the villages of Camusterrach and Toscaig to the south, but the villages to the north were neglected. And if you think that's incredible, there's something else. It was not until 1976 that the circuit from Shieldaig to Kishorn via Applecross was complete.

You can see what an isolated place Applecross was – by which I mean the entire peninsula, not just the little village which most people think of when they hear the name. Even after the roads were built, it was a lot speedier to go by boat over the sea to Skye, as that song has it, than venture into the interior. The coastal villages' remoteness may have saved them from attack from the rear, but they were a sitting target on the seaward side from the Scandanavian menace.

Fearnmore is the most north-westerly point of the peninsula and, shortly after rounding the bend, we stop at a viewpoint where, out to sea, we can see the dark smudge of the chain of distant islands that are Rona, Raasay and Scalpay, although the latter is hidden by a bend in the road. Behind them, the Black Cuillins of Skye are peeking over their shoulders, giving a jagged edge to the horizon where they reach for the low-lying clouds. While it might have been nice to see it in the sunlight, the scene has a certain brooding dramatic intensity which I'm not sure I don't like better.

Just before Sand and its aptly-named bay of the same name, there is an ancient rockshelter. In 2000, Edinburgh University's "First Settlers Project" conducted an excavation here. They were particularly interested in the midden. You can tell a lot about people by looking at the things they throw away. It will come as no surprise to anyone that they found a great deal of shells, limpet shells mainly, as well as tools made of bone, antler and stone. The latter is evidence that these Mesolithic people travelled to Rum and Skye. Isn't that an incredible thing! They also found some items of jewellery: shell beads and a carved boar's tusk.

In 2006, Channel Four's *Time Team* excavated the broch at the end of Shore Street, Applecross village's one and only thoroughfare. They found both the inner and outer walls, with stairs and a hearth which they reckoned was used to work iron. Amongst other items, they uncovered the fragment of a decorated antler comb, a dagger in a leather pouch, a copper-alloy ring and a metal pin.

The name "Applecross" is said to have come about after someone in days of yore planted apple trees in the form of a cross. A romantic story. Alas, it's a complete fallacy. The chronicler Tighernac Ua Braín (died 1088), abbot of Clonmacnoise in Ireland, tells us (in Latin) in the *Annals of Tighernac,* that in 673 Maelrubha founded the Church of "Apercrossan", meaning the "mouth of the (river) Crossan". Later it became known as *A Chomraich* – the Sanctuary.

We first picked up the trail of Maelrubha in Strathnaver and he has been popping up now and again ever since, but this is where his tale really begins and ends. About a mile before the village is Clachan cemetery, and it is here his venerable bones really lie. A Celtic Cross on the other side of the wall stands over us as we read the information boards outside the cemetery gates. As you would expect, there is much about Maelrubha.

He was born in Bangor in what is now Northern Ireland on 3rd January 642, and in 673 found what he had been looking for – a place to found his monastery. According to legend, he spent his first night at Eilean an Naoimh – or Saint's Island – just offshore from the tiny village of Camusterrach, just a mile or so on the other side of the Applecross Inn. From here he probably eyed up the natives and wondered how hostile they might be to receiving the Word he wanted them to hear.

He must have thought they didn't look too scary, for right here, where the church and cemetery are now, is where he built his monastery. And it was from this place his influence spread far and wide. As well as the church and living accommodation for the monks, it also had a hospitium, a place where travellers could expect to be provided with food and lodging – the Premier Inn of its day. It was a lot more than that, however. On a practical level, there was a blacksmith's forge and a carpenter's workshop, while – on a cultural level – there was a scriptorium and a stonemasons' workshop. Both slow, painstaking work, but whether the pen or the chisel was the more laborious it's hard to say when you think of those wonderful illuminated manuscripts like the *Book of Kells.* It must have taken hours to write one of those letters that begins a chapter. Just how long it took to carve a Celtic knot I could not say.

Thanks to the unwanted attention of the heathen Viking invaders who raised hell in this peaceful sanctuary, the monastery lasted a mere 120 years; a mere blink of the eye in the history of the world. Maelrubha lived only a little less longer than the monastery – for 80 years, not a bad age for those days. Perhaps Someone was looking after him, which is more than can be said for his successor, Failbhe MacGuaire, who in 737 had his life cut short when, along with twenty-two of his followers, he drowned in the Sound. It is a reminder that while these waters look tranquil now, they can whip up a storm with little warning.

Despite the claims of Strathnaver, as well as another claim that he was murdered on the Moray Firth by the Vikings, the fact of the matter is he died here on Tuesday 21st April 722, peacefully in his bed, just as the *Annals* record. Alas, there is no marker to distinguish the grave – or "Cladh Maree" as it is called – in the south-east section of the cemetery, only the information that it is near two rounded stones.

We make our way towards the roofless remains of the 15th century chapel which housed the remains of the Mackenzies, who were the landowners here until 1857. Nearby, in a corner, four stones are poking through the grassy sward and, indeed, two of them are rounded. Behind them is a mound. So here is it – under that green grass, a stone sarcophagus lies concealed, containing the bones or the dust of the saint. It's astonishing really that's all there is to see. Only Columba, in whose tradition he followed, did more to convert the Picts to Christianity and leave a mark on this country. They may have made him a saint, but you would have thought they might have put up a marker of some sort to show where he has been sleeping the Big Sleep all these centuries. Even if this is not actually the precise spot, it's close enough, and with modern technology, they could easily find out where the sarcophagus is if they wanted to. Perhaps they don't...

There are some other persons of note buried here (though I have never heard of them), and one person described as an "infamous body snatcher" who is allegedly interred here too. Ask anyone to say the first word that comes into their head when they hear the word "body snatcher" and most people will come up with "Burke and Hare", although that's three words. Partners in crime they may have been, but there is nothing like the rough feel of hemp around your neck to make you contemplate your mortality. As most people know, William Hare turned king's evidence, was pardoned and given a new identity.

He went initially to Dumfries where he called himself "James Maxwell", a surname not uncommon in those parts. One day he disappeared and nothing was heard of him for a while until he turned up in a hospital in the south of England, where he had been admitted after a severe facial injury. After his discharge, he arrived in Applecross where he set up as a weaver, telling people little of his past but explaining the reason for his disfigurement was he had been injured in a blasting accident whilst employed on building a road.

One day he disappeared again, but this time only for a few weeks before returning with a woman whom he said was his wife. In due course they had a son, William (please note), and a daughter, Myria, who became pregnant to

William Paterson, a footman at Applecross House who admitted to being the father. When the Middletons, who had been the owners of the estate since 1864, moved to England, he went too and was never seen or heard of again. On her deathbed, however, Mrs Norris, as Myria now was, confessed the real father of her son was a guest at the Temperance Hotel, as the Inn was then called, and that she and William were well paid for concealing his identity.

On the way to the church, I keep my eye open for Maxwell's headstone but without success. I suppose he has one. The church was built in 1817, and the second I step inside it takes my breath away like some cathedrals do. Having said that, you never saw anything less like a cathedral in your life. What impresses me so much is its awesome simplicity: bare walls, arched windows of clear glass, rows of hard-backed chairs in a V-shape to face the white, three-tiered pulpit – and, get this, oil lamps on long chains suspended from the ceiling.

On the way to the Heritage Centre we pause to have a closer look at the standing stone at the cemetery gates. It is pretty hard to make out anything because of the thick growth of lichen that covers it from top to toe, but we can just about make out the faint trace of the unfinished cross that we knew to look for. It is said to mark the grave of Ruaraidh Mor MacAogan, Abbot of Applecross, the last Celtic abbot. He is not there, however, as – for some reason, at some time – the stone was moved from its original site somewhere near the river. You couldn't move a big hulking stone like that in a hurry, so you have to wonder why they went to all that bother. He died in 801, in Bangor, having had to flee from the Vikings, but his body was taken back here to his spiritual home. It was a brave and risky thing to do, and the unfinished cross is surely a sign that those who took him here had to leave in a hurry.

The light and airy Heritage Centre presents a detailed story of Applecross from Mesolithic Times through Maelrubha to the present day. It also houses collections of old photographs and, in its own words, everything from "matchboxes to whale bones", as well as crofting, farming and household items. There are also a couple of fragments of intricately carved stones, but what I'm drawn towards is the reconstruction of a coracle, the sort of thing Maelruhba and his monks used to paddle across to Raasay and elsewhere.

Like the upturned shell of a turtle, it instantly reminds me of the three men who went to sea in a tub, the sort of thing you'd have a bath in, rather than put your faith in to take you across the sea. Nevertheless, this is the sort of thing Maelrubha and his monks trusted in – this fragile latticework of willow covered in hide, with a coating of tar to make it waterproof. I wouldn't care to cross a pond in it, never mind the Inner Sound to Raasay. No wonder Failbhe MacGuaire and his men were drowned. It would, however, be very easy to transport overland, I grant you that, to where you could peddle the Word to the next lot of heathens.

The other thing, right next to it actually, under a glass dome like the sort of thing you see in baker's shops to cover cakes, is a model of the monastery as it was Maelrubha's day. And like a cake, the monastery grounds were circular and divided into segments where crops were grown or livestock grazed. The modest little church is built of stone, with the thatched-roof workshops clustered nearby. Encircling the whole thing was the vallum, a ditch of turf and stone, like the Antonine Wall. It certainly looks more of a defensive than a hospitable place, where weary travellers would know they could be assured of a bed for the night or the persecuted could receive sanctuary, but it was meant as a deterrent against wolves and bears which still roamed the land in those days. They were blissfully unaware of the Vikings who were yet to come. In addition to that, there was also an inner wooden wall like a palisade running around the church and its associated buildings, thus separating the secular from the non-secular world, a defence against any temptation the monks might be exposed to from outside.

And now we are about to be exposed to the most challenging drive the NC500 has to offer, if the big blue sign at the bottom of the road is anything to go by. It's the Bealach na Bà. It was built in 1822, which makes it a lot older than the coast road, and despite all the talk there has been of sheep recently and regardless of however much it may sounds like one, it has nothing to do with the bleating of sheep. It means "Pass of the Cattle", from which you will deduce it was another Drove Road. It was not one of *the* Drove Roads however; this just served the Highlands.

At 2,053 feet, it is one of the highest roads in Scotland, winding down to join the A896 at Tornapress at the head of Loch Kishorn. The sign warns motorists of hairpin bends and a gradient of one in five. It goes on to say it is not suitable for learner drivers, caravans or very large vehicles, but it does *not* say you musn't, on pain of a fine.

Four zig-zaggy miles or so later we make it safely and without incident to the summit. The bends and the steepness, our trusty steed took in its stride. White lines at the side guided us away from soft verges and passing places were a-plenty, not that we needed them often. The other motorists must all be in the Applecross Inn if the number of cars parked outside was anything to go by. Here there are some cars, but plenty of room to park and admire the view. So far, so good.

We still have to go down again, like the Duke of York's men, but the dangers and warnings would seem, like Mark Twain's death, to be greatly exaggerated. It's a bit of a skoosh actually. It's not the road that's the problem; it's the drivers. For the locals, the NC500 must be something of a curse; tourists clogging up the single-track roads of which there have been a great many miles since Melvich. Even that they might regard as an acceptable price to pay for dwelling amongst the most splendid scenery Scotland has to offer – if only the tourists observed the code of the road. It's quite simple, really. It means not driving in convoy, which clogs up the passing places, and not parking in them while you take a photo or twenty, in the quest for the perfect shot. Tourists on holiday may have all the time in the world, but locals, going about their daily lives, have appointments to keep.

As far as the Pass of the Cattle is concerned, you can see it makes sense to suggest caravans and large vehicles should not use it. Just one of those longitudarians would occupy an entire passing space. And should you be unlucky enough to meet one of those big bully boys between passing places, who do you think it is who would have to back down and reverse? But that's not the real problem. More than likely, other cars will be behind you. Result – a traffic jam as bad as any city can conjure up. Let me put it another way. You wouldn't put paper towels instead of tissue paper down the toilet would you? So why would you clog up the pass by taking a caravan up there?

The view from the top really takes your breath away, and definitely not because of the effort and energy expended on getting here. Just think – in a matter of minutes, without any huffing and puffing, we are at a height that hill

walkers take hours to reach, and perhaps never see if the mist descends as it is prone to do in Scotland. God bless the internal combustion engine and Carl Benz – the patron saint of people like me who prefer to take the path of least resistance for maximum gain.

A plaque with radiating lines, presented by the AA in 1978, helpfully points out the direction and miles to landmarks – some we can see, some we can't – such as Broadford in Skye, thirty miles away to the west. It's a study in chiaroscuro – the darkness of the clouds, hills and water contrasted with the lighter shades of those clouds with silver linings, and – where there is a break in them – the sunlight slanting down, creating pools of light on the Sound where, like a stage lit with spotlights, you half-expect something to appear from the heavens like a *deus ex machina*. It certainly is dramatic. After a few moments I rudely turn my back on it and see, far to the east, over the rucked-up landscape, blue hills in the distance.

Back in the car, the descent to the community of Kishorn is another breathtaking experience. This is the view I knew was coming, the view that inspired me to take this, the anticlockwise route. Below us, the road snakes downwards through the tired and ancient rocks which have seen it all before. Miles of crash barriers keep motorists on the twisty and narrow, and I can see why. The bends have been banked up extremely high with hundreds of rocks so we can be taken down gradually. It's an engineering achievement all right, the only thing making it easier there being no shortage of material – the hillside is littered still with masses of boulders, rocks and stones.

But that's not what makes it really outstanding, hugely impressive though that may be. No, what really tops everything off is the way the road threads its way through, and is dwarfed by, the Coire na Bà on the left and Meall Gorm and Creag a' Chumhaing on the right, with Loch Kishorn nestling at the bottom. You can't help but get that fjord feeling. Then raising your eyes, at the other side of the loch, more hills can be seen rising to greet the horizon.

If, like *Desert Islands Discs*, I had to choose just one spectacular view from the many along the NC500 to take with me to my desert island, then this would be it. And that is why, in my view, you should do the NC500 anticlockwise, especially if the scenery is your main reason for setting out on it. To do it the other way around would be an anticlimax. I have always believed in keeping the best to last, or nearly last, in this case.

I am aware, however, that some people prefer to begin with the best and that is up to them. Whilst the west coast may be said to be more scenic than the east, take my word for it, the descent into Applecross from the top of the Bealach na Bà is not a patch of that into Kishorn.

Chapter Thirty-Eight

Loch Carron: Tartan and Gardens

THEY'VE gone now and I'm not saying they would have been a blot on the landscape exactly, but on the other hand they would hardly have enhanced it either. Had you had been driving down this road in the Seventies and Eighties, from 1975-87, to be precise, you would have seen oil platforms here in the making. Show me someone who says they have seen a beautiful oil platform and I'll show you someone who needs a pair of specs.

The largest one ever built here was the Ninian Central Platform, and at 600,000 tonnes, at the time of its construction in 1978 it was the largest man-made moveable object in the world. It improved the landscape no end when it was moved out to the North Sea by seven tugs, and that's where it is to this very day.

In this small and scattered community of six villages that is known as Kishorn, where you will not find a village of that name, the influx of 3,000 workers was accommodated in a purpose-built village on site as well as two converted car ferries moored out in the loch. One of the reasons it was chosen was because of the depth of its waters, as deep as a fjord (I told you it looked like one) in Norway, that other country involved in drilling for black gold in the North Sea. It was here too that the caissons for the Skye Bridge were built in 1992.

We're at the junction of the A896 at Tornapress. To the left is the shortcut to Shieldaig avoiding the Pass of the Cattle, through Glenshieldaig Forest, but just up the road a little is Rassal Ashwood, the most northerly ashwood in Britain. It was designated a Natural Nature Reserve in 1956. It's a bit of an anomaly, and something of a rarity in these parts where all around is heather. The explanation is that the trees are growing on an outcrop of limestone which, as I said before, provides excellent drainage – essential for vegetation which does not like getting its roots wet.

The wood has been here for six thousand years. It was once cultivated, and animals grazed on stone terraces within a stone enclosure. Similar sites have been found in Scandinavia, so if you ever want to know what the Vikings did for us, this might just be the answer. The leaves would have provided fodder for the sheep and cattle as well as shade and shelter. In return, the animals provided the three Ms – manure, meat, and milk. The wood was turned into tools; now the bark provides a home for a rare type of epiphytic lichen. That means it is not a parasite; it lives in perfect harmony with its host. Just like me and the Missus.

Plans are afoot to restore the wood, or at least some of it, by weeding out the seedlings and younger trees, leaving the old ones to create a glade. And very pleasant it all sounds too. You are welcome to walk in the wood; a mile-long trail begins at the car park.

On the right of the junction, the road heads south and west towards Lochcarron, the village and the loch. From here another little detour on a minor road goes down the west side of the loch, through the sleepy-sounding Slumbay (well it's either that or an unsanitary place to live), to the very much-ruined Strome Castle which occupies a strategic position on a rocky little promontory where the loch narrows. Built in the fifteenth century, it was a fortified tower house and the focus of inter-clan warfare between the incumbents, the MacDonalds of Glengarry and the Mackenzies of Kintail.

Its demise came about in 1602 when, during a siege, some "silly women" as a contemporary chronicler put it, in the dark, mistook the water barrel for the one holding the gunpowder and poured the water they had drawn from the well into it. Naturally when the MacDonalds found out, they were not best pleased and whatever adjectives they used to describe the women, you can bet "silly" wasn't one of then. Worse followed when, during the stramash, a Mackenzie prisoner made his escape by leaping out a window into a dung heap and came up smelling of roses when he told the besieging Mackenzies what he had heard. The MacDonalds realised the game was up, surrendered in order to spare their lives, and mercifully were granted safe passage out of the area. The castle, however, was blown sky-high, leaving the wee bit heap of stone and rubble that you see today.

Carry on to the end of the road at Ardaneaskan and you will find a small crofting museum. "Small" is the operative word. It's not very long, not very wide, not very high and not a museum in the well-organised, well-presented sense of the word. Just as Macbeth was astonished when he stabbed King Duncan to death that his body had so much blood in it, so am I to find this little building could contain so much stuff. It's an amazing display, if that's not too

grand a word, of objects, a veritable pot-pourri of artefacts. It's as if the philosophy of whoever is responsible for this "museum" must be as time "creeps in with petty pace from day to day", so the objects gradually gain some sort of rarity value and should be preserved. Today's commonplace object becomes tomorrow's curio.

I'm not going to try and describe the indescribable. You need to see it for yourself. There are things you might never have seen before, depending on how old you are, or you can become reacquainted with objects you last saw in your childhood. Here is a slate in a wooden frame such as I used in my first years at primary school. And here is the Bakelite telephone whose heavy black handset was almost as good an antidote to long telephone calls (which in those days were paid for by the minute) as my parents yelling at me to "get off that damned phone!" And here is a washboard like the one my mother scrubbed the clothes on and which Lonnie Donegan, and others, used to play.

There is no logic to the layout; it's a complete jumble. It's an Aladdin's cave of delights, or dusty objects, if you prefer to put it that way. It's hard to see, however, what the attraction is in a tower of old paint tins.

There's more on the outside. Leaning against the walls are various wheels. To the left of the door, one has come from some piece of abandoned farm machinery, and propped in front of it, a big, yellow 30. It could have been an enormous house number, the sort that you might expect to see on a door in Brobdignag, only the "museum" stands it in splendid isolation. I imagine it was once a reminder to train drivers not to exceed the speed limit.

In the field are some rusting farm implements such as I last saw in my uncle's farm in the Fifties. It does not bring back happy memories, but late summer days of back-breaking work during harvest-time. Here is a binder which cut the grain and bound it into sheaves, then spewed them out where we gathered them into stooks, aligned east-west to get the most benefit from the drying sun. In my eyes it was a grim reaper as it remorselessly cut a swathe through the golden corn and it was a great relief when it broke down, giving us poor agricultural labourers a chance to rest our backs. Usually it was just enough time to gather up its dead before it clattered into life again.

You might wonder if it is worth coming all the way to see this eclectic mix of objects. Probably not. The view from the beach here is the real reason you should come – a view down the loch with the Applecross peninsula to your right, Plockton to your left and, in the distance, Raasay, Scalpay and Skye. The "museum" is a bonus, one of the serendipitous little discoveries that fall into your life sometimes.

On the way back to Lochcarron, about halfway up the peninsula, is an attraction you might well want to visit. It might appeal particularly to overseas visitors with Scots blood in their veins. But even if you are a native, it's worth stopping to check out Scotland's second most-famous product – tartan. And if the range of artefacts in the "museum" is amazing, then be prepared to be astounded by the range of tartans, tweeds, wools and associated products in the Lochcarron Weaver's Shop. It stocks more than seven hundred different types of tartan. Who would have thought there were so many? If they don't have it here, they won't have it anywhere. But what is this tartan treasure trove doing in this out of the way place?

Actually it dates back to just before the War when, in 1938, Mr Wood was sent from Galashiels, where the company had been set up a few years previously, to teach the craft of weaving to the people of Lochcarron. He was accompanied by Josephine Buchan, the mother of the founder, John Morris Buchan, and whose job it was to manage the weavers. Back then they did not weave tartan, only tweeds, white blankets and rugs. It was not until 1949 that the first tartan was woven here, after looms were sent from Galashiels. No weaving is done here now but at the back of the shop, where an old loom has pride of place, are some old photographs and videos providing some information about the history and growth of the company.

In 1962, seventy years after Peter Anderson set up his modest little weaving business in Galashiels, Morris bought it from Peter's surviving son, Thomas. By that time it was a considerably larger concern. Peter himself died in 1945, aged 86. Today Lochcarron of Scotland is the world's leading manufacturer of tartan, exporting the iconic product worldwide. What better souvenir could you have of Scotland than something from here?

At the head of the loch, the A896 takes the NC500 traveller to Achnasheen, and we will come back to it presently. But before that we are going on a detour down the other side of the loch as far as Stromeferry, which stands directly across the loch from the castle. A sign points to our destination in Gaelic and English which is followed, for the avoidance of any doubt with "(No ferry)". Mind you, it wouldn't take you very long to find that out for yourself – it's only a hop, skip and a jump from the junction.

The ferry service began in 1809 and the railway arrived in 1870, the terminus for the Dingwall and Skye line. From here passengers would board the steamer for Portree and Stornoway. In 1898 the line was extended to Kyle of Lochalsh, and that tolled the death knell for the ferry. Stromeferry could go back to sleep for the next three-quarters of a century until the train began ferrying in those oil-platform constructors who did not arrive by sea. Now the station is lucky if it has as many as half-a-dozen passengers a day who alight here, which I suppose is six more than the station at Adlestrop, Gloucestershire, in Edward Thomas's famous poem.

You get the impression it was the sort of place where nothing exciting ever happened but, on June 3rd 1883, Stromeferry station saw a great deal of excitement indeed. On that memorable day, more than two hundred fishermen gathered here to stop fish being loaded onto the train on a Sunday. The police being powerless to break up the demonstration, the army was called in and ten men were arrested. Questions were asked in the House of Commons. Some people have their day in court; sleepy little Stromeferry had its day in Parliament.

It's about ten miles from the Strathcarron junction, if you'd like to call in here at what would be no misnomer to call "The Place that Time Forgot". One thing you won't be able to do, however, is stay at the Stromeferry Hotel, which is all boarded up and has a very forlorn sort of air. It was built in 1874 with stables and other buildings being added in 1882. In 1992 it was broken into and fittings were stolen and damaged. In 1993 a fire broke out, not just once but twice. To have one fire may be regarded as misfortune, to have two within a month of each other looks like carelessness or wanton vandalism. In 2000, further thefts were reported, and get this – of floors and fittings, skirtings and staircases, and partitions and plasterwork! I suppose, to look on the bright side, it gives anyone who buys it with a view to restoring it, a pretty clean slate on which to start. I could also add it creates a bit of symmetry with the castle across the loch, though it's not quite in such a ruined state as that yet. However, there are some very nice old-fashioned slates still on the roof that must be worth a bit, and which – if removed – could expedite that process enormously.

This is where our little detour ends and, on our way back, we call in at the Attadale Gardens. Their genesis can be traced back to when John Matheson became bankrupt and was forced to sell his estates. His son, Alexander, left home to seek his fortune in the Far East. He was made a partner in his Uncle James's business. What a useful thing it is to have connections. Whilst in India, James had met a certain ship's surgeon, William Jardine (1784-1843), with whom he formed an unholy alliance, smuggling opium into China, as well as the more legitimate commodities of tea and cotton. They founded a company in Guangzhou in 1832 and it was this that Alexander joined as a junior partner. Today Jardine Matheson Holdings, Jardines for short – I expect you have heard of them – is still in business and doing very nicely, thank you very much.

Having made his fortune, Alexander returned to Scotland in 1839 and set about re-acquiring Attadale as well as some other estates too numerous to mention. As chairman of the Northern Railway, he was responsible for extending the line from Dingwall with the intention of it terminating here, but the water proved too shallow for the steamers to dock and the line had to be continued to Strome.

Alexander's life terminated in 1886, by which time he had been a Liberal MP, been knighted and created First Baron of Lochalsh. On his death, the Attadale Estate was leased to Baron Schroder, a son of the wealthy German merchant banker. He bought the estate in 1910, the year of *his* death as it happens. And it was *his* son, Captain William Schroder, a keen plant collector, who created the gardens. He died in 1945, which is just as well, as he would surely have died broken-hearted because in 1980 his pride and joy was destroyed by fierce storms. He is buried in the garden along with his wife, Judith, and a very nice secluded spot it is too. I imagine he's very happy to be planted in this earthly paradise. As for Schroders plc (which you might also have heard of) despite a recent downturn in fortunes, it is also doing very nicely too, like Jardines.

These days the gardens are in the hands of the Macpherson family. It's an artists' paradise, if such a place could be said to belong to any particular section of the human race. I call it so, not only because of the way artists and photographers will be inspired by the reflections in the water, nor because of the way the plants have been grown to frame the view beyond the gardens, provided you set up your easel just so. No, it's because of the seventeen sculptures which enhance your visit as you stroll around. (Beware the cheetah leaping out at you from the undergrowth. That overgrown pussy hath a mean and hungry look.)

Near the start you will find the Water Garden. In yet another artistic connection, it is inspired by Monet's garden at Giverny with its charming Japanese bridge and framed by trees and flowers, but be careful of the giant *Gunnera* which I first came across at Dunvegan and which has too much of the triffid about it for my liking.

Also very large is what is charmingly called the "Old Rhododendron Dell" – giant rhododendrons, tall as trees; more of a wood than a dell, a word that conjures up primroses, bluebells and daffodils, whatever the season. It's not to say I don't like it – I do – but this, for me, brings to mind a different scenario altogether. I imagine it could easily be haunted and, should I venture into its dim interior, I wouldn't be in the least surprised to come across the wolf lying in wait for Little Red Riding Hood on her way to visit grandma. I wouldn't be scared. Why would he eat a tough old geezer like me when there is more tender meat on the menu? But wait a minute: he did eat grandma too, didn't he? No fears. I am not venturing any further into the dell.

Next, and a lot more soothing on the nerves, is the Japanese Garden which does exactly what a Japanese garden is meant to do – induce an atmosphere of quiet contemplation. And it might, if I could first figure out what it means. As we enter, we come first to what looks like a doll's house on a pedestal which is standing next to a bamboo water spout, at the bottom of which is a little square stone basin with a long-handled cup. Curiouser still is a mysterious circular arrangement of seven boulders of various sizes encircled by furrows traced in the gravel. What can it mean? Fortunately hand-held boards have been placed nearby with the explanation.

The doll's house is a lantern, Japanese-style of course, and the whole thing has to do with purifying oneself before the tea ceremony. It is a great leveller. The basin is always on the ground, so everyone from emperor to peasant has to stoop to get the water. As for the stones with the rings in the gravel, it's all to do with a 6th century Taoist legend. According to that, the Immortals lived on seven islands off the coast of Korea. Wishing to become immortal himself, the Emperor had a cunning plan – or at least thought he had. He had seven islands built in the palace lake by which he hoped to entice them to take up residence and from whom he hoped he would learn the secret of everlasting life.

As far as I know, there are no reports of him being alive and well and living somewhere in Japan. Presently, that country has 61,000 centenarians who obviously have a long way yet to go before achieving the ultimate goal. But the longest journey begins with the first step, and they have taken a good many towards it even if some are faltering now.

The desired state of peaceful contemplation this place is meant to induce, in my opinion, is much more likely to be achieved by the green oasis of the sunken fern garden and the geodesic dome – home to even more ferns. And, if by then, you've *still* not had your fill of ferns, there are more in the conservatory. Some may find them utterly fascinating, just as, I suppose, vegetarians might find the ranks of serried rows of vegetables in the Kitchen Garden something to swoon over. The children of carnivores, however, are more likely to have nightmares at the sight of a never-ending supply of greenery which their parents force them to eat, as even they concede vegetables are part of a balanced diet.

Whatever your persuasion, what must surely intrigue everyone is the enormous sundial, thirty-five feet in diameter. The thing that casts a shadow on a sunny day, the gnomon, is supported by a cat, rusty, rampant, in homage to the Macpherson coat of arms, because the present owner is a person of that ilk – Nicky, to be precise – whose father Ian bought the estate from the Schroders in 1952.

There are more than 2,000 trees from all over the world here, but one of the things of which the garden is justly proud is its *Meconopsis grandis* collection, or blue Himalyan poppy, and of which I am also particularly fond. It is the national flower of Bhutan, and first became known in this country after Mallory's ill-fated Everest expedition of 1924. They are notoriously difficult to grow. I know. I have tried, but then my fingers are not particularly green. Unfortunately for me, they are not in season at the moment.

Having visited the Sunken Garden and felt the weight of the satisfyingly round and smooth grinding stone that nestles in the 4500 BC saddle quern like an egg in a nest, we make our way to the exit. On the way we stop to pay our respects to the founder and his wife in their private little cemetery. We're not quite finished our visiting yet, however.

About a mile before the Strathcarron Hotel is the *Carron Pottery, Craft Shop and Gallery*, a four-star Scottish Tourist Board attraction in the former school and schoolhouse. If, like Jerome K Jerome, you like to watch people at work, you can see Rob Teago potter about. It's also another chance, if you still have a hole burning in your pocket after the tartan experience, to buy silverware, knitwear, jewellery and more, if you are in search of another souvenir of your NC500 tour.

We cross the Conon, turn right onto the A890 and head east, initially on a single-lane road through trees, and then along the banks of Loch Dùghail until, at Achnashellach Forest, we hit the fast-track, the two-track road to Achnasheen.

It's a sign the end of the NC500 is nigh.

Chapter Thirty-Nine

Acnasheen and Beauly: Completing the Circuit

ACHNASHEEN, on the banks of the Bran, is situated at the junction of two Thomas Telford roads, the A832 from Gairloch and the one we are presently on which will take us through the strath to Dingwall. Been there, done that. We are going to Beauly, before Inverness, thus completing our circuit of the NC500. Its Gaelic name, *Achadh na Sine*, means "field of storms". Presumably there is a good reason for the name though not today, thankfully.

As you approach the village, both the road and railway cut through what is known as the "Achnasheen Terraces", three distinct flat-topped tiers rising above the river valley. They look artificial, but they come from a time that predates the foot of man. They are raised beaches from a glacial lake that once covered this land about 10,000 years ago, give or take a few thousand years.

Achnasheen's most famous resident was Sir Arthur Bignold (1839-1915), the thirteenth son of Sir Samuel Bignold, which certainly wasn't very lucky for him as it put him very far down the pecking order. Still, the boy "done good" as the saying goes. He went to Cambridge University, spoke five languages including Gaelic, was a member of the London Stock Exchange, founding member of the Kennel Club, Fellow of the Royal Zoological Society, Fellow of the Royal Geographical Society and a Conservative MP. There were some other things besides, but we'll not go into them. He was a bit of a benefactor to the people on his estates: built a church in Lochluichart in memory of his first wife; gifted a house and grounds in Wick to be used as a cottage hospital in memory of his second; and a public park in Kirkwall in gratitude for being given the Freedom of the City. However, his kindness did not extend to deer, as you shall shortly see.

Home to him was Lochrosque Castle on the shores of Loch a' Chroisg on the A832 heading towards Gairloch. In September 1914, Winston Churchill, First Lord of the Admiralty, was passing by on his way to inspect the fleet at Loch Ewe and was astonished to see a burning and a shining light coming from the roof of the castle. He continued to the loch, where he was told an unidentified aeroplane had been seen in the area. In 1914 that was a very rare thing indeed.

Churchill suspected what he had seen was a guiding light for Zeppelins and, with an armed bodyguard, returned to the castle. Sir Arthur explained the light was to catch the "gleam in the eyes of the deer" on the hillside, to make them all the easier to stalk and shoot the next day. A likely story you might think, and so did the First Lord of the Admiralty who ordered the light to be dismantled and background checks made on Bignold, his guests, his friends and even his servants, lest they were German spies. They weren't. Sir Arthur, the deerslayer, was speaking nothing less than the truth. Nowadays a lot more than the light has been dismantled – the whole flaming castle has.

In the early 20th century it became the property of a Harley Street dentist, John Mackenzie. He had two sons, Stuart and Dougal, who successfully bankrupted the family, and the castle was sold to a rich American. The story goes it was taken apart, stone by stone, and shipped to the United States. Incredible, but is it true? It might be. After all, London Bridge was dismantled and shipped to Lake Havasu City, Arizona in 1967. The trouble is, no-one seems to know who the rich American was, or where the castle was rebuilt. The lodge remains, but if it knows anything, it's not telling. Fortunately photographs of it exist, one which clearly shows the lamp on the tower. The United States may be a very large country indeed but you can't plonk down a baronial mansion like this without someone noticing it, I wouldn't have thought.

Here is another story about Achnasheen which is probably less apocryphal. On September 12th 1877, at 4.45 precisely, the royal train drew in at Achnasheen and Queen Victoria, Princess Beatrice, her Majesty's physician, her special friend John Brown, her pet dog, as well as some others, all alighted. They were on their way to Loch Maree, an account of which visit I gave earlier. From here the royal party intended to continue by carriage, only the carriages were delayed and the unmerry monarch's entourage had to spend the night in Achnasheen. Where exactly is not known; a residence known as "The Cottage" has been suggested, but that seems very unlikely indeed. The Station Hotel would have to be the most likely suspect, so you would think.

The owner was a certain Murdo MacIver, who also ran the mail service between Kinlochewe and Gairloch. He was commissioned to carry the Queen's mail to her in Loch Maree, but said it was against his religion to do so on a Sunday. Long gone are the days when such a response would have evoked an extreme response like the Queen of Hearts'. And so the affairs of state ground to a halt thanks to Queen Victoria's not so humble subject, Mr MacIver.

Six miles after Achnasheen, a sign points us to Cnoc na Bhain cemetery at Achanalt. Here lie the mortal remains of Captain Bertram Dickson (1873-1913), Captain in the Royal Regiment of Artillery, soldier, aviator and explorer. If you've never heard of him and would like to know why he is deemed worthy of a brown sign directing you to his grave, an explanation is provided by a noticeboard nearby. Or I can tell you now.

Before he became interested in aeroplanes he led the sort of life you might expect to read in the *Boy's Own Paper*, only his exploits were true. We will pass over them, however, as it's only the aviation part we are interested in. He learned to fly at Chalons in France, getting his pilot's licence in 1910. (Remember that the first powered flight took place at Kitty Hawk in December 1903.) In May 1910 he won the Aéro-Club de France's competition at Tours for flying the furthest aggregate distance with the next-placed miles behind. The following month, he achieved another landmark in the history of aviation when he carried a passenger on a flight that lasted two hours.

Before it turned into the real thing, the Army used to play war games on Salisbury Plain. In September 1910, Dickson took off to spy on the enemy "Blue Force", landed, and reported by telephone to his "Red Force" superiors what the Blues were up to. Thus he became the first aerial spy, or should I say "reconnaissance officer"? The young Home Secretary, Winston Churchill, who was watching the proceedings, was impressed.

Just a week later to the day, poor Bertram achieved another unenviable first – a mid-air collision with a French pilot over Milan. It wasn't his fault. The French pilot crashed into him from above. Somewhat unfairly you might think, the one to blame sustained a few scratches but poor Bertie was so badly injured he never flew again. In fact it was to be the death of him. Whilst visiting his friend, Sir Arthur, at Lochrosque, in September 1913, he died of a burst blood vessel, a legacy from his crash three years and a day previously. September, it seems, not April as T.S. Eliot would have us believe, was the "cruellest month" for him. But before that unhappy day, he continued his interest in aeroplanes in Civvy Street by advising plane manufacturers on how to improve their designs.

Yes, all very interesting but not worthy of a brown sign surely? And indeed his claim to fame – and the reason for it – is because in 1911, the Prime Minister, Asquith, asked the Technical Sub-committee for Imperial Defence (TSID) to look into what role aeroplanes would be likely to play in warfare in the future. In his submission to the committee, Dickson foretold a time would come when aeroplanes would be used to spy on the enemy, both sides would seek to prevent that happening, and that would inevitably lead to aerial conflict.

The TSID took his forecast seriously. On April 13th 1912, the forerunner of the RAF – the Royal Flying Corps – was founded. And that is why he has been accorded the honour of the brown sign. He did not live to see his forecast come true and never heard of the jet engine, but they disturb his rest now as low-flying military jets roar overhead on flying practice.

At Gorstan we come to a parting of the ways with an old friend, the A832, which we had picked up again at Achnasheen. Our new road, the A835, sweeps round the southern side of Loch Garve and presently we arrive at a sign pointing to Rogie Falls.

The Falls are on the Black Water, a tributary of the Conon, and can be viewed from a suspension bridge. On the far side, an artificial ladder has been made to allow the salmon to by-pass the main falls. They make it so easy for them nowadays. August and September are the months when you will see them battling upstream, returning to the place of their birth where they will spawn, then die. And you can't say these massive leaps onwards and upwards towards death are due to the sex drive either. Sex, if you are salmon, is hardly exciting for either party as there is no bodily contact at all. She scoops what is called a "redd" in the gravel of the riverbed with her tail into which she deposits her eggs. He comes alongside, lets go his cargo of sperm and that's him done, an absent father. She disturbs the gravel a little further upstream which the current will carry down to cover her little nest of eggs, about 5,000 in number. She may make as many as seven redds. That's an awful lot of kids for a single parent to bring up, but she never gets to see any of them. Most of them will not survive to maturity and in any case, in just a few days, she will most probably be dead herself.

It seems a hell of a thing to have to do, in the last days of your life, to battle your way to death like this. Yet despite the ladder, some of them choose to do it the hard way by climbing the falls. If at first you don't succeed...

And don't go thinking that those who elect to do it this way rather than climb the ladder are of little brain. If they can navigate their way across the Atlantic to this river, the very one where their life's journey began and where it's destined to end, I think that shows a very high degree of fishy intelligence indeed. No wonder Bertie Wooster attributed Jeeves' vast intellect to his nourishing of the brain with fish. But I wonder, do any of those about to die think to themselves "Sod this for a game of soldiers! I'm not going to all that effort. I'd rather die peacefully in any old riverbed".

Contin is next, the scene of the massacre I mentioned quite early in this narrative. What I did not tell you then is that its church is dedicated to St Maelrubha, whom you know quite a lot about now and which lets you see just how widespread his influence was.

We cross the River Conon at Moy Bridge taking the A832 again to Muir of Ord in the Black Isle, midway between Beauly to the south and Cononbridge to the north. After the rivers on which they stand were bridged in 1814 by that man Telford again, it became a very handy place for cattle drovers from the north to pasture their cattle as they wended their way south on the Drove Road to the famous Falkirk Tryst at the centre of Scotland's narrow waist. I suppose that means you could call Falkirk the "nation's bellybutton", but as far as I know, no-one has, until now. As for this place, this fertile plain continued to be cattle-rearing country even after the invasion of the sheep.

Muir of Ord has the distinction of having the only surviving malt whisky distillery in the Black Isle. In the early 19th century, there were nine! Well, something had to be done with all that surplus barley. The Glen Ord Distillery was founded in 1838. It doesn't much look like a distillery – more like any building you would expect to see in an industrial estate except, perhaps, for the long and slender chimney at one end, with a tip at the top like the little pencil you used to get in Lett's pocket diaries. But there it is; the writing on the wall that tells you it is indeed a distillery and, if you were in any doubt, through the massive windows you can see a gleam of burnished copper. This is the still house, arguably the most important part of any distillery. There are three wash stills and three spirit stills producing four or five million litres of whisky a year. That's enough to float a battleship I would have thought, but what a waste!

Most of the whisky is blended, but what is special about this distillery is it is one of a very few that does its own malting nearby. Most other distilleries buy the maltings from elsewhere. You can't help but feel this is a backward step, and something of the subtlety that distinguishes one whisky from another must be lost in the process. That makes the kilns, with their distinctive pagoda roofs where the malted barley is dried, redundant. Two have been retained, however, to preserve that feeling of former times. It also makes the place *look* like a distillery.

You can take a tour or just stay in the visitor centre, where the whole process is explained in a well-laid out exhibition. You will not be amazed to learn there is a tasting room and a shop. A last chance to buy a souvenir of your NC500 trip. Other distilleries are available and I wouldn't presume to say which one you should visit, but I would have thought a visit to at least one is a must for any non-native visitor. But perhaps you are a whisky aficionado, have visited every single one on the NC500 – in which case this will be a sad occasion for you.

The railway line came to Muir of Ord in 1862, linking it with Inverness and Dingwall. Before then, in the days of the drovers, it was known as "Tarradale" but, in their wisdom, the Railway Board changed its name. Ours not to reason why. Because of the Beauly Firth, this was a busy place, all road traffic heading north and south had to come through here. Then in 1982 the Kessock Bridge was built and the two other villages of Conon Bridge and Muir of Ord found themselves by-passed by that major artery, the A9.

In 1564, Mary Queen of Scots came to Beauly where we are now, saw and said, *"C'est un beau lieu"*. Hence Beauly. You might wonder why the Queen of this nation, born in Linlithgow Palace in 1542, on first seeing the place, didn't exclaim instead, "It's a braw place!" and therefore why the town isn't called "Brawly", even if the Railway Board might have wanted to rename it. Here's the reason.

Mary's hand in marriage was much sought after. At six months old, under the Treaty of Greenwich, she was betrothed to Prince Edward, Henry VIII's only son, the marriage to take place when she was ten. But the "best-laid plans of mice an' men gang aft agley", as the poet said, and the Scottish Parliament revoked the treaty in 1543.

In 1547 another treaty was signed, this time with Henri II of France, in which Mary was betrothed to the three-year old Dauphin. Aged five, she was shipped off to France for safekeeping, out of the way of the auld enemy. After all, we had been friends with the French against the common foe since 1295; what is known as the "Auld Alliance".

At sixteen she married, not her prince but the Prince that had been designated for her. A year later she was a widow. She came back to Scotland the following year, in 1559, and four years after that, married her cousin, Darnley. The rest gets even more astounding but that's not part of my story and since you probably know it already, I'll say no more about it. My point is, it's no wonder when she first came to Beauly that she spoke in French. After all, her mum was French and she had spent the majority of her childhood in France.

Alas, Beauly's name has nothing to do with her at all, but rather the French monks who inhabited the Priory here more than three hundred years earlier. It was founded in 1230 by an Anglo-French nobleman, John Byset, following the example of Alexander II who, in the same year, founded another Valliscaulian Priory at Pluscarden, near Elgin. By 1272, the Priory at Beauly was complete and ready to receive its first body. Step up, in 1287, Sir Simon Fraser of Lovat, the ancestor of "Simon the Fox" the Eleventh Lord (see Chapter

One), who was buried in front of the altar in the chancel.

They were a bit of an obscure lot, the Valliscaulians, only one other priory in addition to the two above, ever being established outside France, at Ardchattan in Argyll. The name comes from the order's origin in Val des Choux in Burgundy. Yes, that's right – the Valley of the Cabbages, though I am still not clear how that translates into "Valliscaulian". Cauliflowers, yes, but not cabbages.

The order was suppressed by Pope Julian II, aka "The Fearsome Pope" and "The Warrior Pope", who personally led his troops into battle on at least two occasions. On the other hand, he was also the one who commissioned Michelangelo to paint the chapel of the Sistine Chapel, so the holiest man in Christendom wasn't wholly bad. And so it was in 1510 that the Priory became Cistercian. And so it stayed until it was disestablished in 1634 and its lands acquired by the Bishop of Ross.

After the Protestant Reformation in 1560 the grounds became a burial ground for the local people, but the biggest change of all came in 1653 when it joined the ranks of the buildings whose stones Cromwell used to build his fort in Inverness, of which nothing now remains but a single tower. Apart from part of the chancel, only the nave of the priory church remains today, roofless and a shadow of its former self. It has a deserted, forlorn sort of air, but an artist's impression of just how splendid it was back in the 16th century is provided by a noticeboard with an artist's impression showing us what it was like in those days with its wooden furnishings and cloisters.

Ah, yes, all very nice, but the monastic life doesn't appeal to me at all. I may have the hairstyle for it now but I could never have been a monk in the days when I would have been required to have a circle shorn on my crown. I imagine such a ridiculous style was only dreamed up to keep women at bay. I can testify that it works. Ever since I involuntarily adopted the style, hand on heart, I have never received an offer.

Hairstyle apart, not to mention the hairshirt worn next to the skin, a bigger deterrent by far for me would have been the early start to the day. I would have struggled to get up for matins – the first prayers of the day, at 2am. The last was compline, bedtime prayers, at 6pm. Early to bed and early to rise makes a monk a very boring person indeed. I would have been complaining from matins to compline, muttering inwardly to myself of course, as I would also have taken a vow of silence. I am not a morning sort of person. Still, since I was praying for the salvation of my immortal soul, I might have been motivated to make the sacrifice. If that's what it takes, so be it. Whatever heaven is like, it has to be better than this life, so hell must be truly horrible.

Another noticeboard nearby is in praise of scaffolding of which there is a great deal here at the moment. It's by way of an apology, an innovative way of saying "Sorry for the inconvenience, but these repairs are necessary". I see and I understand. *Te absolvo.*

Come to dust, we all must, and as well as the large number of graves on the outside for the hoi polloi, there are some notable graves in the body of the kirk, so to speak – but with headstones you would normally expect to see in the graveyard, not here. Near the entrance is the grave of Sir Kenneth MacKenzie who won the battle of Blàr na Pàirce, the Battle of the Field, round about 1485 and which I told you about earlier.

And here lies another Mackenzie, Alexander the Prior, who died in 1479. He would have known his namesake, Kenneth. And here lies Alexander Chisholm of Chisholm who died in 1793 at the tender age of 44 and is joined in death, not by his wife, but his "relict", Elizabeth Wilson, who died in 1826 aged 68. Imagine going to a ball and the footman announcing to the assembly – "Mrs Chisholm, the relict of Alexander Chisholm of Chisholm". It's enough to make you want to marry a much younger man.

Some of the stones have interesting carvings on them as old gravestones often do, and in 1818, Keats and his friend Charles Brown paid a visit here and were inspired – as Romantic poets often were – by ruins and death. Here they were inspired to write a collaborative poem entitled *On Some Skulls on Beauley Abbey.* Keats wrote the first couple of lines and you can just see him saying, "Okay, Charlie boy, now finish it off," and Charles getting stuck and Keats writing the first four lines of the second verse and telling him to get on with it. Then seeing Charles was still struggling, dashing off three verses. There are sixteen in all and some are doggerel. But what do I know? The experts who do know about such things reckon that was how the poem was divvied up, anyway.

They also collaborated on *Walks in the North* about their trip and after they got back, a play *Otho the Great* which was never staged in their lifetime. Neither of them knew it, but Keats had only two-and-a-half years left to live.

And so we take our leave of Beauly on the A862, driving along the southern shore of the Firth. Presently the elegant Kessock Bridge appears, soaring over the water where it and the massive Moray Firth meet. It marked our beginning and now it marks our ending. Our NC500 is complete.

We've done a lot more than five hundred and sixteen miles once you add up all our detours. But that's the thing about the NC500 – it will certainly take you through some of Scotland's most remote and beautiful scenery and worth doing for that alone, but it's a lot more than that. If you have the time, do not follow it slavishly but allow yourself to be sidetracked. The NC500 is the means to an end, not the be-all and end-all.

NC500 traveller, whatever your reasons for doing the trip may be, go forth, explore and enjoy!

Clach an Tiompain: The Sounding Stone

Tarbat Peninsula

The Tower of Major-General
Sir Hector Archibald MacDonald

Jail Dornoch

Dunrobin Castle

Gardens of Dunrobin Castle

Carn Liath

John O'Groats

About the Author

A native of Banff, Scotland, David M. Addison is a graduate of Aberdeen University. In addition to essays in various publications, he has written eight books, mainly about his travels.

As well as a short spell teaching English as a foreign language in Poland when the Solidarity movement at its height, he spent a year (1978-79) as an exchange teacher in Montana.

He regards his decision to apply for the exchange as one of the best things he ever did, for not only did it give him the chance to travel extensively in the US and Canada but during the course of the year he made a number of enduring friendships. The third instalment in his *Innocent Abroad* series, entitled *Less Innocent Abroad,* is forthcoming from Extremis Publishing.

Since taking early retirement (he is not as old as he looks), he has more time but less money to indulge his unquenchable thirst for travel (and his wife would say for Cabernet Sauvignon and malt whisky). He is doing his best to spend the children's inheritance by travelling as far and wide and as often as he can.

An Innocent Abroad

The Misadventures of an Exchange Teacher in Montana: Award-Winner's Edition

By David M. Addison

When, in 1978, taking a bold step into the unknown, the author, accompanied by his wife and young family, swapped his boring existence in Grangemouth in central Scotland for life in Missoula, Montana, in the western United States, he could never have foreseen just how much of a life-changing experience it would turn out to be.

As an exchange teacher, he was prepared for a less formal atmosphere in the classroom, while, for their part, his students had been warned that he would be "Mr Strict". It was not long before this clash of cultures reared its ugly head and the author found life far more "exciting" than he had bargained for. Within a matter of days of taking up his post, he found himself harangued in public by an irate parent, while another reported him to the principal for "corrupting" young minds.

Outwith the classroom, he found daily life just as shocking. Lulled by a common language into a false sense of a "lack of foreignness", he was totally unprepared for the series of culture shocks that awaited him from the moment he stepped into his home for the year – the house from *Psycho*.

There were times when he wished he had stayed at home in his boring but safe existence in Scotland, but mainly this is a heart-warming and humorous tale of how this Innocent abroad, reeling from one surprising event to the next, gradually begins to adapt to his new life. And thanks to a whole array of colourful personalities and kind people (hostile parents not withstanding), he finally comes to realise that this exchange was the best thing he had ever done.

This award-winning book, the opening volume of the *Innocent Abroad* series, charts the first months of the author's adventures and misadventures in a land which he finds surprisingly different.

An Award-Winning Book in the 2015 Bookbzz Prize Writer Competition for Biography and Memoir

Still Innocent Abroad

Further Misadventures of an Exchange Teacher in Montana

By David M. Addison

In the sequel to his award-winning *An Innocent Abroad*, Scot David M. Addison continues his account of a year spent as an exchange teacher in Missoula, Montana in the western United States.

When he embarked on the exchange, the author vowed he would embrace every experience (within reason) that came his way and mostly they *were* reasonable, though there were some he would not care to repeat.

In the course of this book, he experiences seasonal activities such as Hallowe'en (American style), Kris Kringle and Thanksgiving. He also sits his driving test in his wreck of a wagon which he not-so-fondly dubs "The Big Blue Mean Machine" and whose malfunctions continue to plague him in this book, just as they did in the last.

Nevertheless the author and his young family put their trust in it to take them, in winter, on the 1,200 mile round trip over the snow-clad Rockies to visit relations in Canada – just for a long weekend. Which just goes to show you that although he may have learned some things, this author from a small island is still very much an innocent abroad in this vast and mountainous land to even contemplate embarking on such an expedition – particularly since he set out so ill equipped.

Meanwhile, at school, he is on his best behaviour as he tries not to repeat the shocks and alarms of the first few days when he found himself up to his neck in trouble with parents out to get his guts for garters. The reader will not be disappointed to discover that he still finds some parents and students challenging. At the same time, he is also on his guard for attacks from the "enemy" within – his practical-joker colleagues who are all too keen to exploit his innocence for their own amusement.

The narrative ends with the traumatic events on Christmas Day. It would have been a memorable day whatever happened, but no-one bargained for the Addisons turning their hosts' Christmas Day into one they would not forget in a hurry.

The Spectrum of Adventure

A Brief History of Interactive Fiction on the Sinclair ZX Spectrum

By Thomas A. Christie

The Sinclair ZX Spectrum was one of the most popular home computers in British history, selling over five million units in its 1980s heyday. Amongst the thousands of games released for the Spectrum during its lifetime, the text adventure game was to emerge as one of the most significant genres on the system.

The Spectrum of Adventure chronicles the evolution of the text adventure on the ZX Spectrum, exploring the work of landmark software houses such as Melbourne House Software, Level 9 Computing, Delta 4 Software, the CRL Group, Magnetic Scrolls, and many others besides.

Covering one hundred individual games in all, this book celebrates the Spectrum's thriving interactive fiction scene of the eighties, chronicling the achievements of major publishers as well as independent developers from the machine's launch in 1982 until the end of the decade in 1989.

A Righteously Awesome Eighties Christmas

Festive Cinema of the 1980s

By Thomas A. Christie

The cinema of the festive season has blazed a trail through the world of film-making for more than a century, ranging from silent movies to the latest CGI features. From the author of *The Christmas Movie Book*, this new text explores the different narrative themes which emerged in the genre over the course of the 1980s, considering the developments which have helped to make the Christmas films of that decade amongst the most fascinating and engaging motion pictures in the history of festive movie production.

Released against the backdrop of a turbulent and rapidly-changing world, the Christmas films of the 1980s celebrated traditions and challenged assumptions in equal measure. With warm nostalgia colliding with aggressive modernity as never before, the eighties saw the movies of the holiday season being deconstructed and reconfigured to remain relevant in an age of cynicism and innovation.

Whether exploring comedy, drama, horror or fantasy, Christmas cinema has an unparalleled capacity to attract and inspire audiences. With a discussion ranging from the best-known titles to some of the most obscure, *A Righteously Awesome Eighties Christmas* examines the ways in which the Christmas motion pictures of the 1980s fit into the wider context of this captivating and ever-evolving genre.

The Craft of Public Speaking

By Colin M. Barron

Public speaking is one of the most important skills in personal and professional life. Yet too often this key ability is neglected, leading to presentations which are dull, uninspired and poorly delivered.

The Craft of Public Speaking examines some of the crucial aptitudes which are fundamental to delivering an effective presentation for listeners. These include preparation, structure and rehearsal, in addition to some of the more overlooked aspects of oration such as the use of visual aids, adding humour, and dressing for success. As well as discussing how to deliver effective live addresses in public settings, the book also covers interview techniques for TV and radio along with how to organise seminars and conferences.

Dr Colin M. Barron has delivered hundreds of lectures and presentations to audiences during a long career, giving speeches on a wide variety of different subjects over many years. In *The Craft of Public Speaking*, he shares the essential knowledge that you will need to become a truly successful public speaker.

Planes on Film
Ten Favourite Aviation Films

By Colin M. Barron

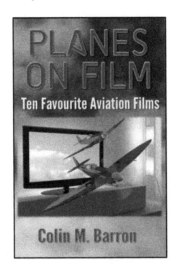

One of the most durable genres in cinema, the aviation film has captivated audiences for decades with tales of heroism, bravery and overcoming seemingly insurmountable odds. Some of these movies have become national icons, achieving critical and commercial success when first released in cinemas and still attracting new audiences today.

In *Planes on Film: Ten Favourite Aviation Films*, Colin M. Barron reveals many little-known facts about the making of several aviation epics. Every movie is discussed in comprehensive detail, including a thorough analysis of the action and a complete listing of all the aircraft involved. With information about where the various planes were obtained from and their current location, the book also explores the subject of aviation films which were proposed but ultimately never saw the light of day.

With illustrations and meticulous factual commentary, *Planes on Film* is a book which will appeal to aviation enthusiasts, military historians and anyone who has an interest in cinema. Written by an author with a lifelong passion for aircraft and their depiction on the silver screen, *Planes on Film* presents a lively and thought-provoking discourse on a carefully-chosen selection of movies which have been drawn from right across the history of this fascinating cinematic genre.

For details of new and forthcoming books from
Extremis Publishing,
please visit our official website at:

www.extremispublishing.com

or follow us on social media at:

www.facebook.com/extremispublishing

www.linkedin.com/company/extremis-publishing-ltd-/